To Improve the Academy

To Improve the Academy

Resources for Faculty, Instructional, and Organizational Development

VOLUME 26

Douglas Reimondo Robertson, Editor
Northern Kentucky University

Linda B. Nilson, Associate Editor
Clemson University

Professional and Organizational Development Network in Higher Education

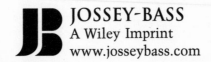

JOSSEY-BASS
A Wiley Imprint
www.josseybass.com

Published by Jossey-Bass
A Wiley Imprint
989 Market Street, San Francisco, CA 94103–1741
www.josseybass.com

Readers should be aware that Internet Web sites offered as citations and/or sources for further information may have changed or disappeared between the time this was written and when it is read.

Jossey-Bass books and products are available through most bookstores. To contact Jossey-Bass directly call our Customer Care Department within the U.S. at 800-956-7739, outside the U.S. at 317-572-3986, or fax 317-572-4002.

Jossey-Bass also publishes its books in a variety of electronic formats. Some content that appears in print may not be available in electronic books.

Composition: Deerfoot Studios

Printed in the United States of America
FIRST EDITION
HB Printing 10 9 8 7 6 5 4 3 2 1

To Improve the Academy

To Improve the Academy is published annually by the Professional and Organizational Network in Higher Education (POD) through Jossey-Bass Publishers/Anker Publishing Company, and is abstracted in ERIC documents and in Higher Education Abstracts.

Ordering Information

The annual volume of *To Improve the Academy* is distributed to members at the POD conference in the autumn of each year. To order or to obtain ordering information, contact:

John Wiley & Sons, Inc.
One Wiley Drive
Somerset, NJ 08875–1272
Voice   877-762-2974
Fax   317-572-4002
Email   consumer@wiley.com
Web   www.josseybass.com

Permission to Copy

The contents of *To Improve the Academy* are copyrighted to protect the authors. Nevertheless, consistent with the networking and resource-sharing functions of POD, readers are encouraged to reproduce articles and cases from *To Improve the Academy* for educational use, as long as the source is identified.

Instructions to Contributors for the Next Volume

Anyone interested in the issues related to instructional, faculty, and organizational development in higher education may submit manuscripts. Manuscripts are submitted to the current editors in December of each year and sent through a blind peer-review process. Correspondence, including requests for information about guidelines and submission of manuscripts for Volume 27, should be directed to:

Linda B. Nilson, Director
Office of Teaching Effectiveness and Innovation
Clemson University
445 Brackett Hall
Clemson, SC 29634
Voice   864-656-4542
Fax   864-656-0750
Email   nilson@clemson.edu

Mission Statement

As revised and accepted by the POD Core Committee, April 2, 2004.

Statement of Purpose

The Professional and Organizational Development Network in Higher Education is an association of higher education professionals dedicated to enhancing teaching and learning by supporting educational developers and leaders in higher education.

The Professional and Organizational Development Network in Higher Education encourages the advocacy of the ongoing enhancement of teaching and learning through faculty, TA, instructional, and organizational development. To this end, it supports the work of educational developers and champions their importance to the academic enterprise.

Vision Statement

During the 21st century, the Professional and Organizational Development Network in Higher Education will expand guidelines for educational development, build strong alliances with sister organizations, and encourage developer exchanges and research projects to improve teaching and learning.

Values

The Professional and Organizational Development Network in Higher Education is committed to:

- Personal, faculty, instructional, and organizational development

- Humane and collaborative organizations and administrations

- Diverse perspectives and a diverse membership

- Supportive educational development networks on the local, regional, national, and international levels

- Advocacy for improved teaching and learning in the academy through programs for faculty, administrators, and graduate students

- The identification and collection of a strong and accessible body of research on development theories and practices

- The establishment of guidelines for ethical practice

- The increasingly useful and thorough assessment and evaluation of practice and research

Programs, Publications, and Activities

The Professional and Organizational Development Network in Higher Education offers members and interested individuals the following benefits:

- An annual conference designed to promote professional and personal growth, nurture innovation and change, stimulate important research projects, and enable participants to exchange ideas and broaden professional networks

- An annual membership directory and networking guide

- Publications in print and in electronic form

- Access to the POD web site and listserv

Membership, Conference, and Programs Information

For information contact:
Hoag Holmgren, Executive Director
The POD Network
P. O. Box 3318
Nederland, CO 80566
Voice   303-258-9532
Fax   303-258-7377
Email   podnetwork@podweb.org

Table of Contents

About the Authors

The Editors

Douglas Reimondo Robertson is assistant provost and professor at Northern Kentucky University. He has helped to start or reorganize four university professional development centers (Portland State University; University of Nevada–Las Vegas; Eastern Kentucky University; and Northern Kentucky University). He is a member of the Professional and Organizational Development Network in Higher Education Core Committee and chair of its Publication Committee. He is senior editor of a book series on college teaching (New Forums Press) and a current or past member of the editorial boards for *Innovative Higher Education, Journal for Excellence in College Teaching,* and *Kentucky Journal for Excellence in College Teaching and Learning.* Doug is a Fulbright Senior Specialist Candidate, available through federal international programs to provide consultations for overseas universities. He has provided more than 135 consultations to a diverse array of education, health care, human service, government, and business organizations. He has authored or co-edited six books, including *Making Time, Making Change: Avoiding Overload in College Teaching* (New Forums Press, 2003) and *Self-Directed Growth* (Brunner-Routledge, 1988). In total, he has authored or coauthored 110 scholarly or creative publications and presentations. He can be reached at robertsond2@nku.edu.

Linda B. Nilson is founding director of Clemson University's Office of Teaching Effectiveness and Innovation (OTEI) and the author of *Teaching at Its Best: A Research-Based Resource for College Instructors,* now in its second edition (Anker, 2003), and *The Graphic Syllabus and the Outcomes Map: Communicating Your Course* (Jossey-Bass, 2007). She also co-edited *Enhancing Learning with Laptops in the Classroom* (Jossey-Bass, 2005). In addition, she has published many articles and book chapters and has presented workshops and sessions at universities and conferences both nationally and internationally on dozens of topics related to teaching effectiveness, assessment, scholarly productivity, and academic career matters. Along with her OTEI duties, Linda teaches a graduate course called "College Teaching." Before coming to Clemson, she directed teaching centers at Vanderbilt University and the University of California–Riverside and was on the sociology faculty at the University of California–Los Angeles. She can be reached at nilson@clemson.edu.

The Contributors

Stacie Badran is assistant professor of mathematics at Embry-Riddle Aeronautical University. She has a Ph.D. in curriculum and instruction in mathematics education from Florida State University. Her research interests include faculty development, teacher education, teaching awards programs, and the scholarship of teaching and learning. She can be reached at stacie.badran@erau.edu.

Andrea L. Beach is an assistant professor in the Department of Educational Leadership, Research, and Technology at Western Michigan University, where she teaches in the higher education leadership doctoral program. Her research centers on issues of organizational climate in universities, support of innovation in teaching and learning, and faculty development as an organizational change lever. She is a coauthor of *Creating the Future of Faculty Development: Learning From the Past, Understanding the Present* (Anker, 2006), and she has published on the variation of faculty work, characteristics of the faculty development community, faculty development priorities at Historically Black Colleges and Universities, and faculty learning communities. She can be reached at andrea.beach@wmich.edu.

Victoria Mundy Bhavsar is an instructional consultant at the Teaching and Academic Support Center (TASC) at the University of Kentucky (UK). Her academic and professional life, including her doctorate in soil science from UK, was in the agricultural sciences until she joined TASC in 2004. In addition to faculty development, she teaches about food issues in the UK Honors Program and participates in curriculum development for sustainable agriculture in the UK College of Agriculture. She can be reached at toria@uku.edu.

A. Jane Birch is assistant director for faculty development at the Brigham Young University (BYU) Faculty Center. She directs the BYU Faculty Development Series, an intensive 18-month new faculty program, and the Scholarship Workshop, a semester-long program on scholarly productivity. Jane's passion is helping faculty make connections between religious faith and their work as teachers and scholars. She also gets excited about the comprehensive faculty development database she designed, developed, and maintains. She can be reached at jane_birch@byu.edu.

Judith N. Burstyn is professor of chemistry and pharmacology at the University of Wisconsin–Madison. She was lead scholar for the Diversity Institute of the Center for the Integration of Research, Teaching, and Learning, a faculty director of the Women in Science and Engineering Residential Learning Community, and a long-time teacher of freshman chemistry. Her research is in bioinorganic chemistry, studying the function of metal-containing proteins and metal-based compounds and materials in gas sensing. She can be reached at burstyn@chem.wisc.edu.

Susanna Calkins received her Ph.D. in European history from Purdue University in 2001. She is presently a senior program associate in faculty development at the Searle Center for Teaching Excellence at Northwestern University. She can be reached at s-calkins@northwestern.edu.

Michael Famiano is assistant professor of physics at Western Michigan University. He received his B.S. from the University of Michigan and his Ph.D. from The Ohio State University. He has worked at the National Superconducting Cyclotron Laboratory and the Institute of Physical and Chemical Research in Wako, Japan. His research focuses on the characteristics of exotic astrophysically interesting nuclei, and on dense nuclear matter to better understand the interior of neutron stars. He can be reached at michael.famiano@wmich.edu.

L. Dee Fink presently works as a national consultant in higher education and is the author of *Creating Significant Learning Experiences: An Integrated Approach to Designing College Courses* (Jossey-Bass, 2003). He is a former president of the Professional and Organizational Development Network in Higher Education (2004–2005) and served as the founding director of the Instructional Development Program at the University of Oklahoma (1979–2005). He can be reached at dfink@ou.edu.

Katherine A. Friedrich is an associate editor at the Center for the Integration of Research, Teaching, and Learning (CIRTL). She is a journalist and a former mechanical engineer. She holds a master's degree from the University of Wisconsin–Madison. Her thesis research focused on media framing of the Arctic National Wildlife Refuge drilling controversy. In addition to writing articles, planning outreach, and editing books for CIRTL, she often does freelance writing about science issues relevant to ethnic minority communities. She can be reached at friedrich@wisc.edu.

Richard A. Gale is a senior scholar at The Carnegie Foundation for the Advancement of Teaching, where he serves as director for the Carnegie Academy for the Scholarship of Teaching and Learning Higher Education Program and works with the Integrative Learning Project. His publications and research interests include aesthetic literacy, integrative learning, critical pedagogy, pedagogy and theater of the oppressed, theater and national identity, the meanings of place, and the scholarship of teaching and learning. He can be reached at gale@carnegiefoundation.org.

Tara Gray is associate professor of criminal justice and director of the Teaching Academy at New Mexico State University (NMSU). She has published three books, including her most recent, *Publish and Flourish: Become a Prolific Scholar* (NMSU, 2005). Tara has been honored at NMSU and nationally with six awards for teaching or service. She has presented faculty development workshops to 3,000 participants in more than 20 states as well as in Canada, Mexico, Guatemala, and Thailand. She can be reached at tgray@nmsu.edu.

Charles Henderson is an assistant professor at Western Michigan University with a joint appointment in the physics department and the Mallinson Institute for Science Education. Much of his research focuses on understanding and promoting change in educational systems from both empirical and theoretical perspectives. His primary teaching assignments have been in the introductory calculus-based physics sequence where he has worked with his colleagues to develop courses consistent with the results of educational research. He can be reached at charles.henderson@wmich.edu.

Matthew Kaplan is senior associate director of the Center for Research on Learning and Teaching at the University of Michigan. His work currently focuses on campus-wide and national initiatives, such as a Ford Difficult Dialogues grant examining the role of religion in a public university. Matt has a Ph.D. in comparative literature from the University of North Carolina, and he has published on teaching evaluation, diversity, and interactive theater. He has served on the Professional and Organizational Development Network in Higher Education Core Committee and was editor of *To Improve the Academy* in 1998 and 1999. He can be reached at mlkaplan@umich.edu.

John Kucsera is a doctoral student in the Department of Educational Psychology at the University of Texas at Austin. He has been involved with teacher training and holistic education in K–12 and postsecondary institutions since 2001. His research centers on teacher motivation, college teaching effectiveness, and educational programs for social equality. He can be reached at kucserajohn@hotmail.com.

Greg Light is director of the Searle Center for Teaching Excellence and associate professor in the School of Education and Social Policy at Northwestern

University. He received his doctorate from the University of London. Before coming to Northwestern, he was on the faculty and was head of the Lifelong Learning Group at the Institute of Education in London. His research focuses on the theory and practice of learning, teaching, and research in higher and professional education. He can be reached at g-light@northwestern.edu.

Jane Love brought her background in philosophy, literature, and women's studies to Furman University in 2001, when she accepted her present position as director of the Collaboratory for Creative Learning and Communication, a multiliteracy peer support center serving students and faculty. Her recent integrative experiences include participation on Furman's Curriculum Review Committee and the design team for Furman's new Center for Teaching and Engaged Learning. She can be reached at jane.love@furman.edu.

Deborah S. Meizlish is coordinator of social science faculty development at the Center for Research on Learning and Teaching (CRLT) at the University of Michigan. She has a Ph.D. in political science. Deborah consults with administrators, faculty, and graduate student instructors on course and curricular issues and facilitates university-wide programs on pedagogy. She co-taught CRLT's Preparing Future Faculty Seminar and supervised the center's graduate teaching consultants. Her interests include academic hiring, graduate student pedagogical training, academic integrity, and course and curricular design. She can be reached at debmeiz@umich.edu.

Joan Middendorf is associate director of the Campus Instructional Center and an adjunct professor at Indiana University. With David Pace she developed the "Decoding the Disciplines" method for teaching disciplinary thinking, facilitating annual faculty learning communities. A frequent guest speaker on assessment and the scholarship of teaching and learning, she has published widely. She serves as a co-principal investigator for the Indiana University History Learning Project and as an assessment specialist and senior researcher on "just-in-time" teaching National Science Foundation grants. She can be reached at middendo@indiana.edu.

Kim M. Mooney is founding director of the Center for Teaching and Learning at St. Lawrence University. The center was established in 2001, during her five-year term as associate dean for faculty affairs. Kim is also the special assistant to the president for assessment and associate professor of psychology. Her teaching and research interests include the effects of food choices on impression formation and the professional experiences of women psychologists at small colleges. She can be reached at kmooney@stlawu.edu.

Bonnie Mullinix is assistant academic dean at Furman University, where she is responsible for coordinating the Center for Teaching and Engaged Learning. An adult educator with more than 25 years of national and international experience, Bonnie has served as faculty at Monmouth and Drexel Universities, established two teaching and learning centers, and has been supporting faculty development as a member of the Professional and Organization Development Network in Higher Education since 1999. Her professional work has involved exploration of educational innovation, technologies, evaluation, and the integration of participatory, learner-centered approaches. She can be reached at bonnie.mullinix@furman.edu.

Christopher O'Neal is the senior consultant for institutional initiatives at the Center for Research on Learning and Teaching at the University of Michigan. His research interests include the impact of early evaluation on teacher performance, the value of interactive theater for building multicultural competencies in educators, and the impact of teaching assistants on student retention in the sciences and engineering. He can be reached at coneal@umich.edu.

David Pace is professor of European history and co-director of the Freshman Learning Project at Indiana University. He is a fellow in the Carnegie Academy for the Scholarship of Teaching and Learning and the Mack Center for Inquiry on Teaching and Learning, as well as coauthor of *Decoding the Disciplines* (Jossey-Bass, 2004) and numerous articles on teaching and learning. He has received the American Historical Association's Eugene Asher Distinguished Teaching Award and Indiana University's Frederic Bachman Lieber Award in recognition of distinguished teaching. He can be reached at dpace@indiana.edu.

Dolores Peters is associate professor of history at St. Olaf College. She received her Ph.D. in modern European history from the University of Minnesota. Her research includes the history of medicine in 20th-century France and topics in the scholarship of teaching and learning (SoTL): developing authentic settings for using primary sources to foster historical thinking, the impact of popular culture on undergraduates' understanding of revolution, and identification of factors determining faculty "readiness" for SoTL inquiry. She can be reached at petersdo@stolaf.edu.

Susan Polich is an instructional consultant at Virginia Commonwealth University and former assistant professor of clinical physical therapy and assessment coordinator for the Center for the Enhancement of Teaching and Learning at the University of Cincinnati. She has more than 20 years of experience in clinical faculty development, working with preceptors to improve the internship training of students. Her current interests are in the process of faculty change, especially faculty in the sciences. She can be reached at smpolich@vcu.edu.

Lois Reddick is an instructional consultant at the Center for Innovation in Teaching and Learning at New York University and a member of the Professional and Organizational Development Network in Higher Education Core Committee. She also does consulting work for the Center for Teaching Excellence at New York University and is director of Cultivating Our Sisterhood International Association, a women's social support network that develops events and programs designed to nurture women's academic, professional, and personal life goals. She can be reached at lar8@nyu.edu.

Michael Reder is director of the Center for Teaching and Learning at Connecticut College and a member of the Professional and Organizational Development Network in Higher Education (POD) Core Committee. He chairs the POD Small College Committee and has run a variety of workshops on small college teaching and learning, including starting successful centers and creating programs that address the needs of untenured faculty. Michael consults regularly on these topics and on writing at small liberal arts colleges. He has served on the faculty of the National Institute for New Faculty Developers and serves on the editorial boards of *Essays in Teaching Excellence, Innovative Higher Education,* and *Thriving in Academe.* He teaches courses on contemporary literature, culture, and theory in the English department. Michael is the author of several chapters on Salman Rushdie, and is the editor of *Conversations with Salman Rushdie* (University Press of Mississippi, 2000), a collection of interviews. He can be reached at reder@conncoll.edu.

Janet Riekenberg is a doctoral candidate in the Department of Educational Psychology at the University of Texas (UT) at Austin. She received a master's of education in counseling from UT–Austin in 2004. Janet has combined her interest in faculty development and counseling in her dissertation titled "Intra- and Inter-personal Processes: An Exploration of Possible Correlations Between Teacher Intrapersonal Dimensions, Student Sense of Classroom Community, and Student Ratings of Teacher Effectiveness." She can be reached at jjinks@mail.utexas.edu.

Rochelle Roberts is a doctoral student in the Department of Educational Psychology at the University of Texas at Austin. She is presently involved in research projects concerning faculty development and college student well-being. Her interests include faculty development in general and, more specifically, improving the effectiveness of instruction at the postsecondary level. She can be reached at trmendiola@mail.utexas.edu.

David Schodt is founding director of the Center for Innovation in the Liberal Arts and a professor in the Department of Economics at St. Olaf College. He has a bachelor's degree in electrical engineering from Cornell University and a Ph.D. in economics from the University of Wisconsin–Madison. He has written widely about political and economic development in Ecuador and about case method teaching in international affairs at the undergraduate level. He oversees the scholarship of teaching and learning program at St. Olaf, and is one of the organizers of the biennial conference "Innovations in the Scholarship of Teaching and Learning at the Liberal Arts Colleges." He can be reached at schodt@stolaf.edu.

Dieter J. Schönwetter works as an administrator in the Faculty of Dentistry at the University of Manitoba, where he is also an assistant professor and education specialist. He has cross-appointments with the Department of Psychology, the Department of Medical Education, and the Faculty of Education. As a social psychologist, he enjoys exploring the cognitive dynamics between effective teaching and student learning in higher education. These dynamics include different teaching behaviors (e.g., expressiveness and organization) and teaching styles, as well as different student learning predispositions (e.g., locus of control, test anxiety, self-esteem). He can be reached at schonwet@cc.umanitoba.ca.

Sherrill L. Sellers is assistant professor in the School of Social Work at the University of Wisconsin–Madison. Her research program centers on the examination of the impact of social inequalities on mental and physical health and in social institutions. She has published extensive projects using both quantitative and qualitative research methods, including articles in journals such as *Gender & Society*, *Ethnicity and Disease*, and *American Journal of Public Health*. Sherrill is a co-leader of the Center for the Integration of Research, Teaching, and Learning Diversity Team, funded by the National Science Foundation to promote the development of a national faculty in science, technology, engineering, and mathematics committed to implementing and advancing effective teaching practices for diverse student audiences as part of their professional careers. She can be reached at slsellers@wisc.edu.

Shana Shaw is in her second year of a doctoral program at the University of Texas at Austin, where she is also an assistant instructor in the College of Education. Her research interests in faculty development include investigations of divergent instructional methods and techniques instructors can use to evaluate learning in the classroom. She can be reached at shanashaw@mail.utexas.edu.

Steven J. Skinner is the Rosenthal Professor in the Gatton College of Business and Economics at the University of Kentucky, where he teaches courses in marketing strategy. He has authored or coauthored several books and numerous articles in the area of marketing strategy and sales management. He can be reached at mkt210@uky.edu.

Marilla Svinicki is former director of the University of Texas at Austin's Center for Teaching Effectiveness and is a former president of the Professional and Organizational Development Network in Higher Education. She left the center after 30 years to become a full-time professor of educational psychology. Her work focuses on the integration of theory and practice in teaching and learning. She can be reached at msvinicki@mail.utexas.edu.

Michael Sweet works in the Division of Instructional Innovation and Assessment at the University of Texas at Austin. He has been in faculty and teaching assistant development at both research universities and community colleges since 1995. His educational psychology research focuses on collaborative learning at the college level. He can be reached at msweet@austin.utexas.edu.

Franklin A. Tuitt is assistant professor of higher education at the University of Denver. His research explores a range of topics related to access and equity in higher education, teaching and learning in racially diverse college classrooms, and diversity and organizational transformation. Frank is a co-editor and contributing author of the book *Race and Higher Education: Rethinking Pedagogy in Diverse College Classrooms*. He is a former co-chair of the *Harvard Educational Review* (Harvard Education Press, 2003) and a 2003 Ed.D. graduate from the Harvard Graduate School of Education. He can be reached at ftuitt@du.edu.

Mary Walczak is associate professor and chair of chemistry at St. Olaf College. She has a bachelor's degree in chemistry from the University of St. Thomas and a Ph.D. in physical chemistry from Iowa State University. Her research interests are focused on promoting scientific literacy among general education students, interdisciplinary teaching and learning, and measuring student learning outcomes. Mary will serve as interim director of the Office of Academic Research and Planning during 2008. She can be reached at walczak@stolaf.edu.

Joshua Walker is pursuing his Ph.D. in educational psychology at the University of Texas at Austin. He was a Korean linguist in the U.S. Marine Corps before earning his bachelor's degree in psychology and theology. His current areas of research include faculty development, developmental education, collaborative learning, and personal epistemology. Josh supervises graduate student instructors as an assistant coordinator for a multisection learning-to-learn course. He can be reached at josh.walker@mail.utexas.edu.

Stephen Walls is a doctoral student in educational psychology at the University of Texas (UT) at Austin. His research focuses on student motivation and faculty development in postsecondary education settings. He received his MBA in 1996 and is presently a faculty member in UT–Austin's marketing department. He can be reached at stephenwalls@austins.rr.com.

Mark Weisberg is a member of the law faculty at Queens University as well as an educational development faculty associate at the Queens Centre for Teaching and Learning. He is interested in ethics and professionalism, how people learn and develop as professionals, as well as in all forms of writing. He has taught graduate courses on teaching and learning for students interested in a teaching career. Mark has received provincial and national teaching awards for his work with students and teachers. He can be reached at weisberg@post.queensu.ca.

Mary C. Wright is coordinator of graduate student initiatives for the Center for Research on Learning and Teaching (CRLT) at the University of Michigan. Her work at CRLT focuses on Preparing Future Faculty programs and graduate student development. She received her Ph.D. in sociology from the University of Michigan. Mary's research and teaching interests include faculty-institutional congruence of values, attrition in the sciences, and qualitative methods. Her book, *Always at Odds? Creating Alignment between Faculty and Administrative Values,* is forthcoming from SUNY Press. She can be reached at mcwright@umich.edu.

Erping Zhu is an instructional consultant and coordinator of instructional technology at the Center for Research on Learning and Teaching at the University of Michigan (U-M). She provides consultations to faculty on teaching and course design with emphasis on integrating technology into instruction and online teaching. She collaborates with colleagues from U-M technology units to present services and programs to faculty such as the Enriching Scholarship program, and she co-directs the Teaching with Technology Institute. She can be reached at ezhu@umich.edu.

Preface

This year is the last of my four-year editorial term for *To Improve the Academy* (two years as associate editor and two years as editor). These four years have impressed upon me the remarkable, even marvelous, nature of this volume, a high-quality, peer-reviewed, useful collection of scholarly work on educational development that is delivered annually to members of the Professional and Organizational Development Network in Higher Education and the larger higher education community. It is a collection that is created collectively. This year, 131 people were involved as authors, reviewers, editors, or project managers. In the span of a few months, some of which include end-of-the-year holidays, this huge band, most of whom do not interact with each other, somehow performs a monumental, cooperative effort to produce the miracle of this volume for little reward other than the deep satisfaction of a job well done for a cause that is larger than one's self.

Many people deserve thanks. First, I want to thank the many colleagues who submitted their good work for review, all 109 of them. This generosity of spirit, impulse to share, and willingness to risk is the heart and soul of developing our professional literature. In order to grow a scholarship of educational development, our challenge is similar to nurturing a scholarship of teaching and learning: We must make our work public, express it in a form that can be circulated easily, and present it for review by our peers. All of the people who submitted their work for review this year, whether or not it was accepted, have advanced this important cause and merit our gratitude and praise.

Members of the review panel for TIA 26 somehow managed to read carefully and provide thoughtful comments for up to 10 manuscripts each during a compressed turnaround period over the holidays, a truly remarkable accomplishment and one without which this volume could not have been produced. So also earning high praise are the 17 members of TIA 26's review panel who altogether provided 162 reviews: David Ametrano, Danilo Baylen, Donna Bird, Phyllis Blumberg, Frances Johnson, Patricia Joyce, Jean Layne, Virginia Lee, Rachel Levin, Alice Macpherson, Edward Nuhfer, Candyce Reynolds, Elizabeth Sandell, Maren Schierloh, Yianna Vovides, Susan Weaver, and Mary Wright.

Another critical member of the team that produced this volume is Associate Editor Linda Nilson. I appreciate Linda not just for what she does, which is wondrous, but for who she is, which is even more marvelous. Dependable, intelligent, sophisticated, informed, principled, spirited, compassionate, and witty, Linda has contributed immeasurably to this volume with her editorial talent, abundant energy, and sparkling insight. She has provided me with deeply valued colleagueship and consistently candid and wise counsel. As Linda assumes her two-year appointment as TIA editor, I know that her work will be exemplary, and I am already looking forward to reading volumes 27 and 28.

Keeping track of manuscripts, authors, reviewers, reviews, biographies, contributors' agreements, and so forth, for a project involving 131 different people, is a huge administrative challenge. Conquering this logistical behemoth with her inspired determination (and Access database) was Patty Wilsey, coordinator of the Professional and Organizational Development Center at Northern Kentucky University. Without Patty's administrative brilliance, remarkable attention to detail, and unshakable can-do spirit, this volume would not have appeared, and I cannot thank her enough for her essential contribution.

Also noteworthy is the work of Carolyn Dumore, who not only provided timely support and editorial acumen but served as a crucial and much-appreciated anchor for this project as the publication of TIA moved from Anker to Jossey-Bass just as the final draft of this manuscript was taking shape. I greatly appreciate Carolyn's well-informed, reliably responsive, and always kind help with this project.

Finally, I want to thank two people who helped fundamentally to produce this volume without realizing it. They are my wife, Dr. Sue Robertson Reimondo, director of Counseling and Psychological Services at Berea College, and my daughter, Maura Eileen Robertson, seventh-grade honors student and all-around good person. They teach me daily the connection between love and work and how crucial it is for who you are and what you contribute to get that connection right.

Douglas Reimondo Robertson
Northern Kentucky University
Highland Heights, Kentucky
April 2007

Introduction

This volume offers a spectrum of generative contributions that can be organized into six themes: evaluating teaching, the scholarship of teaching and learning, the scholarship of educational development, educational development and diversity, educational development centers and professionals, and faculty and instructional development.

Section I: Evaluating Teaching

This section includes two chapters that examine issues related to the thorny problem of evaluating teaching, a challenge that has vital importance because of its connection to faculty reward systems and thereby to motivating faculty to give time, energy, and passion to improving their teaching.

Chapter 1. L. Dee Fink presents a thoughtful, comprehensive model for evaluating teaching that applies across disciplines and missions. If faculty evaluation systems meaningfully reward good teaching at least on a par with scholarly and creative productivity, then more faculty will give more attention to the quality of their teaching. The central problem is being able to evaluate teaching validly and reliably. Fink's model provides an intriguing solution.

Chapter 2. Stacie Badran discusses her national study of the criteria used to evaluate the quality of teaching in teaching awards programs in research-productive mathematics departments. The results are telling and contribute to our understanding of the significance of context in supporting instructional development.

Section II: Scholarship of Teaching and Learning

This section has three chapters that explore different aspects of the important endeavor of continuing to develop the scholarship of teaching and learning.

Chapter 3. Richard A. Gale notes the long-standing and problematical privilege given to individualistic frames regarding accomplishment in higher education and, within the context of the scholarship of teaching and learning (SoTL), argues in favor of the benefits of collective and collaborative work. Gale develops useful frameworks and concrete examples for conceptualizing and doing meta-individual SoTL.

Chapter 4. Joan Middendorf and David Pace present an ingenious and effective approach to getting faculty involved with formal assessment, one of the more promising approaches to this difficult challenge to be advanced in recent years.

Chapter 5. Dolores Peters, David Schodt, and Mary Walczak present a similarly clever approach to encouraging and supporting faculty engagement in the scholarship of teaching and learning within the context of a teaching-intensive liberal arts college, particularly in its general education curriculum.

Section III: Scholarship of Educational Development

This section contains two chapters that extend the emerging scholarship of educational development, a growing area of work in which educational developers conduct research on a variety of issues, especially the outcomes of their practices and programs.

Chapter 6. Michael Sweet, Rochelle Roberts, Joshua Walker, Stephen Walls, John Kucsera, Shana Shaw, Janet Riekenberg, and Marilla Svinicki provide a valuable service to the field by presenting a primer on a well-established research method called "grounded theory," a radically inductive approach that employs qualitative research techniques to generate theory. Both pure and applied research in educational development can benefit from this research method.

Chapter 7. Susan Polich presents a rare formal study of the outcomes for participants in a popular but little-researched faculty development tool called "faculty learning communities." Her provocative results suggest that faculty learning communities, although valuable for many reasons, are not deeply transformative of faculty participants' personal epistemologies (notwithstanding their self-reports to the contrary) and that participants tend to self-select into communities with which their beliefs are already consonant.

Section IV: Educational Development and Diversity

This section presents two highly complementary chapters that investigate different ways in which educational developers can contribute to a culture of inclusiveness in colleges and universities.

Chapter 8. Franklin A. Tuitt and Lois Reddick review the research literature related to stereotype threat, one of the more powerful and generative constructs to come out of social psychology in the last 10 years. Although research has focused on race and gender, the concept has use for situations in which any identity stereotype is operant (e.g., sexual preference, religion, ability, class, etc.). In addition, Tuitt and Reddick develop 10 concrete, research-based suggestions for reducing stereotype threat in instructional environments.

Chapter 9. Katherine A. Friedrich, Sherrill L. Sellers, and Judith N. Burstyn present a thoughtful, well-informed, and succinct discussion of an effective approach to helping faculty and teaching assistants who are teaching science, technology, engineering, or mathematics courses to increase the inclusiveness of their teaching and their classrooms.

Section V: Educational Development Centers and Professionals

This section consists of three chapters that deal with the work of educational developers in various institutional contexts.

Chapter 10. Victoria Mundy Bhavsar and Steven J. Skinner address the common problem of raising campus awareness at a large university through an educational development unit by the synergistic and novel means of collaborating with students in a senior-level marketing capstone course to develop a marketing plan for the educational development unit.

Chapter 11. Kim M. Mooney and Michael Reder provide a useful service by thoughtfully identifying trends, issues, and choices for promoting educational development roles and programs within the context of small and liberal arts colleges.

Chapter 12. Bonnie Mullinix discusses results from an empirical study of 100 educational developers from colleges and universities in 39 U.S. states as well as in Canada, Japan, and Korea. Rich with information about the educational developer's role in a wide variety of institutions, the discussion usefully focuses on the issue of the perceived significance of faculty status for educational developers.

Section VI: Faculty and Instructional Development

This section comprises eight chapters that present a range of fascinating approaches and tools for facilitating the development of faculty and their teaching. Noteworthy is the promising number of authors who include the scholarship of educational development as part of their practice of faculty and instructional development.

Chapter 13. Andrea L. Beach, Charles Henderson, and Michael Famiano provide a discussion of both a cost-effective instructional development technique (co-teaching as opposed to team teaching) and a good example of the scholarship of educational development (actually conducting a study of the outcomes of using the technique).

Chapter 14. Susanna Calkins and Greg Light model good practice by attaching the scholarship of educational development to an impressive instructional development technique that they use with new faculty. The technique involves a sustained, yearlong project and includes participant reflection, a key element that, unfortunately, is often missing in the developmental activities of busy professionals.

Chapter 15. Tara Gray and A. Jane Birch discuss and document (again practicing the scholarship of educational development) a highly effective team approach to mentoring junior faculty. The way in which the approach engages the faculty participants in their own development and builds over time is particularly intriguing and impressive.

Chapter 16. Matthew Kaplan, Deborah S. Meizlish, Christopher O'Neal, and Mary C. Wright use their scholarship and experience to establish the widespread use of teaching philosophy statements, to develop a rubric for writing such statements, and to evaluate the effectiveness of the rubric. The chapter provides an excellent, research-based tool to assist with the common need of helping faculty and teaching assistants to formulate and express their teaching philosophies.

Chapter 17. Jane Love discusses ad hoc connectivity, a profoundly interesting programmatic solution to the challenge of integrative learning that uses face-to-face faculty workshops ("unplugged" forms) and online search tools ("plugged" forms) to help teachers recognize naturally occurring conceptual connections among their courses. The work encourages and supports integrative learning without the use of sometimes costly and politically vulnerable special courses and formal team teaching.

Chapter 18. Dieter J. Schönwetter describes the benefits for teaching assistants, new faculty, scholars of teaching and learning, and educational developers of creating teaching resource portfolios, annotated bibliographies on teaching and learning that grow over a career and can be shared with others.

Chapter 19. Mark Weisberg deals with the sine qua non of deep professional development: reflection. He works with this foundational practice within the context of Teachers' Reading Circles, Teachers' Writing Circles, and a hybrid workshop that he facilitated at the 2006 Professional and Organizational Development Network in Higher Education Conference. Poignant, powerful, and authentic, his chapter provides a rich resource for educational developers who are interested in the use of contemplative practice in professional development.

Chapter 20. Erping Zhu identifies common barriers to faculty integrating instructional technologies into their practice and develops 12 well-founded and insightful recommendations for supporting faculty in overcoming these barriers.

With this volume, thanks to its many contributors, the professional literature related to educational development grows meaningfully, both quantitatively and qualitatively. As editor, I hope that you find the volume worthwhile. I have a long-standing objective for faculty development workshops that I facilitate: that each participant takes away at least one concrete technique to use right away and at least one big idea on which to chew for a while. So it is with this volume. May each of you find in this book something that is immediately useful for you as well as something that, through your working with it over time and making it your own, ultimately takes you to a higher ground of understanding and practice.

Ethical Guidelines for Educational Developers

Preamble

Educational developers, as professionals, have a unique opportunity and a special responsibility to contribute to improving the quality of teaching and learning in higher education. As members of the academic community, we are subject to all the codes of conduct and ethical guidelines that already exist for those who work or study on our campuses and in our respective disciplinary associations. In addition, we have special ethical responsibilities because of the unique and privileged access we have to people and information, often sensitive information. This document provides general guidelines that can and should inform the practice of everyone working in these development roles.

Individuals who work as educational developers come from many different disciplinary areas. Some of us work in this field on a part-time basis, or for a short time; for others, this is our full-time career. The nature of our responsibilities and prerogatives as developers varies with our position in the organization, our experience, and our interests and talents, as well as with the special characteristics of our institutions. This document attempts to provide general ethical guidelines that should apply to most developers across a variety of settings.

Ethical guidelines indicate a consensus among practitioners about the ideals that should inform our practice as professionals, as well as those behaviors that we would identify as misconduct. Between ideals and misconduct is an area of dilemmas: where each of our choices seems equally right or wrong; or where our different roles and/or responsibilities place competing—if not incompatible—demands on us; or where certain behaviors may seem questionable but there is no consensus that those behaviors are misconduct.

It is our hope that these guidelines will complement individual statements of philosophy and mission and that they will be useful to educational developers in the following ways:

- In promoting ethical practice by describing the ideals of our practice

- In providing a model for thinking through situations which contain conflicting choices or questionable behavior

- In identifying those specific behaviors which we agree represent professional misconduct

Responsibilities to Clients

- Provide services to everyone within our mandate, provided that we are able to serve them responsibly

- Treat clients fairly, respecting their uniqueness, their fundamental rights, dignity, and worth, and their right to set objectives and make decisions

- Continue services only as long as the client is benefiting, discontinuing service by mutual consent; suggest other resources to meet needs we cannot or should not address

- Maintain appropriate boundaries in the relationship; avoid exploiting the relationship in any way; be clear with ourselves and our clients about our role

- Protect all privileged information and get informed consent from our client before using or referring publicly to his or her case in such a way that the person could possibly be identified

Competence and Integrity

Behavior

- Clarify professional roles and obligations

- Accept appropriate responsibility for our behavior

- Don't make false or intentionally misleading statements

- Avoid the distortion and misuse of our work

- When providing services at the behest of a third party, clarify our roles and responsibilities with each party from the outset

- Model ethical behavior with coworkers and supervisees and in the larger community

- Accept appropriate responsibility for the behavior of those we supervise

Skills and Boundaries

- Be reflective and self-critical in our practice; strive to be aware of our own belief system, values, biases, needs, and the effect of these on our work

- Incorporate diverse points of view

- Know and act in consonance with our purpose, mandate, and philosophy, integrating them insofar as possible

- Ensure that we have the institutional freedom to do our job ethically

- Don't allow personal or private interests to conflict or appear to conflict with professional duties or the client's needs

- Continually seek out knowledge, skills, and resources to undergird and expand our practice

- Consult with other professionals when we lack the experience or training for a particular case or endeavor and in order to prevent and avoid unethical conduct

- Know and work within the boundaries of our competence and time limitations

- Take care of our personal welfare so we can take care of others

Others' Rights

- Be receptive to different styles and approaches to teaching and learning and to others' professional roles and functions

- Respect the rights of others to hold values, attitudes, and opinions different from our own

- Respect the right of the client to refuse our services or to ask for the services of another

- Work against harassment and discrimination of any kind, including race, gender, class, religion, sexual orientation, age, nationality, etc.

- Be aware of various power relationships with clients (e.g., power based on position or on information); don't abuse our power

Confidentiality

- Keep confidential the identity of our clients, as well as our observations, interactions, or conclusions related to specific individuals or cases

- Know the legal requirements regarding appropriate and inappropriate professional confidentiality (e.g., for cases of murder, suicide, or gross misconduct)

- Store and dispose of records in a safe way; comply with institutional, state, and federal regulations about storing and ownership of records

- Conduct discreet conversations among professional colleagues; don't discuss clients in public places

Responsibilities to the Profession

- Attribute materials and ideas to their authors or creators

- Contribute ideas, experience, and knowledge to colleagues

- Respond promptly to requests from colleagues

- Respect your colleagues and acknowledge their differences

- Work positively for the development of individuals and the profession

- Cooperate with other units and professionals involved in development efforts

- Be an advocate for our institutional and professional mission

- Take responsibility when you become aware of gross unethical conduct in the profession

Conflicts Arising from Multiple Responsibilities, Constituents, Relationships, Loyalties

We are responsible to the institution, faculty, graduate students, undergraduate students, and our own ethical values. These multiple responsibilities and relationships to various constituencies, together with competing loyalties, can lead to conflicting ethical responsibilities, for example, when:

- An instructor is teaching extremely poorly, and the students are suffering seriously as a result

  Conflict: responsibility of confidentiality to client teacher versus responsibility to students and institution to take some immediate action

- A faculty member wants to know how a TA, with whom we are working, is doing in his or her work with us or in the classroom

  Conflict: responding to faculty's legitimate concern versus confidentiality with TA

- We know firsthand that a professor is making racist, sexist remarks or is sexually harassing a student

  Conflict: confidentiality with professor versus institutional and personal ethical responsibilities, along with responsibility to students

- A fine teacher is coming up for tenure, has worked with our center or program for two years, and asks for a letter to the tenure committee

  Conflict: confidentiality rules versus our commitment to advocate for good teaching on campus and in tenure decisions

In such instances, we need to practice sensitive and sensible confidentiality:

- Consult in confidence with other professionals when we have conflicting or confusing ethical choices

- Break confidentiality in cases of potential suicide, murder, or gross misconduct; in such cases, to do nothing is to do something

- Inform the other person or persons when we have to break confidentiality, unless to do so would be to jeopardize our safety or the safety of someone else

- Decide cases of questionable practice individually, after first informing ourselves, to the best of our ability, of all the ramifications of our actions; work to determine when we will act or not act, while being mindful of the rules and regulations of the institution and the relevant legal requirements.

Conflicts Arising from Multiple Roles

As educational developers, we often assume or are assigned roles which might be characterized as, for example, teaching police, doctor, coach, teacher, or advocate, among others. We endeavor to provide a "safe place" for our clients; we are at the same time an institutional model and a guardian or a conscience for good teaching. These multiple roles can also lead to ethical conflicts.

Some educational developers, for example, serve both as faculty developers and as faculty members. As faculty we are on review committees, but through our faculty development work have access to information that probably is not public but is important to the cases involved. Given these multiple roles, it is important always to clarify our role for ourselves, and for those with whom and for whom we are working. When necessary, recuse ourselves.

Summative Evaluation

A particular case of multiple roles needing guidelines is the summative evaluation of teaching. Faculty and administrators (chairs, deans, etc.) have the responsibility for the assessment of teaching for personnel decisions.

In general, educational developers do not make summative judgments about an individual's teaching. In particular, we should never perform the role of developer and summative evaluator concurrently for the same individual, other than with that person's explicit consent and with proper declaration to any panel or committee. However, we may provide assessment tools, collect student evaluations, help individuals prepare dossiers, educate those who make summative decisions, and critique evaluation systems.

Conclusion

These guidelines are an attempt to define ethical behaviors for the current practice of our profession. The core committee welcomes comments and suggestions as we continue to refine this document in light of the changes and issues confronting us as educational developers in higher education. The guidelines will be updated on a periodic basis.

We would like to thank our many colleagues who offered their thoughtful comments on earlier drafts.

In creating this document, we have referred to and borrowed from the ethical guidelines of the following organizations: American Psychological Association, American Association for Marriage and Family Therapy, Guidance Counselors, Society for Teaching and Learning in Higher Education, Staff and Educational Development Association.

Prepared by Mintz, Smith, & Warren, January 1999. Revised March 1999, September 1999, and March 2000.

Section I
Evaluating Teaching

Evaluating Teaching: A New Approach to an Old Problem

L. Dee Fink
Instructional Consultant in Higher Education

The approach to evaluating the quality of teaching described in this chapter starts by developing a Model of Good Teaching. This model is then used to create a set of evaluation procedures based on four key dimensions of teaching: design of learning experiences, quality of teacher/student interactions, extent and quality of student learning, and teacher's effort to improve over time. The challenges and benefits of using these procedures are discussed.

American higher education badly needs to find a better way to evaluate teaching. Like any organization, colleges and universities need good procedures for knowing how well the people responsible for accomplishing the primary purposes of the organization are succeeding. For the educational portion of their mission, universities need to know how well their faculty members are succeeding in their role as professional educators—that is, in their assigned responsibilities for teaching tuition-paying students.

As with any organizational feedback procedure, this process needs to be done in a way that supports two important organizational needs. The individuals who teach need feedback that both motivates and enables them to know how well they are doing but also to know how to get better—that is, how to engage in continuous professional development. In addition, organizational leaders (chairs, deans, and provosts) need reliable information about who are and who are not performing well in their roles as professional educators. They need to know who are not performing well so they can encourage them to make a stronger effort to improve, and they need to know who are performing well so they can reward them and encourage them to share their performance insights with others.

Current procedures for evaluating teaching in American higher education are failing miserably on both counts. In a survey of 600 liberal arts colleges, Peter Seldin found that almost 90% use student questionnaires (Seldin & Associates, 1999), and many institutions reduce their assessment of the complex task of teaching to data from one or two questions to rank order faculty members as teachers. In an effort to determine how research universities evaluate teaching, Larry Loeher surveyed 62 Association of American Universities. He found that 98% of them used student questionnaires as "the primary method of evaluating teaching," and that only 77% of the institutions required faculty to evaluate all courses every term (Loeher, 2006).

These practices are clearly not driving any widespread faculty effort to improve teaching. What they are doing is creating widespread cynicism about teaching evaluations. Many faculty view student ratings as popularity contests, and more than one eyebrow has been raised about the recipients of teaching awards when these are based primarily or solely on student evaluations.

What can be done about this situation? What we do not need is another technical fix—that is, a new technique or procedure that is added to student ratings. This will be rejected as simply adding to the work of evaluating teaching without adding any sense of the need and reason for doing it right. Instead, we need to rethink what teaching is and what teachers should be doing to be "good teachers." Then we need to develop a set of procedures for evaluating teaching based on this Model of Good Teaching.

In the process of developing a Model of Good Teaching, one has to be careful not to focus on specific ways of teaching or specific teaching strategies. There are different specific ways of being "good." The model should strive to identify the general principles that cut across and transcend different ways of being successful as a teacher. An analogy would be the challenge of identifying success in sports. In basketball, for example, some teams use a fast "run and gun" type offense; others use a slower, more deliberate style of offense. On defense, some teams use a few basic types of defense well while others deliberately mix up their defensive schemes to keep the other team off balance. Whatever the different specifics, teams can be evaluated in terms of how successful their offense and defense are, and in terms of their ultimate success: Do they score more points than they allow their opponents to score? Similarly, in teaching there are some common tasks that can be assessed and we can look for the ultimate measure of success: Does the teacher succeed in promoting high-quality learning in a high percentage of students?

In this chapter, I will lay out a description of the basic tasks involved in teaching and, based on this, propose an enlarged Model of Good Teaching. Although professors have disparate and sometimes conflicting views about teaching, this model has the potential to gain widespread acceptance because it focuses on general teaching practices rather than on specific activities or specific ways of teaching. Then I will describe procedures for evaluating teaching based on this enlarged Model of Good Teaching. Finally, I will present a case study from a university that used procedures very close to what is proposed here. This case illustrates important points about what good evaluation procedures can accomplish and what else is needed for them to fulfill the organizational needs mentioned earlier—that is, promoting faculty efforts to improve their teaching and giving organizational leaders reliable information about institutional success in its educational mission.

What Teaching Is: Four Fundamental Tasks

Most professors, given the lack of pre-service study of college teaching in graduate school, view their responsibilities as teachers in a rather simple-minded way: "My job as a teacher is to know my subject well and communicate my knowledge to students in a reasonably clear and organized manner." In fact, teaching involves much more than that. After 30 years of being a college teacher, working with college teachers as a faculty developer, and reading the literature on college-level teaching, I have come to view all teaching as involving four fundamental tasks (see Figure 1.1).

FIGURE 1.1

Four Fundamental Tasks of Teaching

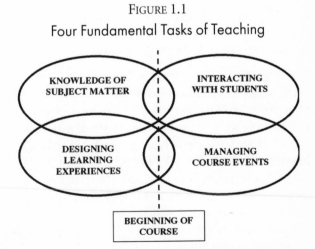

This is what is involved in each of these tasks:

- *Knowledge of subject matter.* Whenever we teach, we are trying to help someone learn about something. The "something" is the subject of the teaching and learning, and all good teachers have some advanced level of knowledge about the subject.

- *Designing learning experiences.* Teachers also have to make decisions ahead of time about what the learning experience is going to include and how they want it to unfold. For example: What reading material will be used? What kinds of writing activities will they have students do? Will there be field experiences? Will the teacher use small group activities? How will student learning be assessed? Collectively, these decisions represent the teacher's design or plan for the learning experience.

These first two tasks happen primarily before the course begins but continue to a lesser degree during the course as well. Once the course is under way, the other two components come into play in a major way:

- *Interacting with students.* Throughout a course, the teacher and the students interact in multiple ways. Lecturing, leading whole class or small group discussions, email exchanges, writing comments on student papers, and meeting with students during office hours—these are all different ways of interacting with students.

- *Course management.* A course is a complex set of events that involves specific activities and materials. One of the responsibilities of the teacher is to keep track of and manage all of the information and materials involved. A teacher needs to know who has enrolled in the course and who has dropped it, who has taken a test and who was absent, who got what grade on their homework and exams, and so forth.

These four tasks are involved in all teaching, whether traditional or innovative, excellent or poor. Everyone—for better or worse—invokes his or her own knowledge of the subject, makes decisions about the learning experience, interacts with students, and manages information and materials.

My belief is that there is a direct relationship between how well a teacher performs these four fundamental tasks and the quality of the students' learning experience. If the teacher does all four well, students will have a good learning experience. To the degree that the teacher does one or more poorly, the quality of the learning experience declines.

After working closely with college teachers for many years, my observation is that we are not equally well prepared for each of these four tasks:

- With but few exceptions, college teachers have a reasonably good knowledge of their subject. Graduate school training as well as most hiring and tenure procedures are focused on determining whether the person has an in-depth knowledge of their particular discipline.

- Our knowledge about course design, however, is a different matter. The vast majority of college teachers have not had any formal training in instructional design. This is one of the reasons that poor course design is the underlying problem behind many of our teaching problems (Fink, 2003).

- Teachers' ability to interact with students varies widely. As a faculty developer, I have observed a lot of teachers interact with their students. Our teacher-interaction skills range from very bad to incredibly good.

- As for course management, the majority of teachers handle this task adequately. However, I have seen a few teachers who were so disorganized (handouts not ready on time, materials not put together properly) that it negatively affected the quality of the students' learning experience.

Because these fundamental tasks are involved in all instances of teaching, we will need to incorporate them in some way into our procedures for evaluating teaching. But this variation in preparation and performance will affect which ones we include.

However, before we move to constructing better procedures for evaluating teaching, we need to look at two other important processes involved in good teaching.

An Enlarged Model of Good Teaching

What is it that we would like to see all teachers do, that would in a general sense constitute "good teaching"? The proposition put forth here is that teachers are good if they do each of the following three things:

- Perform the *fundamental tasks* of teaching well.

- Teach in a way that leads to *high-quality student learning*.

- Work continuously at *getting better over time* as a teacher.

The basic idea here is that any teacher, to be a good teacher, needs to pay attention to—that is, gather information about and act on—all three factors. In this section, I will elaborate on the meaning of these three factors. The next section will show how this model offers a powerful framework for laying out a new way of evaluating teaching.

Fundamental Tasks of Teaching

It is worth noting that the creator of one of the more comprehensive approaches to evaluating teaching, Raoul Arreola (2000), also identified four "defining roles" of teaching: content, delivery, design, and management. These are essentially identical to the four fundamental tasks described here and shown earlier in Figure 1.1.

This suggests there may be growing consensus about the central tasks involved in all teaching. To the degree that this is true, we need to include them in some way in our evaluation of teaching.

The Quality of Student Learning

The quality of student learning occurs in three phases. The desired quality of student learning in each phase can be described in the following way:

- *During the course:* Students are *engaged.* They attend class regularly, they pay attention, they participate in class discussions, they do the work of learning.

- *At the end of the course:* Student engagement has resulted in *significant learning that lasts.* Some student learning is not significant and doesn't last. Good learning is significant and does last.

- *After the course:* That which students learn *adds value to their lives.* It might do this by enhancing their individual lives (e.g., history, literature), preparing them for the world of work, or preparing them to contribute to the many communities of which we are all a part: family, local community, nation state, global interest groups, and so on.

We want all three of these to occur. But if the teacher finds a way to make the second kind of learning happen—significant learning that has been developed up to and by the end of the course—this greatly increases the likelihood of getting the other two to happen: engaging students during the course and generating learning that adds value to their lives after the course is over. How then might we define "significant learning"?

Elsewhere (Fink, 2003) I have offered a Taxonomy of Significant Learning that builds on the well-known taxonomy of Benjamin Bloom and his associates but tries to incorporate newer kinds of learning that recent writers have advocated. In this taxonomy, like in Bloom's, there are six categories. But, unlike Bloom's, these are interactive rather than hierarchical (see Figure 1.2).

FIGURE 1.2

Taxonomy of Significant Learning

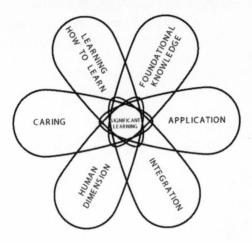

Teachers have found that by using good course design, they can get all six kinds of learning to occur in a single course. In such courses, students are able to:

- *Understand and remember* the key concepts, terms, relationships, and the like (foundational knowledge).

- Know how to *use* the content (application).

- *Relate* this subject to other subjects (integration).

- Identify the *personal and social* implications of knowing about this subject (human dimension: self and others).

- *Value* this subject—as well as value further learning about this subject (caring).

- Know *how to keep on learning* about this subject—after the course is over (how to keep on learning).

But the main point here is that, whether they use Bloom's taxonomy or this taxonomy of significant learning, good teachers strive for many students to achieve high-quality learning—learning that includes but goes well beyond simply learning the content.

Getting Better Over Time

The real goal of any teacher should be more than just striving to be a "good" teacher. The real goal should be to get better at teaching—year after year after year. Teaching is a profession, and all good professionals know they must work continuously to improve their competence in whatever they do.

Professional educators need to recognize that, like everyone else, they have the potential to improve as a teacher. If you ask award-winning teachers whether they can get better, they inevitably say yes. If there is room for improvement in *their* teaching, there is definitely room for the rest of us to get better as well.

Teachers who do get better over time regularly engage in a set of specific activities that I call "The Cycle for Improving Teaching," shown in Figure 1.3.

FIGURE 1.3

The Cycle for Improving Teaching

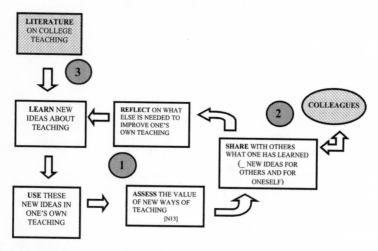

Note. The numbered circles indicate three ways by which faculty can acquire new ideas about teaching and learning.

The cycle begins when a teacher:

- *Acquires a new idea about teaching or learning.* Professors can and usually do learn from their own experience when they observe and analyze their own teaching (Circle 1). They can also acquire new ideas from talking with colleagues, participating in workshops, and the like (Circle 2). However, there is a rich literature on college teaching that has grown exponentially in the last 15 years. This is what most professors are not accessing but need to (Circle 3). See Fink (2005) for a review of some of this literature, a list of the books and associated ideas that have been especially valuable to me.

- *Uses that idea by changing something in their teaching.* Without changing something, it is not possible to improve.

- *Assesses the change by collecting and analyzing information from the course.* This allows them to know whether the change improved something or not (e.g., the quality of student learning, more engaged students, greater joy in teaching, etc.). Only then can they make a good decision about whether to keep the change or discard it.

- *Shares by engaging in dialogue with colleagues about teaching.* Sharing may take place either informally or formally as in conference presentations or journal articles. Formal sharing constitutes the scholarship of teaching and learning and has the potential to benefit both the presenter and the recipient of the sharing.

- *Reflects on what else they might* learn *that could improve their teaching.*

- *Begins another round of the cycle.*

Integrating the Three Factors Involved in Good Teaching

The three factors that we have just examined are linked to each other in important ways, as shown in Figure 1.4.

FIGURE 1.4

A Model of Good Teaching

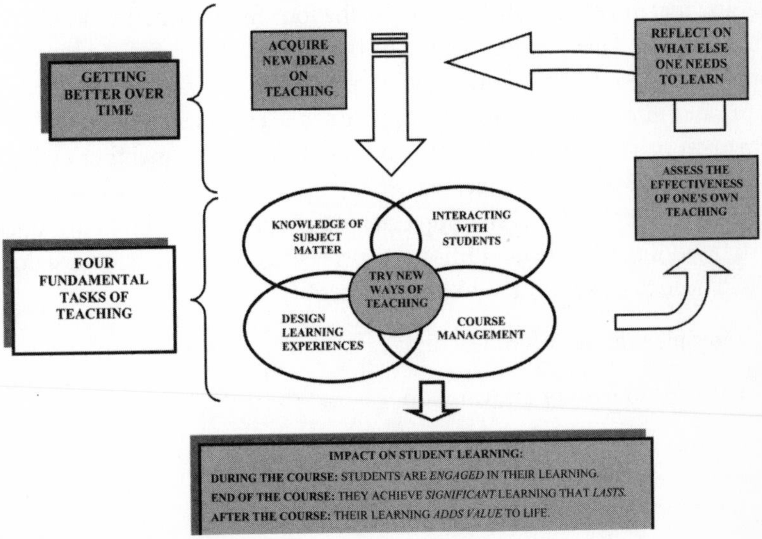

The teacher's ability to adequately perform the fundamental tasks of teaching affects the quality of students' learning experiences. And feedback on the quality of both these factors can and should shape the professor's efforts to improve. The goal is for this cycle to continue—year after year after year.

Now that we have a basic understanding of the Model of Good Teaching, we are ready to use it as a basis for constructing new procedures for evaluating teaching.

Procedures for Evaluating Teaching

The most common way of evaluating teaching at the present time is to use student questionnaires. To be sure, the systematic gathering of information from students is preferable to no evaluation system at all or to letting the department chair base his or her evaluation on one or two random conversations with students. However, student questionnaires have significant limitations as well. First, students only have information about one part of teaching, not the many dimensions identified here. Second, when student questionnaire data are the only data used, they are susceptible to manipulation by teachers who make themselves popular with students by being entertaining, giving easy grades, and so on.

In recent years, more sophisticated procedures for evaluating teaching have been developed and introduced into higher education. One of the best of these is the approach developed by Raoul Arreola (2000). His model calls for academic departments to allocate points to the four role components of teaching that are essentially the same as the four fundamental tasks identified in this chapter. This method is a major improvement over most college questionnaires in two ways: It looks at a broader range of teaching roles and it incorporates information from multiple sources. However, it does not call for information about student learning or about the faculty member's efforts to improve as a professional educator.

The procedures for evaluating teaching proposed here build on Arreola's work by adding these two additional aspects of good teaching. As we do this, we will need to pay attention to how we identify:

- Multiple dimensions of teaching

- Relevant sources of information

- Criteria and standards for excellence

Multiple Dimensions of Teaching

Although Arreola used all of the four fundamental tasks of teaching and nothing more, I propose using only two of the fundamental tasks and then adding the other two components in the Model of Good Teaching described earlier.

I suggest dropping "knowledge of the subject matter" and "course management" from the list of fundamental tasks used to evaluate teaching. The reason for this is simply my observation that, for the majority of professors, these two tasks are not the primary bottlenecks to better teaching and better student learning. However, if the leaders in an academic unit believe there are significant variations in these two capabilities that are important enough to affect the teaching and learning process, then they can and should add one or both of these tasks back into the set of evaluation procedures.

I also propose condensing or collapsing the subfactors in the other two major components of this model: "student learning" and "getting better over time." We can gather information about student learning during and by the end of the course; but getting information about the degree to which that learning "adds value to one's life after the course," while important, is generally beyond the scope of annual evaluations or even evaluations for tenure. Information about the various steps in getting better over time is incorporated into one general report on this aspect of teaching.

Hence, the procedures proposed here call for gathering information about these four dimensions of teaching:

- The *design* of the learning experience

- The quality of *teacher-student interactions*

- The *learning* achieved by students (during and by the end of the course)

- The teacher's *efforts to improve* over time

Relevant Sources of Information

Before we can start assessing teaching, there must also be a good source of information for each dimension. Because we now have multiple dimensions of teaching, we also need multiple sources of information (Arreola, 2000; Seldin, 1999).

The sources that seem appropriate for each of these four dimensions are shown in Table 1.1.

TABLE 1.1

Sources of Information for Four Dimensions of Teaching

Criteria	Primary Source of Information
• The design of courses	• Course design materials
• Teacher-student interaction	• Student questionnaires, peer observations
• Quality of student learning	• Samples of student learning materials
• Getting better over time	• Teacher self-report, documentation

Course design materials. Teachers should assemble a variety of materials that reflect how they designed the course. These would include the syllabus as well as examples of assignments and exams. (With the advent of more computer-enhanced teaching, "course materials" will need to include information about the course web site and perhaps reference to off-campus web sites used, such as learning objects from the MERLOT web site.)

Student questionnaires and peer observations. These are in common use now. But if we can develop a more focused rationale for the kinds of teacher-student interactions that are important for promoting high-quality learning, we will be able to formulate questions that give us better information about desirable kinds of interactions. We can also ask peers or faculty developers to observe our classes and provide feedback.

Student learning materials. Teachers should assemble a set of materials produced by students: exams, projects, writing assignments, and so forth. These should include a sampling of A level work, C level work, and F work. We would also want to know what percentage of the students received As, Bs, Cs, Ds, Fs, and Ws.

Teacher self-report and documentation. Teachers should provide a report of their own performance on all four dimensions. A major part of this report should focus on what they did to improve their teaching—what they did to learn new ideas, what they changed in their teaching, how they assessed the impact of those changes—preferably with accompanying documentation.

Criteria and Standards for Excellence

What are needed next are indicators of quality for each of these four dimensions of teaching. This is necessary to answer questions such as: What makes one course design better than another? What makes one set of teacher-student interactions better than another (or better than the same teacher's interactions at an earlier time)?

Table 1.2 identifies the quality indicators I would suggest for each of these dimensions of teaching. However, individual departments or institutions can modify these or develop their own criteria and standards if they deem it appropriate to do so, still using this conceptual framework.

TABLE 1.2

Criteria for Assessing Excellence in Teaching

Course Design	• *Situational factors:* Course decisions should be based on solid information about multiple situational factors (e.g., the number of students, their prior knowledge, their feelings about this subject, etc.). • *Learning goals:* Are focused on higher level learning, more than just content coverage. • *Learning activities:* Are active and not primarily passive. • *Feedback and assessment:* These procedures enhance the learning process (i.e., they constitute educative assessment) and are more than just a basis for assigning grades. • *Level of integration:* The learning goals, teaching and learning activities, and the feedback and assessment procedures reflect and support each other.
Interaction with Students (individually and collectively)	Students perceive the teacher as: • Competent • Trustworthy • Dynamic (or energetic) • Challenging • Stimulating • Making students feel included and valued, regardless of age, ethnicity, class, nationality, etc.
Overall Quality of the Student Learning Experience	A high percentage of students: • Are engaged in their learning *during* the course. • Have achieved significant kinds of learning by the end of the course.
Improvement Over Time	• Seeks out new ideas on teaching. • Innovates and tries new ideas in one's own teaching. • Evaluates one's own teaching thoroughly. • Reflects continuously on "What do I need to learn about and do next to improve my teaching?"

Developing specific standards. For each dimension and subdimension of teaching, we need to develop specific standards that differentiate higher quality from lower quality teaching. This will be challenging at first because few academics have experience doing this.

The procedures I would recommend for developing these standards are as follows. First, respected members of an academic unit should be selected to do this task, and they should begin by taking time to acquire and develop a shared conceptual framework, one possibility being the framework described here. Second, they should collect materials from their colleagues' courses as described earlier. Third, they should identify characteristics of the best and worst examples of each criterion. As they do this, they may also want to incorporate ideas from the literature on college teaching that indicate what is "possible" on the high side. This would give even the best teachers something additional to strive for.

To get started, it may work best to just generate two descriptions of high and low quality. For example, the standards for high- and low-quality course design could be described as shown in Table 1.3.

TABLE 1.3

Standards for One Dimension of Teaching: Course Design

Low	High
• Is based on only a casual or cursory job of collecting information about the *situational factors.*	• Is based on a careful and thorough job of obtaining information on and analyzing *situational factors.*
• Does not have a clear statement of *learning goals,* only a list of topics to be covered.	• Has a clear statement of *learning goals,* and the goals go well beyond just learning the content and simple application skills.
• Does not use active learning, only *passive learning* (i.e., lectures and readings).	• In-class and out-of-class learning activities include *active learning* (e.g., experiential and reflective activities).
• Does not give frequent and immediate *feedback* to students on their learning, only one or two midterms and a final.	• Students receive *feedback* on their learning, weekly and at times daily, un-graded as well as graded.
• Does not use a dynamic or powerful *teaching strategy;* most classes are repetitions of the same learning activities, over and over.	• Teacher uses a *teaching strategy* with a combination and sequence of learning activities that build on each other and culminate in powerful, integrated learning.

With time and experience, evaluators will see enough examples of good and bad materials that they will be able to expand the number of categories and become skilled enough to write specific, focused descriptions for each category.

One Disadvantage of this Model—and a Solution

Every method for evaluating teaching has its advantages and disadvantages, and this method is no exception. We need to identify possible problems and try to find solutions.

The biggest problem is almost certainly the fact that this approach will require more time, compared to collecting and rank-ordering student questionnaire data. It will require more time by the teacher to collect and organize all of this information, and more time for someone else to analyze and make judgments about those materials. Is there a solution to this problem?

For me, the solution lies in the observation I hear from most department chairs, that the evaluations of a given teacher do not ordinarily change much from year to year. If this is true, then perhaps we do not need an in-depth evaluation of teachers every year. We could ask teachers to do an in-depth evaluation, say, every two to four years. It might be done annually during the pre-tenure years but only every two to four years after that. And it would always be done when someone is being nominated for a promotion or teaching award. In between those times, teaching could be evaluated in a less time-consuming way (e.g., student questionnaires plus a self-report from the teacher) but in a way that also ensures continued serious attention to the quality of teaching.

A Case Study: Important Lessons

In the 2000 edition of his book on evaluating teaching, Arreola included an appendix that described how Frostburg State University adopted a major change in their procedures for evaluating teaching based on his model. However, at that time, Frostburg State had only begun to use it. Therefore, I contacted the person identified in his book as the principal initiator of that effort, Tom Hawk, a professor in the business college, to see what had happened since then.

First, it is important to note that Frostburg State ended up doing more than what Arreola proposed and less than what I have proposed. In addition to collecting information on Arreola's four defining roles, they included a call for evidence of what the professors did for their own "professional development as an educator, teacher." However, they did not ask for specific information about what the teachers changed in their teaching nor about the extent and quality of student learning.

In the business college where Professor Hawk was able to exert some influence, this new way of evaluating teaching did result in a discernible increase in faculty activities in professional development as educators. Roughly 90% of the professors in the management division currently attend at least one workshop on teaching and the majority attends two or more. In the business college overall, he estimates that 65% attend at least one workshop on teaching every year (T. Hawk, personal communication, June 2006). But it has not had the hoped-for impact on the rest of the campus. Why?

First, the faculty's strong belief in professional autonomy as educators apparently overcame any felt need for professional responsibility and accountability. Hence, the evaluators (chairs and members of the evaluation committee) did not hold professors to a high standard and accepted almost anything as sufficient evidence of "professional development."

Second, there was a lack of any clear and important connection to rewards. If the people doing annual evaluations and making promotion and tenure decisions do not give real and meaningful weight to high-quality teaching, high-quality student learning, and high-quality professional development, faculty will respond accordingly and allocate their time elsewhere.

Third, there was no strong support for faculty development. Because the institution did not have a well-supported faculty development program, it was difficult for low performing faculty to know what to do to improve. There was also limited institutional financial support to attend conferences and seminars.

Lessons To Be Learned

This case provides several important lessons for other institutions. First, having a more systematic and sophisticated evaluation system did improve the faculty behavior that it focused on—where it was properly applied. Faculty in the business college discernibly increased their engagement in professional development activities. Second, it is essential for upper level administrators (provost and deans) to make it clear that they expect good teaching and that means having and using a good system to evaluate teaching. They need to cultivate a culture that values good teaching. In such a culture, the institutional members are automatically encouraged to know when good teaching is occurring and when it is not. Third, the evaluation system will be stronger if it includes the two features that were omitted at this institution: evidence of student learning and specific evidence of how faculty members actually change their teaching. Fourth, if an institution values continuous professional development, it needs to provide support for it. In this situation, this would mean having a well-supported faculty development program where faculty can go to learn about new ideas on teaching and where they can seek answers to individual questions and problems.

Conclusion

If an institution can accept the ideas embedded in the model of good teaching described here and use the associated procedures for evaluating teaching, that institution is likely to realize three major benefits:

- *First benefit.* The model would provide professors with the tools and motivation to self-assess and improve their own teaching. The criteria themselves would communicate the expectations of the institution. By regularly collecting data on these criteria and reflecting on them, teachers would already know how well they are doing and what needs to be improved. They would also have an incentive to engage in the ongoing professional development that is necessary for them to become increasingly more competent as educators. Hence, over time it should result in significantly better teaching by the majority of the faculty at a given institution.

- *Second benefit.* The model gives academic units and the institution in-depth knowledge of who is really excelling in their teaching, information that goes well beyond "students like them." This provides a much stronger foundation for annual evaluations, tenure decisions, and teaching awards decisions. With the proper collecting and tracking of this information, it can provide senior administrators with richer and more specific information to share with important outside constituents (e.g., parents of prospective students, donors, and accrediting agencies) about the quality of teaching that is occurring in the institution and how it is improving over time.

- *Third benefit.* Institutional leaders can use these ideas to strengthen the whole institution. At the present time many institutions fall into the trap of *valuing what can be easily measured.* That is why we have come to value so strongly some easily measurable characteristics (e.g., admission rates, graduation rates, levels of external funding, the quantity of faculty publications). However, effective organizations find a way of *measuring what they value.*

If indeed we value good teaching as we all claim to, we must find better ways to measure it. To date, we have not known how to do this in a way that is persuasive, either to ourselves or to outside constituents. This chapter addresses that need by offering a new model for defining what constitutes good teaching and new assessment procedures that give a fuller picture of what faculty members do as professional educators.

References

Arreola, R. A. (2000). *Developing a comprehensive faculty evaluation system: A handbook for college faculty and administrators on designing and operating a comprehensive faculty evaluation system* (2nd ed.). Bolton, MA: Anker.

Fink, L. D. (2003). *Creating significant learning experiences: An integrated approach to designing college courses.* San Francisco, CA: Jossey-Bass.

Fink, L. D. (2005). *Major new ideas that can empower college teaching.* Unpublished manuscript. Retrieved May 14, 2007, from www.finkconsulting.info/files/ Fink2006MajorNewIdeasToEmpowerCollegeTeaching.doc

Loeher, L. (2006, October). *An examination of research university faculty evaluation policies and practices.* Paper presented at the 31st annual meeting of the Professional and Organizational Development Network in Higher Education, Portland, OR.

Seldin, P., & Associates. (1999). *Changing practices in evaluating teaching: A practical guide to improved faculty performance and promotion/tenure decisions.* Bolton, MA: Anker.

Resources

The following is a brief list of additional resources that either comment on the need for better procedures for evaluating teaching or provide ideas that can enhance the quality of teaching and learning in higher education.

Association of American Colleges and Universities. (2002). *Greater expectations: A new vision for learning as a nation goes to college.* Washington, DC: Author.

AAC&U has laid out a challenge and a general blueprint for a liberal education curriculum that will produce "empowered, informed, and responsible" learners.

Bain, K. (2004). *What the best college teachers do.* Cambridge, MA: Harvard University Press.

Many writers have looked at what good college teachers do, but Bain's analysis of what he found is unusually clear and meaningful.

Bok, D. (2006). *Our underachieving colleges: A candid look at how much students learn and why they should be learning more.* Princeton, NJ: Princeton University Press.

With the balance and incisiveness that one might expect from the former president of Harvard University, Bok examines eight major kinds of learning in American higher education and finds we are falling short of where we should be.

Gardiner, L. F. (1994). *Redesigning higher education: Producing dramatic gains in student learning* (ASHE-ERIC Higher Education Report No. 7). Washington, DC: The George Washington University, Graduate School of Education and Human Development.

This book provides a good summary of research and ideas about teaching and learning that would, as the title says, produce a dramatically different result in the quality of student learning—if used.

Hersh, R. H., & Merrow, J. (Eds.). (2005). *Declining by degrees: Higher education at risk.* New York, NY: Palgrave Macmillan.

The DVD relating to this work (available from PBS) interviews professors and students at four representative colleges in the U.S. and discovers major problems. The book provides an analysis of why this is happening.

Kuh, G. D., Kinzie, J., Schuh, J. H., Whitt, E. J., & Associates. (2005). *Student success in college: Creating conditions that matter.* San Francisco, CA: Jossey-Bass.

Kuh, the director of the National Survey of Student Engagement, summarizes lessons from the universities that have used this instrument to show what some are doing that makes them better than most.

Svinicki, M. D. (2004). *Learning and motivation in the postsecondary classroom.* Bolton, MA: Anker.

An excellent summary and interpretation of the research on learning and motivation in higher education.

Weimer, M. (2002). *Learner-centered teaching: Five key changes to practice.* San Francisco, CA: Jossey-Bass.

Weimer suggests that teachers share decision-making power with students, and she notes how that will change the role of the teacher and of the students as well as the function of the content and of feedback and assessment.

2

Investigating Indicators of the Scholarship of Teaching: Teaching Awards in Research Universities

Stacie Badran
Embry-Riddle University

Results from a nationwide study of teaching awards programs in mathematics departments of U.S. research universities show that only a small percentage even offers such awards. Those that do either use ad hoc procedures and criteria for making awards or prioritize curricular contributions over instructional and pedagogical knowledge in selecting award winners. In addition, mathematics faculty reserve the term scholarship *for research in the discipline rather than research on teaching of the discipline.*

> We're a research university, and the first thing we look at [when hiring] is the scholarship.

> It's good and bad to win the award. [It is] good in that you won the award and receive recognition for good teaching; bad in that you have to chair the committee the next year. (Badran, 2004, p. 50)

These quotes from faculty participants of a nationwide study (Badran, 2004) encapsulate how mathematics faculty at American research universities perceive winning a teaching award and how much they value the scholarship of teaching, a concept first coined by Boyer (1990) and later expanded on by others (Cross & Steadman, 1996; Hutchings & Shulman, 1999; Kreber, 1999, 2001a; Kreber & Cranton, 1997, 2000; Paulsen, 1999; Rice, 1992; Shulman, 1987; Weimer, 1995). This study explores the award procedures, criteria, and specific indicators that the selectors (those who choose award recipients) use, and compares them to the indicators created and recommended by Kreber and Cranton (2000).

The Literature on Teaching Awards

"The purpose of teaching is to help students learn more effectively and efficiently than they would on their own" (Angelo, 1996, p. 57). Along with this opportunity comes a responsibility to understand what exemplary teaching is. According to Smith (2001), "faculty must develop their own expertise in helping students learn before they can help students develop expertise" (p. 69). Lowman (1996) offers insight into exemplary teachers, defining them as enthusiastic and engaging speakers as well as approachable, concerned, accessible, demanding, and dedicated. But these criteria are not universally endorsed. Without a clear, agreed-upon definition of exemplary teaching, we cannot determine what constitutes appropriate criteria for rewarding superior teaching (Kreber, 1999).

The structure of a program to honor exemplary teaching reveals important messages about the department's or institution's teaching standards (Svinicki & Menges, 1996). Research studies (Dunkin & Precians, 1992; Forsythe & Gandolfo, 1996; Jenrette & Hays, 1996; Lunde & Barrett, 1996; Miller, 1995; Quinn, 1994; Wergin, 1993; Zahorski, 1996) have explored the types of awards used for institutional and departmental recognition, the procedure involved in these programs, and the criteria selectors use for choosing the exemplary teacher. These studies have been conducted in various sizes and types of institutions of higher education. Research is lacking on the *indicators* of the criteria used for selection.

Wergin (1993) looked into "departmental awards," which universities award to an entire department for its collaborative efforts in teaching, several of which were initiated by major universities in 1992–1993 alone. They reflected an effort to reform faculty roles and rewards systems to deemphasize individualism and provide incentives for departments to act as "self-directed collectives, working cooperatively toward goals derived from a well-articulated institutional mission" (p. 24).

Exploring how two-year colleges honor exemplary teaching, Jenrette and Hays (1996) found that most colleges solicit nominations and make awards using a competitive model rather than a standards-driven model. The awards vary from temporary endowed teaching chairs to project funding to various salary enhancements and public recognition. Many colleges define and publicize the nature of excellent teaching in brochures, applications, and other print material.

Lunde and Barrett (1996) describe the effort of four departments "to precisely identify ways that teaching activity might be better documented, so that effective teaching might be better rewarded and faculty members thus motivated to improve instruction" (p. 94). These departments assigned committees to develop award recommendations from studying how other units conferred awards, reviewed the teaching records of colleagues, and provided formative peer feedback to both nontenured and tenured faculty. This process of peer review raised the importance of teaching to that comparable of research and other scholarly activities, thereby integrating the evaluation of teaching into the "fabric of the department's personnel processes" (p. 96).

Dunkin and Precians (1992) explored award-winning university faculty's concepts of teaching excellence in Australia. They interviewed recipients from a broad range of disciplines and academic ranks and discovered that these award winners had an elaborate set of criteria for evaluating teaching. The award group believed in obtaining the evaluation of others about the quality of their own teaching and in considering longer-term student learning.

In her investigation of four U.S. research universities, Miller (1995) uncovered that 54% of faculty were familiar with the criteria for award selection but didn't approve of them, and 58% believed that faculty didn't have enough input into defining the criteria. The faculty did concur, however, that the university-wide awards carried the most prestige. Quinn (1994) found that award winners themselves in research universities had reservations about the fairness of award programs and preferred that the criteria be more specific and procedures more open.

From this literature summary, it is clear that departments and universities do not follow clearly defined, agreed-upon criteria or procedures in making teaching awards. However, institutions do tend to use the same *indicators* in teaching effectiveness for promotion and tenure, but they do so without a theoretical framework. Two large national studies (Franklin, 2001; Seldin, 1984) documented that more than 90% of all institutions in the United States use student ratings to measure teaching effectiveness for merit, promotion, and tenure reviews. Not that student ratings lack validity and reliability, but they should not be used as the sole criterion (Cashin, 1990; Cohen, 1980a, 1980b; Feldman, 1977, 1978, 1987, 1989a, 1989b, 1996; Levinson-Rose & Menges, 1981; L'Hommedieu, Menges, & Brinko, 1988, 1990; Marsh, 1984, 1987; Marsh & Dunkin, 1992).

While most researchers believe that students offer a significant and unique perspective on the effectiveness of a teacher, Gray and Bergmann (2003) contend that administrators rely on student ratings largely out of convenience and due to the "increased attention to customer satisfaction that has developed with the move toward the corporate model in higher education and its concomitant diminishing of the role of faculty in university governance" (p. 46). These questionable reasons tempt faculty to cheat, forcing the administration "to invent demeaning procedures to prevent cheating" (p. 46). As one professor stated,

> Instead of saying, "Here is a great scholar and teacher; learn from her what you can," the administration of evaluation forms says to students, "We hired these teachers, but we are not sure they can teach or have taught you enough. Please tell us whether we guessed right." (Gray & Bergmann, 2003, p. 46)

Most researchers argue that administrators should consider many sources of data in assessing teaching, such as letters from students, peer observations, evidence of teaching outside the classroom, and the many other items that go into a teaching portfolio (Centra, 1996; Kreber & Cranton, 1997; Svinicki & Menges, 1996; Zahorski, 1996). In addition, administrators should compare faculty against an absolute standard of effective teaching. As Seldin put it, "There are some folks who just think it's inappropriate to try to measure teaching. But my notion of measuring teaching is whether someone is reasonably effective, not whether they are a 4.8 on a 5.0 scale" (qtd. in Bartlett, 2003, p. A9).

A Theoretical Framework for Exemplary Teaching

Perhaps the scholarship of teaching can add a theoretical framework in which to ground the notion of exemplary teaching. According to Kreber (2001b), "the scholarship of teaching requires knowledge of the discipline as well as knowledge of how students learn, the thoughtful integration of the two resulting in pedagogical content knowledge" (p. 79). Kreber and Cranton (2000) contend that the scholarship of teaching has been misconstrued as teaching excellence in regard to outcome measures. Rather it *should* focus on both practice and research on practice, and both the acquisition of teaching knowledge and the application of that knowledge. Weston and McAlpine (2001) agree, and they describe three phases of growth that faculty experience as they pursue the scholarship of teaching. In the first phase, faculty become aware of their own teaching and their students' learning. In phase two, they exchange their knowledge about teaching and learning in their discipline with their colleagues. Finally, in the third phase, enough faculty apply their knowledge in their classrooms that they impact the institution and the field.

As presented in Table 2.1, Kreber and Cranton (1997) describe three components of the scholarship of teaching, which are combined with the levels of reflection Mezirow (1991) posited as the way individuals learn and develop: content, process, and premise reflection.

TABLE 2.1

A Model of the Scholarship of Teaching:
Content, Process, and Premise Reflection on Instructional, Pedagogical, and Curricular Knowledge

Instructional Knowledge	
(Knowledge about the various components of instructional design)	
Content reflection	*What* should I do in course design, method selection, student assessment?
Process reflection	*How* did I do? Were my course design, methods, assessments effective?
Premise reflection	*Why* does it matter that I use these designs, methods, assessments?
Pedagogical Knowledge	
(Knowledge about student learning and how to facilitate it)	
Content reflection	*What* should I do to best facilitate student learning?
Process reflection	*How* did I do? Am I successful in facilitating student learning?
Premise reflection	*Why* does it matter if I consider how students learn?
Curricular Knowledge	
(Knowledge about the goals, purposes, and rationale for courses and programs)	
Content reflection	*What* do I know about the goals and rationale for my course or program?
Process reflection	*How* did I (we) arrive at the goals and rationale for courses or programs?
Premise reflection	*Why* do our goals and rationale matter?

Source. Kreber (2001b, p. 84). Reprinted with permission.

In Kreber and Cranton's (1997) view, "pedagogical knowledge stands at the core of teaching scholarship" (p. 7), and this study adopts their model as its theoretical perspective. But do institutions widely recognize pedagogical knowledge in their award standards?

Kreber and Cranton (2000) also provide a list of criteria and indicators for rewarding exemplary teaching awards on three dimensions: instructional, pedagogical, and curricular knowledge. Instructional knowledge reflects the strategies used in teaching, curricular knowledge addresses *why* we teach the way we teach, and pedagogical knowledge involves how students learn. Table 2.2 lists the indicators for each dimension.

This theoretical framework is one used in this study to compare and assess the way mathematics departments in the United States conferred teaching awards.

Methodology

The 149 institutions in this study of teaching award criteria were selected using *The Carnegie Classification of Institutions of Higher Education, 2000 Edition* (The Carnegie Foundation, 2001) to identify doctoral universities and the National Science Foundation (2003) listing of science and engineering doctorates awarded for 2002 to identify research-productive doctoral universities. During fall 2003, mathematics department chairs of these universities were contacted via email and/or phone to answer questions about the teaching awards programs in their departments, specifically those in which *faculty* award *faculty*. Those who served on the award selection committee during the 2002–2003 academic year were identified and contacted for a tape recorded phone interview. They were also asked to submit the procedures and criteria for award selection. Surprisingly, only three departments had such documents. The semi-structured interviews asked a short list of open-ended questions that allowed for in-depth probing.

Findings

Of the 149 mathematics departments surveyed, only 23 (15%) offered faculty teaching awards conferred by other faculty. Ten members of the award committees, representing eight different mathematics departments, agreed to participate in interviews. Thus, the sample represents 34.8% of mathematics departments that offered teaching awards to faculty.

The transcripts were coded first according to a preassigned coding system that corresponded to the research questions (Bogdan & Biklen, 1998), but subsequent themes emerged from the data, and each was given a unique code. Every coded segment was linked to its corresponding participant and institution. Occasionally themes were consolidated into categories.

TABLE 2.2

Indicators of the Three Dimensions of Knowledge Involved in the Scholarship of Teaching

	Content Reflection	Process Reflection	Premise Reflection
Instructional Knowledge	• Discussing materials and methods with students or colleagues • Reading articles on "how to" teach • Keeping a journal or log of methods and materials used	• Collecting data on students' perceptions of methods and materials • Asking for peer review of course outline • Comparing results of research on teaching to results in own classroom	• Experimenting with alternatives and checking out results • Writing critiques of methods, articles, or books • Challenging the departmental or institutional norms or values regarding teaching methods
Curricular Knowledge	• Reviewing goals of the session, course, or curriculum • Reading articles and books about the goals of higher education • Including a rationale and goals in course outlines	• Conducting a review of curriculum goals including a comparison to current practices • Tracing the history of program goals • Reading books on the goals of higher education and comparing these goals to those underlying the programs offered in the department	• Checking with employers, business industry, etc. to find out their expectations and goals for graduates of the program • Writing an article envisioning what higher education without curriculum goals may look like • Initiating or joining a committee on program goal review
Pedagogical Knowledge	• Administering learning styles or other inventories to students • Reading articles or books on learning theory, critical thinking, self-directed learning • Writing an article on how to facilitate learning in the discipline	• Gathering feedback from students on their learning the concepts of the discipline • Conducting an action research project on student learning • Comparing classroom experience to formal research results on student learning	• Writing a critique of an article on student learning in the discipline • Seeking out literature that questions the importance of learning styles, self-directed learning, etc. • Participating in philosophical discussions on student learning

Source. Kreber and Cranton (2000, p. 488). Reprinted with permission.

One key question was the extent to which these mathematics departments used award selection criteria consonant with Kreber and Cranton's (2000) indicators of the scholarship of teaching (as shown in Table 2.2). Table 2.3 displays the answers: All departments used ad hoc procedures for operationalizing selection criteria. Few indicators corresponded to those suggested by Kreber and Cranton (2000), and these focused more on curricular knowledge than on pedagogical or instructional knowledge. In fact, all but one department cited curriculum involvement as an award criterion. This involvement translated into service on committees dedicated to curricular reform and other curricular work both inside and outside the department. In terms of the types of reflection valued, departments mentioned indicators of process reflection most often, followed closely by premise reflection, and then content reflection. This ranking reflected the faculty's emphasis on curricular reform, curricular development, and student evaluations.

TABLE 2.3

Number of Mentioned Indicators from
the Eight Interviewed Departments (Out of 23 Offering Awards)
Using Kreber and Cranton's (2000)
Indicators of the Scholarship of Teaching

Combined Results	
Instructional knowledge	13
Curricular knowledge	21
Pedagogical knowledge	5
Content reflection	9
Process reflection	17
Premise reflection	13

All eight departments that were interviewed considered student evaluations among the award criteria, an indicator corresponding to Kreber and Cranton's (2000) process reflection under instructional knowledge (collecting data on students' perceptions of methods and materials). Only one department asked its award nominees about their students' opinions of their teaching methods and materials. This atypical department also used five of Kreber and Cranton's indicators in defining exemplary teaching: conducting action research on student learning, administering learning styles or other inventories to students, experimenting with and assessing alternative methods, challenging the departmental norms (periodically reviewing procedures), and comparing one's classroom research results to those in the literature. One other atypical department drew on four of these indicators to reward faculty for "doing innovative things in class." These two departments defined exemplary teaching at a level of sophistication that set them apart from the rest.

Another interesting finding of this study is that the mathematics faculty used the term *scholarship* only to refer to research in the discipline. When asked about the value of teaching in their departments, respondents stated that disciplinary research received more weight than teaching. Even in the case of one professor's calculus reform project, which required extensive research on teaching, the respondents used the term *research* only to refer to research in mathematics rather than in teaching or mathematics education. This type of thinking is hardly unusual (Kreber, 2001a), and it reflects the disciplinary research-based standards for promotion that exist in all fields (Cahn, 2004; Gray, Froh, & Diamond, 1992; Ralph, 1998).

Discussion

This study finds that research-oriented mathematics departments in the United States prioritize curricular knowledge, followed by instructional knowledge, in selecting faculty for teaching awards, *if they use any formal documented criteria at all.* Pedagogical knowledge is relatively unimportant. The degree of reflection about goals or rationale involved in a faculty member's curricular knowledge does not seem important either. However, selectors do look favorably on a colleague's membership on a program review committee, which suggests at least some premise reflection on the curriculum.

Chism (2006) also finds little formal documented criteria in a study of teaching awards programs of many different types of institutions with teaching centers. In many cases, only global statements were made which referred to teaching excellence, and some seemed to believe teaching excellence is not definable. Chism states,

> Many awards programs seem to assume that it is not important to specify particular characteristics or to define teaching excellence for purposes of identifying and discriminating among candidates. By contrast, they list very specific requirements for such things as whether the nomination materials are to be bound or unbound, how many copies are needed, and what font and margin sizes are to be employed. (p. 592)

Programs either imply that criteria are ephemeral, obvious, or make apologetic statements about the criteria they do name. These findings are consistent with those of the present study. Although some departments list criteria, evidence does not match as indicators for criteria. Overall, Chism states there seems to be confusion about the use of the terms *criteria, evidence,* and *standards.* Chism's reasons for this may also explain the reason for the findings of the present study. That is, teaching awards may serve as a symbol of a focus on teaching, rather than as a function of the individual reward system, teaching excellence is difficult to define or identifiable when one sees it, and there is a lack of knowledge and/or trust of the literature on teaching. Another important thought is that program administrators may view the obscurity and vagueness as room for freedom in the selection process, and that "this freedom is worth more than credibility" (Chism, 2006, p. 602).

As the literature pushes for clear guidelines for awards procedures, Kreber and Cranton offer theoretically grounded indicators based on the scholarship of teaching to help faculty identify exemplary teachers among their peers (Cranton, 1998; Kreber 2001a, 2001b; Kreber & Cranton, 1997, 2000). Truly exemplary teaching incorporates the types of knowledge that comprise the scholarship of teaching, and teaching award procedures should seek evidence of this knowledge in nominees. For example, if a search committee valued process reflection in instructional knowledge, it would ask nominees the extent to which they sought student feedback about their methods and materials, solicited their colleagues for advice on course design, and compared their student outcomes to those reported in the literature (Kreber & Cranton, 2000). Virtually none of the mathematics departments in this study considered such indicators of exemplary teaching. Most likely the faculty in these departments had never heard of Kreber and Cranton's model.

Kreber (2001b) recommends evaluating teaching primarily on the basis of the instructor's pedagogical knowledge—that is, knowing how to teach creative thinking, effective verbal and oral communication, critical reflection, collaborative learning, mathematical reasoning, self-directed learning, and self-regulated learning. Specifically, she stated, "Opportunities for university teachers to learn about how to teach these skills [should] be included as an integral part of programs intended to foster the scholarship of teaching" (p. 86). Many researchers agree that institutions shouldn't expect all faculty to conduct scholarship on teaching, but they should expect all faculty to be scholarly in their teaching (Paulsen, 2001; Richlin, 2001; Smith, 2001; Theall & Centra, 2001; Weimer, 2001; Weston & McAlpine, 2001).

References

Angelo, T. A. (1996). Relating exemplary teaching to student learning. In M. D. Svinicki & R. J. Menges (Eds.), *New directions for teaching and learning: No. 65. Honoring exemplary teaching* (pp. 57–64). San Francisco, CA: Jossey-Bass.

Badran, S. (2004). Honoring exemplary teaching: Departmental teaching awards in mathematics departments of research institutions. *Dissertation Abstracts International, 67* (4), 96. (UMI No. 3217013)

Bartlett, T. (2003, December 12). What makes a teacher great? *The Chronicle of Higher Education,* p. A8.

Bogdan, R. C., & Biklen, S. K. (1998). *Qualitative research for education* (3rd ed.). Needham Heights, MA: Allyn & Bacon.

Boyer, E. L. (1990). *Scholarship reconsidered: Priorities of the professoriate.* Princeton, NJ: The Carnegie Foundation for the Advancement of Teaching.

Cahn, S. M. (2004, January–February). Taking teaching seriously. *Academe, 90*(1), 32–33.

The Carnegie Foundation for the Advancement of Teaching. (2001). *The Carnegie classification of institutions of higher education, 2000 edition.* Menlo Park, CA: Author.

Cashin, W. E. (1990). Assessing teaching effectiveness. In P. Seldin & Associates, *How administrators can improve teaching: Moving from talk to action in higher education* (pp. 89–103). San Francisco, CA: Jossey-Bass.

Centra, J. A. (1996). Identifying exemplary teachers: Evidence from colleagues, administrators, and alumni. In M. D. Svinicki & R. J. Menges (Eds.), *New directions for teaching and learning: No. 65. Honoring exemplary teaching* (pp. 51–56). San Francisco, CA: Jossey-Bass.

Chism, N. V. N. (2006, July/August). Teaching awards: What do they award? *Journal of Higher Education, 77*(4), 589–617.

Cohen, P. A. (1980a). Effectiveness of student-rating feedback for improving college instruction: A meta-analysis of findings. *Research in Higher Education, 13*(4), 321–341.

Cohen, P. A. (1980b). A meta-analysis of the relationship between student ratings of instruction and student achievement. *Dissertation Abstracts International, 41* (05), 2012. (UMI No. 8025666)

Cranton, P. (1998). *No one way: Teaching and learning in higher education.* Dayton, OH: Wall & Emerson.

Cross, K. P., & Steadman, M. H. (1996). *Classroom research: Implementing the scholarship of teaching.* San Francisco, CA: Jossey-Bass.

Dunkin, M. J., & Precians, R. P. (1992, December). Award-winning university teachers' concepts of teaching. *Higher Education, 24*(4), 483–502.

Feldman, K. A. (1977). Consistency and variability among college students in rating their teachers and courses: A review and analysis. *Research in Higher Education, 6*(3), 223–274, 277.

Feldman, K. A. (1978). Course characteristics and college students' ratings of their teachers: What we know and what we don't. *Research in Higher Education, 9*(3), 199–242.

Feldman, K. A. (1987). Research productivity and scholarly accomplishment of college teachers as related to their instructional effectiveness: A review and exploration. *Research in Higher Education, 26*(3), 277–291.

Feldman, K. A. (1989a). The association between student ratings of specific instructional dimensions and student achievement: Refining and extending the synthesis of data from multisection validity studies. *Research in Higher Education, 30*(6), 583–645.

Feldman, K. A. (1989b). Instructional effectiveness of college teachers as judged by teachers themselves, current and former students, colleagues, administrators, and external (neutral) observers. *Research in Higher Education, 30*(2), 137–194.

Feldman, K. A. (1996). Identifying exemplary teaching: Using data from course and teacher evaluations. In M. D. Svinicki & R. J. Menges (Eds.), *New directions for teaching and learning: No. 65. Honoring exemplary teaching* (pp. 41–50). San Francisco, CA: Jossey-Bass.

Forsythe, G. B., & Gandolfo, A. (1996). Promoting exemplary teaching: The case of the U.S. Military Academy. In M. D. Svinicki & R. J. Menges (Eds.), *New directions for teaching and learning: No. 65. Honoring exemplary teaching* (pp. 99–104). San Francisco, CA: Jossey-Bass.

Franklin, J. (2001). Interpreting the numbers: Using a narrative to help others read student evaluations of your teaching accurately. In K. G. Lewis (Ed.), *New directions for teaching and learning: No. 87. Techniques and strategies for interpreting student evaluations* (pp. 85–100). San Francisco, CA: Jossey-Bass.

Gray, M., & Bergmann, B. R. (2003, September–October). Student teaching evaluations: Inaccurate, demeaning, misused. *Academe, 89*(5), 44–46.

Gray, P., Froh, R., & Diamond, R. (1992). *A national study of research universities: On the balance between research and undergraduate teaching.* Syracuse, NY: Syracuse University, Center for Instructional Development.

Hutchings, P., & Shulman, L. S. (1999, September/October). The scholarship of teaching: New elaborations, new developments. *Change, 31*(5), 10–15.

Jenrette, M., & Hays, K. (1996). Honoring exemplary teaching: The two-year college setting. In M. D. Svinicki & R. J. Menges (Eds.), *New directions for teaching and learning: No. 65. Honoring exemplary teaching* (pp. 77–83). San Francisco, CA: Jossey-Bass.

Kreber, C. (1999). *Defining and implementing the scholarship of teaching: The results of a Delphi study.* Paper presented at the annual meeting of the Canadian Society for the Study of Higher Education, Sherbrooke, Quebec.

Kreber, C. (2001a). Observations, reflections, and speculations: What we have learned about the scholarship of teaching and where it might lead. In C. Kreber (Ed.), *New directions for teaching and learning: No. 86. Scholarship revisited: Perspectives on the scholarship of teaching* (pp. 99–104). San Francisco, CA: Jossey-Bass.

Kreber, C. (2001b). The scholarship of teaching and its implementation in faculty development and graduate education. In C. Kreber (Ed.), *New directions for teaching and learning: No. 86. Scholarship revisited: Perspectives on the scholarship of teaching* (pp. 79–88). San Francisco, CA: Jossey-Bass.

Kreber, C., & Cranton, P. (1997). Teaching as scholarship: A model for instructional development. *Issues and Inquiry in College Learning and Teaching, 19*(2), 4–12.

Kreber, C., & Cranton P. (2000, July/August). Exploring the scholarship of teaching. *Journal of Higher Education, 71*(4), 476–495.

Levinson-Rose, J., & Menges, R. J. (1981, Fall). Improving college teaching: A critical review of research. *Review of Educational Research, 51*(3), 403–434.

L'Hommedieu, R., Menges, R. J., & Brinko, K. T. (1988). *The effects of student ratings feedback to college teachers: A meta-analysis and review of research.* Unpublished manuscript.

L'Hommedieu, R., Menges, R. J., & Brinko, K. T. (1990, June). Methodological explanations for the modest effects of feedback from student ratings. *Journal of Educational Psychology, 82*(2), 232–241.

Lowman, J. (1996). Characteristics of exemplary teachers. In M. D. Svinicki & R. J. Menges (Eds.), *New directions for teaching and learning: No. 65. Honoring exemplary teaching* (pp. 33–40). San Francisco, CA: Jossey-Bass.

Lunde, J. P., & Barrett, L. A. (1996). Decentralized/departmental reward systems. In M. D. Svinicki & R. J. Menges (Eds.), *New directions for teaching and learning: No. 65. Honoring exemplary teaching* (pp. 93–98). San Francisco, CA: Jossey-Bass.

Marsh, H. W. (1984). Students' evaluations of university teaching: Dimensionality, reliability, validity, potential biases, and utility. *Journal of Educational Psychology, 76*(5), 707–754.

Marsh, H. W. (1987). Students' evaluations of university teaching: Research findings, methodological issues, and directions for future research. *International Journal of Educational Research, 11*(3), 253–388.

Marsh, H. W., & Dunkin, M. J. (1992). Students' evaluations of university teaching: A multidimensional approach. In J. C. Smart (Ed.), *Higher education: Handbook of theory and research, Vol. VIII* (pp. 143–234). New York, NY: Agathon Press.

Mezirow, J. (1991). *Transformative dimensions of adult learning.* San Francisco, CA: Jossey-Bass.

Miller, E. (1995). Rewarding faculty for teaching excellence/effectiveness: A survey of currently available awards including faculty comments and desires in regard to the whole process of rewards. *Dissertation Abstracts International, 56* (6), 2133. (UMI No. 9534400)

National Science Foundation, Division of Science Resources Statistics. (2003). *Science and engineering doctorate awards: 2002* (NSF Publication No. 04–303). Arlington, VA: Author.

Paulsen, M. B. (1999). How college students learn: Linking traditional educational research and contextual classroom research. *Journal of Staff, Program, and Organizational Development, 16*(2), 63–71.

Paulsen, M. B. (2001). The relation between research and the scholarship of teaching. In C. Kreber (Ed.), *New directions for teaching and learning: No. 86. Scholarship revisited: Perspectives on the scholarship of teaching* (pp. 19–29). San Francisco, CA: Jossey-Bass.

Quinn, J. (1994, January). *Teaching award recipients' perceptions of teaching award programs.* Paper presented at the second annual American Association for Higher Education Forum on Faculty Roles and Rewards, New Orleans, LA.

Ralph, E. G. (1998). *Motivating teaching in higher education: A manual for faculty development.* Stillwater, OK: New Forums Press.

Rice, R. E. (1992). Toward a broader conception of scholarship: The American context. In T. G. Whiston & R. L. Geiger (Eds.), *Research and higher education: The United Kingdom and the United States* (pp. 117–129). Buckingham, UK: Society for Research into Higher Education & Open University Press.

Richlin, L. (2001). Scholarly teaching and the scholarship of teaching. In C. Kreber (Ed.), *New directions for teaching and learning: No. 86. Scholarship revisited: Perspectives on the scholarship of teaching* (pp. 57–68). San Francisco, CA: Jossey-Bass.

Seldin, P. (1984). *Changing practices in faculty evaluation.* San Francisco, CA: Jossey-Bass.

Shulman, L. S. (1987, February). Knowledge and teaching: Foundations of the new reform. *Harvard Educational Review, 57*(1), 1–22.

Smith, R. (2001). Expertise and the scholarship of teaching. In C. Kreber (Ed.), *New directions for teaching and learning: No. 86. Scholarship revisited: Perspectives on the scholarship of teaching* (pp. 69–78). San Francisco, CA: Jossey-Bass.

Svinicki, M. D., & Menges, R. J. (1996). Consistency within diversity: Guidelines for programs to honor exemplary teaching. In M. D. Svinicki & R. J. Menges (Eds.), *New directions for teaching and learning: No. 65. Honoring exemplary teaching* (pp. 109–113). San Francisco, CA: Jossey-Bass.

Theall, M., & Centra, J. A. (2001). Assessing the scholarship of teaching: Valid decisions from valid evidence. In C. Kreber (Ed.), *New directions for teaching and learning: No. 86. Scholarship revisited: Perspectives on the scholarship of teaching* (pp. 31–43). San Francisco, CA: Jossey-Bass.

Weimer, M. (1995). Why scholarship is the bedrock of good teaching. In R. J. Menges, M. Weimer, & Associates, *Teaching on solid ground: Using scholarship to improve practice.* San Francisco, CA: Jossey-Bass.

Weimer, M. (2001). Learning more from the wisdom of practice. In C. Kreber (Ed.), *New directions for teaching and learning: No. 86. Scholarship revisited: Perspectives on the scholarship of teaching* (pp. 45–56). San Francisco, CA: Jossey-Bass.

Wergin, J. (1993, July/August). Departmental awards. *Change, 25*(4), 24.

Weston, C. B., & McAlpine, L. (2001). Making explicit the development toward the scholarship of teaching. In C. Kreber (Ed.), *New directions for teaching and learning: No. 86. Scholarship revisited: Perspectives on the scholarship of teaching* (pp. 89–97). San Francisco, CA: Jossey-Bass.

Zahorski, K. J. (1996). Honoring exemplary teaching in the liberal arts institution. In M. D. Svinicki & R. J. Menges (Eds.), *New directions for teaching and learning: No. 65. Honoring exemplary teaching* (pp. 85–92). San Francisco, CA: Jossey-Bass.

Section II

Scholarship of Teaching and Learning

3

Points Without Limits: Individual Inquiry, Collaborative Investigation, and Collective Scholarship

Richard A. Gale
The Carnegie Foundation for the Advancement of Teaching

This chapter proposes that a scholarship of teaching and learning focused on collaborative and collective inquiry can be more effective and have greater impact on student learning and the advancement of knowledge than investigations accomplished by individual faculty and students working in isolation. This conclusion is arrived at as a result of examining the work of Carnegie Scholars and the Carnegie Academy for the Scholarship of Teaching and Learning Campus Program participants since 1998.

There is a perspective about the practice of scholarship that celebrates the work of the individual over the collective. From this point of view, scholarly pursuit is solitary pursuit, exemplified by isolated investigation, idiosyncratic discovery, and individual genius. But virtually all scholarship requires some collaborative effort, and the most important insights tend to result from the most collective endeavors. Such is the case with the scholarship of teaching and learning, which not only thrives on association but strives for the abolition of pedagogical solitude. Even when acknowledged as a communal act, the scholarship of teaching and learning is often viewed in terms of individual faculty members working within the microclimates of their own classrooms. Teaching and learning scholars are seen as reaching out to larger audiences for the purpose of dissemination and review, but not for the processes and practices of inquiry. This tendency may be an artifact of the tenure and promotion

39

process, which clearly privileges individual over communal efforts, but it might also result from a too-limited view of what it means to imagine, engage in, and produce scholarship. For although much ground is to be gained from the work of individual faculty conducting focused inquiry into student learning, even more mileage can be achieved when two or more scholars work collaboratively, and the distance that can be covered by collective approaches to scholarship (within the department, program, school, institution, and system) is certainly significant, if not "without limits."

In his book *Arctic Dreams* (1986), Barry Lopez devotes a lyrical and informative chapter to the mythology, history, biology, and social significance of the narwhal, a (perhaps magical) creature with the appearance of a pike-tipped torpedo, whose pronounced tooth was traded as a unicorn horn in the Middle Ages, and whose very existence has been a source of doubt and legend and misunderstanding for generations. While Lopez offers a good deal of history, science, and lore to help readers understand this member of the whale family, what stands at the heart of his chapter is the value of shared understanding brought to bear on what can only be described as an enduring mystery. Lopez engages the reader with the idea of how observation, investigation, examination, and application all combine, under the right conditions, to create knowledge that leads to action.

> Because you have seen something doesn't mean you can explain it. Differing interpretations will always abound, even when good minds come to bear. The kernel of indisputable information is a dot in space; interpretations grow out of the desire to make this point a line, to give it a direction. The directions in which it can be sent, the uses to which it can be put by a culturally, professionally, and geographically diverse society, are almost without limit. (Lopez, 1986, p. 127)

This idea can be applied to the more general process by which we see and understand anything in the world. It begins with the perceived: an observation, or the simple act of seeing. When seeing is coupled with inquiry, the process of investigation begins, and we have the toehold of "indisputable information," or "a dot in space" with meaning, if not with magnitude. Investigation leads to interpretation, which when combined and coordinated with other interpretations creates a line, a point with direction that not only indicates source but predicts the future and can hence be put to use by the aforementioned "culturally, professionally, and geographically diverse society." This is the process that leads to knowledge building. This is also the course of scholarship, and the way in which investigation moves from individual, to collaborative (between individuals), to collective (involving systematic or institutionally structured) inquiry.

Whether the object at hand is (with apologies to Hamlet) a whale or a weasel, a hawk or a handsaw, the necessities of discovery require that what is seen be documented, what is evident be backed by evidence, what serves as proof be subject to corroboration and evaluation, and what is reviewed be made public for additional analysis and future expansive use. Such is the established pattern of scholarship within the realm of disciplinary journals and professional publications of all kinds. This scenario also serves as well for the scholarship of teaching and learning, which has grown into a global movement with its own dedicated publication outlets, an international society, and widespread currency on campuses around the world. All of this was made possible through the work of individual students, faculty, and administrators, campus teams and centers for teaching and learning, and broad coalitions of institutional and disciplinary partners. Furthermore, whether inquiry is solitary, shared, or formally coordinated, what sits foursquare at the center of this scholarship is evidence of student learning.

Individual Inquiry

Individual inquiry forms the bedrock of the scholarship of teaching and learning, for this process begins with attempts to understand and improve student learning in specific curricular contexts. Yet as with all intellectual work of scope and scale, the scholarship of teaching and learning seeks not to improve one classroom context but to add knowledge to the field and thereby have an impact on how students learn and how faculty teach in multiple educational contexts. Through the gathering of evidence of student learning, the investigation of classroom teaching, and the peer review of significant results, this scholarship seeks to expand the landscape of understanding within and beyond a specific pedagogical or disciplinary context. It utilizes a cycle of inquiry involving observation, investigation, examination, and application: taking note of some aspect of student learning, constructing an inquiry project to gather evidence informing that observation, making the results available for peer review, and going public so that new knowledge can inform practice and make change beyond the local. This represents the most prevalent form of the scholarship of teaching and learning, and the place where most individual scholars of student learning begin. However, if the goal is a better understanding of how students learn, with an eye to changing teaching practice for the better, then individual inquiry cannot be the end of the process, even if it is made public and "passed along" to other interested and influential audiences.

When most effective, individual inquiry leads to application within the discipline, the department, the institution, and beyond—sparking additional individual inquiry or, when possible, collaborative investigation.

Collaborative Investigation

Collaborative investigation might be described not as "many hands make light work" but rather as "two or more heads are better than one." The premise is that collaborative efforts among two or more scholars produce additional evidence, improved insight, and more meaningful results (a position that is now almost commonplace, well documented, and verified in the extensive research on collaborative work but not entirely transparent in the literature on the scholarship of teaching and learning). These collaborations might take several forms, but in general they can be categorized according to the questions asked and the settings in which they take place. Questions might be identical (common), linked in some concrete and logical way (connected), or sufficiently similar so that they can be put side by side and yield meaning (comparable). Likewise, settings might be common (the same course), connected (courses in sequence or in tandem), or comparable (the same course within another department or at another institution). In thinking about this approach to collaborative investigation, the real issue is the evidence generated, and one way of thinking about evidence in a collaborative inquiry environment is represented in Table 3.1.

TABLE 3.1

Collaborative Investigation Settings, Questions, and Evidence

	Common Questions	Connected Questions	Comparable Questions
Common Settings	Common evidence	Connected evidence	Comparable evidence
Connected Settings	Connected evidence	Connected evidence	Comparable evidence
Comparable Settings	Comparable evidence	Comparable evidence	Complementary, not comparable, evidence

When two or more scholars share both question and setting (e.g., how students learn to integrate life experience into two different sections of a Great Books course) the evidence yielded can be viewed as a common set. When scholars' questions are common (integrating life experience), but the settings are not (connected, as in sequential Great Books courses at the same institution, or comparable, as in the same course at another institution), the evidence can be viewed as either connected or comparable, but not as common. However, when both questions and settings are merely comparable (perhaps with one scholar examining the integration of life experience into a Great Books course and the other examining the integration of cocurricular experiences into a modern literature course, or two scholars working at very different kinds of institutions), the evidence must be viewed as complementary, not comparable—informative but not supportive. Such complementary evidence might inform the individual research of each scholar, but the results would be too dissimilar to serve as a true collaboration.

One example of paired inquiry (common, connected, and perhaps comparable as well) can be found in the team-based approaches of Gerald Shenk and David Takacs at California State University–Monterey Bay, who were interested in how students acquire new historical understanding and use that knowledge to inform political action and ongoing civic engagement. They used the common setting of a team-taught course and common questions, jointly developed, to produce common evidence of student learning. That evidence was collected and evaluated jointly, with the different perspectives of the two scholars (the former from history and the latter from environmental studies) producing a triangulation of analysis, as well as a combination of research methodologies from two different disciplinary practices. The paired inquiry resulted in a broader sense of the student work and in a clearer interpretation of student learning (Shenk, 2001; Takacs, 2001).

Catherine Berheide and Michael Marx at Skidmore College took a similar approach to their team investigation of the habits of mind that lead students to critical thinking, and of the metacognitive strategies that contribute to deep and persistent learning. They created an Idea Notebook to help students understand their own responses to course materials, thus bringing to the surface students' cognitive processes:

> One of the common goals of a college education is to develop students' critical thinking skills. We designed the Idea Notebook—a semester-long activity asking students to reflect on their thought processes—to promote critical thinking. We piloted it in an honors course for sophomores serving as tutors in Liberal Studies 1: Human Dilemmas, Skidmore College's required first-year seminar. (Berheide & Marx, 2004)

Their collaboration focused on the recognition of a common observation, the development of a connected question, and then the application of that strategy to connected settings.

One project under way at this writing involves chemistry faculty at Carleton and Hope colleges (Tricia Ferrett and Joanne Stewart, respectively) adopting a decidedly hybrid approach to looking at how students integrate multiple scientific perspectives, social and political influences, and religious predispositions around the topic of abrupt climate change. Teaching two similar courses on two different campuses in sequential terms, this collaborative pairing of scholars provides a unique opportunity to see the ways in which student learning can be observed in comparable settings, with initially common questions, yielding evidence that is interpreted by two informed investigators with complementary interests (Ferrett, 2006; Stewart, 2006). The results of this initial investigation are then applied to a new context, one with shared origins and questions, but distinctly different circumstances, producing a very different but somehow connected dataset that can be compared with the original evidence. Together, the two currents of evidence create a confluence of understanding, almost estuarial in its mixed yet unmixed nature.

> Joanne and I . . . can now articulate which questions we share (what does integrative science learning look like in the context of our courses, different context, student ages and populations) and which ones are unique to our institutional project (Joanne's bit on how students combine who they are with science learning and beliefs and values). And we are both working hard together on describing the pedagogy which we share, and the developmental aspects of student learning that are emerging in our evidence. (T. Ferrett, personal communication, May 26, 2006)

It is a complicated process, difficult to keep in alignment, but the results of this pairing will likely be a much richer and more realistic sense of how student learning can inform a developing teaching practice.

In all of these, the goal has been to make the strongest case possible based on correlated evidence from more than one source, gathered in a collaborative manner, and coordinated for collaborative purposes. Another approach to collaboration involves faculty partnering with students to answer important questions about learning. This strategy can also take the forms mentioned earlier and has added pedagogical benefits for all involved, especially in terms of the collateral impact that such collaboration has on the students who often go on from an initial inquiry to become more intentional about their own learning processes. Perhaps the best examples of this kind of collaboration can be found at institutions like Western Washington University, where faculty and students have been working together under the auspices of the Teaching-Learning Academy to develop comparable questions in common settings, and

North Seattle Community College, where students have taken the initiative to create inquiry tools for asking important learning questions across institutional contexts. My own introduction to the scholarship of teaching and learning was in the form of student collaboration, while a 2000–2001 Carnegie Scholar at Sonoma State University, where I worked with student investigators to develop a unified question set and group of inquiry tools to learn how students were using a program portfolio for the purposes of intentional learning (Gale, 2003). Regardless of the form, these collaborative approaches, shown in Table 3.2, serve to advance the knowledge of student learning and the practice of thoughtful and reflective teaching, while also building a particular kind of scholarly community around issues of importance to classrooms everywhere.

TABLE 3.2

Examples of Collaborative Investigation

	Common Questions	Connected Questions	Comparable Questions
Common Settings	How students acquire new historical understanding and use that knowledge to inform political action and ongoing civic engagement	How students use program portfolios for the purposes of intentional learning	Students working together to develop comparable questions in common settings
Connected Settings		Habits of mind that lead students to critical thinking, and of the metacognitive strategies that contribute to deep and persistent learning	Students creating inquiry tools for asking important learning questions across institutional contexts
Comparable Settings			How students integrate multiple scientific perspectives, social and political influences, and religious predispositions around the topic of abrupt climate change

Collective Scholarship

Yet what if this approach to collaboration were taken to the next level of complexity and incorporated into structures and communities already in existence? What if inquiry were shared not only among individual scholars, but among an entire department, college, or university system? This is the premise behind collective scholarship, which seeks to ask the question: What can we learn in concert that we cannot learn as well, or at all, in isolation? For if collaboration among individual scholars can produce deeper understanding and improved practice, then surely collective scholarship within a program, a discipline, or even a regional network of campuses might yield the answers to significant shared questions.

Like the collaborative investigations described earlier, collective scholarship relies on the work of individual scholars conducting inquiry projects in local settings. But unlike these collaborations, collective inquiry is based on a coordinated and aggregating philosophy wherein multiple inquiry projects, configured in different settings and from different investigative standpoints, all have as their objective a deeper understanding of a communal question. Such collective inquiry requires a substantial level of coordination—coordinated goals, investigations, evidence gathering, and dissemination. Its benefits are just as substantial, indeed, perhaps more so, because they address directly and consistently one of the central difficulties of the scholarship of teaching and learning—going public and passing on the results of the investigation. Collective scholarship begins with a single question asked across a community, builds on the knowledge and experience within that same community, shares evidence and application throughout the community, and then asks all of the members to be involved in more widespread dissemination. Such scholarship, when coordinated, has the potential to yield comparable and complimentary evidence that can in turn influence programmatic, institutional, and trans-institutional understanding of student learning, as suggested in Table 3.3 and the following examples.

Examples of this kind of inquiry are more nascent, but often early steps provide a valuable window into what can be accomplished through a more structural and collective scholarship of teaching and learning. At Gustavus Adolphus College, the Department of History has embarked on a collective scholarship project, coordinated among the faculty and connected to multiple courses, that seeks to answer the question: "How are our students learning to think like historians?" (Huber & Hutchings, 2005, p. 81). This distinctly disciplinary question is being asked within a programmatic context that will, hopefully, yield evidence of how local learning informs and is informed by

TABLE 3.3

Collective Scholarship Settings, Inquiry, and Evidence

	Mission-Oriented Inquiry	Mandate- or Policy-Driven Inquiry	Metacognitive Inquiry
Department or Program Level	Programmatic evidence	Institutional evidence	Trans-institutional evidence
Institution or Discipline Level	Institutional evidence	Institutional evidence	Trans-institutional evidence
System-Wide or Regional Level	Trans-institutional evidence	Trans-institutional evidence	Trans-institutional evidence

disciplinary understanding. Similarly, the Center of Inquiry in the Liberal Arts at Wabash College has, in a series of workshops and presentations, challenged colleagues to turn their scholarly attention to what makes student learning in the liberal arts distinctive, what makes their experience different and (most believe) better. While institutional in scope and mission oriented in focus, this inquiry will produce not only institutional evidence, but perhaps a framework for use within other liberal arts settings, thus expanding the reach to a trans-institutional level.

At a 2005 gathering in Washington, DC, representatives of three biological science disciplinary societies discussed and began planning for a collective inquiry into the teaching and learning of evolution using a coherent group of committed individuals to better understand what is essentially a policy issue. Perhaps most significant, because it is so rare, the University of Wisconsin System recently instituted a collective scholarship project designed to better understand student learning in the creative, fine, and performing arts. This project, coordinated through the Office of Professional and Instructional Development, builds on the depth of knowledge developed by faculty in the University of Wisconsin System and on its commitment to the scholarship of teaching and learning, while also acknowledging that more needs to be understood about how students learn aesthetic literacy, creative confidence, and other important capacities found in arts disciplines. This trans-institutional collaboration will certainly produce evidence that has applicability beyond the institutions of the system itself, and in that way becomes perhaps omni-institutional in its impact.

Less obvious might be the categories under which these examples operate, the forms such collective scholarship might take. As Table 3.3 suggests, there are three types of inquiry that seem particularly well suited to the ways and means and outcomes of collective scholarship. Mission-oriented inquiry is generally directed at one of two questions: Who are you? or Who do you want to be? Collective scholarship of this sort seeks to address changing or uncertain institutional identity and aspirations, concerns about student engagement with campus values, or the impact of signature programs. Mandate- or policy-driven inquiry uses the scholarship of teaching and learning to respond to external influences such as accreditation reviews or calls for accountability and increased productivity, or to address internal reevaluation of what matters, such as diversity initiatives, program development, or student retention. Metacognitive inquiry tries to address issues with wider implications; it also attempts to build knowledge across multiple contexts by understanding what students learn (aesthetic literacy, integrative perspectives, quantitative reasoning), how students learn (the academic seminar, field experience, service-learning, study abroad), or why students learn (ethical reasoning, political engagement, world citizenship). Therefore, a mission-oriented inquiry at the system-wide level might include collective scholarship focusing on successful integration of disciplinary knowledge and local service-learning opportunities in senior capstone courses. Likewise, a mandate-driven inquiry at the program level might involve investigation of how required electronic portfolios help students transition from general education to the major. Finally, a metacognitive inquiry could range from the examination of how mapping software impacts global literacy in an honors seminar (program level), to how study abroad influences global awareness among seniors (institution level) or sociologists (discipline level).

These brief and often speculative examples remind us that the scholarship of teaching and learning is perhaps most effective and most likely to contribute to the academic culture and intellectual advancement of a department, campus, and so on when it is integrated into ongoing initiatives and preexisting structures, or when linked to other data sources already being used at the institutional level (National Survey of Student Engagement, Collegiate Learning Assessment, etc., as well as home-grown surveys and information-gathering mechanisms). Likewise, it brings to the fore one of the central issues surrounding work in the scholarship of teaching and learning: institutional support and scaffolding. All those who have engaged in this form of inquiry understand the need for validation and valorization of teaching and learning scholarship; indeed, the question of how such scholarship is valued by departmental and campus colleagues in the retention, tenure, and promotion process has always been important and is far from being resolved in most settings. At many institutions, the key to support has been the creation of infrastructure: establishing a center for teaching and learning that has part of its mandate the encouragement of inquiry into student learning; creating dedicated pathways and conduits for classroom investigation with dedicated (on-going) funding sources, mentoring opportunities, and dissemination vehicles; building a culture of inquiry that exposes all faculty to this kind of scholarship, provides multiple opportunities for asking questions and sharing results, and celebrates the accomplishments of teaching and learning scholars.

This is particularly important when approaching the challenges of collective scholarship, and in fact might be more likely and more fruitful under those circumstances. Obviously, pursuing this kind of inquiry directly benefits the students, faculty, and others on a campus or within a system. This is especially true when the investigation addresses a felt need or an institutional mandate. It also helps expand the knowledge and practice of the scholarship of teaching and learning such that individuals might build on their experiences and create new kinds of inquiry beyond the collective; in this way, collective scholarship strengthens and encourages collaborative and individual inquiry. But more than that, collective inquiry supports and nurtures the internal/institutional, disciplinary, and international community of scholars, forging connections and building networks within to what Mary Taylor Huber and Pat Hutchings (2005) have termed *the teaching commons.*

Of course, the use of the term *commons* for the shared space of ideas is, if you will, quite common, and has gained particular currency in the 21st-century world of new media and online communications; nevertheless, it is a useful designation for the overlapping work of teaching, learning, and scholarly pedagogical inquiry. The teaching commons, as described by Huber and Hutchings, is a place (occasionally physical, usually metaphorical, and often virtual) where "communities of educators committed to pedagogical inquiry and innovation come together to exchange ideas about teaching and learning, and use them to meet the challenges of educating students for personal, professional, and civic life in the twenty-first century" (p. x). This sense of the commons spans as far and wide as the imagination can reach, including students, faculty, and administrators and staff committed to its ideals, and encompassing much of the practice of teaching and learning, as well as all of its scholarship. But central to the commons is that it is made up of nested communities, and that the totality (if such an amorphous and changeable thing can ever be in toto) is made up not of parts, but of other wholes. Thus, collective scholarship builds on and creates a teaching commons for the department or program, institution or discipline, system or region that chooses to take on the inquiry and organize the intellectual capital to see it through. Aside from breaking down the pedagogical solitude of most faculty, this view of a commons is the natural next step, the structural manifestation of teaching and scholarship as community property first proposed by Lee Shulman (1993).

This, in turn, harkens back to Ernest Boyer's *Scholarship Reconsidered* (1990) which proposed "a *shared* vision of intellectual and social possibilities—a community of scholars" engaged in a "campuswide, collaborative effort around teaching," and championed "cooperative research" because "investigators talk increasingly about 'networks of knowledge,' even as individual creativity is recognized and affirmed" (p. 80).

Conclusion

Boyer's reminder about networks and the individual is as true today as it was then. But the kind of collective work described here requires more than a group of committed experts, and more than a local view of learning and scholarship. It is premised on strong pedagogical leadership; leadership with a vision or ideology based on knowledge and practice, supported by incentives or rewards and tempered by critical judgment, enhanced through the process of reflection and the involvement of a thoughtful community (Shulman, 2004). Such leadership develops out of an intimate knowledge of place and purpose, an empathetic understanding of the work of faculty and students, and above all from a clear and discerning sense of what has been, what is, and what can be. Leaders of this sort might hold positions of prominence within departments or colleges or systems, but they might also be found within a changing student body or a faculty subcommittee. Educational leaders support this kind of scholarship through structural means such as the organization of peer-review panels and the revision of tenure guidelines, but they also work below the radar through campus conversations and student learning initiatives. The who and the where are variable, and not nearly as important as the what and the when and the how. With that said, however, it must be acknowledged that several questions remain: How can educational leaders (variously defined) influence the culture of an institution? What will be the nature and source of support for this kind of scholarship? Where can faculty (and graduate students and administrators) begin? The answers are often bound to institutional culture, disciplinary predisposition, and the vagaries of higher education economics. But they are also the starting point for a broader understanding of student learning, faculty work, and campus accountability.

All of this suggests a longer view of learning and teaching and scholarship, and a more coherent and directed sense of community and common cause. Much of the work of the scholarship of teaching and learning has been local and small scale—individual faculty pursuing bounded inquiry from which they hope to make a difference. Often this kind of scholarship begins with intellectual curiosity and the desire to make things better (or at least different) in a teacher's own classroom. This is a noble pursuit, and when made available for peer review and public use, such endeavors are the foundation of knowledge building and pedagogical improvement. But with collaborative and especially collective scholarship, the focus shifts dramatically and intentionally to a place outside the local. The question becomes not, What would make this course better? or, Is this working in my class? or, How do I think about assessing for this? Instead, it becomes, Will this lead to better student learning in the department and the discipline? or, How does this fit with the larger curricular goals of the institution? or, What gets assessed, and why, and how often?

Change has always been the goal of the scholarship of teaching and learning: deeper understanding of the processes of student learning; clearer knowledge of what contributes to better student learning; more imaginative approaches to learning from student learning. But that devotion to change has, as its corollary, a commitment to broad-based, widespread, and long-ranging improvement beyond the single classroom, department, or campus. And while the effort of individuals will always be at the heart of this and all forms of scholarship, it is the coordinated work of scholars, students, and administrators sharing communal goals, processes, and evidence that will ultimately bring the most light to the often opaque environment of student learning.

As Lopez (1986) suggested, our curiosity and commitment and desire for change always begins as a single point; and scholarship that remains in place exists forever as a point in space, without breadth or trajectory or influence. But when isolated inquiry becomes scholarship, when investigation becomes public, that point becomes a line with scale and purpose and significance. Geometry teaches us that there is another stage, a way in which multiple lines combine to form a plane that reaches to infinity. And this is what we are about when we move the scholarship of teaching and learning beyond the local, the individual, even the collaborative. It is the moment when lines become landscape, when direction becomes dimension, and when insight becomes impact that can change teaching and learning practice writ small and large, locally and beyond, now and into the future.

References

Berheide, C. W., & Marx, M. S. (2004). *Thinking about thinking: Using an Idea Notebook to develop critical thinking skills.* Retrieved May 14, 2007, from www.cfkeep.org/html/snapshot.php?id=68820745934565

Boyer, E. L. (1990). *Scholarship reconsidered: Priorities of the professoriate.* Princeton, NJ: The Carnegie Foundation for the Advancement of Teaching.

Ferrett, T. (2006). *First year students "go beyond" with integrative inquiry into abrupt change.* Retrieved May 14, 2007, from www.cfkeep.org/html/snapshot.php?id=28615862064637

Gale, R. (2003). *Portfolio assessment and student empowerment.* Retrieved May 14, 2007, from www.cfkeep.org/html/snapshot.php?id=2478563

Huber, M. T., & Hutchings, P. (2005). *The advancement of learning: Building the teaching commons.* San Francisco, CA: Jossey-Bass.

Lopez, B. (1986). *Arctic dreams.* New York, NY: Vintage Books.

Shenk, G. (2001). *California history and political action.* Retrieved May 14, 2007, from www.carnegiefoundation.org/programs/project_summary.asp?scholar=114

Shulman, L. S. (1993, November/December). Teaching as community property: Putting an end to pedagogical solitude. *Change, 25*(6), 6-7.

Shulman, L. S. (2004). Visions of educational leadership: Sustaining the legacy of Seymour Fox. In M. Nisan & O. Schremer (Eds.), *Educational deliberations: Festschrift in honor of Seymour M. Fox* (pp. 451–472). Jerusalem: Keter Publishers.

Stewart, J. L. (2006). *Integrative learning in the sciences: Decision making at the intersection of science knowledge and student beliefs and values.* Retrieved May 14, 2007, from www.cfkeep.org/html/snapshot.php?id=70824690508493

Takacs, D. (2001). *Teaching to inspire political participation in communities.* Retrieved May 14, 2007, from www.carnegiefoundation.org/programs/project_summary.asp?scholar=115

4

Easing Entry into the Scholarship of Teaching and Learning Through Focused Assessments: The "Decoding the Disciplines" Approach

Joan Middendorf, David Pace
Indiana University

Students' difficulty in mastering material can motivate faculty toward the scholarship of teaching and learning (SoTL) if instructors' frustration can be framed as a researchable question, and they have practical models for assessing learning outcomes. The "decoding the disciplines" approach supports this shift from reflective teaching to SoTL. By focusing on narrowly defined bottlenecks to learning, faculty define researchable questions convincing to their disciplines. The specificity of these inquiries makes the assessment of learning much easier through the application of existing tools, such as those provided in Angelo and Cross's Classroom Assessment Techniques *(1993). Example of specific assessments are provided.*

Getting Past the "A" Word

There is nothing quite like the word *assessment* to clear a room of faculty. It immediately evokes images of mindless evaluations imposed by an educational bureaucracy that has no real understanding of the forms of knowledge or the traditions that shape academic disciplines. And even instructors who are willing to entertain the possibility of finding ways to assess learning in their classes often find it difficult to form effective strategies to accomplish this goal.

This situation poses serious problems for the scholarship of teaching and learning (SoTL). If the work in this new field is to have a real impact on what actually happens in the classroom, its findings must have legitimacy in the eyes of those who are positioned to implement them. This requires some form of assessment that makes claims in the SoTL literature credible. But the creation of such assessments often seems to be beyond the abilities of the faculty who are conducting this research. Those faculty who are new to SoTL often assume that it requires the kind of evidence long identified with traditional social sciences. Faculty who have never had a day's training in quantitative methods set out on a fruitless quest for numbers to crunch, double-blind tests of pedagogical efficacy to administer, and variables to correlate. Not surprisingly, such efforts generally fail. Even those who are better prepared to use such methods usually come to realize that the preconditions for such research do not exist in most of the real-life situations in which SoTL is typically generated.

The irony is that in many cases these methodologies would not produce the desired effect even if they were successfully implemented. Although higher education has attempted to discover generalizable principles to improve student learning, Shulman (2002) found, through his research on medical schools, that teaching is content and context specific: "Domain specificity is likely to be the hallmark of inquiry, learning, and teaching in a discipline" (p. vii). Large numbers of faculty are not apt to be swayed by arguments couched in an unfamiliar language and based on forms of legitimization that are alien to those accepted in their own disciplines. Professors of literature, for example, are only slightly more likely to change their approaches to instruction in response to scholarship based on strict statistical procedures than their counterparts in a mathematics department are to be swayed by a literary analysis.

The difficult task of generating assessments that are convincing to a member of a particular discipline is made even harder by the fact that faculty often begin by seeking to evaluate large and ill-defined qualities such as critical thinking. Such broadly defined skills are generally an aggregation of simpler operations, each of which must be present and functioning correctly for the learning to take place. A global assessment of critical thinking cannot tell us which ones have not been sufficiently mastered.

Thus, if SoTL is to realize its potential, it will be necessary to find ways to focus the attention of its practitioners on clearly defined, manageable questions and to assess the results of classroom modules in a language that is meaningful to members of the relevant academic disciplines. We believe that the "decoding the disciplines" methods developed in the Indiana University Freshman Learning Project may be useful in overcoming these obstacles.

This chapter describes how we encouraged faculty who were deeply engaged in their disciplinary research to become involved in SoTL and to avoid the common mistakes of naïve teaching and learning research, such as we describe next. It provides examples of specific projects in a variety of disciplines.

Naïve Attempts at Assessment

There are currently 41 discipline-specific teaching journals in higher education (Weimer, 2006). The articles that comprise these journals often lack compelling evidence that learning has taken place. The standard format for these articles is to tell a "story," a detailed account of a new technique that a teacher has developed, often with no literature review and usually no assessment data beyond a claim that the students liked the new approach or that course evaluations improved. If they do present data, it commonly takes one of four forms. The first is a standard course evaluation showing improvement in the ratings following the implementation of a new approach (see the example in Table 4.1).

TABLE 4.1

Course Evaluation Improvement

Overall I would rate the quality of this course as outstanding.	
Before new method	49%
After new method	83%

In the second type, the course evaluation has been customized to allow students to rate themselves on a particular skill, the focus of the innovation (see the example in Table 4.2). Students rating themselves as improved at thesis writing are not providing very specific feedback to their instructor; thesis writing consists of many subskills.

TABLE 4.2

Student Skill Self-Rating

My skills at formulating a thesis:	
A. greatly improved	17
B. improved	44
C. stayed the same	38
D. regressed	2

The third approach to providing evidence that a learning innovation succeeded is to show improved exam scores the semester after a new technique is used (see the example in Table 4.3).

TABLE 4.3

Exam Score Increases Following Innovation

	Percent Increase
First exam	6%
Second exam	11%

Finally, naïve educational researchers often attempt method comparison studies, in which the instructor compares the outcomes for two courses delivered in two different ways, such as lecture versus discussion or lecture versus computerized practice exercises. The problem with this research design is that in hundreds of such studies, the main result has shown that the medium has no effect on the learning (Clark, 1983; Russell, 2001). Another challenge of good research design is described by W. J. McKeachie, who writes that there are so many extraneous variables affecting student learning (from instructional methods, to media attributes, to learning style, etc.) that "any study in a natural setting is lucky to account for 3% to 5 % of the variance" (personal communication, October 13, 1997). We have found it useful to help faculty avoid inappropriate research methodologies by showing them how to create their own focused assessments of student learning outcomes.

The FLP and Preparation for Assessment

Since 1998 the Freshman Learning Project (FLP) has been taking faculty through a two-week summer workshop in which they seek to develop new ways to increase learning in their classes. The seven-step "decoding the disciplines" process that is at the heart of the program has been described at length in other publications (Pace & Middendorf, 2004). This process (see Figure 4.1) has proven highly effective in helping faculty find new ways to increase learning, and it has played a crucial role in reenergizing many faculty at mid-career. But it has also served the unanticipated function of drawing faculty into SoTL and of providing them the tools with which they can assess the results of the implementation of new teaching strategies. Moreover, it has given the FLP participants (called "fellows") ownership over the assessment process, assured that the qualities that are evaluated are central to their goals, and produced evaluations of success that are couched in terms familiar to other faculty in that discipline.

FIGURE 4.1

Decoding the Disciplines:
Seven Steps to Overcome Obstacles to Learning

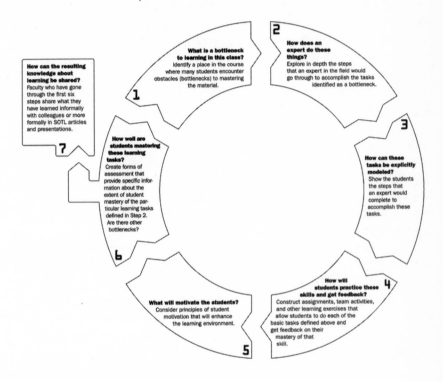

Source. Pace and Middendorf (2004, p. 3). Reprinted with permission.

At the beginning of this decoding the disciplines process each faculty fellow defines a bottleneck—that is, a place in one of his or her courses at which significant numbers of students fail to master material that is essential to the course. This might involve a complex theoretical issue such as the inability of students to understand the ways that light interacts with matter in an astronomy course or the characteristics of a painting that indicate that it was created in 16th-century Amsterdam. Or the bottleneck may involve a seemingly simple issue, such as how to distinguish between productive and unproductive details in the text of a literature course or how to generate objections to an argument in philosophy. Faculty find bottlenecks to be interesting problems to solve and they become as engaged in them as they are in their disciplinary research. Every discipline has numerous bottlenecks that deserve further exploration. (See Figure 4.2 for examples of bottlenecks grouped according to social sciences, sciences, and humanities.)

Once the bottlenecks have been clearly defined, fellows go through a lengthy interview in which they try to describe what steps an expert in the field would take to overcome the bottleneck. Their automatic responses are often somewhat superficial and jargon laden, but the interviewers probe to get beyond these to reveal the micro-operations that an expert does automatically and often unconsciously.

This process of defining bottlenecks and the procedures actually employed by experts in the field to overcome them may seem far removed from the assessment of learning, but, in fact, it can be a crucial step in reaching that end. This process focuses attention on specific, concrete forms of student behavior, whose presence or absence at various points in the course can be assessed, and it assures that the competencies being measured are in fact those that faculty members themselves have judged to be central to learning in their courses. By translating abstract critical thinking into concrete, discipline-specific sets of operations, a faculty member begins with a clear focus on defined skills that can be measured.

The details of the next several steps in the decoding the disciplines process (modeling the operations for students, giving them a chance to practice and receive feedback, and developing a strategy to motivate students to remain involved in the process), while somewhat peripheral to the issues of this chapter, often produce information that is highly useful in the assessment process, and they give faculty a motivation to conduct assessment because they are naturally curious about whether their interventions have proven effective.

Getting Started in Assessment

How do faculty who are untrained in pedagogical assessment move from the definition of learning operations to the evaluation of the success of particular interventions designed to teach these carefully defined ways of thinking? Before seeking to answer this question, it is worth noting that the form of the question may lead us to assume that there is a single process of evaluation that is appropriate to all teaching situations. As we noted earlier, such a one-size-fits-all approach ignores the differences in disciplinary practice and epistemology, and it can easily lead to assessments that are unacceptable or even

FIGURE 4.2

Bottleneck Examples from Varied Disciplines

Social Sciences

- Economics: Students cannot correlate two dimensions of data on a graph.

- Logic: Students can translate simple logical propositions (e.g., p and q) into colloquial language but get stuck translating nested, more intricate ones. For example, (a = > (b or not c)).

- Sociology: For some students it is almost heretical to question the taken for granted cultural assumptions (success as wealth, inequalities, etc.) and structures (capitalism, democracy, globalization). This in turn blocks an understanding of what ideology even is.

Sciences

- Life science: Students seem unable to grasp why certain numbers are used for certain parts of the equation, what they represent, and how to look at their numbers and understand the values they are getting.

- Computer science: Students have difficulty distinguishing between conceptual design (real-world entities and the relationships among them) and logical design (representations of the real world which describe the levels among entities, the connections, data types, etc.).

- Biology: Students, who have been successful at memorization, do not know how to move beyond memorizing to start the problem-solving process.

- Genetics: Students are unable to move from terminology and verbal descriptions to visualizations of function or processes.

- Chemistry: Students do not grasp the formative mechanisms of acids and bases, and the similarities/differences between them. They are making incorrectly charged molecules.

- Chemistry: Students are intimidated by a problem with more than one math step. It is not the chemical principles that are confusing them but the mathematical manipulation required.

Humanities

- Art history: Students cannot apply the historical/contextual elements that influence artists and their work.

- Theater: Student actors find it difficult to maintain their courageous openness when they are in front of people and the pressure is on.

- Language: Students in a language class struggle to comprehend an unfamiliar word because they don't observe patterns of word endings and articles.

- English: The conflict or paradox of students asking for "freedom" when given a writing assignment and yet also wanting to know precisely what they "need" or "must" do to be successful.

Note. What may be perfectly simple in one discipline, may become a bottleneck if it is transferred to another.

unintelligible to the very faculty it is designed to convince. As Shulman (2002) argues, "if different disciplines value particular forms of evidence and argument, narrative and explanation, then the pedagogies should reflect the same forms of representation and exposition" (p. vii).

Instead, the decoding the disciplines model encourages faculty to approach assessment within the context of the language and methods of their own fields. And the process of assessment does not need to be methodologically complex. In many cases the simple application of one of the strategies outlined in Angelo and Cross's *Classroom Assessment Techniques* (1993) can yield results that are quite adequate to convince members of a discipline of the effectiveness of a particular intervention.

In the FLP summer seminar we start simple:

- Fellows try one CAT per day to evaluate that day's session.

- We give them the Angelo and Cross book.

- We recommend three to five likely CATs to evaluate their lesson to narrow their choices.

- They select and use one CAT following their lesson.

- They complete CATs following the presentations of the 11 other FLP fellows.

- In small groups they recommend CATs relevant to other participants.

As part of the follow-up to the FLP seminar, fellows are expected to teach and assess their model lesson in a real class. They can either use the CAT they planned in the seminar, or they can meet with a team of assessment specialists, including an institutional review board consultant, to design the assessment that will be the basis for their SoTL project.

Sample Assessments

Here are some examples of the assessments that grew out of the decoding the disciplines process and were published by novices to SoTL (Pace & Middendorf, 2004). Note the specificity and the variety.

Assessing Learning in a Literature Class

As Gutjahr defined a bottleneck, "Students often cannot see the 'double and triple meanings' in a passage of text, and when I teach this, some students feel

I am making the obvious obscure and even absurd" (Ardizzone, Breithaupt, & Gutjahr, 2004, p. 50). To assess student ability to analyze text, he used CAT #2, Focused Listing, before and after the lesson. Presented with an unfamiliar passage of text, students were asked to list as many meanings as they could. Results showed that following the lesson, 70% more of the students were able to go beyond plot summary to list at least two different possible interpretations of the text (see Figure 4.3). His analysis of the CAT revealed that the students had recognized more complex patterns and meanings in the text, and had to a greater degree than ever before unlocked the author's code of word choice and rhetorical strategy that are an important part of literary analysis.

FIGURE 4.3

Improvement in Meaning Interpretation

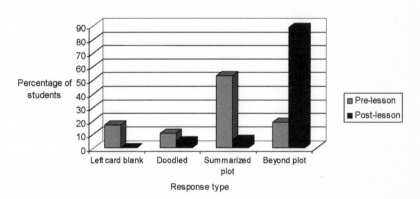

Assessing Learning in an Astronomy Class

Pilachowski noticed astronomy textbooks include many schematic diagrams to illustrate astrophysical concepts. To a scientist these diagrams contain the kernels of astrophysical concepts, while the text serves primarily to flesh out the idea with further detail. In contrast, students' experience in other courses leads them to see illustrations and images as decoration or enrichment rather than as primary content. Students find it difficult to think visually in order to identify and master critical astronomy concepts (Durisen & Pilachowski, 2004). With this bottleneck in mind, she applied CAT #16, Concept Maps, asking students to sketch the Milky Way galaxy at the beginning of class and again at the end, including as much detail as they could. The frequency of particular features in the first and second drawings were counted and compared (see Figure 4.4).

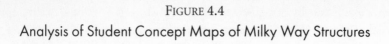

FIGURE 4.4

Analysis of Student Concept Maps of Milky Way Structures

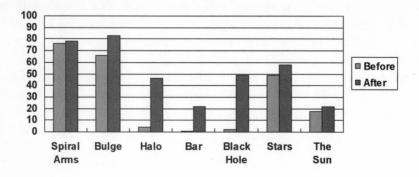

Not only did the students provide more detail at the end of the class than at the beginning, but she could identify the specific concepts where the increase was greatest or least, and thus gained insights into the specific details of visualizing astronomy.

Materials for Practice Designing Assessments

If you would like to have a faculty group practice turning the bottleneck and expert thinking into assessments, Appendix 4.1 provides examples from four disciplines that specify concrete forms of learning for you to work with. Small groups can use these materials as the basis for discussion about how we would know if students could do this kind of thinking and create some assessments for each example.

Moving from Assessments to SOTL

In the "Sample Assessments" section, the questions and data analysis may seem crisp, and the generation of such data may seem straightforward. But the iterative process of getting to such results is often messy and complex (see Figure 4.5), as faculty follow the decoding disciplines steps, repeatedly revisiting the bottleneck and expert thinking to disaggregate the operations. When implementing their lesson with an actual class, the FLP fellows use several CATs because it is not always clear which one will provide the most constructive feedback. They may end up with several sets of student responses, but these are often initially ambiguous and require focused analysis. Because the results of such assessment have not been reported widely in the literature, we don't have a good order of magnitude estimates to judge whether a teaching strategy may be deemed successful. But these are the kinds of problems that faculty are already quite good at solving, and this process is fortunately often facilitated by the material on "Turning the Data You Collect into Useful Information," which follows each CAT in the Angelo and Cross book.

FIGURE 4.5

Iterative Decoding the Disciplines Process to Produce SoTL

1. Define the bottleneck and the steps by which an expert successfully addresses the bottleneck.

2. Repeat Step 1 several times to disaggregate the bottleneck and expert thinking operations.

3. Design a module to teach the bottleneck (following decoding disciplines Steps 3 through 6).

4. Implement and assess the module in an actual class.

5. Analyze the data.

6. Redefine the bottleneck and the steps by which an expert successfully addresses the bottleneck.

7. Write up the process using the decoding the disciplines steps as a framework.

In the literature assessment example, for instance, the literature professor, having read how the data from a Focused Listing can be used, compiled student answers into useful categories that showed the specific kinds of mistakes students made in finding the double and triple meaning in the text. Once he totaled the items in each category, he could write up his results in a way that would make sense to his colleagues. It was in analyzing and organizing the assessment results that he ascertained his orderly description for SoTL.

This process has narrowed the gap between classroom experience and published classroom research. Like many of their colleagues, the FLP fellows have "stories" to tell about strategies they have used to increase student learning. But unlike most of their colleagues, these instructors have a means to actually demonstrate the extent to which their experiments have been successful. Thus, it is not surprising that 16 of the fellows have published articles on their FLP projects, 18 have presented papers, and 4 have been awarded a total of almost $3.5 million in grants to continue such work. This was the first foray into SoTL for most of these instructors, and several of them now make this work a regular part of their research agendas.

But beyond the usual academic outcomes, one of the most surprising aspects of decoding the disciplines has been its enthusiastic reception by faculty. By setting up a community of smart teachers, each one having identified a bottleneck, and providing them with the tools to explore their bottleneck, momentum is created, like a laboratory of rich questions. No longer is teaching a problem to be "fixed" (Bass, 1999). We have observed faculty literally run to their offices following a Step 2 interview, so eager are they to get their ideas on paper. Even several years after the summer seminar, faculty show up at meetings excited to discuss their ongoing efforts to explore bottlenecks. And the clarity of the method makes it easier to attract faculty into the process. When it was proposed to a large department to investigate the bottlenecks in their upper division courses, the proposal was accepted with unanimous acclamation—cheering and applause at a faculty meeting. The affective reactions to decoding the disciplines have impelled the project along as much as anything has.

Conclusion

If SoTL is to become an important part of higher education, it will be necessary to find effective mechanisms for drawing faculty into this new field of research. We believe that the combination of the decoding the disciplines process from the FLP with the CATs devised by Angelo and Cross provides such a mechanism. Bottlenecks serve as specific, visible points of entry to inquiry about student learning. The process of identifying them and of defining expert thinking focuses faculty from the outset on discrete operations that will allow them to later assess whether the bottleneck modules have actually had an impact on learning. The CATs can play a useful role in guiding instructors who are new to assessment through the process. The entire operation begins with problems that were defined by faculty themselves and, thus, is less likely to generate resistance to the process. The assessments do not require faculty to completely retool their methodologies, and the results are presented in a language that will not be foreign to other members of their discipline.

Appendix 4.1

Practice Turning Bottlenecks and Expert Operations into Assessments for Small Group Discussion

Read the bottleneck and the expert thinking (Steps 1 and 2) for your disciplinary area. What evidence would indicate whether students could do this kind of thinking? Choose two or three applicable assessments from the Angelo and Cross CATs book, or invent your own.

Philosophy (O'Connor, 2006)

Step 1: Define the bottleneck:

Many students are unable to distill the basic structure of an author's argument.

Step 2: Define the steps an expert would follow to overcome this bottleneck:

a. Scan the entire passage to find the author's conclusion or thesis and the general line of argument.

b. Return to the text and identify the main points, dubious arguments, and unfamiliar terms.

c. Reconstruct the argument in a formal manner, making each step explicit, recognize the logical steps and the gaps in the argument.

d. Consider the best possible objections to premises that are most likely to be disputed.

Creative Writing (Dorsey, 2006)

Step 1: Define the bottleneck:

Students cannot distinguish between writing an autobiographical "chronology" of events ("plodding") from a carefully constructed fictional plot that gives the reader a sense of the causal relationship between the series of events and puts the dramatic situation into motion toward its inevitable conclusion through the actions of the character ("plotting").

Step 2: Define the steps an expert would follow to overcome this bottleneck:

1. Recognize that a chronological succession of events is not the same as a tightly integrated plot.

2. Generate realistic characters and a world within which the action can take place by asking:

a. Who is it happening to? Who are the characters involved?

b. Where is it happening?

c. Why to this character and why now?

d. How does this character behave, react? How is tension created?

e. What is at stake? What does a reader need to know about the character's situation to care about the outcome?

f. When *(the most important plot question)* do they need to know each detail for maximum dramatic tension?

Marketing (Rubin & Krishnan, 2004)

Step 1: Define the bottleneck:

Marketing decisions hinge on an accurate understanding of consumers and their decision processes. Although students generally understand how consumers make decisions, they are not able to reverse perspective and think like marketing managers. In particular, the bottleneck students face is that they do not know how to use information about consumer decision making to design actions that would influence those decisions.

Step 2: Define the steps an expert would follow to overcome this bottleneck of reversing perspectives:

a. Identify the set of attributes consumers use to make decisions about a product.
b. Describe the weights consumers assign to these attributes based on their underlying purchase motivations.
c. Translate how differences in motivation lead to the formation of decision rules.
d. Understand how to group consumers into different segments based on decision rules.
e. Identify the possible range of actions that could influence consumer decision rules.
f. Match specific actions with the types of decision rules used by consumer segments.

Geology (Johnson & Middendorf, 2007)

Step 1: Define the bottleneck:

When faced with questions involving geological time, students do not understand that time is continuous. Students cannot move from the diagrams in the textbook to a meaningful understanding of geological time. They do not recognize that the events identified as a single point in time on the diagram (e.g., the origin or extinction of the dinosaurs) were actually spread over a great period of time. See the Geologic Time Scale at www.geosociety.org/science/timescale/timescl.htm.

Step 2: Define the steps an expert would follow to overcome this bottleneck:

a. Break down the geological column into its largest division, the eras, and explain the terminology.
b. Recognize that the bottom of the chart represents the oldest period, and the top the newest.
c. Identify where the present day is located on the time scale.
d. Identify and define the division boundaries and state their relation to origination and extinction events.
e. Remain aware that segments on the charts each represent long periods of time in which considerable change occurred.

References

Angelo, T. A., & Cross, K. P. (1993). *Classroom assessment techniques: A handbook for college teachers* (2nd ed.). San Francisco, CA: Jossey-Bass.

Ardizzone, A., Breithaupt, F., & Gutjahr, P. (2004). Decoding the humanities. In D. Pace & J. Middendorf (Eds.), *New directions for teaching and learning: No. 98. Decoding the disciplines: Helping students learn disciplinary ways of thinking* (pp. 50–55). San Francisco, CA: Jossey-Bass.

Bass, R. (1999, February). The scholarship of teaching: What's the problem? *Inventio, 1*(1). Retrieved May 15, 2007, from the George Mason University, Division of Instructional Technology web site: www.doit.gmu.edu/Archives/feb98/randybass.htm

Clark, R. E. (1983, Winter). Reconsidering research on learning from media. *Review of Educational Research, 53*(4), 445–459.

Dorsey, R. (2006). *Decoding creative plot development.* Unpublished manuscript, Indiana University, Bloomington.

Durisen, R., & Pilachowski, C. (2004.) Decoding astronomical concepts. In D. Pace & J. Middendorf (Eds.), *New directions for teaching and learning: No. 98. Decoding the disciplines: Helping students learn disciplinary ways of thinking* (pp. 33–43). San Francisco, CA: Jossey-Bass.

Johnson, C., & Middendorf, J. (2007). *Decoding geologic time.* Manuscript submitted for publication.

O'Connor, T. (2006). *Decoding a philosophical argument.* Unpublished manuscript, Indiana University, Bloomington.

Pace, D., & Middendorf, J. (Eds.). (2004). *New directions for teaching and learning: No. 98. Decoding the disciplines: Helping students learn disciplinary ways of thinking.* San Francisco, CA: Jossey-Bass.

Rubin, B., & Krishnan, S. (2004.) Decoding applied data in professional schools. In D. Pace & J. Middendorf (Eds.), *New directions for teaching and learning: No. 98. Decoding the disciplines: Helping students learn disciplinary ways of thinking* (pp. 67–73). San Francisco, CA: Jossey-Bass.

Russell, T. (2001). *The "no significant difference phenomenon"* (5th ed.). Montgomery, AL: International Distance Education Certification Center.

Shulman, L. S. (2002). Foreword. In M. T. Huber & S. P. Morreale (Eds.), *Disciplinary styles in the scholarship of teaching and learning: Exploring common ground* (pp. v–ix). Sterling, VA: Stylus.

Weimer, M. (2006). *Enhancing scholarly work on teaching and learning: Professional literature that makes a difference.* San Francisco, CA: Jossey-Bass.

5

Supporting the Scholarship of Teaching and Learning at Liberal Arts Colleges

Dolores Peters, David Schodt, Mary Walczak
St. Olaf College

Although the liberal arts college, with its traditional focus on teaching, may seem like a natural environment for the scholarship of teaching and learning (SoTL), few such institutions participate in national SoTL initiatives. Our associates' experience since 2001 suggests a model for supporting SoTL in teaching-intensive contexts based on faculty ownership, a focus on general education, and some emerging rules of engagement. Because faculty reward systems must validate SoTL if it is to become part of the institutional culture, we also describe one department's efforts to reform its review criteria in order to define scholarly activity broadly.

Since 2000, St. Olaf College has encouraged and supported faculty interested in pursuing the scholarship of teaching and learning (SoTL). Approximately 200 colleges and universities have participated in the Carnegie Academy for the Scholarship of Teaching and Learning's (CASTL) Campus Program (2000–2006), which worked with "institutions of all types to cultivate the conditions necessary to support the scholarship of teaching and learning" (The Carnegie Foundation for the Advancement of Teaching, 2006), but St. Olaf is one of only three liberal arts colleges represented among the 96 institutions to have participated in the most recent Campus Program.[1] We find these statistics somewhat paradoxical given our sense that liberal arts colleges should be fertile ground for SoTL. While we do not pretend to resolve this paradox, we do offer one model for supporting SoTL at liberal arts colleges and at other institutions that share their salient characteristics of relatively small size and a focus on undergraduate education.

Numbers alone might seem to provide an explanation for the low representation of liberal arts colleges. These institutions comprise a small percentage of the higher education universe, accounting for only 4%–5% of students and a somewhat higher percentage of faculty members. For several reasons, however, we would expect their involvement with SoTL to be greater. Faculty choose liberal arts colleges out of a strong commitment to undergraduate teaching, and smaller classes facilitate the exploration of new approaches to teaching and learning. While most liberal arts colleges have relatively high expectations for traditional scholarship, they typically rank excellence in teaching above research in the reward structure. A recent survey of nearly 500 faculty development leaders showed that 60% of respondents from liberal arts colleges ranked advancing new initiatives in teaching and learning among their top three goals, compared with 45% at research institutions (Sorcinelli, Austin, Eddy, & Beach, 2006). In short, liberal arts colleges appear to be ideal incubators for innovations in teaching and natural candidates for widespread engagement with SoTL.

However, SoTL does not happen automatically, even in contexts where excellent teaching flourishes. As we learned from our experiences at St. Olaf, neither faculty commitment to undergraduate teaching nor a corresponding institutional commitment necessarily translates into SoTL. Most graduate programs do not prepare future faculty for engagement with SoTL, and an institutional commitment to excellence in teaching may not extend beyond the hiring of good faculty who want to teach or an emphasis on teaching in the reward structure.

Nevertheless, supporting SoTL in the liberal arts context makes a great deal of sense, precisely because such institutions, unlike many research universities, do not have to make an argument for the importance of undergraduate teaching. Yet even faculty already heavily invested in teaching and open to new approaches are usually unfamiliar with the vast body of literature that has developed on effective teaching practices. And, despite the supportive environment at liberal arts colleges, the substantial amount of pedagogical innovation that does take place is rarely communicated beyond the individual faculty member's classroom, a result of what Lee Shulman (1993) has identified as pedagogical solitude. SoTL's emphasis on connecting the exploration of one's own teaching problems to an existing body of scholarship on teaching, and on making public the results of these inquiries, addresses both of these problems. For faculty, SoTL can be another way to connect research and teaching; for students, it can provide new opportunities for undergraduate research. Furthermore, the results of this inquiry help make the case for liberal arts colleges to constituencies that may be increasingly skeptical of the value of this particular form of higher education. Finally, SoTL offers a way to create a public repository of good practices at the institution and beyond. It can form part of a college's assessment, building from the bottom up on faculty members' genuine interests in teaching well.

Generalizing from the experiences of seven diverse institutions, Cambridge's (2004) recent report on progress in adopting SoTL identifies the following elements as important in fostering this work: involving academic administrators, ensuring a diversity of participants, communicating the results, and working with the reward system. Key to the success of programs designed to support SoTL, however, is the specific way these elements are deployed to match the institutional context in which they function. For example, department chairs may be key academic administrators at some institutions, but not at others where this position may be filled with short-term, rotating appointments. Although having a reward system congruent with SoTL is essential, also significant are whether teaching or research is the highest of the three traditional categories in that system, and in which category SoTL is counted.

A survey of faculty development at a variety of institutions identifies a difference between liberal arts respondents and others that is relevant to the success of programs supporting SoTL. Responses from many liberal arts colleges (and from comprehensive universities) argued for the importance of strong faculty ownership of faculty development. By contrast, at research institutions, the more common perception was that faculty development priorities were set by senior-level administrators (Sorcinelli et al., 2006). Our own experience, while reinforcing the importance of supporting SoTL in ways that are responsive to institutional priorities, also suggests that faculty ownership of these programs cannot be overemphasized. To ensure success in the liberal arts context, programs need to begin by addressing faculty interests, building on local expertise, and creating indigenous models for doing SoTL.

St. Olaf's program for supporting SoTL began with the establishment of our Center for Innovation in the Liberal Arts (CILA). While this learning and teaching center identified SoTL as one of its founding goals, we decided early on to support SoTL as one of many types of activities taking place along a continuum. We wanted to provide direct support for a small number of faculty who would undertake SoTL projects, but we also wanted to encourage larger numbers of faculty who might only be interested in less formal ways of thinking about student learning, such as classroom assessment and "just-in-time" teaching.

A cohort of faculty engaged in SoTL is critical to shifting institutional culture from one in which "good teaching" is expected and rewarded to one where vibrant conversations about learning are grounded in why and how this learning takes place. This cohort can provide local, credible models for how others might begin to think in new ways about teaching. In economists' language, the spillover effects from even relatively small numbers of faculty engaging in SoTL can be quite large. However, just as it is important to support SoTL, it is equally important to create a "big tent where there is space for small-scale efforts aimed mostly at local improvement as well as more ambitious, sustained, work of a larger scale" (Huber & Hutchings, 2005, p. 30). Each nourishes the other.

In this chapter, we focus on two aspects of our experience. First is the program of CILA associates. Associates anchor our efforts by creating local models for SoTL inquiry. Each associate receives a one-course released-time award to undertake an SoTL project. Associates also help support CILA's broader activities. As we recount here, their experiences to date have led us to make some important modifications to this program, including the addition of SoTL Learning Communities and the Writing Residency.

Although responsibility for changing the faculty reward system falls outside CILA's administrative mandate, a system that provides appropriate incentives is a vital component of the institutional context that supports SoTL. The second part of this chapter, then, describes our chemistry department's experience revising its standards for tenure and promotion in a way that supports not just excellent teaching, but also a broad definition of scholarship that includes SoTL. St. Olaf's review process is more decentralized than that of some institutions: Statements of Professional Activity developed by individual departments serve as the standard for evaluating faculty work. Nevertheless, as at most liberal arts colleges that rank teaching excellence first among the traditional categories for review, the debate over SoTL at St. Olaf is about whether and how it will be included in scholarship, the second-ranked category for tenure and promotion. Although the process and outcome we describe are specific to our institutional context, we think the work undertaken by the chemistry department illustrates the spillover effect that even a small core of SoTL inquiry can produce and can be a useful model for other departments and colleges.

SoTL and the CILA Associates Program

Since 2001, five cohorts of CILA associates (11 faculty), have undertaken 12 projects that represent the core of SoTL on our campus. Associate professors have provided the highest percentage of participation (7 of 11 associates). Their predominance reflects both campus demographics and national data on faculty careers indicating a broadening of professional activities at this rank. A distinctive feature of SoTL on our campus is its engagement of faculty at both extremes of the academic ranks. Full professors' involvement (three associates) is not surprising since senior faculty at liberal arts institutions continue to be fully engaged in teaching. Participation by an instructor in an adjunct position reflects CILA's philosophy of encouraging good teachers at all ranks as well as St. Olaf's policy of considering instructors and adjuncts eligible for many types of faculty development. No assistant professors have yet been associates. Their conspicuous absence probably reflects local and national uncertainty about the status of SoTL in the reward system. For example, at Illinois State University, the lead institution in the CASTL cluster to which St. Olaf belonged, respondents to a survey who were generally favorable toward SoTL were ambivalent about its value and use on campus (McKinney et al., 2003).[2] Although important initiatives introducing SoTL to junior faculty exist (Reder & Gallagher, 2007), assistant professors at St. Olaf, as elsewhere, seem more likely to focus on classroom teaching and traditional scholarship than on SoTL.

The humanities, the largest division of the St. Olaf faculty, have provided the largest number of associates (see Table 5.1). Chemistry's prominence among the sciences builds on its long-standing interest in student learning as a legitimate focus of professional activity. Finally, since the environmental studies project in fact focused on visual literacy, there have been two SoTL projects in the fine arts. CASTL has noted fine arts' underrepresentation in SoTL work done in the United States, so our relative overrepresentation of fine arts is atypical.

What Does SoTL at St. Olaf Look Like?

SoTL inquiry at St. Olaf (see Table 5.2) is similar to the work emerging nationally that Hutchings (2000) has described. Associates are interested in examining what works in the classroom. For example, one studied PowerPoint's effectiveness in introducing visual images into a course. Another wondered which classroom assessments best measure chemistry students' understanding of scientific content and their pre- and post-course attitudes about science. Some studies describe what student learning looks like by observing or articulating constituent components of a classroom experience or technique. An associate examining the effects of EndNote wanted to know how this software for managing bibliographic references encourages students' development as researchers. Still others sought to determine whether the addition of certain desirable components, even if not

TABLE 5.1

Distribution of SoTL Projects by Area and Department

Area	Total Number of Projects
Humanities	
English	1
History	1
Religion	2
Social and Applied Sciences	
Political science	2
Psychology	1
Natural Sciences and Math	
Chemistry	2
Fine Arts	
Music	1
Interdisciplinary and General Studies	
Environmental studies	1
Integrative studies	1

strictly cognitive, enhances student learning. For example, a notion of the "expertise of discovery" informs the projects of three associates: a historian who wanted students to experience the *thrill* of constructing meaning out of a mass of primary sources; a political scientist who wanted students to be skillful researchers and to experience the *immediacy* of researching politics during a presidential primary; a chemist who is *passionate* about the responsibility of educating informed citizens. "The urgency of training the next generation of scientists," the chemist argued, "occurs in tandem with the need for increasing [scientific and technological literacy] among all citizens. [This urgency] argue[s] for a science-literate population as a means to realizing the life-enhancing potential of science and technology" (CILA Associates, 2005, report 0405C, p. 1). Finally, as is the case nationally, associates did not focus on explicitly developing new conceptual frameworks that affect teaching practices.

TABLE 5.2

SoTL Questions Asked by CILA Associates

Hutchings's Taxonomy of SoTL Questions	Questions Posed by Associates
What works in the classroom?	Is PowerPoint an effective pedagogical aid?
	What correlations exist between computer-assisted visual presentations and learning styles?
	How can classroom assessment techniques be used to measure chemistry students' understanding of scientific content and their pre- and post-course attitudes about science?
	How can the web enhance English majors' research skills, especially in the collaborative process of drafting and revising papers?
What does student learning look like?	What is the effect of bibliographic database management software (EndNote) on student learning and competence in political science research?
	Can technologically mediated drills in music theory provide greater interactivity, integration, individualization, and immediate feedback for students than existing practices do?
	How can the hyperlink capacity of the web foster students' development of integrative skills from related fields of study and support the transferability of knowledge across the boundaries of those fields?
	How can image-and-text pedagogy enhance students' capacity to create sophisticated image-text compositions?
	What kind of capstone course best supports seniors with individually designed majors in their understanding of interdisciplinarity?
What is possible?	How can web technology be used in a history survey to enhance student engagement and provide authentic opportunities for "doing history"?
	How can technology enable students to do political science research in a more immediate and iterative way, especially in the field?
	Can technologically mediated assignments based on mainstream news articles enhance the scientific and technological literacy of chemistry students?
	How can one develop a model of skill-based virtue ethics in computer science to support students' capacity to integrate ethical concerns with their design of technology?

Note. Adapted from Hutchings (2000, pp. 4–5).

SoTL on our campus is overwhelmingly course based and situated in the classroom experiences of individual instructors rather than addressed to the entire curriculum or an academic discipline. Eight projects originated in individual courses where a question or problem had been identified. Even the three projects involving multiple course clusters were based on faculty members' close knowledge of students' patterns of movement through the curriculum, whether across a four-course sequence for music theory majors or three *levels* of political science coursework.

The majority of our SoTL projects focus on general education (GE) courses. At this point in our SoTL experience, it is unclear whether this characteristic is a differentiating one. In her 2005 keynote address at the first national conference on "Innovations in the Scholarship of Teaching and Learning in Liberal Arts Colleges," Hutchings suggested the tantalizing possibility that SoTL at liberal arts institutions may be particularly well suited to "making connections." In our case, three projects emphasize development of literacies (specifically, visual, scientific, and technological) that transcend particular courses; similarly, one project focuses explicitly on developing ethical thinking. Five focus on research competencies (e.g., gathering and evaluating data, recursive thinking in developing a topic) that students can generalize to a variety of classes. Associates have designed SoTL projects that help students make connections within/across course(s) by integrating old and new knowledge. And the political science project on political analysis during a presidential primary—set in part in New Hampshire—helped students connect experiences inside and outside the classroom by demonstrating that disciplinary research can be experiential learning and even service-learning.

The leitmotiv of GE in associates' work also reveals commonalities with SoTL inquiry nationally. First, since our GE courses are discipline based, the projects reinforce the differentiation of SoTL from traditional educational research. Second, targeting GE courses in research on student learning reflects an emerging consensus that the teaching and learning of critical thinking is grounded in making disciplinary methodology explicit for students and providing them with authentic opportunities to practice it (Wineburg, 2003). Emphasis on teaching critical thinking is shared by faculty across categories of institutional classification: In the Higher Education Research Institute's (HERI) 2004–2005 faculty survey, 99% of respondents considered development of students' ability to think critically to be "very important" or "essential"; helping students master knowledge in a discipline garnered the second highest endorsement (94%) as an appropriate goal for undergraduate education (Lindholm, Szelény, Hurtado, & Korn, 2005).[3]

This profile of associates' work highlights faculty ownership of SoTL at St. Olaf, where projects grow out of classroom experience rather than departmental or administrative directives. At the same time, SoTL is not detached from our institutional priorities. All applications for associate positions require a sign-off from the relevant department chair to ensure that discussion has occurred regarding the assignment of faculty time and energy. Moreover, senior faculty's participation means that those conducting SoTL studies may already have been chairs or are chairs during their project year. Nevertheless, our experience clearly suggests a bottom-up rather than top-down pattern of SoTL adoption.

How Does St. Olaf Do SoTL?

Four informal rules of engagement are emerging as SoTL has developed on campus. First, like many SoTL practitioners, associates have employed a range of methodologies (see Table 5.3) to gather and analyze data and frequently combined methodologies. Similarly, some discovered the need to develop new methodological expertise beyond their own discipline's practices. While this experience is common for faculty new to SoTL, it also has implications for dissemination of SoTL, as we will discuss. The associates' methodological preferences also reveal traces of a particular institutional context. On a campus where faculty frequently solicit student feedback on teaching, student self-reporting is a favorite source of both quantitative and qualitative data. Campus conversations about the pedagogical potential of hyperlink technology echo in the three projects that used electronic portfolios to target cognitive processes or to assess learning outcomes.

A second rule of engagement is the tendency not to use control groups in project design and assessment. A pragmatic explanation for this practice, directly related to institutional context, arises from our low number of multiple-section courses and the fact that even when they exist, responsibility for them is distributed among several faculty. Yet the ethics of SoTL inquiry provide a more complex context for understanding the absence of control groups. Early on, The Carnegie Foundation raised the problematic issue of ethics in a field that straddles traditional research with human subjects, typically requiring review by an institutional review board (IRB), and the collection of classroom data in the aggregate, which has not typically required such review (Hutchings, 2002). In addition, many campuses have recently reconsidered their guidelines for research with human subjects or, in some cases, established IRBs for the first time. St. Olaf is an example of the former; reconsideration of our IRB's organization and procedures occurred just as the first associates

TABLE 5.3

Methodologies Used in CILA Associates' SoTL Projects

Methodology	Number of Projects
Student surveys	7
Electronic portfolios	4
Student questionnaires	3
Student journals and logs	2
Researcher journal and logs	2
Content analysis of student assignments	2
Measurement of student achievement	2
Classroom assessment techniques	1
Focus groups	1
Longitudinal tracking of changed practices	1

launched their projects. Like all IRBs, ours strives both to protect the rights of human participants and to facilitate research. Like many, ours currently permits expedited review of research involving the collection of anonymous, aggregate classroom data.

We might consider whether an ethos distinctive to teaching-intensive institutions exists in SoTL inquiry. For example, two associates, in disciplines familiar with IRB review, *intentionally* rejected the use of control groups. One, a political scientist, rejected the practice in part precisely because of ethics: "Despite the explanatory advantages offered by experiments with randomly selected or self-selected test and control groups, I conclude that these experimental research designs suffer from logistical, ethical and/or accuracy problems that outweigh their possible methodological benefits" (CILA Associates, 2003, proposal 0304A, pp. 2–3). Interestingly, this statement reflects faculty opinion frequently expressed in CILA conversations: Using control groups is equivalent to withholding good teaching from students and so is unethical.

A third feature of SoTL engagement involves assessment. SoTL is emerging as a powerful factor in helping to establish a culture of assessment at St. Olaf because it highlights efficacy rather than accountability. At the same time, the range of expertise in assessment is wide, even among advocates of an evidentiary culture. Associates' initial expertise ranged from complete bafflement to the development of a portable set of classroom assessment techniques, to an attempt to study changes in student practices across the arc of their undergraduate careers. This range is similar to that among St. Olaf faculty in general. Almost half of those responding to a survey on faculty development in spring 2005 were uncertain how to measure the impact on their students of their participation in CILA conversations about teaching. On the other hand, 31 of the 45 faculty indicating that adoption of new teaching practices had a positive impact on student learning could provide a variety of evidence for this impact (St. Olaf College, 2005).

A final rule of engagement emerged on our campus: SoTL will thrive only if it exists as part of a range of systematic inquiry about teaching and learning. A majority of respondents to the survey reported that they had introduced new teaching practices or changed existing ones as a result of participating in CILA opportunities. Such openness, however, seems unlikely to translate into mass participation in SoTL, at St. Olaf or elsewhere. (At Illinois State, for example, where survey data reveal a generally positive attitude toward SoTL and a significantly higher level of participation in SoTL than on our campus, a statement that all faculty should do SoTL research elicited a neutral response rather than agreement [McKinney et al., 2003].) Perhaps the point is not that *even* at institutions with a tradition of excellence and innovation in teaching, but rather *especially* at such institutions, faculty are committed to sustaining choice in the level and nature of their involvement in teaching-related conversations and activities enhancing teaching and learning. Faculty commitment to a range of options echoes even in the plaintive statement of this associate: "During my year as a CILA associate, I have often felt that I am being asked to make a conversion, a full confession of faith in SoTL, when in fact, I have primarily been interested in thinking intentionally about teaching and learning" (CILA Associates, 2005, report 0405B, p. 3). The desire to sustain an environment rich in opportunities to address issues in teaching and learning is the obverse of faculty ownership of SoTL and corresponds to Huber and Hutchings's (2005) notion of a "teaching commons" as a broad context supported, but not monopolized, by SoTL.

The SoTL imperative to "go public" with one's findings has not been lost on the associates, who have presented their work in regional, national, and international venues (see Table 5.4). To date, however, little of this work has been published.

Future Challenges and Opportunities

As we look to the future of SoTL at St. Olaf, we recognize both challenges and opportunities. Some challenges arise from the needs of faculty engaged in SoTL; others relate to institutional culture.

TABLE 5.4

Dissemination of CILA Associates' SoTL Work

Type of Dissemination	Number of Presentations/Publications
On-Campus Presentation	
CILA brown-bag conversation	14
Departmental	2
Workshop or Symposium	
Regional	2
National	1
Conference Paper	
Regional	2
National	5
International	2
Conference Poster	
Regional	2
National	2
International	0
Publication	
Regional article	0
National article	2
Article in preparation	6

One challenge for faculty engaged in SoTL is the unexpectedly long time from project inception to publication, as associates' experience suggests. To address this issue, we have established biennial Writing Residencies. Each residency involves three or four faculty in a three-day, off-campus workshop facilitated by an individual experienced in working with faculty on SoTL projects. Participants arrive at the residency with their research completed and five pages (minimum) of a proposed article drafted. During the residency, participants share work, receive constructive feedback, and write intensively. Each participant's goal is to leave with 15 pages written and a clear plan for completing the article. Our writing residency is modeled after the successful Visible Knowledge Project (VKP) centered at Georgetown University (http://cross roads.georgetown.edu/vkp/index.htm). Although the VKP involves faculty from multiple and diverse institutions, its main features are translatable to the individual liberal arts college. And, in the interests of sustainability, associates are trained to become in-house facilitators.

Conversations with past associates helped us understand that the primary obstacle to moving SoTL projects to the publication stage is not time but unfamiliarity with how to write in a new scholarly area. Faculty engaged in SoTL projects often need to stretch beyond their disciplinary training. The skills needed to conduct SoTL research overlap only partially with prior training and experience. A quantitative scientist probably lacks training in the kind of qualitative research frequently conducted in the social sciences.

We also learned that interaction with interested colleagues is critical for gaining expertise as faculty undertake SoTL projects. CILA associates have reported feeling isolated at times as they pursue their projects without formal opportunities to engage in sustained conversation with others interested in teaching and learning. For other faculty, lack of experience with SoTL has prevented them from realizing that their work was sufficiently mature to be shared with a wider audience. To support collegiality, we established SoTL Learning Communities, groups of five faculty led by a CILA associate, who spend a year together exploring a teaching and learning topic of common interest. This model of faculty collaboration has been successful on our campus for exploring "just-in-time" teaching and Bransford, Brown, and Cocking's *How People Learn* (2000).

The Faculty Reward System

St. Olaf faculty are evaluated in three traditional areas: teaching, scholarship (research), and service. Teaching is the primary consideration in faculty evaluation, as expected at a liberal arts institution. Because scholarship differs across fields, each department has created a Statement of Professional Activity defining scholarly work in its field. After they are approved by a college committee and the dean, these statements are used in the faculty review process. When a candidate is considered for tenure and/or promotion, a copy of the appropriate statement is included in the dossier and sent to the external reviewers of the candidate's scholarship.

St. Olaf's chemistry department has successfully adapted its statement to define scholarship broadly, including SoTL. It has 11 faculty members distributed across all ranks. Historically, its faculty have engaged in traditional laboratory-based scholarly work in the early years of their careers and have branched out into different areas, including SoTL, at some point following tenure. This pattern is consistent with the institutional data presented earlier indicating that associate professors are more likely than those at other ranks to engage in SoTL at St. Olaf.

Developed without the involvement of most of the current faculty, the original statement (1986) defined professional activity as "creative and scholarly work in laboratory research, development of new laboratory experiments, and curriculum innovation." This definition explicitly included teaching-related work, as one would expect at a liberal arts institution. It recognized refereed publications as the typical outcome of scholarly work and listed specific works and activities considered scholarship (see Table 5.5).

TABLE 5.5

Evolution of the Chemistry Department's Standards for Professional Activity, 1986–2004

Examples of Acceptable Professional Activity		
1986	**2001**	**2004**
Book	Laboratory/theoretical investigation of scientific phenomena	Applying/securing resources for individual growth or maintenance of department's professional status
Refereed articles (published/accepted)	Innovative development/adaptation/implementation of pedagogy/course content materials	Classroom/laboratory/theoretical investigation
Grant, award	Scientific writing/presentation for various audiences, using library/other forms of investigation	Consulting, patent
Review of current research	Participation/leadership in professional organization	Participation/leadership in faculty development workshop
Invited presentation at national meeting	Consulting, patent	Innovative development/adaptation/implementation of pedagogy/course content materials
Refereed presentation at a national meeting	Securing resources for individual professional growth or maintenance of department's professional status	Involvement in professional organization from attending meeting to holding leadership position
Activity in national professional organization	Peer reviewing grant proposal/publication	Peer reviewing grant proposal/publication
Patent	Scientific writing/presentation for various audiences	Consulting

Departmental review of the statement in 2001, in preparation for launching a tenure-track search, resulted in a revised document that reflected its members' professional diversity and significantly expanded the definition of scholarship. Two full professors led the revision, which was based on Ernest Boyer's *Scholarship Reconsidered* (1990). The revised statement endorsed "all professional activity that promotes faculty and student development" and noted the special value of activities involving student collaborators. A broader list of *examples* of such activities, not intended to be restrictive, emerged (see Table 5.5). For instance, writing and presentations were no longer significant only if peer reviewed or presented at a national meeting. In addition, successful grant writing on behalf of the department was recognized along with grants for individual work.

At the conclusion of its discussions in 2001, the department agreed to review the statement biannually. This review has become a valuable exercise that reminds both current and new faculty members of the range of professional activity in chemistry at St. Olaf.

In 2004 two tenure-track assistant professors and an associate professor proposed broadening the statement further. The revision states that the chemistry faculty "have a diverse set of gifts and talents and we expect members to participate in commensurate professional activities." In addition to activities that promote faculty and student development, the department endorses those that promote programmatic or institutional development. It also reiterates its commitment to faculty-undergraduate collaborations.

An introductory statement delineates what professional activity involves: "Professional activity requires expertise; is conducted cognizant of goals, with the proper preparation and using appropriate methodologies; is recorded and disseminated; is significant to others; and is predominantly assessed by peer review." This revised statement even explicitly names the four areas of scholarship promoted by Boyer and The Carnegie Foundation: those of discovery, application, engagement, and teaching and learning, with brief appended descriptions.

Consistent with its experience and its promotion of professional diversity, the chemistry department states that faculty may choose to conduct different kinds of scholarship at different stages of their careers and need not engage in all kinds. The alphabetically arranged list of examples of scholarly activities discourages ranking one type of activity above another. It recognizes grant proposal preparation (with or without an award), classroom investigations (SoTL), participation in or leadership of faculty development workshops, and diverse forms of involvement in professional organizations (see Table 5.5).

The department recognizes that diverse forms of professional activity require diverse forms of assessment. While traditional forms of peer review are effective for some products of scholarship, other activities require alternative forms of assessment. The department chair will work with a candidate for tenure and/or promotion who presents such professional activity to determine an appropriate way to assess it. For example, if a faculty member attended a series of faculty development workshops in an effort to improve his or her teaching, evidence of the impact of those efforts could be assessed by examining how the workshop ideas were incorporated into the faculty member's courses.

An important goal of advancing SoTL is its incorporation into faculty evaluation systems. Other departments and institutions will follow different paths to include SoTL in theirs. As an institutional member of the CASTL cluster centered on "Organizing to Foster the Scholarship of Teaching and Learning," St. Olaf helped develop language that can be adapted for use on other campuses to incorporate SoTL into the faculty review process. The cluster's model document focuses on SoTL as work that exhibits methodological rigor, has evident and substantive implications/outcomes, is peer reviewed, and is made public (American Association for Higher Education & Carnegie Campus Cluster, 2004).

Conclusion

Engagement with SoTL is consistent with the mission of most liberal arts colleges. It has clear benefits for the institution, and the innovations in teaching and learning that are cultivated in this rich environment can be valuable to faculty in many other institutional settings. Yet as our experience illustrates, engagement with SoTL does not happen even in liberal arts contexts without effective support. To be effective, support for SoTL must be tailored to the particular institutional environment. In the case of the liberal arts colleges and, we suspect, other teaching-centered institutions, the development of credible, local models is critical to success.

Author Note

We would like to thank the Bush Foundation of St. Paul, Minnesota, for its support of the Center for Innovation in the Liberal Arts at St. Olaf College. We also want to thank Assistant Provost Arnie Ostebee for his unflagging support for faculty development in general and for the scholarship of teaching and learning in particular.

Endnotes

1. Liberal arts colleges were identified using the *U.S. News & World Report* classifi-
    cation. The Campus Program involves significant institutional commitment,
    unlike the Carnegie Scholars Program, which is more individual. Seven out of
    162 scholars were from liberal arts colleges.

2. In addition, 94% "indicated that the impact of doing SoTL on their career would
    be neutral (48%) or negative (46%)" (McKinney et al., 2003, p. 5).

3. According to the institutional profile provided by HERI, the numbers for St. Olaf
    on these two items are 99.1% and 92%, respectively.

References

American Association for Higher Education & Carnegie Campus Cluster. (2004). *T and P SoTL language*. Retrieved May 15, 2007, from www.cfkeep.org/html/snapshot.php?id=9244212

Boyer, E. L. (1990). *Scholarship reconsidered: Priorities of the professoriate*. Princeton, NJ: The Carnegie Foundation for the Advancement of Teaching.

Bransford, J. D., Brown, A. L., & Cocking, R. R. (Eds.). (2000). *How people learn: Brain, mind, experience, and school* (Expanded ed.). Washington, DC: National Academy Press.

Cambridge, B. L. (Ed.). (2004). *Campus progress: Supporting the scholarship of teaching and learning*. Sterling, VA: Stylus.

The Carnegie Foundation for the Advancement of Teaching. (2006). *CASTL campus program*. Retrieved May 15, 2007, from www.carnegiefoundation.org/programs/sub.asp?key=21&subkey=68&topkey=21

Center for Innovation in the Liberal Arts Associates. (2001–2006). *Proposals and final reports* (0102A–0506B). Northfield, MN: St. Olaf College.

Huber, M. T., & Hutchings, P. (2005). *The advancement of learning: Building the teaching commons*. San Francisco, CA: Jossey-Bass.

Hutchings, P. (Ed.). (2000). *Opening lines: Approaches to the scholarship of teaching and learning*. Menlo Park, CA: The Carnegie Foundation for the Advancement of Teaching.

Hutchings, P. (Ed.). (2002). *Ethics of inquiry: Issues in the scholarship of teaching and learning*. Menlo Park, CA: The Carnegie Foundation for the Advancement of Teaching.

Lindholm, J. A., Szelény, K., Hurtado, S., & Korn, W. S. (2005). *The American college teacher: National norms for the 2004–2005 HERI faculty survey.* Los Angeles, CA: University of California–Los Angeles, Higher Education Research Institute.

McKinney, K., Broadbear, J., Gentry, D., Klass, P., Naylor, S., & Virgil, N. (2003). *Summary of on-line questionnaire study on the status of SoTL at Illinois State University.* Retrieved May 15, 2007, from the Illinois State University, Scholarship of Teaching and Learning web site: www.sotl.ilstu.edu/downloads/pdf/sotlonlinequest.pdf

Reder, M., & Gallagher, E. V. (2007). Transforming a teaching culture through peer mentoring: Connecticut College's Johnson Teaching Seminar for Incoming Faculty. In D. R. Robertson & L. B. Nilson (Eds.), *To improve the academy: Vol. 25. Resources for faculty, instructional, and organizational development* (pp. 327–344). Bolton, MA: Anker.

Shulman, L. S. (1993, November/December). Teaching as community property: Putting an end to pedagogical solitude. *Change, 25*(6), 6–7.

Sorcinelli, M. D., Austin, A. E., Eddy, P. L., & Beach, A. L. (2006). *Creating the future of faculty development: Learning from the past, understanding the present.* Bolton, MA: Anker.

St. Olaf College, Office of Academic Research and Planning. (2005). *Faculty development survey results: Quantitative and qualitative results.* Northfield, MN: Author.

Wineburg, S. (2003, April 11). Teaching the mind good habits. *The Chronicle of Higher Education,* p. B20.

Section III

Scholarship of Educational Development

6

Grounded Theory Research in Faculty Development: The Basics, a Live Example, and Practical Tips for Faculty Developers

Michael Sweet, Rochelle Roberts, Joshua Walker,
Stephen Walls, John Kucsera, Shana Shaw,
Janet Riekenberg, Marilla Svinicki
University of Texas at Austin

While autobiographical narratives and case study reflections remain vital to faculty development research, we must also make substantive efforts to build theory in our field. Researchers making claims about collective meanings of observed behaviors and the mechanisms that underlie them (i.e., theoretical claims about social behavior) must be disciplined in how they identify and organize the evidence they use to support those claims. Such systematic, inductive theory-building in the social sciences is called "grounded theory" research. This chapter presents the basics of grounded theory research, describes a grounded theory research program currently being executed by faculty developers, and offers practical tips especially for faculty developers.

As faculty developers, we are constantly drawn into complex stories and relationships at our institutions, and it is natural for us to begin forming hypotheses about "how things work here." Formalizing our hypotheses and investigating them systematically is the scholarly next step that most of us are trained to take. For these investigations, many seek out numerical data like course evaluation scores, GPAs, institutional research data such as retention-attrition rates, and so on. These quantitative data can be informative, but when it comes to collecting data directly from the teachers or administrators with whom we work, the often delicate nature of our professional relationships can make the qualitative data collection process more compatible with our faculty development goals. A trusting, collaborative relationship with our clients is the foundation on which effective faculty development rests (Gillespie, Hilsen, & Wadsworth, 2002), and the interpersonal experience of a qualitative interview or observation can result in more trust-building than filling out a questionnaire.

Our field has benefited greatly from many kinds of qualitative research, and so have a wide array of our client populations, including new and untenured faculty (e.g., Boice, 1992; Mullen & Forbes, 2000; Olsen & Sorcinelli, 1992; Whitt, 1991), graduate students (e.g., Austin, 2002; Damron, 2003; Nyquist et al., 1999; Smith, 2001), women and minorities in academia (e.g., Taylor & Antony, 2000; Ward & Wolf-Wendel, 2004), scholars of teaching and learning (e.g., Schroeder, 2005), and interdisciplinary faculty (e.g., Lattuca, Voigt, & Faith, 2004; Stein & Short, 2001). Moreover, qualitative research has given us insights into our own circumstances as faculty developers and how best to operate within them (e.g., Austin, Brocato, & Rohrer, 1997; Carusetta & Cranton, 2005; King, 2004; Mullinix, 2006).

Given this rich collection of precedents, faculty development will likely continue to benefit from qualitative data and analysis. However, the rigor with which any research is conducted is the measure by which we must judge the knowledge claims it produces. Although autobiographical narratives and case study reflections are vital to the field, researchers making claims about the collective meanings of observed behaviors and the mechanisms that underlie them (i.e., theoretical claims about social behavior) must be disciplined in how they identify and organize the evidence they use to support those claims. Systematic, inductive theory-building in the social sciences is called "grounded theory" research, and its goal of producing theoretical models distinguishes it from "thick description" qualitative methods, which have the more documentary, anthropological goal of rendering new social settings intelligible to the reader. Within the larger sphere of qualitative—and even within grounded theory itself—there are many approaches to the task of building nonquantitative knowledge. Even a brief overview of this diverse landscape is beyond the scope of this chapter, but several good resources exist to inform and guide qualitative research in education (e.g., Bogdan & Biklen, 2003; Camic, Rhodes & Yardley, 2003; LeCompte, Millroy, & Preissle, 1992). One such resource, Strauss and Corbin (1998), describes a rigorous grounded theory approach in no-nonsense terms and the methods reviewed here draw primarily from that source.

This chapter, therefore, has three goals: 1) to introduce the basics of grounded theory research, 2) to describe the steps taken in a grounded theory research program currently being executed by faculty developers, and 3) to offer practical real-world tips to faculty developers conducting grounded theory research.

Grounded Theory Research: The Basics

All research generally includes data inputs, analytical procedures, and some form of reporting output. In this way, qualitative and quantitative methods are no different. Important differences between the two methods lie in the nature of the data, the forms of analysis, and the criteria used to judge the reports they ultimately generate. In terms of *input*, quantitative methods only accept numerical data, while qualitative methods accept many forms of non-numerical data: observations, interviews, focus groups, videotapes or transcripts of social events, and documents of many kinds. In terms of *output*, quantitative and qualitative methods differ in the criteria they use to legitimate knowledge claims. Quantitative research bases its knowledge claims on the extent to which measured observations are significant, reproducible, generalizable, and so on. However, these criteria do not always make sense when applied to research on social phenomena occurring in a natural setting. For example, it is unrealistic to consider complex real-world social events perfectly reproducible. Instead, criteria for judging qualitative research include (among others) the extent to which observations are credible, confirmable, and detailed enough for the reader to judge the transferability of findings from one context to another (Lincoln & Guba, 1985).

Of most practical interest here, however, are the actions between data collection and theoretical output—the actual steps of analysis. Where statistical analysis is used in quantitative social science research, the analysis used in grounded theory research is called "coding" and occurs in a few distinct steps: open coding, axial coding, and selective coding. Grounded theory research is often referred to as a constant-comparative method because coding involves continually comparing new data to old data in pursuit of an ever more accurate description of the explanatory schemas that underlie the observations. This recursive process takes place across the lifespan of the study, up to and through selective coding.

Open Coding

Open coding is a provisional first pass at the data, to identify data that seem important and possible meanings those data might have. This process can be as microscopic as a word-by-word analysis of a transcript, but in practical terms it frequently takes the form of circling words and phrases in transcripts, jotting notes in the margin, and writing reflective "memos" to one's self about possible interpretations of specific data. As these notes accrue, *concepts* begin to emerge—certain things may be repeated, described with great energy, or obvious grounds for some kind of decision. These concepts become more clearly characterized by their *properties* and the *dimensions* along which they vary.

To illustrate the coding process, we will use a phenomenon familiar to most readers of this volume: the academic conference. Often, conversations about a conference begin with "Where is the conference next year?" Conversations about a winter conference held in Honolulu, Hawaii, would unfold in somewhat predictably different ways than if the same winter conference were held in Fairbanks, Alaska. So "location" is obviously a concept that is important to the phenomenon of the academic conference, with one property of location being seasonal weather (varying along the dimension of pleasantness: perhaps from glorious to nasty).

Axial Coding

Axial coding involves *relating* concepts into categories and subcategories and identifying sequences of *cause* → *action/interaction* → *consequence*. To extend our academic conference example, the conceptual category of "conference presentation" has several subcategories (poster, roundtable, paper, symposium, plenary) and a built-in sequence (proposal, acceptance, scheduling, delivery, evaluation). Within these sequences, meaning is created and negotiated by motivated subjects acting/interacting with context-specific results. For the graduate student who has just finished presenting a paper session, seeing the "big name" scholar clearly approaching with the intent to engage may cause a great deal of anxiety. Because the impending interaction means so much to the graduate student, it will likely have significant emotional consequences in the moment and possibly longer term professional consequences as well.

Selective Coding

Selective coding is where we take the concepts we first identified in open coding, then related into categories and sequences during axial coding, and now use them to build theory. Selective coding is the process of identifying a category that can be considered *core* in the sense that one can relate all of the other major categories to it. Core categories must be described abstractly enough to explain many kinds of data. Perhaps, as the conference approaches, we observe a greater frequency of conversation about it, a dramatic increase of anxiety among those who are scheduled to present, and even more anxiety among those responsible for coordinating the event. These observations might lead us to become curious about the sources of this anxiety—the emotional stakes for the people involved in the conference. Upon reviewing a travel reimbursement form, the checkbox under "Reason for travel" labeled "increases the university's reputation" might catch our eye. This could lead us to consider the possibility of "reputation" as the basis for a core category: personal for the presenters, institutional for the schools which send them, and organizational for the body that offers the conference. We may begin to think of our data in terms of whether "Reputation marketplace" or "Intersections of prestige" seem to have explanatory power for much or all of the meanings associated with the academic conference. This step is selective in the sense that it leads us to ask some specific questions and seek specific kinds of data, so we can try on labels for the core category to see how well they fit. Coming to recognize a core category can be the most difficult part of generating grounded theory and the core category criteria described by Glaser (1978) are extremely helpful in this regard. As the core category is selected and refined, the study begins to reach theoretical saturation—that is, when all new data are compared to previously collected data and found to fit into existing categorical schemes without need to adjust or reinvent those categories. This marks the natural point of conclusion for a grounded theory study.

As with any research, there are many agonizing decisions to be made throughout, frustrating setbacks, and dead ends. But for our purposes, we hope the preceding overview prepares the reader for a description of our faculty focused, grounded theory research program that is currently under way.

The following section briefly describes the research goals, data sources, analytical steps, and some preliminary findings that were presented at the annual conference of the American Psychology Association in 2006. For brevity's sake, we have omitted the literature review situating our research amidst existing educational psychology literature, but the interested reader can find it online at https://webspace.utexas.edu/ms416453/TeacherMistakesAPAPaper.pdf. Importantly, this particular study is incomplete: We remain in pursuit of our core category, but we thought "looking under the hood" of a still unpolished piece of grounded theory research could give the reader a realistic sense of the process while it is still under way.

A Live Example of Grounded Theory Research: Teacher Mistakes—A Window into Teacher Efficacy?

Any experienced teacher knows that teaching is not a coldly logical process of problem solving and rationally choosing among clear alternatives. Instead, it may have the same motivational and affective tone that "hot" cognition (Pintrich, Marx, & Boyle, 1993) has for student choices in the classroom, with cognition and emotion intertwined. Indeed, Palmer (1998) says, "As we try to connect ourselves and our subjects with our students, we make ourselves, as well as our subjects, vulnerable to indifference, judgment, ridicule" (p. 17).

If teaching indeed has an emotional charge, it seems one of the most intense experiences for teachers—especially new teachers—may come when they make a "mistake" in the classroom. Unfortunately, little exploratory, much less experimental, work has been done to guide teachers faced with this situation. In addition, research has seldom explored the causes and effects of teacher attitudes and reactions toward mistakes. Drawing from Kegan and Lahey's (2001) notion that "competing commitments" and underlying "big assumptions" can be revealed in negative reactions to events, we wanted to conduct exploratory research into how teachers describe, categorize, and react to their own mistakes. Although research on student attitudes and reactions to failures has flourished (e.g., Firmin, Hwang, Copella, & Clark, 2004; Linnenbrink & Pintrich, 2002; Perry, Hladkyj, Pekrun, Clifton, & Chipperfield, 2005), research has seldom explored the causes and effects of teacher attitudes and reactions toward their own mistakes. Ultimately, we hope to generate both theoretical and practical findings useful to those helping new faculty members acclimate more smoothly to their teaching roles. Through a better understanding of how to interpret and manage their own inevitable "mistakes," we hope to help new faculty accept more openly the new pedagogical strategies and tools that will become available to them throughout their career.

In our discussion around what constitutes mistakes and how we could study them, we were at a loss to come to any agreement or even a guess at what the boundaries of "mistakes" might be for faculty. This was the perfect situation for the use of a grounded theory approach: We needed to let the words of those most intimately involved—the teachers themselves—become the data on which to build our understanding of mistakes.

Data Collection

In the initial phase of our exploratory study, we conducted interviews with demographically representative faculty members at the University of Texas at Austin regarding how they define and react to teaching mistakes they make in the classroom. Faculty participants were identified initially on the basis of personal prior contact or participation in various faculty development opportunities offered on campus. Subsequent faculty participants were identified using a cascading procedure of asking each participant to recommend one other person, who was then contacted individually by a member of our research team.

During interviews, participants were asked to identify an incident that they considered to be a "mistake" they made during class, and to describe their thoughts and feelings during and after that time. Qualitative data from the interviews were coded into categories centering on faculty members' definitions of mistakes as well as their reactions and coping strategies.

Interviews and Transcription

A pilot interview was conducted with a volunteer, and the team discussed possible themes that might emerge in later interviews and the procedures for conducting these interviews (the interview protocol). After developing our initial interview protocol and getting institutional review board (IRB) approval, we began conducting our interviews. The interviews were semi-structured, digitally recorded, and later transcribed by the interviewer. Steps were taken to ensure that the interviewer was not acquainted with the faculty member prior to the interview. A total of 19 faculty were interviewed by 6 different interviewers.

Open Coding

To train and calibrate their coding, all members of the team open coded one transcript, then compared the concepts they saw emerging between that transcript and the pilot interview. Interpretive parameters around emerging concepts were negotiated. Of the themes that began to emerge, the team chose three on which to focus first: what constitutes a mistake, how teachers described their emotional reaction, and how the teachers described their behavioral response.

Two raters (neither of whom was the original interviewer) open coded each transcript separately, then compared coding. When the two raters both agreed on the meaningfulness of a statement, it was coded; when they did not agree, they returned to the original audio of the interview. If they still could not agree on a coding, then the statement was dropped from analysis. Interviews were coded by four coding teams, and coded statements were entered into a spreadsheet by interview number, line number, coding team, and coding label.

Axial Coding

Once the open coding was completed, each coding team's entries were assigned to a different coding team to identify themes *across* the concepts that had emerged. For example, of the 19 teachers interviewed, teams considered whether patterns emerged among teachers who defined "mistakes" in a certain way, who felt certain emotions about those mistakes, or who responded or coped in certain ways. These thematic categories were intended to capture the structures and sequences of the teachers' experiences of their mistakes: in other words, to capture the collective stories that these teachers were telling us.

Selective Coding

The process of selective coding is still under way. Axial coding has proved fruitful enough to justify and guide a second round of interviews, but because theoretical saturation has not yet been attained, a core category cannot yet be determined.

Preliminary Findings

As the faculty members in this study told their stories about mistakes they made in the classroom, three major categories of "mistake" emerged, which we labeled as structural/design mistakes, procedural/execution mistakes, and relational/self mistakes. Interestingly, the Ohio State Teacher Efficacy Scale, which was found to be the most psychometrically sound among eight commonly used teacher efficacy scales (Tschannen-Moran & Hoy, 2001), is organized into three efficacy factors: instructional strategies, classroom management, and student engagement, which appear congruent with the three domains that emerged in our interviews.

Structural/design mistakes included the preparation for and organization of the class material usually either at the beginning of the semester or the beginning of a class period. Underestimating the amount of time for class topics, too rigidly planning the syllabus, creating unclear learning objectives, and designing poor tasks and tests were just some of the examples taken from the interviews. As one faculty member described:

> That's another . . . mistake that I have made over time. In assigning topics for papers. I mean you have to have a middle ground between telling them exactly what they are supposed to do, and giving them a completely open-ended type of assignment. And I think sometimes I haven't made very good paper assignments.

The emotional reactions related to this type of mistake included feeling thoughtful, regretful, discouraged, fearful, and frustrated. However, in general, many faculty members who described a structural/design mistake eventually exhibited a behavioral response to correct the mistake, and most were willing to adapt to the mistake by rethinking the material, taking feedback into consideration, preparing better, being more flexible, and reaffirming themselves.

Procedural/execution mistakes focused more on mistakes during a class and involved class procedures, such as moving through material at an inappropriate pace for students, being inflexible, giving poor instructions, boring students, and being inefficient. Specifically, some faculty members provided examples of giving factual errors to students, going too quickly through PowerPoint slides, and managing classroom behavior inadequately. One faculty member in particular commented on managing students in the classroom: "I think it's a mistake for faculty to let bad behavior go by in a lecture. Because I've been in classes where there's a lot of disruption . . . people moving in and moving out." Emotional reactions to this type of mistake appeared much more ambiguous than those in the other two domains—reactions were not always clearly directed at one particular thing or person; they seemed much more diffused and sometimes directed at various aspects of the learning environment. These ambiguous emotional reactions included feeling insecure, uneasy, confused, anxious, perturbed, and uncomfortable. In one interview, a faculty member mentioned, "And I think it may have been exactly this kind of insecurity that comes from dealing with new material." Perhaps one explanation for these more complex feelings comes from the lack of proper faculty training about effective classroom procedures (Menges & Austin, 2001). Similar to the structural mistakes, behavioral responses or coping strategies remained positive and encouraging for the faculty members who discussed procedural mistakes. In general, the teachers became more flexible, reconsidered their objectives, and attempted different methods in future situations.

Relational/self mistakes referred largely to the faculty member's social interactions with students in the classroom. Faculty who experienced this type of mistake recounted stories of being unprofessional, offending students, shutting down students, and getting angry or losing their tempers with students. Sometimes the faculty member did not even realize the impact of the mistake until much later, as was the case in one interview:

> I think that one of the first mistakes that I made probably was making light of a student in one of the early sessions in a case discussion . . . with a lot of numbers in it. The student hadn't done any numbers

and I said lightly, "Well, what's the matter, was your calculator broken?" And it was the second or third session and I was trying to establish rapport with the class and all that. And I learned later that student's feelings were hurt greatly.

In general, the emotional reactions faculty members reported in response to these kinds of mistakes were much more intense than mistakes in the other two domains. They reported immediate feelings of anger, devastation, and shame when handling mistakes concerning social interactions with students, and as one faculty member experienced after a mistake, ". . . but that was devastating. I thought 'Oh, sh—.' That's almost the worst thing I can imagine . . ." The fact that relational mistakes made the most severe emotional impression lends support to Borich's (1999) description of the teacher-student relationship as one between "significant others." Even in the face of this intensity, however, faculty members mostly demonstrated promising behavioral responses to cope with the mistakes. They turned mistakes into learning opportunities for both themselves and the students, became more sensitive to students, spoke to students individually, and tried to find alternatives to avoid making the same mistakes in the future.

At this point in the process the research team is considering how to gather more data that will help tie these various themes together. In a research paradigm of this sort, the appropriate strategy is both to return to the data already gathered with this in mind and/or to return to the informants for more insights. That is where we stand at this point in time.

Practical Tips: Conducting Grounded Theory Research as a Faculty Developer

As faculty developers, we have limited time to devote to any one dimension of our job. The purpose of this section, therefore, is to share what practical tips we have learned so that others may benefit from our experience.

Tips for Collecting Data

Collaborate, collaborate, collaborate. It is difficult to overstate how helpful collaboration can be for the many interpretive tasks involved in qualitative coding. Having several people code the same data, then compare their coding, and discuss the meanings each saw in the data can help calibrate a research team to generate categorical schema with much greater depth, breadth, and discrimination. Beyond the added texture that collaboration can bring to interpretive analysis, it very simply can make a seemingly insurmountable research project possible. Many faculty developers have neither the training nor the staff to carry out a well-designed qualitative study, so collaborating with a qualitative researcher from elsewhere on campus—or even at another campus—can provide the experienced know-how that the faculty developer might lack. Furthermore, graduate and undergraduate students are frequently looking for real experience on research teams, and can often be the ones who ask the innocent questions that reveal important assumptions, tacit knowledge, and overlooked relationships, making their *lack* of experience a very practical advantage. Of course, each additional team member makes additional person hours available to the project, whether to collect data at a time when no one else is available or get a larger step in the project completed much faster, since "many hands make light work." If working alone is your only option, several methods described by Lincoln and Guba (1985), such as triangulation, audit trails, member-checking, and negative case analysis, can enrich how you understand your data and establish the "trustworthiness" of your findings.

Carefully design—and revisit— your interview protocols. A lesson we learned the hard way was that our interview questions did not generate in our participants the kinds of reflection we had hoped. After all the interviews in our first round were completed, we analyzed the data and found that, in our attempts to brainstorm a core category, we simply were not yet able to. Any attempt to generate a core category from our existing data would require us to make inferences far beyond our comfort level. We learned a great deal about the kinds of mistakes faculty experience and how they experience them, but do not yet have the insights into teacher efficacy we wanted.

We are presently still a considerable distance from theoretical saturation and need to conduct a new round of interviews, this time with similar questions asked in a few different ways. At the very least, we will ask interviewees to be thinking about the topics of our interview questions ahead of time, so we get more reflective and less on-the-spot responses. We may even send our interviewees the entire protocol ahead of time. Doing so would not be giving away anything: If having more than 30 seconds to think about our questions will help them give us richer, more detailed answers, all the better. That said, we would avoid reverting entirely to a virtual email interview because of the difficulty of establishing rapport in a purely electronic medium, and all the para-verbal and nonverbal communication available in the face-to-face setting that can be very helpful in guiding the interview conversation. This last concern—the nuances of interpersonal communication in a face-to-face setting—is especially significant to faculty developers, given the importance to us of our relationships with the people we serve.

Digital is good. If at all possible, record interviews. There are of course conditions when recording is impossible, inappropriate, or simply too intrusive but even with excellent note-taking skills, the human memory cannot always be relied on to notice everything important or retain it for long. Among the best decisions we made at the outset of our project was to use a digital (MP3) recorder instead of traditional audio cassettes. In addition to good sound quality, the digital nature of the audio files made storing the data in a secure—but easily accessible—location very easy. We simply created a special area in our university course management system (a Blackboard "organization") and uploaded the audio files directly to that organization. This allowed only the people on the team simultaneous, round-the-clock access to all the data. This access enabled us to email each other with requests like, "Hey, I am transcribing Interview 12, but I can't figure out what she is saying at 4 minutes and 42 seconds. Can someone download it, have a listen, and tell me what you think?" It is not hard to see how much faster and less frustrating this made the entire transcription process. If you do not already have access to a digital recorder (even an iPod with a recording attachment), many campus technology centers now have them available for loan.

Tips for Analyzing Data

Use to the fullest *the technology you already have.* Software packages like NVivo and ATLAS.ti exist to help facilitate large-scale qualitative research, but our research was not large enough to justify such an investment. We found that some word processing and spreadsheet functions, combined with an LCD projector, were incredibly helpful in organizing and analyzing our data and keeping ourselves calibrated as a team. Specifically, one team member would transcribe an interview in Microsoft Word and add line numbers (Page Setup > Layout > Line numbers), then upload the Word document to our Blackboard organization. Two other team members would then download the transcript separately, and open code it individually. They would then open Microsoft Excel and—still separately—enter their open codings into a spreadsheet with the Excel row numbers corresponding to the line numbers on the transcript. They would then compare their separate spreadsheets, referring to the downloaded audio file when necessary, and produce a combined "interrater" spreadsheet that they would then upload to the Blackboard organization. Finally, when we met as a team, we used the LCD projector to look at all of the coding spreadsheets as a group and discuss what we had found, what categories we felt were emerging, what ambiguities needed resolution, and so on. This made for a very efficient coding process, given the relatively large size of our team. We made liberal use of Excel's ability to include many sheets in a workbook, to color-code cells, and to hide/reveal columns as it suited us. This gave us the ability to keep *all* of our data in a single (large) Excel workbook.

Pay attention to the increasing sensitivity of your coding instruments (you). As you code more, you will become more discriminating at resolving the ambiguity inherent in the task of categorizing real-life data. Category definitions will become more nuanced, as will the criteria you use to include or exclude data from those categories. As you code, make notes about the rationales for why you are coding certain data in certain ways (Excel's Insert > Comment function is handy for this) and be prepared to go back and recode your first few interviews after you have coded a dozen or so: Your categorical rubric will have evolved enough to make this necessary—but that's a good thing.

Tips for Managing Relationships

Ethical considerations. Your campus undoubtedly has some form of IRB with procedures in place for research on human subjects (which is what you are doing). IRBs usually require that a description of your project, your plan for acquiring subject consent, and at least a prototype of your research protocol be approved before you can begin collecting data. Though it is easy to chafe at the extra chore of getting IRB approval, these requirements are in place for good reasons, so learn what you need to do to get the IRB's blessing and do it. Beyond the IRB, one must also consider the ethics of the potential "dual relationship" one can create with a client-turned-research-subject. Here again we see the virtues of having a research team: They allow you to distance yourself as a researcher from any of your own clients who may be participating in the study. If you do not interview your own clients, nor even know who does interview them, nor which interview number corresponds to them—then you can be considered to be taking good-faith measures to keep the boundaries of your relationship clear. That said, participants must always be informed of their right to withdraw from the study at any time. Remember, research must always play second fiddle to the maintenance of good relationships with one's clients.

Courtesy considerations. We recruited our participants with personal invitation letters sent from the senior faculty developer on the team. These letters included the rationale for a faculty developer doing research in the first place, as well as a reassurance about measures taken to protect the participants' privacy. We wrote: "Part of my ability to serve the community is to understand the issues you as instructors face at a deeper level, which means doing some qualitative research. But to maintain confidentiality, I won't be the one interviewing you, and when I see transcripts they will have been made anonymous and devoid of any specific identifiers." After transcribing each interview, researchers gave the faculty participant a copy of the transcript and a handwritten thank-you note from the senior faculty developer. (To maintain confidentiality, these thank-you notes were all written generically at the outset of the study and only later addressed to participants by their particular interviewer.) Finally, faculty who expressed interest in our findings were given copies of the American Psychology Association paper that resulted from the data they helped us collect (Roberts et al., 2006).

Conclusion

So, we end where we began—focusing on the importance of maintaining relationships with our faculty clients while doing the qualitative research necessary to serve them better. As the midcourse corrections in our own research illustrate, qualitative research is a constant learning process requiring collaborative adjustments and flexible attempts to try things a new way. At the same time, qualitative research takes the faculty developer into the lived stories of one's constituents in ways that quantitative research never can—which can make the process both more rewarding and frustrating—but it is a journey that ultimately makes us better at what we do.

References

Austin, A. E. (2002, January/February). Preparing the next generation of faculty: Graduate school as socialization to the academic career. *Journal of Higher Education, 73*(1), 94–122.

Austin, A. E., Brocato, J. J., & Rohrer, J. D. (1997). Institutional missions, multiple faculty roles: Implications for faculty development. In D. DeZure & M. Kaplan (Eds.), *To improve the academy: Vol. 16. Resources for faculty, instructional, and organization development* (pp. 3–20). Stillwater, OK: New Forums Press.

Bogdan, R. C., & Biklen, S. K. (2003). *Qualitative research for education* (4th ed.). Boston, MA: Allyn & Bacon.

Boice, R. (1992). *The new faculty member: Supporting and fostering professional development.* San Francisco, CA: Jossey-Bass.

Borich, G. D. (1999). Dimensions of self that influence effective teaching. In R. P. Lipka & T. M. Brinthaupt (Eds.), *The role of self in teacher development* (pp. 92–117). Albany, NY: State University of New York Press.

Camic, P. M., Rhodes, J. E., & Yardley, L. (Eds.). (2003). *Qualitative research in psychology: Expanding perspectives in methodology and design.* Washington, DC: American Psychological Association.

Carusetta, E., & Cranton, P. (2005, July). Nurturing authenticity through faculty development. *Journal of Faculty Development, 20*(2), 79–86.

Damron, J. (2003). What's the problem? A new perspective on ITA communication. *Journal of Graduate Teaching Assistant Development, 9*(2), 81–88.

Firmin, M., Hwang, C., Copella, M., & Clark, S. (2004, Summer). Learned helplessness: The effect of failure on test-taking. *Education, 124*(4), 688–694.

Gillespie, K. H., Hilsen, L. R., & Wadsworth, E. C. (Eds.). (2002). *A guide to faculty development: Practical advice, examples, and resources.* Bolton, MA: Anker.

Glaser, B. G. (1978). *Theoretical sensitivity: Advances in the methodology of grounded theory.* Mill Valley, CA: Sociology Press.

Kegan, R., & Lahey, L. L. (2001). *How the way we talk can change the way we work: Seven languages for transformation.* San Francisco, CA: Jossey-Bass.

King, K. P. (2004). Both sides now: Examining transformative learning and professional development of educators. *Innovative Higher Education, 29*(2), 155–174.

Lattuca, L. R., Voigt, L. J., & Faith, K. Q. (2004, Fall). Does interdisciplinarity promote learning? Theoretical support and researchable questions. *Review of Higher Education, 28*(1), 23–48.

LeCompte, M. D., Millroy, W. L., & Preissle, J. (Eds.). (1992). *The handbook of qualitative research in education.* San Diego, CA: Academic Press.

Lincoln, Y. S., & Guba, E. G. (1985). *Naturalistic inquiry.* Newbury Park, CA: Sage.

Linnenbrink, E. A., & Pintrich, P. R. (2002). Motivation as an enabler for academic success. *School Psychology Review, 31*(3), 313–327.

Menges, R. J., & Austin, A. E. (2001). Teaching in higher education. In V. Richardson (Ed.), *Handbook of research on teaching* (4th ed., pp. 1122–1156). Washington, DC: American Educational Research Association.

Mullen, C. A., & Forbes, S. A. (2000, April). Untenured faculty: Issues of transition, adjustment and mentorship. *Mentoring & Tutoring, 8*(1), 31–46.

Mullinix, B. B. (2006, April). *Trends across the HE landscape: The faculty status of faculty developers.* Paper presented at the annual meeting of the American Educational Research Association, San Francisco, CA.

Nyquist, J. D., Manning, L., Wulff, D. H., Austin, A. E., Sprague, J., Fraser, P. K., et al. (1999, May/June). On the road to becoming a professor: The graduate student experience. *Change, 31*(3), 18–27.

Olsen, D., & Sorcinelli, M. D. (1992). The pretenure years: A longitudinal perspective. In M. D. Sorcinelli & A. E. Austin (Eds.), *New directions for teaching and learning: No. 48. Developing new and junior faculty* (pp. 15–25). San Francisco, CA: Jossey-Bass.

Palmer, P. J. (1998). *The courage to teach: Exploring the inner landscape of a teacher's life.* San Francisco, CA: Jossey-Bass.

Perry, R. P., Hladkyj, S., Pekrun, R. H., Clifton, R. A., & Chipperfield, J. G. (2005, August). Perceived academic control and failure in college students: A three-year study of scholastic attainment. *Research in Higher Education, 46*(5), 535–569.

Pintrich, P. R., Marx, R. W., & Boyle, R. A. (1993, Summer). Beyond cold conceptual change: The role of motivational beliefs and classroom contextual factors in the process of conceptual change. *Review of Educational Research, 63*(2), 167–199.

Roberts, R., Sweet, M., Walker, J., Walls, S., Kucsera, J., Shaw, S., et al. (2006, October). *Teacher mistakes: A window into teacher self-efficacy.* Paper presented at the annual meeting of the American Psychological Association, New Orleans, LA.

Schroeder, C. M. (2005). Evidence of the transformational dimensions of the scholarship of teaching and learning: Faculty development through the eyes of the SoTL scholars. In S. Chadwick-Blossey & D. R. Robertson (Eds.), *To improve the academy: Vol. 23. Resources for faculty, instructional, and organizational development* (pp. 47–71). Bolton, MA: Anker.

Smith, K. S. (2001, Fall). Pivotal events in graduate teacher preparation for a faculty career. *Journal of Graduate Teaching Assistant Development, 8*(3), 97–105.

Stein, R. B., & Short, P. M. (2001, Summer). Collaboration in delivering higher education programs: Barriers and challenges. *Review of Higher Education, 24*(4), 417–435.

Strauss, A., & Corbin, J. (1998). *Basics of qualitative research: Techniques and procedures for developing grounded theory* (2nd ed.). Thousand Oaks, CA: Sage.

Taylor, E., & Antony, J. S. (2000, Summer). Stereotype threat reduction and wise schooling: Towards the successful socialization of African American doctoral students in education. *Journal of Negro Education, 69*(3), 184–198.

Tschannen-Moran, M., & Hoy, A. W. (2001, October). Teacher efficacy: Capturing an elusive construct. *Teaching and Teacher Education, 17*(7), 783–805.

Ward, K., & Wolf-Wendel, L. (2004, Winter). Academic motherhood: Managing complex roles in research universities. *Review of Higher Education, 27*(2), 233–257.

Whitt, E. J. (1991, Winter). "Hit the ground running": Experiences of new faculty in a school of education. *Review of Higher Education, 14*(2), 177–197.

7

Assessment of a Faculty Learning Community Program: Do Faculty Members Really Change?

Susan Polich
Virginia Commonwealth University

In this study, participants in a faculty learning community (FLC) program were followed to see if they had really changed their epistemological beliefs and teaching methods. Of the 39 FLC participants, 87% reported a change in their epistemological beliefs and 79% reported a change in their teaching methods. Seven participants were followed in-depth to determine if their reported changes actually occurred. Observations suggest that none of the seven appeared to have changed epistemological beliefs although all changed teaching methods. More importantly, the participants adopted their new pedagogy only when the pedagogy was aligned with their beliefs.

Even though Milton Cox has been working with faculty learning communities (FLCs) since 1979 and writing about them since 1995 (Cox, 1995), FLCs are still a relatively new concept in faculty development. Although the exact number of institutions supporting FLCs is not known, only 34 institutions have registered with the Faculty Learning Communities Consortium, a national organization dedicated to promoting FLCs (Miami University, 2004). In another study, Richlin and Essington (2004) reported that 65 institutions claimed to have FLCs.

As a relatively new concept, FLCs have generated little empirical literature about their effectiveness, with most of that coming from Cox's research. Despite Cox's assertion that they are an effective means of enhancing teaching and learning (Cox, 2004; Cox & Richlin, 2004), the literature regarding FLCs in higher education is primarily descriptive, set in the community college level, or gathered via self-report (Goldberg & Finkelstein, 2002; Stevens, 2004). We learn how FLCs have functioned but very little about the changes they, in fact, produce.

This research sought to examine the effectiveness of FLCs at one institution of higher education by validating reported change in teaching methods, and we report here on another finding: limited change in participants' teaching methods when the participants beliefs' about teaching and learning were not aligned with their chosen pedagogy. In discussing this finding, we will consider the importance of epistemological beliefs in making changes to teaching methods and in selecting FLC members.

Discussion of the Current Literature on FLCs

Several studies exist in the educational literature that address teaching improvement programs for cohorts of faculty members who function as loose networks. In these studies, participants reported greatly valuing the impact of their peers on their own teaching. Participants reported their peers provided moral support, shared information, and gave practical day-to-day help with the mechanics of teaching and scholarship (Sekerka & Chao, 2003; Skinner & Welch, 1996). Some participants reported an improvement in their teaching ability, knowledge, academic roles, and scholarship because of their learning community–like experience (Elliot, Skeff, & Stratos, 1999; Houston et al., 2004; Steinert, Nasmith, McLeod, & Conochie, 2003).

These loose faculty networks do not, however, meet the criteria for an FLC as described by Cox (2004):

> A cross-disciplinary faculty and staff group of six to fifteen members (eight to twelve members is the recommended size) who engage in an active, collaborative, yearlong program with a curriculum about enhancing teaching and learning and with frequent seminars and activities that provide learning development, the scholarship of teaching, and community building. (p. 8)

With all of the studies on the effectiveness of teaching improvement programs in college classrooms, only five published pieces plus one unpublished manuscript could be found—all of them described here—that discuss the effectiveness of FLCs, as Cox defines them, in higher education. All of the evidence in these studies, however, is from self-report.

Cox's first report on FLCs discussed a program to improve the teaching and scholarship abilities of new and junior faculty members (Cox, 1995). Cox reports three sets of data for program assessment, including two surveys. Participants rated their impression of the program and its effectiveness as 7.7–8.8 out of a possible 10 points. Cox also measured the tenure rate of participants versus nonparticipants and found a significant difference (p = 0.005) in the number of participants who received tenure (72%) versus nonparticipants who received tenure (55%). However, one should not attribute the higher rate of tenure status directly to participation in the FLC. There is simply not enough evidence to assign causality to Cox's claim.

Cox (2004) also reported that faculty members who participated in FLCs had a higher rate of tenure, lower rate of stress, were more active civically, and were more easily able to integrate work and family life. This study is limited, however, in that it relied entirely on surveys to gather evidence and lacks any description of the population, methods, and instruments used to gather data.

Blaidsell and Cox (2004) report on an FLC for senior faculty members. Their survey showed that the participants rated the colleagueship/learning from other participants, retreats and conferences, and released time as the most important impact of their experience. Again, this information was obtained by self-report.

Stevens's (2004) unpublished manuscript reported on the factors behind the success or failure of FLCs. These factors included prior work with and interest in the pedagogical focus, administrative and financial support, the group members and their backgrounds, creating and achieving goals, continued work after the initial meeting, and individual commitment and passion.

As measured by this body of literature, research on the effectiveness of FLCs is still in its infancy. Although these studies do report change, the evidence for change rests on self-report. An extension of such studies is needed to verify the reported changes and to look for deeper significance underlying the efficacy of FLCs.

Setting and Population

This study took place in a large, public, research-extensive university in the Midwest. The institution is made up of two schools and fourteen colleges, including two that resemble community colleges and one that resembles a technical college. The host institution for this study sponsors a weeklong workshop, the September Institute, that serves as the kick-off event for new FLCs and brings all participants together to learn about various aspects of teaching and learning. Approximately half of the week is given to presentations on various aspects of teaching. During the other half of the week, participants gather together in their individual learning communities to study their pedagogy of interest. The main emphasis of this portion of the week is to begin the process of becoming a community, especially since the individual learning communities need to set the agenda for their upcoming year of working together on their area of pedagogical study.

Each FLC is expected to grow its efforts during the coming academic year, and the September Institute is the week set aside to begin this process. Each learning community is asked to continue to meet at least twice quarterly following the September Institute, with the agenda for and content of these meetings determined by the FLCs themselves as long as they continue to study, plan, and implement their pedagogy.

Participants

A total of 39 full-time faculty members, representing nine colleges and nineteen departments and making up five FLCs, participated in the September Institute. Demographics of these participants can be found in Table 7.1.

In the first part of this study, all participants in the September Institute were surveyed to ascertain their perceptions of the institute. However, in order to verify reported changes and understand the role of the learning community in helping participants make changes to their teaching, a more in-depth study

TABLE 7.1

Demographics: Participants in the September Institute

	Number		
Learning Community Focus	**Participants**	**Colleges Represented**	**Departments Represented**
Introduction to problem-based learning (PBL)	8	5	5
Multidisciplinary course using PBL	7	2	3
Using multimedia/computer graphics	10	4	5
Student transfer and retention of knowledge	8	1	6
Improving large lecture classes	6	2	3

using qualitative methods was needed. Seven participants were chosen to participate in this in-depth study. Participants were chosen via stratified random sampling because it allowed equal representation from each learning community (Patton, 2002). The participants were stratified into the respective FLCs and two members of each FLC were chosen randomly and asked to participate in the in-depth portion of the study.

There was an unequal representation of FLCs in the in-depth portion of the study. Two members of one FLC team-taught a course and wished to participate as a team, and thus one FLC was represented by three, not two, participants. All members of one FLC declined participation despite numerous attempts to contact them; therefore, this FLC is not represented in the in-depth study.

The participants varied in sex, tenure status, academic rank, and teaching experience: five were female, three had tenure, another three were on the tenure track, and one held the rank of adjunct. The number of years at the university ranged from 3 to greater than 20, with a mean of 10. Table 7.2 summarizes the demographic information for the participants for this in-depth study.

TABLE 7.2

Demographic Information: In-Depth Study Participants

Pseudonym	Sex	College	No. Years	Rank	Discipline	FLC
Bob	M	Technical	3	NT	Architecture	PBL-Multi
Lisa	F	2 year	15	T	Biology	Transfer
Joan	F	2 year	20+	A	Criminal Justice	PBL-Intro
Elizabeth	F	2 year	13	T	Business	PBL-Intro
Carol	F	2 year	8	T	English	Transfer
Jennifer	F	2 year	4	NT	Psychology	Transfer
John	M	Technical	4	NT	Computer Science	Learning Objects

Note. College = type of college within the institution; No. Years = number of years teaching at this institution; FLC = the name of the FLC to which the participant belonged; Rank = T (has achieved tenure), NT (has not achieved tenure but is on a tenure track), A (Adjunct).

Methods and Procedure

Four types of data sources were used in this study in order to increase the trustworthiness of the data (Patton, 2002): survey, syllabi reviews, participant interviews, and classroom observations. The institutional review board for the host institution approved this study.

Survey

A cross-sectional, self-administered questionnaire, containing both open-ended and forced-choice items, was designed to gather an impression of the effectiveness of the September Institute on all aspects of academic life. All September Institute participants were invited to complete the survey. A commercially available web site was used to administer and collect the survey data.

In-Depth Study

Qualitative methods were used for the in-depth portion of the study. Participants were asked to supply syllabi and participate in one-on-one, semi-structured interviews and classroom observations.

Syllabi were examined because they must accurately reflect the course (Parkes & Harris, 2002) and therefore any changes the faculty member has made in the course from one year to another should be seen in the syllabus. Participants were asked to submit a syllabus from their courses before and after the September Institute. Syllabi were then examined to determine the number of times the target pedagogy was mentioned and the number of lines used to discuss that pedagogy (Patton, 2002).

The interviews followed a one-on-one, semi-structured format with open-ended questions (Creswell, 2003). The purpose of the interviews was to help determine if teaching and learning beliefs were being affected by the learning community experience. Questions included the reasons to participate in an FLC, if changes in teaching methodology and/or epistemological beliefs were made and why, and the impact of the FLC on making any changes.

Classroom observation was the only method to actually confirm the pedagogy's use (Fraenkel & Wallen, 2003). Each participant's classroom was observed for a minimum of 90 minutes. The interview and the classroom observation were then analyzed using both deductive and inductive analysis (Creswell, 2003; Denzin & Lincoln, 2000) using NVivo software.

Findings

Survey Results

Twenty-four of thirty-nine (62%) of the September Institute participants completed the survey, with the majority of respondents (27 of 29, or 91.7%) believing that the September Institute was moderately to highly useful in their academic careers. A majority (19 of 24, or 79.2%) reported a great to moderate amount of change in their teaching methods, and 21 of 24 (87%) reported a great to moderate change in their beliefs about teaching and learning.

Qualitative Findings

Changes in Teaching Methods

Each participant in the in-depth study actually made some type of change in teaching methodology. This change was reflected in their course documents and classroom observation. Each participant attributed this change to participation in the September Institute and/or their FLC.

Changes seen in syllabi. The percentage of changes in the syllabi ranged from 0% to 29.6%. Changes were noted in all but two syllabi; however, one of these participants, John, was able to show that he made changes via the course web site. The second participant, Joan, made no changes in her syllabus related to her pedagogy of interest.

Changes seen through classroom observation and interviews. Six of the seven participants were seen to employ their pedagogy as prescribed by their FLC, although the amount of pedagogy usage varied. For example, both Bob and Elizabeth used their pedagogy, problem-based learning (PBL), as their only teaching method, and they used it as prescribed by other PBL practitioners (Barrows & Tamblyn, 1980; Savin-Baden & Major, 2004). Others used their pedagogy along with other teaching methods. For example, John used his pedagogy, multimedia learning objects, to support his students in their studying. His pedagogy was thus not seen in the classroom but rather as a support method on the course web site. Students could access the course web site and see a video of John performing and narrating a complex computer programming task he had previously discussed and demonstrated in class. Thirteen times during a two-hour class session, Carol and Jennifer demonstrated the use of transfer techniques such as concept association, elaboration, retrieval practice, and spacing repetition within and across the lecture (deWinstanley & Bjork, 2002; Murphy & Alexander, 2002). Joan was the only participant of the seven to use her pedagogy, PBL, in a method other than what is prescribed by most practitioners of the pedagogy.

Joan adopted some of the components of PBL such as group work and group process policies. However, her class was highly structured, with Joan clearly leading the class through the lesson plan, relying on lecture and a case study as her teaching methods. Lecture served to supply the students with information, but Joan stated, "I expect them [students] to read outside of class. Lecture is just an outline to follow, it's just a start. I don't give them everything in class." Following the lecture, she used a case study to help students understand how the material related to their discipline and expected students to "show what [they've] just learned in lecture on [their] projects." Joan believed the case study was a derivative of PBL, since the case study employed group work and active learning. However, Joan supplied information via lecture prior to the students acting on the case. Her methodology was contrary to the tenets of PBL, in which the student would receive no didactic information prior to receiving the case (Barrows & Tamblyn, 1980; Savin-Baden & Major, 2004).

Despite making changes inconsistent with her pedagogy, Joan believed her students were performing at a far superior rate than students in previous classes. She noted an increase in enthusiasm, work effort, and attendance. She did not notice a change in grades from previous years; however, she attributed this lack of change to "being harder on them this year because I know what they can do. 'A' papers last year would be 'B' papers this year." She planned to keep using her new teaching and classroom management techniques in future courses.

Why was Joan so different from the others? Why didn't she adopt her pedagogy as completely as the others in this study? Did it have something to do with her beliefs as a teacher?

Participants and Their Teaching and Learning Beliefs

Eighty-seven percent of respondents to the general survey reported a change in their teaching and learning beliefs. However, the participants in the in-depth study did not relate a change in their beliefs, and none of them came to the September Institute with a firm conviction only to have it changed by their FLC experience. Most came to the September Institute with at least an idea of their epistemology, even if that epistemology was subconscious. Their beliefs about teaching and learning were not changed by their experiences with the FLC.

In most cases, the participants' epistemology was either in an infancy stage or fully formed as they entered the learning community. Elizabeth, for example, had a difficult time expressing her beliefs. She did, however, believe that students needed to be self-directed and take responsibility for their learning. She maintained that one of the roles of education was to prepare students for the working world by teaching them not only disciplinary content but also strong work habits, especially teamwork; the instructor's role was thus to guide students and not "spoon feed them." Her beliefs about the role of the student, education, and teacher had not changed because of her learning community experience. Even though she was not able to clearly voice them, those beliefs were consistent with PBL, her chosen pedagogy (Barrows & Tamblyn, 1980).

Bob's September Institute and FLC experience served as an enlightening experience. He stated, "I now know how to teach and what teaching is all about." He was slowly coming to his beliefs before the FLC experience and maintains that he might have been able to find them given enough time, with his experiences with his learning community only speeding up that process. As he stated, "It put me in my path. I might have gotten there eventually, maybe not."

Lisa held a mixed opinion about the role of her FLC and her beliefs. She did admit wanting a change when she realized how poorly students were acting in the classroom. As she stated, "When I looked out at my students I got the glazed eye look, deer in the headlights." She credited reading a book on course design for changes in her beliefs and methodology. However, she realized she would not have found the book without her learning community and would not have been open to the change if she hadn't heard about her pedagogy and discussed effective teaching with her community members. Like Elizabeth, she came to the learning community experience seeking a more effective teaching technique but then left with a clearer idea of her core beliefs about the nature of teaching and learning.

Carol, Jennifer, and John are the few members who didn't credit epistemological formation or change to their learning community experience. In the cases of Carol and Jennifer, their previous training had created their beliefs. Carol had previous education in pedagogy and Jennifer in cognitive psychology. They may not have changed their beliefs, but they did change their teaching methods. Their learning community experience helped them to find the techniques that supported their beliefs. John firmly felt his beliefs had changed, but this change was due to his ongoing doctoral studies in teaching and learning. His doctoral education was supplemented by a growing movement in his discipline, a "movement . . . toward social constructivism," an education theory that John firmly espoused and that was reflected by his changing teaching methods.

Unlike other participants, Joan's changes seem to have been made only in teaching methodology. When asked about these developments, or her learning community's role in these changes, she consistently returned to the changes made in teaching methods. Even in follow-up questions that attempted to discover her beliefs, Joan only spoke about changes made in classroom management, course/classroom policies, or teaching methods. She felt her students needed more guidance and structure than PBL, used in its pure format, allowed. She was grateful to the learning community for giving her techniques to help with the classroom guidance and structure her students needed, but she voiced strong concern about her students' ability to succeed if she used the pedagogy to its full capacity.

Why was Joan so different from the others? Why did she not adopt her FLC's pedagogy as did the others? In the bigger picture, what impact might Joan's actions and example have on the way FLCs are formed and conducted in the future?

Discussion, Implications, and Further Studies

The intention of this study was to determine if faculty members in higher education who participated in FLCs really made changes in teaching methods and beliefs about teaching and learning as they had reported in a survey. Findings support that FLCs can be an effective method of creating faculty change, under the right conditions. One of these conditions might be the alignment of participants' beliefs about the nature of teaching and learning with the type of pedagogy studied.

This need for alignment can be argued from the case study of Joan. No evidence of the pedagogy, as described by experts in the field, was seen in her syllabus or during classroom visits. She had adopted bits and pieces of the pedagogy to better manage her classroom, such as course policies outlining how students were to conduct themselves inside the classroom, and a teaching technique that allowed students to apply the course material through a case study. These policies could, of course, just as easily be used in a non-PBL classroom.

Differences between Joan's beliefs and the belief structure implicit in her selected pedagogy might have been the reason she did not change her teaching methods so as to model her pedagogy. Joan believed that her students would be less successful without her firm guidance and course structure. She thus had a classroom format that was very organized, with a syllabus that clearly delineated course policies and procedures. Such an approach is in direct opposition to PBL, which espouses a more learning-centered epistemology and approach.

Implications and Further Studies

Perhaps in order for FLCs to be successful, the participants must share some fundamental beliefs about teaching and learning or, at least, the same beliefs as espoused by the pedagogy. Asking a faculty member who holds teacher-centered beliefs to adopt a pedagogy requiring learner-centered beliefs may be asking too much. Might faculty members who participate in learning communities be matched to that community through their teaching and learning beliefs? It might be possible to identify teaching and learning beliefs through such instruments as Schommer's Epistemological Beliefs Questionnaire (Clarebout, Elen, Luyten, & Bamps, 2001) or Schraw, Bendixen, and Dunkle's Epistemic Beliefs Inventory (2002), or through interviewing and observing the potential community members.

Limitations

This study has several limitations. First, there is no way to completely confirm or deny that the changes could have been made without the FLC experience. There was no comparison to change in the general faculty community. Second, participants in the in-depth portion of the study came from only two colleges and did not represent the entire faculty. Third, one FLC was not represented in this study.

Conclusion

This study examined the efficacy of FLCs at one institution of higher education. FLCs do appear to be effective in producing change. Using survey research and qualitative techniques, the study showed that all participants made changes to their teaching methods. Despite the pedagogical changes, however, no change was shown in the teaching and learning beliefs of the seven participants enrolled in the qualitative portion of the study. One participant whose teaching and learning beliefs were contrary to those underlying the pedagogy made changes to her teaching methods, but these changes were not completely consistent with her pedagogy. However, students in this participant's class were judged by her to be performing at a better rate than students in previous classes.

Further work should be performed to determine if matching FLC members by teaching and learning beliefs may lead to better success of the community and may expand and quantify the changes or nonchanges in teaching and learning beliefs. Such research may further determine if persons participating in FLCs have some fundamental beliefs that differentiate them from the faculty community at large.

Author Note

I would like to express my thanks to Wayne Hall, vice provost for faculty development at the University of Cincinnati, for his guidance and assistance with this study.

References

Barrows, H. D., & Tamblyn, R. M. (1980). *Problem-based learning: An approach to medical education.* New York, NY: Springer.

Blaidsell, M. L., & Cox, M. D. (2004). Mid-career and senior faculty learning communities: Learning throughout faculty careers. In M. D. Cox & L. Richlin (Eds.), *New directions for teaching and learning: No. 97. Building faculty learning communities* (pp. 137–148). San Francisco, CA: Jossey-Bass.

Clarebout, G., Elen, J., Luyten, L., & Bamps, H. (2001, March). Assessing epistemological beliefs: Schommer's questionnaire revisited. *Educational Research and Evaluation: An International Journal on Theory and Practice, 7*(1), 53–77.

Cox, M. D. (1995). The development of new and junior faculty. In W. A. Wright & Associates, *Teaching improvement practices: Successful strategies for higher education* (pp. 283–310). Bolton, MA: Anker.

Cox, M. D. (2004). Introduction to faculty learning communities. In M. D. Cox & L. Richlin (Eds.), *New directions for teaching and learning: No. 97. Building faculty learning communities* (pp. 5–23). San Francisco, CA: Jossey-Bass.

Cox, M. D., & Richlin, L. (2004). Editor's notes. In M. D. Cox & L. Richlin (Eds.), *New directions for teaching and learning: No. 97. Building faculty learning communities* (pp. 1–4). San Francisco, CA: Jossey-Bass.

Creswell, J. W. (2003). *Research design: Qualitative, quantitative, and mixed methods approaches* (2nd ed.). Thousand Oaks, CA: Sage.

Denzin, N. K., & Lincoln, Y. S. (Eds.). (2000). *Handbook of qualitative research* (2nd ed.). Thousand Oaks, CA: Sage.

deWinstanley, P. A., & Bjork, R. A. (2002). Successful lecturing: Presenting information in ways that engage effective processing. In D. F. Halpern & M. D. Hakel (Eds.), *New directions for teaching and learning: No. 89. Applying the science of learning to university teaching and beyond* (pp. 19–31). San Francisco, CA: Jossey-Bass.

Elliot, D. L., Skeff, K. M., & Stratos, G. A. (1999). How do you get to the improvement of teaching? A longitudinal faculty development program for medical educators. *Teaching and Learning in Medicine, 11*(1), 52–57.

Fraenkel, J. R., & Wallen, N. E. (2003). *How to design and evaluate research in education* (5th ed.). New York, NY: McGraw-Hill.

Goldberg, B., & Finkelstein, M. (2002, Summer). Effects of a first-semester learning community on nontraditional technical students. *Innovative Higher Education, 26*(4), 235–249.

Houston, T. K., Clark, J. M., Levine, R. B., Ferenchick, G. S., Bowen, J. L., Branch, W. T., et al. (2004, December). Outcomes of a national faculty development program in teaching skills. *Innovations in Education and Clinical Practice, 19,* 1220–1227.

Miami University. (2004). *Faculty learning communities: Participating institutions and their communities and directors.* Retrieved May 16, 2007, from the Miami University, Faculty Learning Communities web site: www.units.muohio.edu/ flc/participating.shtml

Murphy, P. K., & Alexander, P. A. (2002, Spring). What counts? The predictive powers of subject-matter knowledge, strategic processing, and interest in domain-specific performance. *Journal of Experimental Education, 70*(3), 197–214.

Parkes, J., & Harris, M. B. (2002, Spring). The purposes of a syllabus. *College Teaching, 50*(2), 55–61.

Patton, M. Q. (2002). *Qualitative research and evaluation methods* (3rd ed.). Thousand Oaks, CA: Sage.

Richlin, L., & Essington, A. (2004). Overview of faculty learning communities. In M. D. Cox & L. Richlin (Eds.), *New directions for teaching and learning: No. 97. Building faculty learning communities* (pp. 25–39). San Francisco, CA: Jossey-Bass.

Savin-Baden, M., & Major, C. H. (2004). *Foundations of problem-based learning.* New York, NY: Open University Press.

Schraw, G., Bendixen, L. D., & Dunkle, M. E. (2002). Development and validation of the Epistemic Belief Inventory (EBI). In B. K. Hofer & P. R. Pintrich (Eds.), *Personal epistemology: The psychology of beliefs about knowledge and knowing* (pp. 261–275). Mahwah, NJ: Lawrence Erlbaum.

Sekerka, L. E., & Chao, J. (2003, Winter). Peer coaching as a technique to foster professional development in clinical ambulatory settings. *Journal of Continuing Education in the Health Professions, 23*(1), 30–37.

Skinner, M. E., & Welch, F. C. (1996, Fall). Peer coaching for better teaching. *College Teaching, 44*(4), 153–156.

Steinert, Y., Nasmith, L., McLeod, P. J., & Conochie, L. (2003, February). A teaching scholars program to develop leaders in medical education. *Academic Medicine, 78*(2), 142–149.

Stevens, M. C. (2004). *What makes a faculty learning community effective?* Unpublished manuscript.

Section IV

Educational Development and Diversity

8

Stereotype Threat and Ten Things We Can Do to Remove the Threat in the Air

Franklin A. Tuitt
University of Denver

Lois Reddick
New York University

The purpose of this chapter is to present an overview of the literature related to stereotype threat in an effort to provide faculty members and instructional developers with a better understanding of what the phenomenon is and what can be done about it in college classroom settings. To this end, we reviewed several of the major studies published on the subject between 1995 and 2005 and compiled a list of strategies that reflected both the major empirical findings on stereotype threat and our own research and experiences with faculty and students in college settings. Given the enormity of the subject, we focused heavily on the features of stereotype threat that relate specifically to race but acknowledged that the complexity of the subject required attention to other aspects of identity that may function to lessen, or in some cases increase, the intensity of stereotype threat. The overall findings suggested that there are several ways in which faculty and instructional developers can help to create learning environments that serve to mitigate the impact of stereotype threat, and that more work needs to be done to examine the ways in which faculty and instructional developers can strive to create environments that improve the quality of students' perceptions and academic performances.

Research has shown that for some populations of high-achieving students, taking a difficult exam can produce feelings of anxiety that are rooted in a fear of confirming a negative stereotype about an affiliated group, and that these feelings can result in deficits in performance (Marx & Roman, 2002;

Spencer, Steele, & Quinn, 1999; Steele & Aronson, 1995). This phenomenon labeled *stereotype threat* is generally activated when three situational conditions are present: 1) students must be explicitly or implicitly exposed to a negative stereotype about a group with which they can be associated, 2) the testing or learning conditions must pose a challenge to the students, and 3) the testing or learning domain must be of some importance to the students (Steele & Aronson, 1995). Stereotype threat is strongest among the highest achieving students because academic performance is an integral part of their collective identities. In fact, low-achieving students, who do not perceive the academic domain to be an important indicator of their personal success, are less susceptible to this threat (Major, Spencer, Schmader, Wolfe, & Crocker, 1998).

Empirical research on stereotype threat demonstrates its impact on the performance of a wide range of student populations, including women (Désert, Gonçalves, & Leyens, 2005; Quinn & Spencer, 2001; Shih, Pittinsky, & Ambady, 1999; Spencer et al., 1999), Latinos (Aronson, Quinn, & Spencer, 1998; Aronson & Salinas, 1997; Gonzales, Blanton, & Williams, 2002), Asians (Shih et al., 1999), gay white males (Bosson, Haymovitz, & Pinel, 2004), and even white male students who do not traditionally suffer from negative stereotypes in academic domains (Inzlicht & Ben-Zeev, 2000). In this chapter, we center our discussion on the impact of stereotype threat as it relates to black students in academic settings. Specifically, we provide an overview of the literature related to stereotype threat in an effort to provide faculty members and instructional developers with a better understanding of what this phenomenon is and what can be done about it.

Stereotype Threat: What Is It?

According to Steele and Aronson (1995), the educational experiences of black students are uniquely affected by the sociopsychological threats that arise when they are engaging in academic activities for which a negative stereotype about their group may apply. This predicament threatens students with the possibility that they may be judged or treated stereotypically and that their academic performance may confirm the stereotype. Taylor and Antony (2000) describe this as the social and psychological sense of peril that negative racial stereotypes may be unfairly applied to black students solely on the basis of their skin color. This threat of being racially stereotyped produces a climate of intimidation that can hamper academic performance (Steele & Aronson, 1995). Black students may also disidentify with academic goals because of the anxiety that is produced by widely held stereotypes that they are intellectually inferior (Steele, 1997).

The Impact of Stereotype Threat Related to Race

Good, Aronson, and Inzlicht (2003) argue that "being evaluated in a stereotyped domain is sufficient to trigger the trademark responses associated with stereotype threat such as a lack of enjoyment of the educational process, increased anxiety and stress, and ultimately, underperformance" (p. 647). These "trademark responses" can contribute to students' underperformance when their academic profiles might suggest otherwise. For example, Steele (1997) argues that when gifted black students sit down to take a difficult exam, "the extra apprehension they feel in comparison with whites is less about their own ability than it is about having to perform on a test and in a situation that may be primed to treat them stereotypically" (p. 52). This conclusion suggests that talented black students who perceive their learning environment to be racialized may not perform up to their ability (Carter & Tuitt, 2006). This underperformance appears to be rooted less in black students' self-doubt than in their social mistrust of the learning environment (Steele, 1999).

While stereotype threat is commonly known for the detrimental impact it has on standardized test scores, research also indicates that individuals may suffer negative performance outcomes such as less engagement with academics because of the burden black students may experience when confronted with "the prospect of confirming cultural stereotypes impugning their intellectual and academic abilities" (Good et al., 2003, p. 647). According to Osborne (2001), there is empirical support for the assertion that black students do in fact have increased anxiety or arousal that can inhibit participation when performing in academic arenas. He argues that the racial performance gaps may be explained through "the cognitive effects of increasing anxiety, which include decreasing cognitive capacity, reticence to respond, attention deficits, and distracting thoughts" (p. 293). This evidence suggests that for some black students the "threat in the air" existing in predominantly white classrooms may not simply be a figment of their imagination (Tuitt, 2003).

Removing the Threat in the Air

Although a significant amount has been written about the impact of stereotype threat and what can be done about it, this information is not widely disseminated among those who work within the field of higher education and faculty/teaching assistant development. The identification of pedagogical interventions and learning strategies that potentially reduce the impact of stereotype threat is vitally important if we are to create teaching and learning environments in which all students have a chance to reach their potential.

Creating Identity-Safe Learning Environments

According to Davies, Spencer, and Steele (2005), attempting to eliminate all potentially threatening cues from the learning environment would be a futile exercise, but it may be possible to create environments that effectively reduce the risk of experiencing stereotype threat. In addition, Taylor and Antony (2000) suggest that students' academic performance can be improved through instructional strategies that reduce stereotype threat and assure students that they will not be cast in the shadow of negative stereotypes. Essentially, professors have the responsibility of creating identity-safe environments where their students' sense of the institution is not a barrier to their academic success (Davies et al., 2005). According to Davies et al., identity-safe environments challenge the validity, relevance, or acceptance of negative stereotypes linked to stigmatized social identities. These identity-safe environments would remove the threat in the air, allowing stigmatized individuals to enter previously threatening situations without the risk of confirming a negative stereotype targeting their social identity (Markus, Steele, & Steele, 2002; Steele, 2004).

Ten Strategies for Removing the Threat in the Air

In the next section, we discuss ten strategies that instructors can employ to create identity-safe environments and combat stereotype threat in the classroom. These recommendations emerge out of the current literature on stereotype threat and provide educators with some pedagogical practices they can undertake to remove the potential threat in the air.

1. Create optimistic and personalized teacher-student relationships.

Steele and Aronson (1995) suggest that the prevailing stereotypes based on prior experiences with racism make it reasonable for talented black students to worry that professors in their institutions will doubt their academic abilities. Steele (1997) proposes that one "wise strategy," suitable for all students, is to discredit this assumption through the establishment of potential-affirming faculty-student relationships. Likewise, Baker (1998) found that students were able to develop effective relationships with the faculty members who demonstrated behaviors such as being supportive, caring, knowledgeable, challenging, concerned, and open to establishing an interpersonal relationship. These attributes focus on the faculty member's ability to relate to the student on an interpersonal level and are essential for a positive learning environment (Baker, 1998). In such personalized and optimistic teacher-student relationships, instructors make their confidence in students explicit (Taylor & Antony, 2000).

2. Affirm students' sense of belonging.

According to Steele (1997), negative-ability stereotypes raise the threat that one does not belong in the learning environment: "They cast doubt on the extent of one's abilities, on how well one will be accepted, on one's social compatibility with the domain, and so on" (p. 625). The more that instructors can provide direct affirmation of students' belongingness—that is, assuring individuals that they are welcomed, supported, and valued (Davies et al., 2005) in the classroom—the more effective they will be in removing the threat in air. This affirmation has to be genuine and authentic, and Steele warns that it is important to base this affirmation on the students' intellectual potential.

3. Build students' self-efficacy.

Nauta, Epperson, and Kahn (1998) found that interventions designed to help students develop more accurate views of their past and present performances led to increases in perceptions of self-efficacy, which contributed to higher level aspirations in career achievement for mathematics, science, and engineering majors. Steele (1997), building on Bandura's (1986, 1997) theory of self-efficacy, advises that instructors attempt to develop students' sense of competence and self-efficacy in the schooling domain. He contends that for students who are threatened by a poor reputation and who probably hold internalized doubts about their ability, the Socratic method is one pedagogical intervention that has the potential to create a safe teacher-student relationship where there is little cost of failure and the gradual building of self-efficacy from small gains. In addition, other research indicates that a strong racial identity may serve as a buffer against stereotype threat (McFarland, Lev-Arey, & Ziegert, 2003). For example, Smith and Hopkins (2004) found that students who possess a strong sense of self-determination and pride about self are able to perform better on more complex tasks than others who do not demonstrate these characteristics.

4. Create authentic opportunities for students to affirm their individuality.

Ambady, Paik, Steele, Owen-Smith, and Mitchell (2004) contend that if the salience of group identity is replaced by the salience of individual identity, the risk associated with negative stereotype activation might be attenuated and performance altered to reflect more accurately the unique capabilities of the individual rather than the stereotypes in the group. Moreover, these authors suggest that the disclosure of personal information accentuating one's unique qualities encourages a more multifaceted view that may distinguish a person from his or her in-group and counteract stereotyping. In theory, a person might overcome a self-threat by affirming "the broader self-concept or an equally important, yet different, aspect of the self-concept" (Ambady et al., 2004, p. 405). Thus, if professors are able to create opportunities for their students to represent themselves in genuine, authentic, and meaningful ways, it is more likely that students will trust that their academic efforts will be judged by merit and not some stereotypic impression (Carter & Tuitt, 2006).

5. Hold students to high standards.

Taylor and Antony (2000) argue that providing students with "challenging, rather than remedial expectations and academic work, which builds on promise and potential, not failure" (p. 187) can eliminate the potential threat in the air. For example, Cohen, Steele, and Ross (1999) observed that giving challenging work and critical feedback to students demonstrates a respect for their potential and shows "that they are not regarded through the lens of an ability-demeaning stereotype" (Steele, 1997, p. 625). Baker (1998) observed that "faculty members created a positive learning atmosphere by challenging students and demonstrating concern and belief in the (academic) ability of students" (p. 58).

6. Teach students about the nature of intelligence and stereotype threat.

According to Taylor and Antony (2000), emphasizing the expandability of intelligence lets students know that skills can be learned and extended through education and experience. Steele (1997) posits that the extent to which schooling can stress what Dweck (1986) called the incremental nature of human intelligence—its expandability in response to experience and training—should help to deflect the meanest implication of the stereotype. Aronson (2004) cites empirical research that indicates the benefits of teaching students to view their intellectual abilities as expandable rather than fixed. He contends that stereotypes impose on students the notion that their academic difficulties reflect an "unalterable limitation, a bell curve view of abilities that says that some people are born smart and others dumb" (p. 17). Essentially, Aronson contends that when we teach students about a human being's ability to expand intelligence, we inform our students to think of their minds as muscles: use it and it is strengthened; waste it and it atrophies. Finally, according to Aronson, studies show the value of explicitly teaching students about stereotype threat. Learning that their test anxiety results from a common response to stereotyping helps students interpret their struggles in a less pejorative and anxiety-producing way and results in higher test scores (Aronson & Williams, 2004).

7. Value multiple perspectives.

According to Steele (1997), concerns that students may have about whether they are going to be assessed in stereotypical ways can be addressed by being explicit in regard to the value of multiple perspectives. This refers to strategies that explicitly value a variety of approaches to both academic substance and the larger academic culture in which that substance is considered. "Making such a value public tells stereotype-threatened students that this is an environment in which the stereotype is less likely to be used" (Steele, 1997, p. 625). In Baker's (1998) study, students identified the professor's ability to be "unbiased" and open to diverse perspectives as being very important to the establishment of an effective faculty-student relationship. In this context, openness did not just involve an openness to students but an openness to the diverse perspectives of others as well (Baker, 1998). Another way that faculty members can demonstrate that they value multiple perspectives is to make sure that the course content (readings and examples) is diverse. According to Osborne (2001), the utilization of a truly multicultural curriculum can help to undermine the negative group stereotypes related to intellectual ability. Alternatively, Adams (2005) argues that the absence of a diverse curriculum can cause black students to internalize marginalized status as a result of not seeing themselves reflected in the course readings. Thus, when professors include positive examples of diverse individuals they provide counternarratives that help to delegitimize the potentially negative stereotypes floating in the air (Marx & Goff, 2005).

8. Create cooperative learning environments.

Social psychologists and others examining the impact of stereotype threat have advocated for the development of learning environments rooted in fairness, high expectations, trust, and collaboration, not competition. For example, Aronson (2004) argues that creating cooperative classroom structures in which students work interdependently can produce immediate and dramatic gains in grades, test scores, and engagement of students of color because such environments reduce competition, distrust, and stereotyping among students (Aronson & Patnoe, 1997). Marx, Brown, and Steele (1999) report that creating cooperative learning environments minimizes competition among students, builds trust, and facilitates student success.

9. Provide role models.

Aronson (2004) suggests that exposing students to role models who have triumphed over similar academic struggles with hard work and persistence markedly improves the students' study habits, grades, and test scores.

Specifically, people from the stereotype-threatened group who have been successful in the domain carry the message that stereotype threat is not an insurmountable barrier (Aronson, 2004). "The presence of role models of people who have successfully overcome stereotype threat" demonstrates to students that the potential threat in the air does not have to be a barrier to their success (Taylor & Antony, 2000, p. 106). The research of Marx and Goff (2005) suggests that something as simple as who administers a test (or stands in front of the class) can change the attitudes black students have about how they might be racially stereotyped. In this regard, the extent to which institutions can diversify their faculty and staff may have a tremendous impact on their ability to remove the threat in the air.

■10. Address test taking anxiety.

Several researchers note that explicitly telling students that an exam is racially fair, reporting to students specific aspects of their performance that indicate their capacity to perform at high levels (Spencer et al., 1999; Stone, Lynch, Sjomeling, & Darley, 1999), and exposing students to stereotype-disconfirming evidence (e.g., a mathematics professor of Latino or African descent) all function to mitigate the effects of stereotype threat. In addition, Steele and Aronson (1995) found that decreasing the diagnosticity of an exam by telling students that a given test is not an indicator of their intellectual ability minimizes the impact of stereotype threat.

Conclusion

Although it is virtually impossible to eliminate all of the potentially threatening cues (Davies et al., 2005), professors have the responsibility to create identity-safe environments where their students' racialized sense of the institution is not a barrier to their academic success (Davies et al., 2005). In theory, if faculty do the following, they can clear the air of any potential stereotype threat:

- Create optimistic and personalized teacher-student relationships.

- Affirm students' sense of belonging.

- Build students' self-efficacy.

- Create authentic opportunities for students to affirm their individuality.

- Hold students to high standards.

- Teach students about the nature of intelligence and stereotype threat.

- Value multiple perspectives.

- Create cooperative learning environments.

- Provide role models.

- Address test taking anxiety.

The results of the various studies cited in this chapter have major implications for faculty and for those who do the work of instructional development. It is clear that instructors can create learning environments that produce differential outcomes for students based on their status and sociopsychological location in the classroom. In this regard, it is crucial that educational institutions be capable of developing professors who are cognizant of stereotype threat and the impact it can have on the learning environment. Moreover, institutions need to hold instructors accountable for the role they play in creating identity-threatening learning environments. Assessment and evaluation of instructors at the institutional level is vital. Finally, more attention needs to be paid to how we prepare doctoral candidates for postsecondary teaching. Graduate programs should ensure that there are a variety of opportunities for aspiring professors to hone their teaching skills prior to arriving in their first college classroom as an instructor (Carter & Tuitt, 2006). Graduate programs responsible for preparing the next generation of college professors must ensure that future instructors have the pedagogical knowledge and skills needed to create classrooms where all students, regardless of their background, have the opportunity to achieve at the highest levels—free from the threat of being stereotyped.

References

Adams, T. A. (2005). Establishing intellectual space for black students in predominantly white universities through black studies. *Negro Educational Review, 56*(4), 285–299.

Ambady, N., Paik, S., Steele, J., Owen-Smith, A., & Mitchell, J. P. (2004). Deflecting negative self-relevant stereotype activation: The effects of individuation. *Journal of Experimental Social Psychology, 40*(3), 401–408.

Aronson, E., & Patnoe, S. (1997). *The jigsaw classroom: Building cooperation in the classroom* (2nd ed.). New York, NY: Longman.

Aronson, J. (2004, November). The threat of stereotype. *Educational Leadership, 62*(3), 14–19.

Aronson, J., Quinn, D. M., & Spencer, S. J. (1998). Stereotype threat and the academic underperformance of minorities and women. In J. Swim & C. Stangor (Eds.), *Prejudice: The target's perspective* (pp. 83–103). San Diego, CA: Academic Press.

Aronson, J., & Salinas, M. F. (1997). *Stereotype threat, attributional ambiguity, and Latino underperformance.* Unpublished manuscript.

Aronson, J., & Williams, J. (2004). *Stereotype threat: Forewarned is forearmed.* Unpublished manuscript.

Baker, P. (1998). Students' perception of classroom factors that impact success for African-American students in higher education settings (Doctoral dissertation, Northern Illinois University, 1998). *Dissertation Abstracts International, 59,* 1434.

Bandura, A. (1986). *Social foundations of thought and action: A social cognitive theory.* Englewood Cliffs, NJ: Prentice Hall.

Bandura, A. (1997). *Self-efficacy: The exercise of control.* New York, NY: W. H. Freeman.

Bosson, J. K., Haymovitz, E. L., & Pinel, E. C. (2004). When saying and doing diverge: The effects of stereotype threat on self-reported versus non-verbal anxiety. *Journal of Experimental Social Psychology, 40*(2), 247–255.

Carter, D., & Tuitt, F. (2006, October). *Black achievers' experiences with and responses to stereotype threat and racial microaggressions.* Paper presented at the BOTA Think Tank, Atlanta, GA.

Cohen, G. L., Steele, C. M., & Ross, L. D. (1999). The mentor's dilemma: Providing critical feedback across the racial divide. *Personality and Social Psychology Bulletin, 25*(10), 1302–1318.

Davies, P. G., Spencer, S. J., & Steele, C. M. (2005). Clearing the air: Identity safety moderates the effects of stereotype threat on women's leadership aspirations. *Journal of Personality and Social Psychology, 88*(2), 276–287.

Désert, M., Gonçalves, G., Leyens, J.-P. (2005). *Stereotype threat effects upon behavior: The role of actual control.* Manuscript submitted for publication.

Dweck, C. S. (1986, October). Motivational processes affecting learning. *American Psychologist, 41*(10), 1040–1048.

Gonzales, P. M., Blanton, H., & Williams, K. J. (2002). The effects of stereotype threat and double-minority status on the test performance of Latino women. *Personality and Social Psychology Bulletin, 28*(5), 659–670.

Good, C., Aronson, J., & Inzlicht, M. (2003, December). Improving adolescents' standardized test performance: An intervention to reduce the effects of stereotype threat. *Journal of Applied Developmental Psychology, 24*(6), 645–662.

Inzlicht, M., & Ben-Zeev, T. (2000). A threatening intellectual environment: Why females are susceptible to experiencing problem-solving deficits in the presence of males. *Psychological Science, 11*(5), 365–371.

Major, B., Spencer, S., Schmader, T., Wolfe, C., & Crocker, J. (1998). Coping with negative stereotypes about intellectual performance: The role of psychological disengagement. *Personality and Social Psychology Bulletin, 24*(1), 34–50.

Markus, H. R., Steele, C. M., & Steele, D. M. (2002). Color blindness as a barrier to inclusion: Assimilation and nonimmigrant minorities. In R. Shweder, M. Minow, & H. R. Markus (Eds.), *Engaging cultural differences: The multicultural challenge in liberal democracies* (pp. 453–472). New York, NY: Russell Sage Foundation.

Marx, D. M., Brown, J. L., & Steele, C. M. (1999, Fall). Allport's legacy and the situational press of stereotypes. *Journal of Social Issues, 55*(3), 491–502.

Marx, D. M., & Goff, P. A. (2005, December). Clearing the air: The effect of experimenter race on target's test performance and subjective experience. *British Journal of Social Psychology, 44*(4), 645–657.

Marx, D. M., & Roman, J. S. (2002, September). Female role models: Protecting women's math test performance. *Personality and Social Psychology Bulletin, 28*(9), 1183–1193.

McFarland, L. A., Lev-Arey, D. M., & Ziegert, J. C. (2003). An examination of stereotype threat in a motivational context. *Human Performance, 16*(3), 181–205.

Nauta, M. M., Epperson, D. L., & Kahn, J. H. (1998, October). A multiple-groups analysis of predictors of higher level career aspirations among women in mathematics, science, and engineering majors. *Journal of Counseling Psychology, 45*(4), 483–496.

Osborne, J. W. (2001, July). Testing stereotype threat: Does anxiety explain race and sex differences in achievement? *Contemporary Educational Psychology, 26*(3), 291–310.

Quinn, D. M., & Spencer, S. J. (2001, Spring). The interference of stereotype threat with women's generation of mathematical problem-solving strategies. *Journal of Social Issues, 57*(1), 55–71.

Shih, M., Pittinsky, T., & Ambady, N. (1999, January). Stereotype susceptibility: Identity salience and shifts in quantitative performance. *Psychological Science, 10*(1), 80–83.

Smith, C. E., & Hopkins, R. (2004, March). Mitigating the impact of stereotypes on academic performance: The effects of cultural identity and attributions for success among African American college students. *Western Journal of Black Studies, 28*(1), 312–321.

Spencer, S. J., Steele, C. M., & Quinn, D. M. (1999). Under suspicion of inability: Stereotype vulnerability and women's math performance. *Journal of Experimental Social Psychology, 35*, 4–28.

Steele, C. M. (1997). A threat in the air: How stereotypes shape intellectual identity and performance. *American Psychologist, 52*(6), 613–629.

Steele, C. M. (1999, August). Thin ice: Stereotype threat and black college students. *The Atlantic Monthly, 284*(2), 44–54.

Steele, C. M. (2004). Kenneth Clark's context and mine: Toward a context-based theory of social identity threat. In G. Philogène (Ed.), *Racial identity in context: The legacy of Kenneth B. Clark.* Washington, DC: American Psychological Association.

Steele, C. M., & Aronson, J. (1995, November). Stereotype threat and the intellectual test performance of African Americans. *Journal of Personality and Social Psychology, 69*(5), 797–811.

Stone, J., Lynch, C. I., Sjomeling, M., & Darley, J. M. (1999). Stereotype threat effects on Black and White athletic performance. *Journal of Personality and Social Psychology, 77*(6), 1213–1227.

Taylor, E., & Antony, J. S. (2000, Summer). Stereotype threat reduction and wise schooling: Towards the successful socialization of African American doctoral students in education. *Journal of Negro Education, 69*(3), 184–198.

Tuitt, F. (2003). *Black souls in an ivory tower: Understanding what it means to teach in a manner that respects and cares for the souls of African American graduate students.* Unpublished doctoral dissertation, Harvard University, Cambridge, MA.

9

Thawing the Chilly Climate: Inclusive Teaching Resources for Science, Technology, Engineering, and Math

Katherine A. Friedrich, Sherrill L. Sellers, Judith N. Burstyn
University of Wisconsin–Madison

Although universities are aware of the need to promote diversity in science, technology, engineering, and mathematics (STEM), this awareness has not translated into significant changes in classroom environments. Many STEM instructors would like to offer equal opportunities for success to all of their students, but they are not sure where to begin. We describe an effective group of teaching tools that can empower STEM faculty and graduate students to modify their courses to address diversity at their own pace. These resources extend from awareness exercises to recommendations for action and have been useful tools for course design, teaching assistant training, and faculty development.

Although "diversity in the sciences" has become a common topic of discussion among university administrators and at funding agencies, inclusive teaching has not fully made its way into the college science classroom. Several scholars have suggested directions for this cultural shift (Riley, 2003; Rosser, 1993). However, in practice, science, technology, engineering, and mathematics (STEM) disciplines have been slow to change.

This response is not necessarily due to resistance from scientists. Many scientists with whom we have spoken do not view diversity awareness as essential to their teaching practice because they do not see the connections between diversity and their course content. Many others know that "diversity is important" but are not sure how to approach the topic.

Faculty in technical fields face many challenges, especially when teaching large courses. The content they must convey is often complex and difficult for students to grasp intuitively. Because they need to focus on content delivery, faculty and teaching assistants (TAs) may not attend to the learning styles of their students. Research indicates that the learning styles of faculty and students often differ (Felder, 1996). Faculty traditionally tend to orient courses toward students who are introverted, are abstract thinkers, are logical rather than values oriented, and prefer definite solutions. However, many students do not fit this profile. If a faculty member assumes that his or her students learn best through listening to lectures, for example, he or she may find that students are not retaining the material.

Many STEM faculty and TAs are unaware of the exclusionary aspects of their courses. They are simply teaching their students the way they were taught. Subtle changes to teaching practices, especially in introductory courses, can make a difference for students who are still exploring their career choices. These are the students who are currently dropping out of STEM programs, and they are the ones we need to retain (Seymour & Hewitt, 1997).

The Center for the Integration of Research, Teaching, and Learning (CIRTL) has developed resources to aid in creating discussion among faculty, initiating interventions, and improving classroom climate and course content. Recent evaluations of the resources suggest STEM faculty find the materials to be useful (Burstyn, Sellers, Friedrich, & Gunasekera, 2006).

Why Teach Inclusively?

Encouraging inclusive teaching begins with awareness of the current situation of students from underrepresented groups.

Minority students of high potential often leave STEM fields. For example, African-American students are more likely than majority students to express interest in STEM careers, but few persist through graduate school to complete their Ph.D.s (Maton, Hrabowski, & Schmitt, 2000). Bright students opt out of STEM for a variety of reasons (Seymour & Hewitt, 1997), including the lack of creative engagement in introductory courses (Tobias, 1990), the lack of connection between science and social values (Rosser, 1993), and unwelcoming departmental cultures (Ferreira, 2002).

The problem of stereotypes transcends the classroom. Some studies show that children, even before entering preschool, already consider the typical scientist to be white and male (see Yanowitz, 2004). Students from underrepresented groups may be more likely to eschew a STEM degree because they doubt their technical competence in the face of stereotypes (Moore, Madison-Colmore, & Smith, 2003; Steele, 1997).

In this challenging, sometimes intimidating environment, faculty may be unaware that teaching for inclusion is more than a matter of changing pronouns, last names, or pictures on a PowerPoint slide. Inclusive teaching is a composite of good communication, cultural understanding, effective course design, fair grading, and awareness of interpersonal dynamics (Adams, Bell, & Griffin, 1997; Davis, 1993).

College students from underrepresented groups face subtle challenges to their confidence and barriers to learning (Cabrera & Nora, 1994). Grading often reflects verbal participation, which may be influenced by language or cultural differences. Returning students, international students, and students with disabilities face specific obstacles.

Alienation may be especially problematic for students who have difficulty forming study groups with their peers because of social or demographic differences. For instance, Treisman (1992) found that the underrepresented minority students who were not doing well in his mathematics courses were having difficulties, not because of academic preparation or motivation, but because they were not part of study groups. He initiated an honors program that encouraged students to collaborate on challenging problems in an environment of high expectations. The model has been so successful that it has spread to other universities and colleges throughout the country.

Changing the Climate

Treisman (1992) and others point the way to addressing these questions: What can instructors and administrators do to develop inclusive climates in STEM? And how can organizational developers work with them to accomplish this goal?

Three types of approaches emerged from the CIRTL Diversity Institute, a collaborative effort that brought together STEM faculty and diversity experts to develop resources for inclusive teaching. We group these approaches into the following categories:

- Raising awareness

- Developing intervention programs

- Supporting inclusive teaching

All three prongs of this approach are important. Awareness-raising without action does not lead to sustained change. Intervention program development may address the immediate needs of students from underrepresented groups, but it does not change the culture that surrounds them. Awareness is needed to motivate inclusive teaching, and intervention programs are needed to complement inclusive practice.

Raising Awareness

Faculty, instructional staff, TAs, and administrators can raise their awareness by reflecting on student experiences of diversity in the classroom. Sometimes, people discuss diversity only with others who will agree with them. Providing opportunities where people can disagree respectfully brings the conversation out into the open and raises the awareness of all participants. Organizational developers can create forums for these types of discussion. Clear ground rules are essential for these facilitated conversations.

One useful resource that we have developed is *Case Studies in Inclusive Teaching in Science, Technology, Engineering, and Mathematics* (Sellers, Friedrich, Gunasekera, Saleem, & Burstyn, 2006). This collection of scenarios is designed to introduce educators to issues that faculty and students from underrepresented groups may face in STEM academic programs. The topics covered include nationality, race/ethnicity, gender, sexual orientation, disability, and academic preparation. Each case is written so that it can be addressed from a variety of perspectives. The case studies are presented together with discussion questions, worksheets for individual responses, and group facilitation instructions.

This book has been used successfully in workshops with a variety of audiences and at a range of institutions. For example, we have used these cases in TA training, in faculty development workshops, and with university administrators. We have conducted case-based workshops at research universities, community colleges, and national foundations. The case studies are also available on the Internet; in the future, we plan to produce several of them in a multimedia format.

We have found data, personal experiences, and self-tests to be useful in helping people step outside their usual perspectives and learn about the experiences of students from underrepresented groups. We synthesized these approaches in developing our online self-guided workshop (Sellers & Friedrich, 2006), which contains resources that we found impressive in their honesty and directness. The workshop materials include self-tests for bias, reflective articles on racism, data on educational access and the U. S. labor force, videos on student experiences, and challenging exercises for group work.

Developing Intervention Programs

Once faculty and administrators are aware of the disparities that exist, they may express interest in developing intervention programs. Intervention—creating specialized programs to help students from underrepresented groups succeed in STEM—is a popular method of improving student success and retention. The Diversity Institute literature review (Cabrera et al., 2004) indicates that some of the most successful programs emphasize mentoring, research experience, financial support, collaborative learning, and high expectations for all students (Barlow & Villarejo, 2004; Cabrera et al., 2002; Maton et al., 2000; Stahl, 2005).

In recent years, many universities have created innovative programs to recruit and retain students from underrepresented groups. For example, the Meyerhoff Scholars Program provides extensive advising and career support for future Ph.D.s (Maton et al., 2000). Smith College has initiated a degree program in engineering for women and is pioneering innovative teaching strategies to engage students in critical thinking (Riley, 2003). Many institutions offer support programs for women in science and engineering. For example, the University of Wisconsin–Madison Women in Science and Engineering program is a residential learning community that encourages appreciation for science and the arts and has improved undergraduate STEM students' grades (Allen, 1999). National support programs in mathematics based on the work of Treisman (1992) have been particularly successful. The Wisconsin Emerging Scholars program, a multicultural intensive math program, has improved students' grades in calculus (Alexander, Burda, & Millar, 1997).

Supporting Inclusive Teaching

It is important for faculty and TAs to understand that diversity and teaching excellence are intertwined. This concept is one of the core principles of CIRTL. Inclusive teaching is part of good instruction. Administrators and organizational developers can support faculty in experimenting with techniques and strategies to engage all students.

We developed the teaching manual *Reaching All Students: A Resource for Teaching in Science, Technology, Engineering, and Mathematics* (Sellers, Roberts, Giovanetto, & Friedrich, 2005) with the intention of integrating inclusive practice throughout the educational process, from course planning through evaluation. Rather than being one chapter appended to the guide, diversity is woven throughout the text. We have compiled sections from many existing sources, including *Tools for Teaching* (Davis, 1993) and *Science Teaching Reconsidered* (National Research Council, 1997), and have authored additional material to create a concise handbook that is geared toward STEM instruction. *Reaching All Students* has been used in TA training and in new faculty development, as well as with university staff and experienced faculty.

Reaching All Students is structured around the lifecycle of a course and includes information on the following:

- Course planning guidelines that allow instructors to begin a course in a way that "reaches all students." Inclusion can be accomplished through thoughtful selection of course materials, development of student-friendly syllabi, and outcomes-oriented course planning (also known as "backwards design").

- Recommendations for communicating effectively with students, developing rapport, addressing misconceptions about science, discussing controversial topics, and communicating cross-culturally.

- Teaching methods that include students of diverse learning styles. There are many advantages to introducing active and interactive learning to supplement lecture methods. Within a lecture setting, there are also steps that one can take to encourage student confidence, interaction, and participation.

- Assessment and evaluation methods that provide useful and fair data on student experiences and knowledge. This information can be used to continuously improve course design.

The resources that we have compiled allow STEM instructors to gradually implement more strategies as they have time to do so. The literature review, for example, contains many recommendations for both faculty innovation and institutional change (Cabrera et al., 2004). From creating intervention and support programs to promoting collaborative learning, these actions can foster a welcoming environment for STEM students from underrepresented groups while also improving the academic climate for majority students.

Conclusion

Meeting the need for inclusive teaching requires both faculty and institutional commitment, and organizational developers and administrators play a vital role. Faculty will feel freer to experiment within their classrooms with institutional backing. More specifically, initial innovations may not be welcomed by students familiar with more traditional teaching methods; one possible outcome may be a short-term dip in teaching evaluations. Recent studies show that students who prefer a more didactic style of teaching, for example, may express discomfort with teaching methods that differ from what they expect (Kember, Jenkins, & Ng, 2004; Kember & Wong, 2000). It is the role of administrators and organizational developers to support their faculty through the transition to inclusive teaching methods. Institutional understanding can empower faculty to strive for teaching excellence, thus thawing out the chilly climate.

Author Note

Our resource development has been supported by the National Science Foundation, Grant 0227592. Any opinions, findings, and conclusions or recommendations expressed in this material are those of the authors and do not necessarily reflect the views of the National Science Foundation. We would like to acknowledge the contributions of the current and past members of the CIRTL diversity team, including Alberto Cabrera and Nilhan Gunasekera. Diversity Institute scholars from many universities contributed time and energy to this project. We also would like to thank CIRTL's leaders and staff for their support.

Correspondence concerning this chapter should be addressed to Katherine A. Friedrich, Center for the Integration of Research, Teaching, and Learning, University of Wisconsin–Madison, 552 Educational Sciences Building, Madison, WI 53706. Email: friedrich@wisc.edu.

References

Adams, M., Bell, L. A., & Griffin, P. (1997). *Teaching for diversity and social justice: A sourcebook.* New York, NY: Routledge.

Alexander, B. B., Burda, A. C., & Millar, S. B. (1997). A community approach to learning calculus: Fostering success for underrepresented ethnic minorities in an emerging scholars program. *Journal of Women and Minorities in Science and Engineering, 3*(3), 145–159.

Allen, C. (1999). Wiser women: Fostering undergraduate success in science and engineering with a residential academic program. *Journal of Women and Minorities in Science and Engineering, 5*(3), 265–277.

Barlow, A. E. L., & Villarejo, M. R. (2004). Making a difference for minorities: Evaluation of an educational enrichment program. *Journal of Research in Science Teaching, 41*(9), 861–881.

Burstyn, J. N., Sellers, S. L., Friedrich, K. A., & Gunasekera, N. (2006). [Workshop evaluations of CIRTL Diversity Resources]. Unpublished raw data.

Cabrera, A. F., Crissman, J. L., Bernal, E. M., Nora, A., Terenzini, P. T., & Pascarella, E. T. (2002, January/February). Collaborative learning: Its impact on college students' development and diversity. *Journal of College Student Development, 43*(1), 20–34.

Cabrera, A. F., Doyon, K., Friedrich, K., Roberts, J., Saleem, T., & Giovanetto, L. (2004). *Literature review.* Retrieved May 16, 2007, from the University of Wisconsin–Madison, Center for the Integration of Research, Teaching and Learning web site: http://cirtl.wceruw.org/DiversityInstitute/resources/annotated%2Dbibliography

Cabrera, A. F., & Nora, A. (1994). College students' perceptions of prejudice and discrimination and their feelings of alienation: A construct validation approach. *Review of Education/Pedagogy/Cultural Studies, 16*(3–4), 387–409.

Davis, B. G. (1993). *Tools for teaching.* San Francisco, CA: Jossey-Bass.

Felder, R. M. (1996). Teaching to all types: Examples from engineering education. *ASEE Prism, 6*(4), 18–23.

Ferreira, M. M. (2002). The research lab: A chilly place for graduate women. *Journal of Women and Minorities in Science and Engineering, 8*(1), 85–98.

Kember, D., Jenkins, W., & Ng, K. C. (2004, March). Adult students' perceptions of good teaching as a function of their conceptions of learning—Part 2. Implications for the evaluation of teaching. *Studies in Continuing Education, 26*(1), 81–97.

Kember, D., & Wong, A. (2000, July). Implications for evaluation from a study of students' perceptions of good and poor teaching. *Higher Education, 40*(1), 69–97.

Maton, K. I., Hrabowski, F. A., & Schmitt, C. L. (2000, September). African American college students excelling in the sciences: College and post-college outcomes in the Meyerhoff Scholars Program. *Journal of Research in Science Teaching, 37*(7), 629–654.

Moore, J. L., III, Madison-Colmore, O., & Smith, D. M. (2003, Fall). The prove-them-wrong syndrome: Voices from unheard African-American males in engineering disciplines. *Journal of Men's Studies, 12*(1), 61–73.

National Research Council. (1997). *Science teaching reconsidered: A handbook.* Washington, DC: National Academy Press.

Riley, D. (2003). Employing liberative pedagogies in engineering education. *Journal of Women and Minorities in Science and Engineering, 9*(2), 137–158.

Rosser, S. V. (1993). Female friendly science: Including women in curricular content and pedagogy in science. *Journal of General Education, 42*(3), 191–220.

Sellers, S. L., & Friedrich, K. A. (2006). *Unmasking inequality: A self-guided workshop on educational success.* Retrieved May 17, 2007, from the University of Wisconsin–Madison, Center for the Integration of Research, Teaching and Learning web site: http://cirtl.wceruw.org/DiversityInstitute/resources/workshops/

Sellers, S. L., Friedrich, K., Gunasekera, N., Saleem, T., & Burstyn, J. (2006). *Case studies in inclusive teaching in science, technology, engineering, and mathematics.* Madison, WI: University of Wisconsin–Madison, Center for the Integration of Research, Teaching, and Learning.

Sellers, S. L., Roberts, J., Giovanetto, L., & Friedrich, K. (2005). *Reaching all students: A resource for teaching in science, technology, engineering, and mathematics.* Madison, WI: University of Wisconsin–Madison, Center for the Integration of Research, Teaching, and Learning.

Seymour, E., & Hewitt, N. M. (1997). *Talking about leaving: Why undergraduates leave the sciences.* Boulder, CO: Westview Press.

Stahl, J. M. (2005, January). Research is for everyone: Perspectives from teaching at historically black colleges and universities. *Journal of Social and Clinical Psychology, 24*(1), 85–96.

Steele, C. M. (1997). A threat in the air: How stereotypes shape intellectual identity and performance. *American Psychologist, 52*(6), 613–629.

Tobias, S. (1990, July/August). They're not dumb. They're different. A new "tier of talent" for science. *Change, 22*(4), 10–30.

Treisman, U. (1992, November). Studying students studying calculus: A look at the lives of minority mathematics students in college. *College Mathematics Journal, 23*(5), 362–372.

Yanowitz, K. L. (2004). Do scientists help people? Beliefs about scientists and the influence of prosocial context on girls' attitudes towards physics. *Journal of Women and Minorities in Science and Engineering, 10*(4), 393–399.

Section V

Educational Development Centers and Professionals

10

Marketing Plans for Faculty Development: Student and Faculty Development Center Collaboration for Mutual Benefit

Victoria Mundy Bhavsar, Steven J. Skinner
University of Kentucky

Our faculty development center engaged senior-level business students as consultants to help us inform instructors about our resources. The students argued that organizational and marketing tasks are critical to our pedagogical work as they create opportunities for the pedagogical work to occur. This chapter describes the collaboration, the students' recommendations, and the center's response. Engaging students, our ultimate clients, in setting priorities for our center was a powerful learning experience for both us and them. Other centers may wish to use our experiences as impetus to collaborate with students on their campuses.

Teaching and faculty development centers are sometimes asked to argue their value to their institutions by demonstrating positive impacts in tangible terms, such as helping faculty to raise their student evaluations, make classes more accessible through the use of technology, and perhaps to find ways that they enjoy teaching more and so have higher morale. The catch is that a center can achieve these outcomes only if instructors participate in the center's activities and use its resources. A constant challenge for faculty development centers is to inform faculty and other instructors on their campuses about their services and resources, and a further problem is to convince instructors to use those services. Many centers find themselves struggling to create and maintain a strong presence on campus and to engage instructors. Brookfield (2007) observes, "For many of us, just getting teachers to show up at faculty development events is a triumph in itself" (p. 67). Issues of adding value, communicating to clients, and enticing clients are quite similar to the problems that businesses face when selling their products or services, and in fact faculty development centers have been likened to service firms within larger organizations (Nyquist, 1986).

Strategic marketing plans are often used as part of an organization's overall strategic plan. A marketing analysis provides detailed descriptions of the environment of the organization, the potential clientele or customers, an analysis of the organization itself, and specific goals and implementation plans for marketing the services or products of the organization. Almost any kind of organization can use a marketing plan, and many do, including universities (Cohen, 2006). Certainly teaching and faculty development centers can use strategic marketing plans, but a survey of two decades of *To Improve the Academy,* as well as a search of the Professional and Organizational Development Network's email listserv archives, indicated that centers may not use marketing plans much or at least do not communicate formally about their use of marketing plans. Practices and concepts from the business world are relevant for faculty development centers, but unless a member of a center's staff has a business background, no one in the center may have the expertise to apply business organization tools to the center's needs. Outside consultants can be sought, but they are usually costly.

The University of Kentucky's (UK) teaching center was a fairly new organization on campus and had been grappling with the well-known challenges just described. The center solved the problem of needing expert marketing advice by engaging senior-level business students as expert consultants. These students created full-length strategic marketing plans for the center as a capstone class project. This collaboration provided business expertise for the center, a client-based project for the students to apply their skills, and involved students deeply in teaching improvement initiatives on campus. Although students are the ultimate beneficiaries of a teaching center's services, they are not often included as partners in campus initiatives to improve teaching, and are even more rarely involved in setting priorities for the center (Cox & Sorenson, 2000). This chapter describes the collaboration between the teaching center and the students, the students' recommendations for the center's activities, and the center's response. We end with reflections on the relationship between the students and the center.

Institutional Background

UK is a land-grant research university with very high research activity and several professional schools. It has more than 25,000 students, nearly 2,000 full-time faculty members, approximately 450 part-time instructors, and about 1,900 graduate teaching assistants (GTAs). The Teaching and Academic Support Center (TASC) at UK was created in 2003 by combining several units that provided different kinds of assistance to teachers, including a traditional faculty development center. TASC's mission is to provide services to enhance undergraduate education at the university. Currently, the center has five resource or service groups: audio-visual, instructional technology, distance learning, graphics and multimedia, and educational (faculty) development. The total number of staff is about 50, with 3 devoted to educational development. TASC is located in one of the health science buildings at the southwestern edge of campus and has a small satellite facility in a large classroom building near the center of campus, where many undergraduate classes are held.

Educational development experienced a loss of visibility and usage on campus when the previous faculty development center, the Teaching and Learning Center (TLC), was incorporated into TASC. The TLC had high name recognition on campus. Faculty now talk about the loss of the TLC and its pedagogical resources without realizing that TASC has people who are equipped to help them. TASC itself has been perceived by some faculty and administrators as mostly a technology and audio-visual center. These misperceptions are marketing problems.

The Project

In summer 2005, a TASC staff member in the educational development group contacted the UK Gatton School of Business and Economics to locate a marketing class that would be willing to help address TASC's marketing problems. Dr. Steve Skinner, who taught the senior capstone marketing class, responded. The previous year, 2004–2005, Dr. Skinner had changed the design of the course from content delivery based on lectures, problems, and case studies, to a client-based, experiential class in which teams of students created marketing plans for local businesses or organizations. He had not yet identified local partners for his fall 2005 class and was willing to partner with TASC.

The class was divided into five teams of five students each. Early in the semester, a TASC staff member visited the class to introduce the center, describe its function in the university, and explain why the center wanted help. For the first part of the semester, the course proceeded traditionally, with students learning content through lectures, readings, and so on. In the last week of October, students began to apply their learning to TASC, engaging in a series of five progressive assignments that culminated in the production of their marketing plans. The teams presented their work on a weekly basis to each other and to a business faculty panel arranged by Dr. Skinner. The panel provided detailed, expert critique to the teams, who were directed to improve their work based on the feedback. The teams competed with one another every week for points. Dr. Skinner described the procedure as a cross between the popular television shows *The Apprentice* and *American Idol*, both featuring stiff competition and severe feedback.

During the creation of the plans, the student teams visited TASC, taking the initiative to make contact and set up meetings. They queried the heads of each service group about its clientele and work, perceived barriers to faculty's use of the service, and the service group's plans for the future. The director of TASC informed the students about the center's budget and categories of spending. The teams also examined TASC's web site. Three teams even created an email or phone survey that they administered to a small sample of UK faculty, department chairs, and deans. At the end of the semester, the center received all five marketing plans, and the group with the most points and the best marketing plan identified by Dr. Skinner won the competition. This winning plan was impressive in its thoughtfulness and professional presentation. Team members received a cash prize provided by TASC ($1,000 to split among themselves) and appropriately high grades. Other teams did not receive a prize but received appropriate grades. Every student in the class ended up with an authentic marketing product in hand to display to prospective employers.

The pedagogical benefits of client-based projects are well described in the marketing education literature (for a good summary, see Lopez & Lee, 2005) and include active learning, skill development in a realistic setting, and heightened motivation. The collaboration between Dr. Skinner's class and TASC represented a medium- to large-scale client-based project, one that could be completed in a few weeks but required students to do significant background work and produce a full-scale marketing analysis and plan (Lopez & Lee, 2005).

The Marketing Plans and TASC's Response

The students' reports were typical strategic marketing plans, each including an executive summary, an introduction, a situational analysis, a target market analysis, a SWOT (strengths, weaknesses, opportunities, threats) analysis, and marketing objectives, strategies, tactics, implementations, and controls. As the delineation of sections in marketing plans is not hard and fast, some repetitiveness among sections resulted.

Situational Analysis

The situational or environmental analysis contained the students' detailed descriptions of TASC and its place in the university. Students described objective factors such as the center's organizational structure and history, location, budget, staff complement, physical assets, and the like. This analysis also included legal issues such as confidentiality and adherence to the university's code of conduct, financial issues such as funding streams, and "social" or campus cultural issues such as the perception of TASC and the value placed on teaching improvement around campus. The students identified the center's competitors, the most important being the faculty's competing activities. TASC's limited use of media and technology to advertise itself was also a feature of the environment. In other words, the "situation" was the mise-en-scène in which the center operated.

The students analyzed how these environmental factors affected TASC's activities. One team described the center as having an identity problem owing to its location in the health sciences buildings instead of a central campus location appropriate to undergraduate education. The team described TASC's services as unmemorable because most services represented "just-in-time" problem solving, easily forgotten when the problem was solved, and reported that TASC was hampered by its pattern of waiting for faculty to approach rather than seeking opportunities to develop programs proactively. This team concluded that many of the center's resources were underutilized if instructors were not having (or not dealing with) problems, a result of the reactive ways of working that TASC had developed. While this analysis identified some negative environmental factors not under the center's control, it clearly showed that the center had created other negatives for itself.

Target Market Analysis

The target market analysis described faculty demographics such as age distribution, tenure status, and gender. Three of the five teams proposed ways to segment the target market of "all faculty" so that programs and services could be created for and directed to the people most likely to use them. One team proposed segmentation based on their perception of two major faculty orientations toward teaching improvement: "pioneers" or "set in their ways." Another team divided faculty into "high users" and "low users" of the center's services.

These students found that health science faculty were by far the highest users of TASC's technology and multimedia services, probably because these services had previously been available for health sciences and TASC was physically located in the health science area. Two teams, including the first team mentioned earlier, identified a group of unserved potential clients, GTAs, who were not included in TASC's responsibilities even though GTAs contributed to undergraduate education.

This section of the marketing plans was the least surprising to members of TASC, who were generally aware of the characteristics of teachers on campus. The most important outcome of the target market analyses was having undergraduate students so emphatically identify GTAs as contributing to undergraduate education. This opened the door, administratively, for the center to reach out to GTAs.

Strengths, Weaknesses, Opportunities, and Threats

All student teams identified similar strengths, weaknesses, opportunities, and threats for TASC. TASC's strengths included the wide variety of available teaching services—for example, someone with questions about engaging students could talk to an educational development specialist about active learning and to an instructional technologist about designing online activities. The fact that all of the center's services were free was another strength. In addition, TASC had no direct competition on campus, being the only teaching center. The students also perceived TASC as a resource for the university as it moved toward its goals of rising in the national institutional rankings, and they considered TASC's potential contributions to university goals as a strength.

To the students, TASC's most obvious weaknesses included its noncentral, low-visibility main facility, low name recognition on campus, lack of advertising and marketing, and an unsuccessful web site with an ineffective visual image. Two other weaknesses were more subtle. First, because the center was an amalgamation of several units, its staff did not have a history of working in teams across service unit lines. A lack of synergy, and therefore a lack of effectiveness, was the result. Second, the exclusion of GTAs was the result of an emphasis on dealing with faculty only. To complicate matters, GTA services were housed in the graduate school. The consequence was that TASC did not, and to some extent could not, engage this large segment of people who contributed to undergraduate education.

The students also identified several opportunities that TASC could capitalize on to become more effective around campus. In the marketing plans, "weaknesses" were reclassified as "opportunities" if they could be relatively easily addressed. The web site and the center's visual image were the most obvious of these weaknesses-turned-opportunities. A critical opportunity was the fact that, because TASC was a relatively new unit on campus, it still had time to develop an identity and to market its services. The students described TASC's specialized staff and their ability to learn and adopt new technology as points in its favor. An opportunity to extend the center's reach was the opening of a satellite office on the central campus. Finally, TASC's most vital opportunity was that most faculty on campus wanted to be good teachers and would use available resources for that goal, provided that the resources were the right ones at the right time.

Threats included outside factors that might negatively affect TASC's ability to gain recognition as the campus's central authority and resource for teaching improvement. Interestingly, the students described two issues as threats that, to TASC staff, were not threats at all. First, the students thought that if faculty talked to one another about teaching problems, rather than consult TASC, the center's position as the source of teaching expertise was threatened. Second, the students identified learning tools packaged in textbooks as threats for a similar reason. To the contrary, the center's personnel considered these other resources to be opportunities because they provided openings by which faculty might become interested in getting more and different resources that TASC could then provide.

The students all identified, unerringly, the worst threat to TASC and especially educational development: the lack of time for faculty and other teachers on campus to engage with the center's services. If instructors did not have time to use TASC's resources, the resources themselves would become useless. One team identified an emotional threat, namely faculty's real feelings about having problems with teaching. Educational development personnel had thought that faculty might not want to engage in development activities for fear of their colleagues' reactions ("If you need to go to the teaching center, you must be inferior"). The students found that faculty were actually more concerned about their own feelings of inadequacy ("If I need to go to the teaching center, I must be inferior"). This was a subtle but important distinction in thinking.

Marketing Objectives, Strategies, Implementations, and Controls

All student teams created similar objectives for TASC, although their target numbers differed somewhat. The students intended to increase awareness of TASC among all faculty, GTAs, and other instructors to 90%–100%, and they said that clients' satisfaction with the center's services should be high. All students intended to increase client usage by about 10%–20% per year. Finally, all teams suggested that TASC needed to be perceived positively by its target market. Certainly, these objectives were interrelated. The strength of the marketing plan was the clarity with which the students communicated criteria for success—the objectives were quantifiable and could be monitored. Students suggested strategies for accomplishing the objectives and monitoring progress at a level of detail that included naming the TASC members who should be responsible for implementing each tactic.

Every student team suggested changing the center's visual image on its web site and campus communications. The original visual image was a light, vertically fading teal depiction of the acronym TASC, with no representation of teaching. The students felt that the weak color did not convey strength and innovation, and the lack of a teaching symbol made the image ambiguous; the logo was not identifiable as that of a teaching resource center. Three teams presented new logos that they felt communicated the center's nature more clearly. Although TASC did not use these logos, its graphic and multimedia group did create a new image for the center's web site and communications. This image had bright colors and pictures of teachers and students.

Every student team also suggested refining the center's web site. The original one was composed of existing, unedited content from the web sites of the units that made up TASC. The site was hard to navigate, had no search engine, and few images. Most of the content was in large text blocks unsuitable for on-screen reading. In short, the original web site was unimpressive and unproductive, especially problematic for a center whose services included web site and instructional technology design and deployment. Finally, the site link was buried within the university web page rather than appearing prominently in resource lists for faculty and staff. In the web site redesign, all existing content was updated, corrected, and reorganized, and the educational development group created substantial new content for pedagogy and teaching resources. TASC plans to get a link placed on the university home page.

All of the students recommended increasing general advertising and promotion of TASC through such predictable methods as emails, flyers, posters, brochures, open houses, and promotional items. They suggested creating better signage for TASC's main facility, which was not easy to find in the health science building complex, and for the satellite facility on the central campus. Most importantly, the students emphasized that promotion needed to be "someone's job," rather than "everyone's job" (and therefore no one's job), and three teams suggested hiring a new staff member, or at least an intern or student worker, dedicated to marketing. At the time of this writing, signage has been enhanced for the satellite facility but not the main facility. Promotion and advertising are still haphazard although two recurring communications have debuted: an annual insert in the campus-wide faculty and staff newsletter and a weekly or biweekly educational development announcement email sent to a growing listserv.

Two of the five student teams suggested changing the center's name. TASC is pronounced "task," which is "a matter of considerable labor or difficulty" (Random House, 2006), and the students found this off-putting. Of course, the acronym stands for the "Teaching and Academic Support Center," but the students did not care for the word "support," either, as it implied to them that the center's clientele need crutches or counseling. These are not attractive messages to people whose identities depend on intellectual competence. One team proposed changing the center's name to the "Academic Center for Excellence," or ACE, as a strong, positive representation of the center's goals and position on campus. The other team suggested simply changing the word "support" to "service." Changing the center's name was more complicated than the students realized, and we did not act on this recommendation.

Most of the students realized the significance of enlisting faculty and administrators to promote the center. Although gathering administrative support and faculty buy-in are well recognized as critical steps in promoting faculty development (Aitken & Sorcinelli, 1994; Lang & DeCaro, 1989), students are typically unaware of the status of teaching on campus and the role of administrators in promoting teaching. We felt that the students' insight into the necessity of administrative support was quite impressive. One team proposed a "college ambassador" program in which one or two well-respected faculty members in each college would be paid a small stipend to forward messages and announce TASC events in their colleges. Another team suggested engaging our university's president, himself an enthusiastic former teacher, in a recurring informal event that would bring people together to talk about teaching. The third team recommended working closely with deans' offices to ensure the relevancy of the center's programs and the deans' help in promotion. TASC has begun to engage faculty members as advisors, but not as formal ambassadors, and it has begun cultivating relationships with deans and other upper administrators.

The students were unable to suggest effective solutions to one of TASC's most pressing concerns: how to create a single, cohesive, highly functional organization from five historically separate units. One team at least recognized the problem and proffered a limited solution: a four-step user process in which clients would create an online profile and check in online, meet with an initial consultant, identify and use appropriate services, and complete an evaluation. The purpose of this process was to gather and track data to ensure that clients' needs were completely identified and met, and any problems could be solved quickly and seamlessly. TASC had already implemented the two essential middle steps of this process. The center had also previously tried to create a relational database, which would have accomplished almost exactly what the students suggested. This initiative failed because some people had difficulty with the software and because some service groups were reluctant to participate. TASC is still working to become a fully mature, united, and completely effective organization.

The Students' Response

All of the students who participated in this project have now graduated. We were able to speak to two of the five students involved in the winning team. From the students' perspective, the collaboration provided a client-based situation in which they could learn and practice the skills involved in creating a marketing plan for a real organization. Both students reported that the client-based project was an excellent learning experience, a true capstone in the sense of integrating years of undergraduate learning. The competitive aspect of the project motivated this team and reflected the "real business world"; the prize was a nice bonus but was not the main motivation for their effort. Having the marketing plan to display was a positive factor in their employment searches.

These two students also reported that their team worked well together. They were able to decide which tasks could be effectively divided and assigned to individuals and which tasks needed to be handled face to face. Unlike some of the less successful teams, this team had five highly motivated members and none who dragged. Both students were pleased to have learned to work in teams to prepare themselves for careers that require constant collaboration. Interestingly, both students have been surprised at how much teamwork their jobs require.

Both students expressed appreciation for Dr. Skinner's work in arranging the experience for them. One student reported being disappointed by "knowing from the beginning that [their] ideas probably would not be used." This, of course, was a misperception, as TASC has adopted several of the students' important recommendations, but the student's words underline the need for client partners to follow up with students after projects are completed.

TASC's Response

As already described, the center tangibly responded to this collaborative project by implementing a number of the recommendations in the students' plans. This section explores what TASC staff members, in particular those staff in educational development who spearheaded the project, learned from seeing their organization, and even their profession, from an entirely new and unexpected viewpoint. Cox and Sorenson (2000) describe several ways that students have been invited to share their unique vantage point in teaching development—for example, as short- or long-term consultants or classroom observers, as members of faculty learning communities, and as participants and co-presenters in teaching seminars. All such activities empower students to improve teaching and learning. In this project, we empowered students by inviting them, as experts in their field, to advise us how to run our center and do our work better. What we did is no different from what we want faculty to do by seeking our expert services to improve their teaching.

If the experts have done their job well, a strategic marketing plan is a highly detailed, analytical document, sometimes painfully honest, that seriously addresses an organization's imperfections. As the students were relatively unhampered by considerations of university political issues and the history of our center, we saw our center through the eyes of young businesspeople whose sole concern was to solve our problems and help us sell our services, aggressively if necessary. Their basic themes were refreshingly straightforward: identify clientele and their needs, communicate widely both internally and around campus, and monitor client satisfaction. These tasks are neither difficult nor surprising, but they require constant work that is not directly related to pedagogy, advising, and the scholarship of teaching. The students pointed out that organizational and marketing tasks are as important to our pedagogical work as the pedagogical work itself as they create opportunities for the pedagogical work to occur. For us, this was a significant realization, requiring a shift from insisting on our own priorities to valuing the priorities of our clients. Previously it had been easy to give lip service to client needs while continuing with business as usual, but we could not change our clientele's priorities without changing our own first.

We were surprised at the power these ideas took on because they came from students. For us, the students had a dual identity as outside experts and our ultimate clients. In their roles of outside experts, they did impressively professional work. Because of their roles as our ultimate clients, we could not ignore the students' thoughtful analysis and unequivocal directions. Of course, we cannot say what our response would have been to nonstudent, professional, paid consultants, but our sense is that students' ideas were more meaningful to us, more likely to be taken seriously, especially because their work was so good.

We did not consider our center "weak" because of issues with reaching and engaging our clientele. To reiterate an earlier point, soliciting high participation is a constant challenge for faculty development centers at many universities and colleges. The challenge is more difficult for a newly formed center such as TASC, and we look forward to greater success as we implement our marketing plans. Involving students, our ultimate clients, benefited us, and the students themselves benefited by completing a meaningful project for a real organization on their campus. We hope that our experience with the students will stimulate other faculty development centers to consider partnering with business students on their campuses.

References

Aitken, N. D., & Sorcinelli, M. D. (1994). Academic leaders and faculty developers: Creating an institutional culture that values teaching. In E. C. Wadsworth (Ed.), *To improve the academy: Vol. 13. Resources for faculty, instructional, and organizational development* (pp. 63–77). Stillwater, OK: New Forums Press.

Brookfield, S. D. (2007). A critical theory perspective on faculty development. In D. R. Robertson & L. B. Nilson (Eds.), *To improve the academy: Vol. 25. Resources for faculty, instructional, and organizational development* (pp. 55–69). Bolton, MA: Anker.

Cohen, W. A. (2006). *The marketing plan* (5th ed.). Hoboken, NJ: John Wiley & Sons.

Cox, M. D., & Sorenson, L. D. (2000). Student collaboration in faculty development: Connecting directly to the learning revolution. In M. Kaplan & D. Lieberman (Eds.), *To improve the academy: Vol. 18. Resources for faculty, instructional, and organizational development* (pp. 97–127). Bolton, MA: Anker.

Lang, H. G., & DeCaro, J. J. (1989). Support from the administration: A case study in the implementation of a grassroots faculty development program. In S. Kahn (Ed.), *To improve the academy: Vol. 8. Resources for student, faculty, and institutional development* (pp. 71–79). Stillwater, OK: New Forums Press.

Lopez, T. B., & Lee, R. G. (2005). Five principles for workable client-based projects: Lessons from the trenches. *Journal of Marketing Education, 27*(2), 172–188.

Nyquist, J. D. (1986). CIDR: A small service firm within a research university. In M. Svinicki, J. Kurfiss, & J. Stone (Eds.), *To improve the academy: Vol. 5. Resources for student, faculty, and institutional development* (pp. 66–83). Stillwater, OK: New Forums Press.

Random House. (2006). *Random House unabridged dictionary.* Retrieved May 17, 2007, from http://dictionary.reference.com/browse/task

11

Faculty Development at Small and Liberal Arts Colleges

Kim M. Mooney
St. Lawrence University

Michael Reder
Connecticut College

The notable growth of faculty development programs and centers at small institutions warrants attention before their next stages of growth. We aim to capture and convey the central issues coalescing around the professionalization of teaching and learning activities and the work of faculty developers at small colleges. While this descriptive review draws direct comparisons to other types of institutions, particularly large research and comprehensive universities that serve as the norm for our profession's faculty development practices, its main purpose is to address the distinctive characteristics of professional development at small colleges in general and liberal arts colleges in particular. Toward this end, we identify and explore four key issues: the characteristics and traditions related to teaching and learning in these institutional settings; the models and structures for teaching and learning programs at such colleges; the distinctive components of successful faculty development work at such institutions; and the broad applications that small college programs have for other institutional types and the future of our profession.

The past seven years have witnessed tremendous growth in the professionalization of faculty development at small colleges, particularly at residential liberal arts colleges. We have seen steady growth since 1999 in many relevant areas: small college membership and attendance at the annual conference of the Professional and Organizational Development Network in Higher Education (POD); the number of conference sessions about small college issues at this conference (recently close to a dozen); the creation of a formal Small College Committee within the POD governance system; and the number of subscribers to the small college listserv, from just over a few dozen members in fall 2001, to almost 100 members in 2004, to more than 160 members in fall 2006. In 2002, the conference officially inaugurated the position of small college conference coordinator. According to POD membership data from 2006 broken down by Carnegie institutional classifications, almost 80% of doctoral-extensive (119 out of 151) institutions are POD members, but for baccalaureate liberal arts and baccalaureate general, the percentages are still relatively low: fewer than 15% (34 out of 228) and 10% (32 out of 321), respectively. Therefore, the growth potential among small baccalaureate institutions, in terms of both percentages and raw numbers, is tremendous.

Emerging issues in and changing models of higher education have led to a growing need for faculty development at colleges and universities, including liberal arts colleges (Lieberman & Guskin, 2003; Mooney, Reder, & Holmgren, 2005). Yet with a few notable exceptions (e.g., Sorcinelli, Austin, Eddy, & Beach, 2006), the professional literature has not directly addressed the professional experiences, programming goals, and other potentially distinctive issues and concerns of faculty development at liberal arts and other small colleges. The relatively low representation of small college faculty developers in recent surveys about practices and support structures at different institutional types (Brinko, Atkins, & Miller, 2005; Frantz, Beebe, Horvath, Canales, & Swee, 2005; Mullinix & Chism, 2005) is most likely due to the still relatively small cohort size. Nevertheless, as faculty development programs and centers continue to proliferate at smaller institutions, identifying the distinctive features of this work and the elements of successful small college programs should prove helpful during the next growth stages of this professional sector.

The Characteristics of Teaching and Learning at Small Colleges

We are often asked by our colleagues exactly just what the term *small college* means. With no litmus test for "small," those faculty developers interested in the small college movement and the POD Small College Committee have traditionally self-identified. That said, these self-identifiers generally work at institutions with at least some of these characteristics: the institution is predominantly undergraduate and teaching is a main mission; it has a faculty under 250 and few if any graduate students; classes are usually small, from 15 to upwards of 30 students; the faculty developer may operate with little or no budget, space, or support staff; and most activities and conversations about teaching take place face to face. Of these various traits, overall culture is key, especially the value placed on teaching.

Here we aim to capture and convey the central issues coalescing around the professionalization of teaching and learning activities and the work of faculty developers at small colleges. While this descriptive review draws direct comparisons to other types of institutions, particularly large research and comprehensive universities that serve as the norm for our profession's faculty development practices, its main purpose is to address the distinctive characteristics of professional development at liberal arts colleges and its connection to the type of education these institutions typically offer. Toward this end, we address four key issues: the characteristics and traditions related to teaching and learning in these institutional settings; the models and structures for teaching and learning programs at such colleges; the distinctive components of successful faculty development at such institutions; and the future trends and issues small college faculty developers will likely need to address through their programming and as they continue to shape the future of our profession.

Perhaps more so at liberal arts colleges than anywhere else in American higher education, exceptional teaching is explicitly sought, expected, and valued. But often new faculty at these institutions quickly realize that they lack the pedagogical training necessary to meet these expectations. Authors elsewhere have noted that faculty responsibilities and cultures at liberal arts and small residential colleges differ markedly from those at the research universities in which most of us were trained (Gibson, 1992). Even high-quality, discipline-specific training does not prepare us for the scope and variety of demands we face in small college faculty roles (Reder & Gallagher, 2007; Rice, Sorcinelli, & Austin, 2000).

According to the most recent national data from the Higher Education Research Institute (HERI) (Lindholm, Szelény, Hurtado, & Korn, 2005), the percentage of full-time undergraduate faculty with a major interest in teaching varies by institution type: 17% for public and private university faculty and 35% for public and private four-year colleges. Yet ironically, the most established faculty support at four-year colleges is for disciplinary *scholarship*, especially as most of these institutions offer sabbaticals, many pre-tenure, which are usually geared toward supporting research agendas. Almost universally, colleges and universities have strong systems for funding faculty research and disciplinary conference presentations. They view scholarship as a public enterprise that can and should be replicated, extended, and critiqued by peers.

Even at colleges that claim to value teaching, faculty members do not expect to engage in such communal activity in regard to teaching. As Reder and

Gallagher (2007) argue, small colleges that claim to emphasize teaching must put resources behind "promoting the critical discussion of teaching"; "such schools can no longer get away with giving mere lip service to valuing teaching" (p. 339). At most small institutions, unlike many large universities, teaching is assumed to be important, and this assumption may allow such schools (or faculty) to get away with avoiding teaching issues, relying on the false logic of "We all value teaching; that is why we are here; therefore, we must all be good at it." The increased participation by small college faculty developers in POD and the growing number of small colleges initiating formal faculty development programs and teaching and learning centers reveal growing recognition of the need to formally support continuing pedagogical education. Evidence also suggests that faculty at these institutions are taking advantage of this emerging support. When asked whether they had participated in a faculty development program in the past two years, 79% of the four-year college faculty responded that they had, compared to only 49% of the university faculty, according to the HERI data (Lindholm et al., 2005). Yet both types of faculty overwhelmingly maintain the personal goal of being a good teacher (97% at universities and 98% at four-year institutions) (Lindholm et al., 2005).

In spite of their deep interest in teaching, faculty at smaller colleges report experiencing greater stress from the demands of their teaching loads than do their colleagues at larger universities (Lindholm et al., 2005). They also report spending more time teaching and preparing for teaching, including grading, and they are less satisfied with their teaching loads.

Given the differing teaching expectations and experiences between faculty at small colleges and larger universities, it is no surprise that the nature of faculty development varies by institutional type. According to national survey data (Sorcinelli et al., 2006), faculty developers at liberal arts colleges focus more on creating or sustaining cultures of teaching excellence and advancing initiatives in teaching and learning than do their colleagues at research/doctoral institutions and community colleges. Both groups are more concerned about providing support to faculty having difficulty. The researchers speculate that this finding reflects the continued emphasis on excellent teaching in the liberal arts even while many smaller schools are emphasizing scholarly production. In some ways, this dual focus suits the newer faculty cohorts, which value active scholarship (Stimpert, 2004).

This research suggests that, beyond offering formal programs to support effective teaching, faculty developers need to be aware of the teaching issues that create stress for their faculty. Teaching effectively at a small college, and therefore successful faculty development, is not just about pedagogy; it requires attending to the tenuous and often daunting balance between teaching and scholarly pursuits. Teaching and scholarly expectations at small schools, especially with the growing emphasis on faculty-mentored student research, have important implications for creating and funding faculty development programs that address concerns beyond the confines of the traditional classroom.

Models and Structures of Faculty Development Programs

Sorcinelli et al.'s (2006) data indicate a notable increase during the past 15 years in the number of centralized faculty development units with dedicated staff, when compared to the less formal efforts organized by a single administrator or advisory committee. This trend toward formal structures is particularly evident among research and doctoral institutions, where 72% report a centralized unit dedicated to faculty development. Liberal arts colleges report the smallest percentage of centralized structures (24%) and the largest percentage of "one-person" programs. Small colleges also report the highest reliance on advisory boards.

While larger university centers usually employ a full-time director and often full-time professional and clerical staff, no predominant administrative structure exists for smaller colleges. Faculty development—where faculty engage in conversations about teaching and learning in particular—can and does happen anywhere. But when these diffuse and sometimes haphazard forays become centralized, it is often less about a *physical* space for faculty development than about one person or a group of persons who coordinate and advance the efforts. Whether part of the portfolio of an associate dean, the purview of a faculty development committee, or as the job of a particular individual (frequently with an advisory board), the "center" is often, unlike in our university brethren, a metaphorical one. Indeed, several of the more prominent small college faculty development programs/centers have no physical space. Peter Frederick has long argued that at a small college, having physical space is not necessary and can in fact deter a program's success. We do believe that having a center, even if it is so only in name, gives a program a place and identity on campus, especially on a campus where centers have status (P. Frederick, personal communication, November 26, 2004). A center is the "place" where things happen, where things are embedded and made visible.

Faculty development models and administrative responsibilities vary widely among liberal arts and smaller institutions, and each may be very effective for its campus culture. A number of liberal arts colleges dedicate physical space for centers and are led by a director selected from among the tenured faculty (e.g., Colorado College, St. Lawrence University, and Whitman College). Others have center directors with offices but no dedicated program space (e.g., Connecticut College and Muhlenberg College), while a few are managed out of the dean's office (e.g., Allegheny College and Southwestern University).

Faculty developers often emerge from the tenure-track faculty ranks (Mullinix & Chism, 2005), but at smaller colleges, the job is seldom full-time with a dedicated staff. Although these individuals consider faculty status critical to their credibility (Mullinix & Chism, 2005), their continuing to teach, advise students, publish in their disciplines, and serve on committees creates a challenging "many hats syndrome." In an informal poll of 16 small college faculty developers at a recent 2006 POD small college business meeting, 10 out of 16 (63%) reported time as their most pressing or only challenge. Most of the time pressures derived from the multiple roles directors fulfill on their campuses, followed by the demands of the faculty for whom they design and implement programming.

Not only are small college faculty developers pressed to find time to serve their faculty, but their names often become synonymous with faculty development. The strong identification of one person to this role is more than a function of campus size; it also reflects the nascent stage of faculty development at liberal arts colleges. These two interdependent issues, person-program identity and first-generation developers, present a challenge to the continuity and sustainability of faculty development work at a small college.

Sustainability may be the single most critical issue facing small college faculty development. Because at many small colleges no formal administrative structure for faculty development exists—such as a dedicated staff line that needs to be filled and a predictable, continuing budget to support activities—ongoing programming often sits precariously between success and oblivion. For example, when faculty development is centralized under an individual dean or faculty member, that person's sabbatical or return to the faculty may jeopardize all that he or she accomplished. Faculty development committees may also face the same challenge when the chair rotates and members move on and off, bringing on new people with little knowledge of faculty development. In addition, the faculty development coordinator must single-handedly offer the full range of services, some of which would be distributed to other staff at larger institutions. So the faculty developer running a "single-person" program is under pressure to have command of the ever growing faculty development field.

Because we find ourselves among the first generation of faculty tapped to lead faculty development programs/centers at small colleges, and because this position requires reeducating and retooling beyond our disciplines, many of us lack local mentors or colleagues. On larger campuses with multiperson centers where faculty development has thrived for years, mentors are more readily available. Therefore, the emerging national network of small college faculty developers becomes a significant and often sole source of critical and creative professional feedback. Perhaps equally important, the practitioners at larger institutions who wish to mentor those of us at smaller colleges need to understand the differences and similarities between small college and large university faculty development work.

Features of Successful Small College Faculty Development Work

Peter Frederick, a long-time advocate and original organizer of small college faculty development work and the founder of Carleton College's Learning and Teaching Center, recommends that small college faculty developers look for programming opportunities wherever faculty (or faculty and students) routinely come together within *their* particular campus culture. Specifically, he suggests embedding programs in staff planning meetings, in core and capstone courses, and in team-taught introductory courses. In busy faculty lives where going to a workshop, however inviting, is just one more thing on an overflowing plate, these already established settings are where the best, most practical, and most immediately useful holistic "development" can take place (P. Frederick, personal communication, November 26, 2004).

In spite of the time constraints of those directing faculty development programs at small colleges, the small college publication record in the past four volumes of *To Improve the Academy* (2004–2007) shows that successful programs do get implemented on small college campuses. Whether focusing on mentoring new faculty (Fayne & Ortquist-Ahrens, 2006; Reder & Gallagher, 2007) or promoting innovative pedagogies (Blumberg, 2004; Mooney, Fordham, & Lehr, 2005) or creating opportunities for ongoing special-topic conversations (Holmgren, 2005; Jones, 2005), these programs described in *To Improve the Academy* share several common elements. First and perhaps most importantly, faculty participation was voluntary; no faculty members were remanded or cajoled into attending a single meeting. Second, in five of the six programs just cited, people committed to a series of meetings with the same community of colleagues, even if the designated topics changed. In addition, leaders established regular meeting times, provided common readings, and guided participants in ways to provide regular feedback to one another. Finally, almost all of the programs dedicated time to participant reflection on the learning process and outcomes of their participation in the faculty development program. The differences among these programs are relatively superficial—for example, at least one offered stipends for faculty participation but most did not; at least one was almost entirely electronic; and at least one had fewer than 6 continuing participants while another had more than 15.

Success or failure of faculty development programs on small college campuses has a unique economy of scale, and it is one that we encourage colleagues to consider as they prioritize their program planning. On a small college campus, a workshop that attracts 30 faculty members may reach almost 20% of the total faculty at once and could be a transformative experience for the faculty, exposing a significant proportion of the faculty to something new. However, if the workshop is not well received or perceived as useful, 20% of the faculty are potentially alienated. On a small college campus where the entire faculty knows each other by name, there is also a multiplier effect: If each of those 30 faculty speaks with one other person about his or her experience, whether good or bad, then suddenly 40% of the faculty can be impacted by a single event. In addition, with such a small faculty, where there are a limited number of people to attend seemingly unlimited numbers of campus events, "overprogramming" is always a threat. Colleagues at other small schools have corroborated this problem: With so much going on (e.g., special speakers, job search talks), we often bring to campus well-known (and sometimes expensive) speakers/facilitators, and fewer than 12 people end up coming—even after a lot of effort promoting the event. The faculty are not indifferent, just busy. So we have to plan thoughtfully, develop creative collaborations with other offices and divisions, and diligently use the campus master calendar.

Describing a single faculty development workshop or a semester-long program as successful is certainly a function of the local campus and faculty culture, but in our collective (albeit time-limited) experience in program planning and implementation, we offer seven recommendations to colleagues just starting out as faculty development coordinators or directors on small college campuses (Reder & Mooney, 2004):

- Create an advisory board and include a few "unusual suspects."

- Make your program/center a place of excellence.

- Start with one program and do it very well.

- Use the talent pool on your own campus.

- Generate grassroots interest in your programs *before* announcing them to the faculty.

- Continue to attend conferences in higher education (POD, Association of American Colleges and Universities, etc.).

- Provide refreshments to acknowledge that you value colleagues' time.

As the momentum behind faculty development programs at small colleges continues to grow, not only will this list expand, but so too will the number of contributors to it.

Future Trends in Small College Faculty Development

The changing and multicultural demographics of college students continue to increase new instructional opportunities for and demands on faculty preparation time and workload, and the support faculty developers provide must be responsive to these evolving realities (Rice, 2006; Sorcinelli et al., 2006). The digital literacy of college students and their daily exposure, applications, and saturation levels "lead to pedagogical challenges . . . as (faculty) search for the means to teach Net generation students in a manner that capitalizes on the group's technology-driven lifestyle and fosters quality liberal learning" (Carey, 2006, p. 3; see also Oblinger & Oblinger, 2005). As instructional roles and classroom settings continue to expand and change, the need for faculty to learn new skills and to teach differently will require increased, not compromised, support (Lieberman & Guskin, 2003). Whether differences in the future work for small and large institutions are more about scale and scope than about the nature of the educational issues remains to be seen.

Despite some agreement, there is no clear consensus among faculty developers on the direction of our professional foci over the next 10 years, nor is there tremendous overlap in perceptions of how the field should change and how it is likely to change (Sorcinelli et al., 2006). Undoubtedly, faculty development will respond to the continued emphasis on outcomes assessment generated by regional accreditation agencies and more recently by the Spellings Commission report and higher education's responses to it (U.S. Department of Education, 2006). In addition, the field will address two other engines of change: the role of technology in teaching and learning and the nature of the faculty workforce itself. Even on small college campuses, the impact of technology and new faculty cohorts and appointment types will likely impact faculty development work.

The Role of Technology at Small Colleges

Recent national survey data indicate that faculty developers are well aware of the force behind the movement to integrate technology into teaching, learning, and many other dimensions of higher education, but they do not uncritically embrace technology as a central focus for future faculty development efforts (Sorcinelli et al., 2006). "The electronic learning environment requires thinking differently about delivery, content, and student feedback. It is critical that the academy focuses not only on the importance of technological delivery, but also on the pedagogy involved in this process" (Lieberman & Guskin, 2003, p. 265). Perhaps because technology leaders at small colleges are at a disadvantage in terms of economies of scale, they may feel as if they are always playing catch-up with their peers at larger institutions. Rather than look merely at the current role of technology at small colleges (e.g., see Smallen & Leach, 2004), studies need to explore the *ideal* roles for instructional technology by framing the issue squarely within the literature about student learning and teaching with technology (Chickering & Ehrmann, 1996; Ehrmann, n.d.), as well as within the context of a small college focused on teaching. In various national forums, academic leaders from liberal arts institutions have raised legitimate questions and sometimes conflicting viewpoints about the role that technology can and should play on their campuses, particularly in relation to student learning. This lack of consensus represents a common disparity in perceptions among liberal arts faculty and among faculty developers. What faculty development programs need to do, however, is facilitate the discussions around the role of technology in student learning.

Liberal arts and other small institutions that emphasize small classes and face-to-face interaction are less likely to be spending faculty development time and resources on online course design and implementation, another place where the role of technology at small colleges differs greatly from that at larger institutions. Faculty developers should raise and address questions like these: What role does and should instructional technology play in the distinctive setting of small residential liberal arts colleges? To what degree does technology play into the strengths that small liberal arts colleges have to offer: intimate classes, a great deal of student and faculty contact, and the opportunity for one-on-one individualized study and research? What evidence indicates that teaching with technology plays a central or transformative role in the learning process? Does the faculty member teaching a 12-person seminar at a liberal arts college *need* technology in the same ways that a peer teaching a 300-student lecture course at a larger institution might? At both small and large institutions, technology *does* have the potential to increase student learning, but the distinct issues related to technology and the small college have yet to be studied systematically.

The Faculty Workforce at Small Colleges

Planning future faculty development programming in educational technologies extends beyond training faculty in new classroom pedagogies and applications. Advances in educational technologies lead to the "unbundling of the faculty role" (Rice, 2007, p. 14), and when coupled with the proliferation of nontenure-track faculty appointments, the implications for faculty developers are challenging. Increasingly, faculty developers may be positioned to support instructors who come to teaching with nonacademic backgrounds and assume nontraditional faculty roles in the academy. Although small colleges may not experience the changing nature of faculty appointments as much as larger universities, no institution type is immune from the need to consider how to support and respond to the changing demographics and workload issues of future faculty members.

According to the most recent HERI data, at least 43% of responding faculty perceive mentoring new faculty as among the highest priorities of their institutions, regardless of size (Lindholm et al., 2005). As the small college session topics and attendance at the past three POD conferences attest, small college faculty developers are very interested in implementing constructive new faculty orientation and mentoring programs on their campuses. Far less is known or widely discussed about faculty needs and issues at other points in their careers.

The professional issues and transitions of faculty in post-probationary years are currently ill defined but warrant attention in order for institutions to benefit from the experience of mid-career faculty (Baldwin & Chang, 2006). In a recent study on support for mid-career faculty, Baldwin and Chang (2006) discovered that while colleges and universities are beginning to pay attention to faculty in this career phase, few programs approach their support or programming in coordinated or comprehensive ways. Connecting faculty across generations may be a challenge worth pursuing as senior and junior colleagues have much to gain from each other. Certainly, early-career faculty might benefit from the institutional wisdom a senior colleague might offer about issues ranging from a college's priorities to a deeper appreciation of its students (Rice et al., 2000). On smaller campuses where administrative leadership is less layered and often harvested from faculty ranks, it is critical for more senior colleagues to mentor recently tenured and mid-career faculty to help prepare them for such leadership positions. One constructive byproduct of such mentoring is that the sincere solicitation of senior colleagues' pragmatic advice may encourage detached faculty to reinvest in the institution even as they grow closer to retirement. Creating model programs that include and draw on the experiences of senior faculty to support mid-career faculty is one area where small colleges can make significant contributions. Especially at small colleges, where senior administrators often rise from the faculty ranks, the need to develop the next generation of leadership is overdue for sustained and coherent attention.

Charting Our Course for the Future of Small College Teaching and Learning

What may distinguish small colleges, particularly residential liberal arts colleges, from their larger institutional counterparts is the creation and support of a community of learners. In fact, we believe this mission is central to faculty development programs at small institutions. One reason we employ and favor the term *center for teaching and learning* to describe our work is the idea of a "center," a component that is central for the day-to-day operations of our colleges. Even if a center has no physical space, our programs provide a *metaphorical center* for the many activities related to teaching and learning that occur daily across our campuses. Our programming serves as a crossroads of sorts, where issues as diverse as support for early-career faculty, curriculum design, general education, learning outcomes and assessment, information fluency, and technology all come together under the guiding principle of supporting faculty teaching to enhance student learning.

According to Sorcinelli et al.'s (2006) data, faculty developers at liberal arts institutions believe that their efforts should continue to be planned and directed *by* the faculty in response *to* the faculty. Faculty development programs are distinctively situated at small colleges to play a neutral role focused on improving student learning rather than advancing any partisan cause. At Connecticut College, for example, the president asked the Center for Teaching and Learning (CTL) to run a series of discussions focused on diversity in the curriculum; the dean of the faculty and the faculty curriculum committee requested that the CTL kick-start the revision of the general education program by hosting a series of discussions and dinners; and the main faculty governance committee asked the CTL to design a new program to connect entering faculty with their more senior, tenured colleagues across the disciplines. Similarly, since its inception in 2001, the Center for Teaching and Learning at St. Lawrence University has engaged in a wide range of programming and initiatives and strives to be responsive to emerging curricular issues on campus. For example, in its short history, the annual end-of-the-year May Faculty College has evolved into a strategic planning conference that draws together a significant number of faculty from across the disciplines to discuss the theory and practice of teaching and learning in liberal education. A well-established and productive partnership with the educational technologies staff has generated annual technology programs in August and January and most recently led to the co-development of a best practices web site for faculty to share their pedagogical innovations.

The programming goals of all of these initiatives may seem diverse, but they all are ultimately focused on improving student learning, even those seemingly focused on issues of improving faculty experiences or changing curricula. They go about advancing these goals by creating opportunities for faculty to come together in a public setting to share their ideas about curriculum, classroom teaching, and student learning. While the primary faculty development goals may not differ between larger, more research-oriented universities and smaller, mostly residential colleges, we believe the teaching and learning expectations and faculty development work at these small colleges are sufficiently unique to warrant continued exploration, discussion, and collaboration among faculty development colleagues across the profession.

References

Baldwin, R. G., & Chang, D. A. (2006, Fall). Reinforcing our "keystone" faculty: Strategies to support faculty in the middle years of academic life. *Liberal Education, 92*(4), 28–36.

Blumberg, P. (2004). Documenting the educational innovations of faculty: A win-win situation for faculty and the faculty development center. In C. M. Wehlburg & S. Chadwick-Blossey (Eds.), *To improve the academy: Vol. 22. Resources for faculty, instructional, and organizational development* (pp. 41–51). Bolton, MA: Anker.

Brinko, K. T., Atkins, S. S., & Miller, M. E. (2005). Looking at ourselves: The quality of life of faculty development professionals. In S. Chadwick-Blossey & D. R. Robertson (Eds.), *To improve the academy: Vol. 23. Resources for faculty, instructional, and organizational development* (pp. 93–110). Bolton, MA: Anker.

Carey, S. J. (2006, Fall). From the editor. *Peer Review: Learning & Technology, 8*(4), 3.

Chickering, A., & Ehrmann, S. C. (1996, October). Implementing the seven principles: Technology as lever. *AAHE Bulletin, 49*(2). Retrieved May 17, 2007, from www.tltgroup.org/programs/seven.html

Ehrmann, S. C. (n.d.). *Asking the right question: What does research tell us about technology and higher learning?* Retrieved May 17, 2007, from www.tltgroup.org/resources/Flashlight/AskingRightQuestion.htm

Fayne, H., & Ortquist-Ahrens, L. (2006). Learning communities for first-year faculty: Transition, acculturation, and transformation. In S. Chadwick-Blossey & D. R. Robertson (Eds.), *To improve the academy: Vol. 24. Resources for faculty, instructional, and organizational development* (pp. 277–290). Bolton, MA: Anker.

Frantz, A. C., Beebe, S. A., Horvath, V. S., Canales, J., & Swee, D. E. (2005). The roles of teaching and learning centers. In S. Chadwick-Blossey & D. R. Robertson (Eds.), *To improve the academy: Vol. 23. Resources for faculty, instructional, and organizational development* (pp. 72–90). Bolton, MA: Anker.

Gibson, G. W. (1992). *Good start: A guidebook for new faculty in liberal arts colleges.* Bolton, MA: Anker.

Holmgren, R. A. (2005). Teaching partners: Improving teaching and learning by cultivating a community of practice. In S. Chadwick-Blossey & D. R. Robertson (Eds.), *To improve the academy: Vol. 23. Resources for faculty, instructional, and organizational development* (pp. 211–219). Bolton, MA: Anker.

Jones, L. F. (2005). Exploring the inner landscape of teaching: A program for faculty renewal. In S. Chadwick-Blossey & D. R. Robertson (Eds.), *To improve the academy: Vol. 23. Resources for faculty, instructional, and organizational development* (pp. 130–143). Bolton, MA: Anker.

Lieberman, D. A., & Guskin, A. E. (2003). The essential role of faculty development in new higher education models. In C. M. Wehlburg & S. Chadwick-Blossey (Eds.), *To improve the academy: Vol. 21. Resources for faculty, instructional, and organizational development* (pp. 257–272). Bolton, MA: Anker.

Lindholm, J. A., Szelény, K., Hurtado, S., & Korn, W. S. (2005). *The American college teacher: National norms for the 2004–2005 HERI faculty survey.* Los Angeles, CA: University of California–Los Angeles, Higher Education Research Institute.

Mooney, K. M., Fordham, T., & Lehr, V. D. (2005). A faculty development program to promote engaged classroom dialogue: The Oral Communication Institute. In S. Chadwick-Blossey & D. R. Robertson (Eds.), *To improve the academy: Vol. 23. Resources for faculty, instructional, and organizational development* (pp. 220–235). Bolton, MA: Anker.

Mooney, K., Reder, M., & Holmgren, R. (2005, January). *Transforming teaching cultures: The need for teaching and learning programs at liberal arts colleges.* Paper presented at the annual meeting of the Association of American Colleges and Universities, San Francisco, CA.

Mullinix, B. B., & Chism, N. V. N. (2005, October). *The faculty status of faculty developers: A collaborative construction and collective explorations.* Paper presented at the 30th annual meeting of the Professional and Organizational Development Network in Higher Education, Milwaukee, WI.

Oblinger, D. G., & Oblinger, J. L. (Eds.). (2005). *Educating the net generation.* Boulder, CO: Educause.

Professional and Organizational Development Network in Higher Education. (2006). *POD institutional membership by Carnegie classification.* Internal POD Network Document.

Reder, M., & Gallagher, E. V. (2007). Transforming a teaching culture through peer mentoring: Connecticut College's Johnson Teaching Seminar for Incoming Faculty. In D. R. Robertson & L. B. Nilson (Eds.), *To improve the academy: Vol. 25. Resources for faculty, instructional, and organizational development* (pp. 327–344). Bolton, MA: Anker.

Reder, M., & Mooney, K. (2004, November). *Getting started in small college faculty development.* Roundtable at the 29th annual meeting of the Professional and Organizational Development Network in Higher Education, Montreal, Canada.

Rice, R. E. (2006, Fall). From Athens and Berlin to LA: Faculty work and the new academy. *Liberal Education, 92*(4), 6–13.

Rice, R. E. (2007). It all started in the Sixties: Movements for change across the decades—A personal journey. In D. R. Robertson & L. B. Nilson (Eds.), *To improve the academy: Vol. 25. Resources for faculty, instructional, and organizational development* (pp. 3–17). Bolton, MA: Anker.

Rice, R. E., Sorcinelli, M. D., & Austin, A. E. (2000). *Heeding new voices: Academic careers for a new generation.* Washington, DC: American Association for Higher Education.

Smallen, D., & Leach, K. (2004). *Information technology benchmarks: A practical guide for college and university presidents.* Washington, DC: Council of Independent Colleges.

Sorcinelli, M. D., Austin, A. E., Eddy, P. L., & Beach, A. L. (2006). *Creating the future of faculty development: Learning from the past, understanding the present.* Bolton, MA: Anker.

Stimpert, J. L. (2004, July/August). Turbulent times: Four issues facing liberal arts colleges. *Change, 36*(4), 42–49.

U.S. Department of Education. (2006). *A test of leadership: Charting the future of U.S. higher education.* Washington, DC: Author.

12

Credibility and Effectiveness in Context: An Exploration of the Importance of Faculty Status for Faculty Developers

Bonnie Mullinix
Furman University

This study documents an emerging profile of the faculty status of faculty developers as solicited, compiled, and interactively interpreted with faculty developer practitioners. It used integrated (mixed) methodology and participatory research strategies to gather data and it shares descriptive statistical information on the various positions held by faculty developer respondents; qualitatively analyzed impressions of the importance of faculty status to their credibility and effectiveness as faculty developers; and information regarding respondents' institutional contexts. Findings are further disaggregated across institutional contexts and sex to explore trends, differential perceptions, and other emergent issues as identified by participant researchers.

Centers for teaching and learning (CTLs) represent a wide variety of contexts and historical origins reflected in a significant range of structural identities. These origins influence the degree to which directors and other faculty developers are directly involved in teaching within the institution. Even greater are differences of faculty status associated with positions and faculty developers' perceptions of how this status impacts their effectiveness in working with faculty. Building from Sorcinelli, Austin, Eddy, and Beach's (2006) recent work on mapping the profession and Graf and Wheeler's (1996) findings regarding sex differences in faculty developer status within institutions (75% male/25% female with faculty status [Chism & Mintz, 1998]), this study took an active, constructivist approach to furthering exploration of faculty development as a profession embedded in the higher education context. A participatory research approach allowed for collaborative inquiry, constructing trends from data, adding to it, and interpreting findings together.

The data has its origins in an initial survey of faculty developers invited to participate through the listserv of the Professional and Organizational Development Network in Higher Education (POD). In a five-day period in late December 2004, 31 faculty developers responded to a 16-question online survey; subsequently, this number grew to 35 respondents. Building on the initial analysis of online survey data, this chapter expands the analysis by adding the results collected through two interactive sessions at the POD Network Conference in October 2005. Additional responses solicited in a poster session and follow-on concurrent session are incorporated, along with the analysis and interpretation of the data by faculty developers participating in the sessions.

In its essential form, this chapter documents an emerging profile of the faculty status of faculty developers as solicited, compiled, and interactively interpreted with faculty developer practitioners. It shares:

- Descriptive statistical information on the various positions held by faculty developer respondents

- Impressions of the importance of faculty status to their effectiveness as faculty developers (as captured in a qualitative summary of illustrative themes)

- Information regarding respondents' institutional contexts

- Initial findings disaggregated across institutional contexts and gender disparities to explore trends and differential perceptions (e.g., profiles of small baccalaureate colleges, medium-size master's teaching universities, and larger doctoral/research universities)

- Other emergent issues as identified by survey participants

Methodological Orientation, Data Collection, and Analysis

This study represents an integrated research (also called "mixed methods") approach that strategically incorporates quantitative and qualitative methods. As noted, its origins in a POD listserv query solicited information via an online survey and initial findings were subsequently shared with, added to, and collectively interpreted by practicing faculty developers. Using participatory research strategies, POD conference participants enhanced the research by validating, adding to, and interpreting the quantitative and qualitative data collected around the central question of *the importance of faculty status for faculty developers.*

Data Collection and Sources

The study draws its data from multiple sources. The data collection techniques implemented included online surveys, an interactive poster session, and participatory data analysis and interpretation with participating practitioners. The online survey formed the referential foundation of the study and solicited the following information:

- Position and roles

- How participants came to the position: entry point, history at current institution

- Engagement in teaching: position/appointment and teaching responsibilities, degree/amount of teaching, level of teaching

- Impressions regarding the importance of faculty status to the role of faculty developer

- Description of institutional contexts: types, focus, size, and other defining features

- Respondent gender and geographic distribution

A full version of the survey follows this discussion (see Appendix 12.1). In a five-day period in late December 2004, 31 faculty developers responded to this 16-question online survey as solicited through the POD listserv, the primary professional association for faculty developers (final initial response rate to the survey was 35 respondents by March 2005). In a three-hour interactive poster session at the October 2005 POD conference, the response rate rose to 110 participants who completed the survey and "grew" the visual response graphs by adding their data to the poster presentation of data (incomplete responses dropped the final number of respondents to a remarkably convenient 100). With the assistance of Nancy Chism, this information was compiled as participants completed their surveys and formed the core of the data handouts structured for practical analysis and interpretation by participant researchers in a concurrent session the following day.

Data Analysis

Participatory research principles (Cornwall and Jewkes, 1995; Maguire, 1987; Mullinix & Akatsa-Bukachi, 1998) and grounded theory (Strauss & Corbin, 1998) informed the analysis as researchers and practitioner colleagues identified emergent themes and allowed for their growth and extended validation. Quantitative and qualitative data analysis was further enhanced through the use of Excel and NVivo qualitative software, respectively. Periodic informal and formal discussions among author-researchers and practitioner participant-researchers served as an inductive base to identify themes of topic impact that were further expanded and identified through text analysis. Recoding strategies were utilized to increase validity by generating initial free nodes and subsequently exploring relationships by establishing tree-noded categories, supporting each with quotations and emergent analysis (Richards, 1999). "Live" collaborative data interpretation was undertaken on the expanded dataset collected during the POD conference poster session by faculty developers participating in a concurrent working session, producing patterns of findings and directions for additional research.

Findings and Considerations

As noted, the first-level response to the online survey was 31 participants (71% female, 23% male). This grew to 110 participants in the second round, culled to a straight 100 completing all questions posed (59% female, 34% male, 7% unidentified). This updated gender distribution moves substantially closer to the 54%/44% female/male response distribution recorded in the only known survey of POD membership that asked about gender (Graf & Wheeler, 1996). Hailing from 39 states and from Canada, Japan, and Korea and covering most institutional types, most respondents were from doctoral/research universities (47%) or master's colleges/universities (26%), with the remaining identifying themselves with baccalaureate colleges (11%) and associate degree-granting institutions/community colleges (5%). This institutional breakdown is reasonably close to that reported by Sorcinelli et al. (2006), whose institutional breakdown of respondents included 44% from research and doctoral institutions, 23% from comprehensive I and II, 11% from liberal arts I and II, 9% from community colleges, 5% other, and 8% from Canadian institutions. The majority described themselves as mid-size (10,000–20,000, 38%), with the remainder comparably split between smaller (33%) and larger (28%) institutions.

The exhibits on the following pages provide an emerging profile of faculty developers and the key characteristics that define their roles: their faculty development responsibilities and how they came to faculty development (Exhibits 12.1, 12.2, and 12.3), and their teaching responsibilities and faculty status within their institutions (Exhibits 12.4, 12.5, and 12.6). Out of respect for the contextual variabilities and range of responses, the data are provided without summary descriptive narrative (which tends to relate patterns that may not yet exist). Rather, they are offered in their pure form to encourage continued reflection and allow faculty development colleagues to situate themselves within this data.

EXHIBIT 12.1

Positions and/or Roles*

a) Director of CTL	50	37%
b) Consultative Support	28	21%
c) Training Support	20	15%
d) Technical Support	9	7%
e) Faculty Peer Mentor/Consultant	11	8%
f) Other	16	12%
Note. Multiple responses.		

Positions/Roles

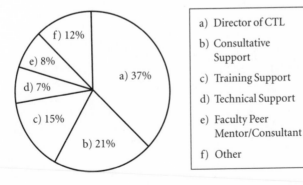

EXHIBIT 12.2

Entry into Faculty Development (Q 2A)

Entry Point

a) From a tenure-track faculty appointment within the institution	36%
b) From a nontenure-track faculty appointment within the institution	7%
c) From an administrative appointment within the institution	10%
d) Hired from the outside with professional faculty development experience	26%
e) Hired from the outside with no faculty development experience, but with higher education faculty/teaching experience elsewhere	6%
f) Hired from the outside with no faculty development or higher education faculty experience, just related/relevant skills	7%
g) Other (indicate in narrative)	8%
Total	**100%**

Note. Goodness of fit test indicates entry points are unequally distributed, c2 (6, N = 100) = 58.9, p < .001.

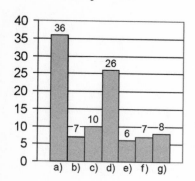

Entry Point

a) From a tenure-track faculty appointment within the institution

b) From a nontenure-track faculty appointment within the institution

c) From an administrative appointment within the institution

d) Hired from the outside with professional faculty development experience

e) Hired from the outside with no faculty development experience, but with higher education faculty/teaching experience elsewhere

f) Hired from the outside with no faculty development or higher education faculty experience, just related/relevant skills

g) Other (indicate in narrative)

EXHIBIT 12.3

History at Current Institution (Q 2B)

Time	%
a) Less than a year	8%
b) 1–3 years	15%
c) 3–6 years	16%
d) 6–10 years	21%
e) More than 10 years	39%
No response	*1%*
Multiple responses	*2%*

Note. Approximate weighted average equals 8.59 years.

History at Current Institution

Engagement in Teaching

Faculty developers report generally being involved with teaching in a variety of contexts from a variety of positions, distributed unequally across categories (χ^2 (5, N = 100) = 22.29, p < .001). Forty-eight percent of those responding to questions about teaching engagement listed multiple levels of engagement (with 38% including "teaching" faculty as part of their work). Likewise, those who do teach are split between those teaching from tenured or tenure-track positions (34%), special faculty appointments (6%), and those teaching as adjuncts (31%, as part of position or for pay).

Exhibit 12.4

Teaching Engagement and Position* (Q 3A)

a) Conduct workshops/training/sessions for faculty only   13%

b) Teach courses as part-time/adjunct faculty
   (outside of normal working hours for pay)   19%

c) Teach courses as part-time/adjunct faculty
   (as part of position/appointment responsibilities)   12%

d) Hold nontenure-track/faculty appointment as part of position
   (specialist faculty, etc.) and teach   6%

e) Hold a tenure-track position at the assistant/associate level   7%

f) Am tenured faculty   27%

Note. Forty-eight percent of respondents offered multiple responses, which are only partially reflected in the selection above. For example, 38% of respondents conduct workshops/sessions for faculty as part of their varied teaching responsibilities.

Teaching Engagement and Position

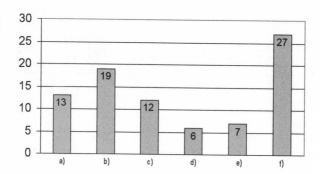

EXHIBIT 12.5
Degree/Amount of Teaching (Q 3B)

a) Conduct workshops/training/ sessions for faculty only	31%
b) 1 course a year	23%
c) 1 course a semester	12%
d) 2 courses a semester	10%
e) More than 2 courses a semester	5%
f) Guest lecture/present/facilitate sessions upon request	2%
g) Other (indicate in narrative)	14%
No response	*3%*
Multiple responses	*25%*

EXHIBIT 12.6
Level of Teaching (Q 3C)

a) Introductory/foundational undergraduate courses (lower level courses)	35%
b Advanced undergraduate courses (upper level courses)	17%
c) Master's-level courses	16%
d) Doctoral-level courses	10%
e) Advising	1%
f) Other (indicate in narrative)	9%
No response	*12%*
Multiple responses	*28%*

The Central Question

A total of 15 thematic responses were revealed through a preliminary analysis of the narrative responses to the central survey question: What are your impressions regarding the importance of holding faculty status as it contributes to your credibility and ability to effectively support faculty within your institution? Exhibit 12.7 provides a basic overview of these emergent themes.

EXHIBIT 12.7

Importance of Faculty Status

	Percentage/Total Responses, N = 100 (*% non-conflicting responses*)
Faculty Status Is Important	79 (*69*)
Critical—very important	48
Adds to credibility	54
Impacts effectiveness	28
Supports personal professional development	12
Tenure is a consideration—titled membership (6), access (4), security (5)	17
Releases tension between faculty and community college	1
Faculty Status May (May Not) Be Important	25
Challenging to balance roles	4
Mixed—hard to judge—context dependent	8
Differing perspectives (to faculty, yes; director, unsure)	3
Is theoretically important	4
Faculty Status Is Not Important/of Limited Importance	30 (*9*)
Teaching experience most/more important	12
Faculty status not important	6
Reputation as an outstanding instructor most important	7
Engage in scholarly activities	2
Teaching not important	3
Totals (average of 2.1 impressions per respondent)	209

Note. χ^2 (2, N = 100) = 56.23, p < .001.

Examples of illustrative quotes identified through qualitative analysis help to bring these themes to life. Respondents who identified faculty status as important (79%) noted it as critical to very important (48%), impacting their credibility (how they were perceived by colleagues, 54%) and/or effectiveness (their ability to do their work, 28%). They clarified the importance of faculty status as follows:

CRITICAL!!! I have no credibility without it. I can negotiate credibility with admin and staff due to my background.

I could not do the work that I have done without being a tenured faculty member; I couldn't do it if I didn't teach. I am a faculty member. I research. I publish. I write curriculum. I present at conferences. I serve on committees. I do all a "regular" faculty member does. . . . This position is also very vital for assuring credibility for the new faculty; they see me as one of them and come out to my workshops.

It's vital. The faculty/administration divide at our institution involves a lot of mutual hostility and suspicion. The fact that I'm faculty, and have faculty interests and experience, makes it much easier for me to do the job.

I have never had faculty status, but I believe it would be VERY helpful in my work with faculty. I have been told (sometimes very directly) that my lack of faculty status makes me less qualified to help certain faculty members (despite my credentials (PhD) and teaching experiences)

I believe that I must remain actively teaching for more credibility. I also believe that I hold more credibility as a faculty member (as opposed to administrator). My position is assistant professor, and I feel this is extremely significant, both for drawing academics into academic development, and for my credibility with clients.

Faculty status and active teaching, at any level, directly impacts effectiveness and credibility. I cannot effectively support faculty if I am not engaged in their challenges and won't know the right questions.

I believe I am MUCH more credible when I can share experiences from my own teaching situations on this campus. The anecdotes and specific examples I can provide are invaluable. It also gives me more confidence in making suggestions to faculty.

In some ways, not being a faculty has caused big [road] blocks, e.g., mailing lists/communication loops, inclusion in faculty meetings/decisions.

Extremely important—librarians have tenure track faculty status and it facilitates conversations about teaching/curricular issues. . . . I believe that heads of teaching and learning centers must have faculty status (as opposed to other kinds of academic appointments) to be perceived by faculty as equals . . . and be at appropriate tables for conversations.

I think that full faculty status on the tenure track would increase my effectiveness on campus and my ability to intervene in important issues regarding student learning.

I believe that being a faculty colleague provides instant rapport and respect with other faculty. I can speak about promotion, tenure, classroom management, online teaching, electronic portfolios from personal experience rather than theory alone.

I cannot imagine being nearly as effective without faculty status.

Those who identified faculty status as not important or of limited importance offered fewer comments or examples. When they did, these occasionally conflicted (21%): "Faculty status would be nice, but experience in the field trumps."

Others offered additional criteria for credibility and effectiveness, such as reputation, experience, or established structures:

I think that my reputation on campus was important. For a long time (10 years) I was administrative faculty. I thought this would be a problem with tenure-track folks, but it really wasn't. 2 years ago, my status was changed to research faculty.

Middle level administrators do not have faculty status, but may teach and advise students. This is a regularized approach at the University and poses no problems to credibility as long as we have teaching experience.

The Context

Descriptive background on the respondents (position, engagement in teaching, sex, and geographic distributions) and their institutional context (type, focus, size, and other defining features, some noted next), help to provide the ability to compile distributed profiles (see Exhibits 12.8 and 12.9).

Initial analysis by institutional context and respondent status/perspective revealed added insights (i.e., smaller teaching colleges/universities find faculty status to be critical, while the highest responses citing faculty status as less/not important were among research universities).

EXHIBIT 12.8

Institutional Type

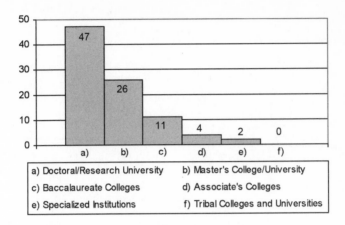

a) Doctoral/Research University   b) Master's College/University
c) Baccalaureate Colleges   d) Associate's Colleges
e) Specialized Institutions   f) Tribal Colleges and Universities

EXHIBIT 12.9

Institutional Size

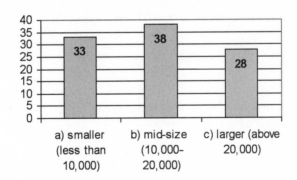

Significant Patterns: Participatory Interpretation of Findings

Bringing voice to faculty developers' insights into their own work is an important part of this study. Built into the data collection strategies have been opportunities for interpretive analysis by faculty developers. Having worked with cross-coded responses to the central questions, 10 faculty developers assisted the researchers by sorting, compiling, and interpreting the findings as captured in Exhibit 12.10.

EXHIBIT 12.10

Patterning Responses Regarding Importance of Faculty Status

Faculty Status:	Is important: 63%	May or may not be: 24%	Is not important: 13%
Key Characteristics	Percentage of Category Respondents		
2A Entry point	• 20% hired from outside with faculty development experience • ~ 50% tenure track	• 50% from faculty positions outside • 50% from all other categories	• 20% faculty • 30% hired from outside
5A Institutional type	• 52% from research institutions	• Reported as "mostly" doctoral/research institutions	• 50% doctoral • 20% master's
5C Institutional size	• 40% small colleges • 38% mid-size • 26% larger	• 11% small • 47% mid-size • 32% larger	• 50% small colleges • 20% mid-size • 30% larger
Gender	• 60% female • 40% male	• 57% female • 26% male • (17% unidentified)	• 50% female • 30% male • (20% unidentified)

Participant analysis of collected data revealed the following interpretations and responses to the key prompts:

- *What do you see in the data?* People seem to report their perceptions based on their own experience. If they come in with faculty status, they believe it's important. If hired as an expert, they may not need it to be effective. In general, a reputation as an excellent teacher may be the most important criterion of all.

- *What does it mean to you?* To support faculty successfully through a promotion and tenure process may require experiential knowledge of the process to support faculty. However, when technical support is the primary focus this may require technical expertise but not necessarily faculty status.

Gender Disparities

Gender disparities may have weakened slightly, but they still persist (see Exhibit 12.11). Among the 59% of female respondents, approximately 46% held faculty status while 54% did not. For the 34% of male respondents, the figures were split evenly between those who held faculty status and those who did not. Among the males who held faculty status, 69% were tenured or tenure track. While proportionally smaller in overall percentage, the women faculty developers who did hold faculty status reported themselves as tenurable/tenured at a rate of 95%. Arguably, this survey data is based on a limited response rate and should be compared against additional data collected on the current state of the field for faculty developers. Meanwhile, however, it is safe to state that the status of faculty developers vis-à-vis faculty roles in the academy has become more dynamic and variable since Graf and Wheeler's 1996 findings, where only 25% of female faculty developers held faculty status. Whether a function of broader definition of faculty developers or increasing range of structural options emerging, it is safe to say that gender disparities in the field are in flux.

EXHIBIT 12.11

Gender Distribution

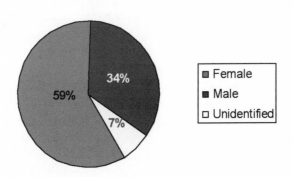

Additional Pathways and Perspectives: A Case in Point

Participant researchers recommended that future analysis consider institutional size as a key reference variable and that follow-on research might also include asking faculty to indicate their perceptions of the importance of faculty status for faculty developers. Long attuned to this interest, I have had the opportunity to explore this perspective, most specifically as a natural part of building a CTL. The design for Furman University's Center for Teaching and Engaged Learning (CTEL) has included the identification of four instructional development consultants (IDCs), experienced teaching and learning specialists associated with each of four academic divisions. A smaller liberal arts university with a focus on teaching and engaged learning for undergraduate students, Furman has approximately 2,600 students and 250 full-time faculty. Poised for major curricular and schedule changes and the institution of a two-course, interdisciplinary first-year seminar sequence, Furman conceptualized CTEL as a vehicle to support faculty and students through this shift. While student support was handled by well-established branches of CTEL (Collaboratory for Creative Learning and Communication and Undergraduate Research and Internships), the faculty development components were the focus of development. IDCs were to be the driving force in faculty support for teaching and learning. As such, significant faculty input into the development and staffing of these positions was critical, as were views on how to create positions that would be most effective within this context.

Explicit conversations with separate faculty focus groups drawn from fine arts, humanities, sciences, mathematics, and social sciences revealed remarkably diverse impressions of the importance of teaching and faculty status to credibility that these faculty developers might hold with faculty. Humanities faculty expressed the importance of having direct experience teaching Furman students (in addition to higher education teaching experience), a Ph.D., and continuing disciplinary scholarly excellence as critical factors in effectively connecting and supporting them and were most vocal regarding faculty status as important. Sciences and mathematics faculty shared concerns about too narrow and deep a disciplinary focus influencing IDC's ability to connect with faculty across departments and described individuals with multiple degrees in different disciplines and perhaps a terminal degree related to instructional design or adult learning that would enable team teaching, guest teaching, and other modeling opportunities. Social sciences faculty were more interested in current technical expertise supporting research, citing past teaching experience as sufficient for connection and credibility. Fine arts faculty were most concerned with candidates having experience as an artist in addition to technological expertise that would support fine and performing arts. In addition, while faculty tended to recognize teaching, team teaching, and faculty status as important to faculty developers, conversations with administrators and technical support staff found this less compelling. While earlier decisions predicated on contextual challenges limited the possibility of advertising positions as faculty positions, latitude was provided to advertise broadly and differentiate each IDC position to reflect the input collected from faculty and capture divergent divisional desires. In this case, prior to and since the arrival of IDCs, departments and new initiatives (first-year seminars) have invited IDCs to teach.

Faculty Status and Faculty Developers

Identification of the natural overlay between faculty developer professional responsibilities and traditional faculty responsibilities serves to facilitate discussions of how faculty developers can be accommodated as faculty, especially within structures to clarify the overlaps with existing tenure and promotion evaluation.

Teaching   "Teaching" faculty + teaching students

Research   Scholarship of teaching and learning, programmatic evaluation and research

Service   Committee service, support of curricular initiatives

During the interpretive analysis session and based on discussion of the data, participant researchers proposed the idea that somewhere within a CTL, someone should have faculty status and that should include a clearly articulated balance of time and responsibilities distributed between faculty and administrative status. This was thought to make for the most effective combination as it seemed to both differentiate between contexts and accommodate varying numbers of positions within given CTLs. It also addressed the interpretive impression gleaned from textual responses: that smaller institutions with greater teaching focus had fewer CTL staff, and faculty expected closer working relationships with faculty colleagues who maintained a direct connection with teaching. At larger research-oriented institutions, faculty might expect to work with professional staff more regularly than faculty colleagues.

Conclusion

Credibility, trust, and appreciation for the teaching abilities and instructional design skills of faculty developers have the potential to impact their effectiveness. This incremental study continues to document faculty developer impressions of the importance of faculty status to their ability to effectively function within their particular institutional contexts. While such profiles of faculty developers are not intended as prescriptive recommendations, they do offer important illustrative insights into current trends and practices across the higher education landscape of faculty development. Even though context continues to be the primary determinant of whether faculty developers actually have faculty status associated with their positions, it is clear that a significant majority of these experienced professionals perceive faculty status to be an important contributor to their credibility, effectiveness, and interactions with faculty colleagues.

Appendix 12.1

Survey on the Faculty Status of Faculty Developers

Instructions

There are five multi-part questions below. Where projected options/responses are proposed as prompts, select as many as are relevant to your situation, adding more wherever necessary. You may circle relevant letters, supply simple lists of letter-coded responses, and/or develop a descriptive narrative that captures your information.

Estimated Response Times

Short version via coded responses, approximately two to five minutes.
Longer descriptive/narrative responses, approximately five to ten minutes.

Thanks in advance for your contribution,

Bonnie Mullinix & Nancy Chism

1. **What position do you hold and/or role do you play in supporting faculty on your campus?**

   1A. Positions/Roles
   - a) Director of CTL
   - b) Consultative Support
   - c) Training Support
   - d) Technical Support
   - e) Faculty Peer Mentor/Consultant
   - f) Other (indicate in narrative): _____

2. **How did you come to this position at your current institution?**

   2A. Entry Point
   - a) From a tenure-track faculty appointment within the institution
   - b) From a nontenure-track faculty appointment within the institution
   - c) From an administrative appointment within the institution
   - d) Hired from the outside with professional faculty development experience
   - e) Hired from the outside with no faculty development experience, but with higher education faculty/teaching experience elsewhere
   - f) Hired from the outside with no faculty development or higher education faculty experience, just related/relevant skills
   - g) Other (indicate in narrative): _____

2B. History at Current Institution
    a) Less than a year
    b) 1–3 years
    c) 3–6 years
    d) 6–10 years
    e) More than 10 years

3. What is your engagement in teaching within your college/university?

3A. Position/Appointment and Teaching Engagement
Teaching Engagement and Position
    a) Conduct workshops/training/sessions for faculty only
    b) Teach courses as part-time/adjunct faculty (outside of normal working hours for pay)
    c) Teach courses as part-time/adjunct faculty (as part of position/appointment responsibilities)
    d) Hold nontenure-track/faculty appointment as part of position (specialist faculty, etc.) and teach
    e) Hold a tenure-track position at the assistant/associate level
    f) Am tenured faculty

Departmental/School Affiliation
    g) Am affiliated with a particular department
    h) Am affiliated with a particular school
    i) Teach courses across departments/schools
    j) Am an active, contributing member of a particular department/school
    k) Other (indicate further in narrative for 3): _____

3B. Degree/Level of Teaching
    a) Conduct workshops/training/sessions for faculty only
    b) 1 course a year
    c) 1 course a semester
    d) 2 courses a semester
    e) More than 2 courses a semester
    f) Guest lecture/present/facilitate sessions upon request
    g) Other (indicate in narrative): _____

3C. Level of Teaching
    a) Introductory/foundational undergraduate courses (lower level courses)
    b) Advanced undergraduate courses (upper level courses)
    c) Master's-level courses
    d) Doctoral-level courses
    e) Advising
    f) Other (indicate in narrative): _____

4. What are your impressions regarding the importance of holding faculty status as it contributes to your credibility and ability to effectively support faculty within your institution?

  4A. Faculty Status Is Important
    A1) Critical—very important
    A2) Adds to credibility
    A3) Impacts effectiveness
    A4) Tenure—contributes to job security
    A5) Supports personal professional development
    A6)
    A7)
    A8)

  4B. Faculty Status May (May Not) Be Important
    B1) Differing perspectives (to faculty, yes; faculty development, unsure)
    B2) Challenging to balance roles
    B3) Mixed—hard to judge—context dependant
    B4) Is theoretically important
    B5)
    B6)
    B7)
    B8)

  4C. Faculty Status Is Not Important/of Limited Importance
    C1) Teaching experience most/more important
    C2) Faculty status is not important
    C3) Reputation as an outstanding instructor most important
    C4) Engage in scholarly activities
    C5) Teaching not important
    C6)
    C7)
    C8)

5. How would you describe your institution?
   (Codes or description pulling from categories/descriptors below are welcome.)

  5A. Type
    a) Doctoral/research university
    b) Master's college/university
    c) Baccalaureate college
    d) Associate's college
    e) Specialized institution
    f) Tribal college and university
    g) Other (indicate in narrative):

5B. Focus
   a) Teaching university
   b) Liberal arts/comprehensive
   c) Research
   d) Professional
   e) Other (indicate in narrative):

5C. Size
   a) Smaller (less than 10,000)
   b) Mid-size (10,000–20,000)
   c) Larger (above 20,000)
   d) Other (indicate in narrative):

5D. Other Defining Features
   a) Public
   b) Private/independent
   c) Multicampus institution
   d) Faculty union
   e) Other (indicate in narrative):

6. Your information: Name, email, and address
   (Optional: If you would like copies of the results.)

   Or please share:
   • Gender
      a) Female
      b) Male
   • Geographical location (state/country):
   • Institution (optional):

Return Surveys (and/or direct questions regarding this study) to:
   Dr. Bonnie B. Mullinix
   Assistant Academic Dean
   Center for Teaching and Engaged Learning
   Furman University
   3300 Poinsett Hwy
   Greenville, SC 29613
   Email: bonnie.mullinix@furman.edu

References

Chism, N., & Mintz, J. (1998). *Who's developing the developers? A survey of job satisfaction, challenges, and disappointments of North American educational developers.* Paper presented at the International Consortium of Educational Developers, Austin, TX.

Cornwall, A., & Jewkes, R. (1995, December). What is participatory research? *Social Science and Medicine, 41*(12), 1667–1676.

Graf, D., & Wheeler, D. (1996). *Defining the field: A survey of the membership of the Professional and Organizational Development Network.* Colorado Springs, CO: Professional and Organizational Development Network.

Maguire, P. (1987). *Doing participatory research: A feminist approach.* Amherst, MA: University of Massachusetts, Center for International Education.

Mullinix, B. B., & Akatsa-Bukachi, M. (1998). Participatory evaluation: Offering Kenyan women power and voice. In E. T. Jackson & Y. Kassam (Eds.), *Knowledge shared: Participatory evaluation in development cooperation* (pp. 167–176). West Hartford, CT: Kumarian Press.

Mullinix, B. B., & Chism, N. V. N. (2005, October). *The faculty status of faculty developers: A collaborative construction and collective explorations.* Paper presented at the 30th annual meeting of the Professional and Organizational Development Network in Higher Education, Milwaukee, WI.

Richards, L. (1999). *Using NVivo in qualitative research.* Thousand Oaks, CA: Sage.

Sorcinelli, M. D., Austin, A. E., Eddy, P. L., & Beach, A. L. (2006). *Creating the future of faculty development: Learning from the past, understanding the present.* Bolton, MA: Anker.

Strauss, A., & Corbin, J. (1998). *Basics of qualitative research: Techniques and procedures for developing grounded theory* (2nd ed.). Thousand Oaks, CA: Sage.

Section VI

Faculty and Instructional Development

13

Co-Teaching as a Faculty Development Model

Andrea L. Beach, Charles Henderson, Michael Famiano
Western Michigan University

Co-teaching is a promising and cost-effective approach to promoting fundamental research-based instructional change. In this chapter, we discuss the theoretical underpinnings of co-teaching and describe our initial experience with it. A new instructor (MF) co-taught with an instructor experienced in physics education research-based reforms (CH). An outsider (AB) conducted separate interviews with each instructor and observed several class sessions. Results include immediate use of research-based instructional practices by the new instructor and a significant change in teaching beliefs over time. Recommendations are made for implementing co-teaching as part of a faculty development program.

Most reforms in college-level teaching call for a significant shift in the role of teachers from content experts who can impart their knowledge to students to facilitators of the learning process (e.g., Barr & Tagg, 1995). The National Research Council's Committee on Undergraduate Science Education calls for undergraduate teaching faculty to "be prepared to use combinations of inquiry-based, problem-solving, information-gathering, and didactic forms of instruction under appropriate classroom circumstances that promote conceptual understanding and students' ability to apply knowledge in new situations" (National Research Council, 2003, p. 27). Research on teaching and student learning has supported the improved learning outcomes of such approaches (e.g., Handelsman et al., 2004), and faculty developers at colleges and universities are key agents in helping faculty learn to teach using such research-based approaches.

Cuban (1999) refers to such a shift in the role of teachers as a fundamental change and distinguishes between fundamental and incremental changes: "*Incremental changes* aim to improve the efficiency and effectiveness of existing structures, cultures, and processes" (p. 63). "*Fundamental changes* are those that aim to alter drastically the core beliefs, behaviors, and structures" (p. 64). This distinction between fundamental and incremental changes is important because fundamental changes always face significant resistance while incremental changes often do not (Elmore, 1996). Thus, it is likely that different faculty development approaches are needed to bring about each type of change.

Obstacles to Fundamental Teaching Change

Research indicates that a major obstacle to faculty development aimed at bringing about fundamental change is that instructors attempting to change traditional practices are acculturated into and surrounded by a culture that reflects their current practices (Ben-Peretz, 1995; Fullan, 2001; Kezar, 2001; Loucks-Horsley, Hewson, Love, & Stiles, 1998). Thus, in order to change, they must undergo a fundamental *internal* change in their views about teaching and learning. Even when instructors are able to successfully make such an internal change, they are typically still immersed in their current situation. Many aspects of this situation likely conflict with their new views of teaching (Kezar, 2001). For example, in an interview study, physics faculty cited strong situational constraints that made it difficult to teach in a nontraditional manner (Dancy & Henderson, 2005). Challenges such as large class sizes, broad content coverage expectations, classroom infrastructure, scheduling constraints, and poor student preparation/motivation all appear to favor traditional instruction.

Students often pose another barrier to teaching change by resisting new instructional strategies (Felder & Brent, 1996). In a traditional science class, for example, students and instructors often abide by a "hidden contract" whereby students are responsible for sitting quietly and asking clarifying questions while teachers are responsible for presenting clear lectures and solving example exercises that are not too different from test questions (Slater, 2003). When an instructor attempts to change this contract, many students feel threatened and resist (Mazur, 1997).

Because of the conflicts with existing cultures (both personal and institutional), new instruction that calls for research-based fundamental changes (e.g., transforming classrooms from passive to active learning) is often altered by instructors and implemented as incremental changes. Although such implementation may keep some of the surface features of the innovation, it is essentially traditional instruction. For example, research suggests that instructors may attempt to implement the peer instruction strategy (Mazur, 1997), but without the peer interaction component (Henderson, 2005; Henderson & Dancy, 2005). Henderson and Dancy (2005) developed the term *inappropriate assimilation* to describe this type of "adoption." Innovations requiring fundamental changes appear to be quite susceptible to inappropriate assimilation (Boyer Commission on Educating Undergraduates in the Research University, 1998; Hutchinson & Huberman, 1993; Spillane, 2004; Stigler & Hiebert, 1999; Yerrick, Parke, & Nugent, 1997).

Common methods of faculty development to promote teaching change include talks, papers, and workshops aimed at convincing individual faculty to change their instruction and giving them information and materials in support of a specific research-based strategy. For instructors to fundamentally change their instruction, however, they must simultaneously transform their personal views about teaching and learning to align with the new instruction as well as use this understanding to adapt the new instruction to their unique situation. Such fundamental change requires more support than these typical faculty development approaches provide (Cox, 2001, 2004; Rice, Sorcinelli, & Austin, 2000).

An additional barrier to standard workshop-based faculty development approaches in promoting fundamental teaching change is the complex nature of teaching itself. Similar to any complex task, much of a teacher's decision-making is implicit (Berliner, 1987; Mitchell & Marland, 1989). It would be an overwhelming task for a faculty developer to make all of the implicit decisions explicit and equally overwhelming for an instructor to attempt to externalize these decisions. The ability to make "correct" decisions implicitly is learned through experience and reflection (Berliner, 1987; Schön, 1983; Van Driel, Verloop, Van Werven, & Dekkers, 1997; Wilson, Shulman, & Richert, 1987).

Establishment of Teaching Styles by New Faculty

Many new faculty, particularly in the sciences, have held teaching assistant (TA) appointments in graduate school. However, relatively few have actually taught a course of their own before their first faculty position. Thus, these first years of teaching are a formative time in the development of an instructor's teaching style and likely an ideal time for interventions aimed at promoting nontraditional instructional practices (Saroyan & Amundsen, 2004).

However, for new faculty on the tenure track, any departure from traditional instruction may be dangerous because such changes may require more time than traditional instruction and result in lower student ratings, especially at first (Seymour, 2001). Studies of new faculty show that it is quite common for them to spend a majority of their time on instructional activities and to receive poor student ratings under normal conditions. Boice (1991) studied 77 new tenure-track faculty at two different universities (one with a research emphasis and one with a teaching emphasis) via interviews and observations. By the middle of their first semester, most of the new faculty complained about the lack of collegial support and reported that lecture preparation dominated their time. Few of the faculty reported teaching skill as depending on anything other than their knowledge of content and clear, enthusiastic presentation. Most described their classes as standard facts-and-principles lecturing and many had no plans for improving their teaching. Boice concludes that new faculty typically teach cautiously and defensively and tend to blame low student ratings on external factors (e.g., poor students, heavy teaching loads, and invalid rating systems). He suggests that new faculty would benefit from programs that helped them find ways to increase student participation and avoid overpreparing facts.

Thus, because new faculty already struggle with learning how to teach, this is the time to assist them in developing a research-based instructional style. Instructional change in new faculty still involves fundamental change because these new faculty were likely involved largely in traditional teaching approaches as students and TAs. We propose co-teaching as one model for promoting such change in new faculty.

What Is Co-Teaching?

The practice of co-teaching was developed by Roth and Tobin as an alternative to the standard student teaching practice associated with most K–12 teacher preparation programs (Roth, Masciotra, & Boyd, 1999; Roth & Tobin, 2002). In standard student teaching, the student teacher typically first observes several of the master teacher's classes, then the student teacher takes over the class on his or her own. Roth argues that student teachers do not often develop the tacit knowledge necessary to be good teachers under this arrangement (Roth et al., 1999). During co-teaching, on the other hand, the student teacher and master teacher share responsibility for all parts of the class. Student teachers "begin to develop a feel for what is right and what causes us to do what we do at the right moment" (Roth et al., 1999, p. 774).

Co-teaching is consistent with a cognitive apprenticeship paradigm of instruction, in which

> novices and experts are from different worlds, and a novice gets to be an expert through the mechanism of acculturation into the world of the expert. Actual participation in this world is critical for two reasons: (a) much of the knowledge that the expert transmits to the

novice is tacit, and (b) the knowledge often varies with context. (Farnham-Diggory, 1994, p. 466)

Co-teaching differs from team teaching in intention (acculturation to teaching vs. interdisciplinary connections), process (cognitive apprenticeship vs. collaboration), and intended outcome (aimed at teaching change primarily and student learning as a secondary vs. student learning primarily) (e.g., Austin & Baldwin, 1991; Erby, 2001). Although we are aware that co-teaching activities have occurred at the college level at other institutions, scant research (Eddy & Mitchell, 2006) has identified its uses, costs, and benefits or documented the results of this approach to fostering fundamental teaching change.

Data Collection and Analysis

The goal of this study was to develop a better understanding of the prospects of co-teaching for promoting fundamental instructional change through the in-depth investigation of one co-teaching experience. This is what Stake (1998) refers to as an instrumental case study. The expectation is that a deep understanding of this single case can be used to provide insight into the use of co-teaching in other similar settings.

The Case

The case under investigation was the fall 2005 co-teaching of the first semester introductory calculus-based physics course at Western Michigan University (WMU) by two of the authors, CH and MF. CH was an experienced instructor in his fourth year of teaching at WMU. He had been involved in the research-based reform of the introductory calculus-based physics sequence at WMU and had previously taught both of the courses in that sequence using reformed methods. He was also an experienced physics education research (PER) researcher with knowledge about many PER instructional interventions. MF was a new tenure-track faculty member in his first semester at WMU. All of his prior teaching experience was as a physics TA while a graduate student at the Ohio State University (OSU). As a graduate student at OSU he had some exposure to PER via his interactions with the OSU physics education research group, which ran a required quarter-long course for TAs. The purpose of co-teaching was to allow MF to gain enough experience with the WMU reforms that he would implement a fundamentally reformed course in subsequent semesters. He was scheduled to teach the same course on his own in spring 2006.

From a cognitive apprenticeship perspective, the goal of co-teaching in the current study was to acculturate MF into research-based physics instruction as embodied in the design principles developed and enacted by the WMU reformers. As discussed earlier, the largely tacit and context-dependent nature of teacher decision-making means that learning to teach in a reform-compatible manner requires more than just talking about teaching; it requires *direct experience* in the practice of teaching. This is especially true because the culture—that is, the assumptions and norms—of reformed teaching is very different from the culture of traditional teaching.

The co-teaching took place in the lecture portion of an introductory calculus-based physics course at WMU. The four-credit course (Phys 2050: Mechanics and Heat) met each weekday for 50 minutes and enrolled about 70 students, mostly engineering majors, in a stadium-style lecture hall with fixed seating. CH and MF were both listed as the instructor of record for the course. There were five basic co-teaching activities. Each of these is described briefly next, then considered from the perspective of a cognitive apprentice instructional framework.

CH and MF alternate being in charge of class each week. Although both of the instructors were present during each class session, they alternated being "in charge" of the class on a weekly basis. The person in charge typically presided over any whole class discussions or presentations. Students spent much of the class working in assigned small groups, during which both instructors circulated around the lecture hall and interacted with the groups. The instructor in charge developed the first draft of the weekly quizzes or exams and shared them with the other instructor for comment.

CH and MF held weekly meetings to reflect on the previous week and discuss initial plans for the coming week. Each Friday, CH and MF met for approximately one hour, during which they talked about how things went the past week and any difficulties that arose. The instructor in charge of the following week then presented his initial plans for discussion. In addition, CH and MF frequently discussed the course more briefly at other times.

CH set up the course structure to reflect design principles supported by educational research. CH based the course structure on his previous successful teaching of the course, reserving much of the class time for students to work together and discuss physics concepts in small groups.

MF had access to materials used by CH in previous offerings of the course. At the beginning of the semester, CH provided MF with electronic copies of all the course activities and assignments used in the previous semester. MF typically used, with minor modifications, about half of these and developed the other half himself.

MF taught the course on his own during the subsequent semester (spring 2006).

Table 13.1 shows how each of the co-teaching activities match with the cognitive apprenticeship instructional model (Collins, Brown, & Holum, 1991). There are six basic aspects of this approach:

- Modeling, in which an expert performs a task so the novice can observe

- Coaching, when an expert observes and facilitates while the novice performs the task

- Scaffolding, in which the expert provides support to help the novice perform the task

- Articulation, when the expert encourages the novice to verbalize his or her knowledge and thinking

- Reflection, when the expert enables the novice to compare his performance with others

- Exploration, when the expert invites the novice to perform additional tasks with decreasing support

These aspects are not linear; they can be woven into multiple activities and are assumed to be iterative, repeating as needed as the novice gains skill and confidence.

TABLE 13.1

Alignment of Co-Teaching Activities Within the Cognitive Apprenticeship Framework

	Modeling	Coaching	Scaffolding	Articulation	Reflection	Exploration
CH and MF alternate being in charge of class each week.	X	X				X
Weekly meetings between CH and MF to reflect on previous week and discuss initial plans for coming week.	X	X		X	X	
Course structure set up by CH to support design principles suggested by educational research.			X			
MF had access to materials used by CH in previous offerings of the course.			X			
MF teaches the course on his own during the subsequent semester.						X

Data Sources

Case study research relies on multiple sources of evidence (Yin, 2003). A faculty member from the college of education (AB) participated in the co-teaching experience as an outsider. She conducted open-ended individual interviews with CH and MF at the beginning, middle, and end of the co-teaching semester. Her interviews focused on the progress of the course, general beliefs about teaching and learning, and the value of the co-teaching. Her final interview was with MF at the end of spring 2006 after he had taught the course on his own. The associated data sources were the interview transcripts of the seven 45- to 75-minute interviews. In addition, AB observed both CH and MF teaching at the beginning, middle, and end of the co-teaching semester. The associated data source was approximately four pages of handwritten field notes taken during each of the six observations following the Reformed Teaching Observation Protocol (RTOP) (Piburn & Sawada, 2000). The final data source was the syllabi used by CH and MF in fall 2005 for co-teaching and by MF in spring 2006 when teaching alone, supported by their own comments on the course structure for each semester.

Data Analysis

Both AB and CH independently analyzed all of the data sources looking for four things: 1) evidence related to MF's instructional practices; 2) evidence related to MF's beliefs about teaching and learning; 3) evidence related to MF's intentions toward future instruction; and 4) any other evidence related to co-teaching that seemed helpful in understanding the experience. After completing this independent analysis, CH and AB compared notes. Their analyses largely concurred and they resolved any differences through discussion. Although not directly involved in the data analysis, MF reviewed and commented on AB's and CH's findings. Therefore, we reached a consensus on all the results reported here.

Results

Our goal was to document changes, if any, and the degree of agreement with the WMU reform principles in MF's teaching practices, beliefs about teaching and learning, and intentions toward future instruction. We examine each of these aspects next.

Teaching Practices

MF and CH received similar scores on the RTOP instrument for each class session as well as similar scores to one another. This suggests that they were both working appropriately within the interactive class structure. AB did notice some more subtle differences, however. For example, in her first observation of MF, she wrote in her field notes, "MF was somewhat more structured than I saw CH to be, but very interactive with students nonetheless. MF presented concepts and then problems that exemplified them. Less of having students generate concepts. More formulas." MF also noticed this small difference:

> I noticed CH's technique [for managing class discussions] is even slightly different from mine. . . . I am not criticizing him at all because this is his technique and it obviously works, but from my point of view, he doesn't mind letting the students hang for a long time and squirm and sweat over this problem. He will ask some, what I consider, very open-ended questions, whereas I will tend to ask something that I consider slightly more leading.

AB did not note any changes in MF's instructional practices during the semester. These observations suggest that the scaffolding provided by the course structure was effective, right from the start, in helping MF teach in a nontraditional way.

MF perceived a shift in his own instruction toward more focus on concepts and less on mathematics.

> As the semester wore on . . . I ended up getting in the habit of . . . going through the concepts, setting up the problem, and saying to the students, "You go figure out the algebra on your own." That allows you to go through many more problems, and it also allows you to spend a larger percentage of time on the physics per problem so that they realize that the problem isn't a massive algebraic equation, but it really is physics.

Without this structure it is likely that MF, much like the new faculty interviewed in Boice's (1991) study, would have put much more emphasis on facts-and-principles lecturing. MF confirmed this during the first interview (conducted during the first week of classes when MF had participated while CH was in charge of the class, but had not yet been in charge himself).

AB: If you were doing this by yourself, if they just said, "Okay, here is your class schedule for the semester. Good luck." What would you be doing? How would you approach preparing for a class like that?

MF: I would probably not actually in all honesty . . . not have done it the same way that we are treating this class. . . . I [would] probably treat it more like a lecture. Of course I tend to be more interactive, so I will still be more interactive, asking the students questions and things. I probably wouldn't do as many in-class activities as we are doing now . . . and so it will probably be a little bit more like the formal lecture.

MF reiterated this thought in response to a similar question during the final interview with MF after the end of spring 2006. His belief that he would not have taught the course in a reformed manner without the co-teaching approach was consistent throughout all interviews.

Beliefs About Teaching and Learning

Although his beliefs about student learning were consistent throughout the semester, MF's beliefs about teaching appeared to change. He envisioned his teaching as being more interactive than a traditional lecture, utilizing the Socratic method to get students involved in answering questions. However, he was initially concerned about the reformed course structure, in which almost all class time is devoted to group-based problem solving, as too much of a departure from the lecture method.

I have really come to appreciate the use of in-class problems. It's surprising to know, because when I first came I was skeptical about having students do nothing but problems in class—just sort of standing by while they do problems. It really seems to be a good method.

MF's largest initial concern appeared to be student resistance to such an interactive class structure. Thus, he did not envision such methods being successful until he experienced the students being engaged and was also convinced by a survey of student perceptions of what helped them learn.

What convinced me about this [the reformed course structure] was that most of the students . . . were really engaged . . . but even more than that at the end of the semester when we gave them the survey, the thing they liked the most was the in-class work. Very strangely surprisingly to me was that they liked doing this and found it to be very helpful to them.

This concern for student opinion was a theme that ran throughout all of the interviews and is consistent with Boice's (1991) finding that new faculty tend to "teach defensively, so as to avoid public failures at teaching" (p. 170).

Intentions Toward Future Instruction

Not surprisingly, as MF's beliefs about teaching changed, his intentions toward future instruction also began to change. From the first three interviews, it appeared that his intentions toward future instruction, specifically the following semester, were changing to become more aligned with a reformed course. By the midterm interview, MF was beginning to become comfortable with the course design but was still largely noncommittal about how these might fit into his future instruction. "You know, it [the co-teaching experience] taught me something that I am going to adopt aspects of in future courses." By the end of the term, though, he seemed to have shifted his perception to be very favorable toward the course structure. "My class [next semester] is going to be very similar to what we did last semester, even the structure will be the same structure. It's going to be almost identical."

Changes MF made to the course after the co-teaching semester and his assessment of those changes revealed lasting change in his teaching beliefs. Even though at the end of the fall co-teaching experience, MF indicated that his spring 2006 course would be "almost identical" to the co-taught course, he later decided to make some changes to the course structure. The spring 2006 course was well within the reformed course structure, but he did pull the course toward a more traditional structure. In addition, he made almost all of these changes to reduce his preparation time or perceived student dissatisfaction. In the final interview at the end of the spring 2006 semester, MF was unhappy with many of the changes that he made and planned to go back to a course structure more closely aligned to the fall 2005 course. He indicated that his direct experience with co-teaching followed by teaching alone convinced him that the course elements were important enough in promoting student learning that they were worth extra time and possible student dissatisfaction.

> I did not do quiz corrections this year, simply because of time constraints involved, and, looking back on that, I think that was a bad idea.... I think students looked at quizzes as sort of a module of the course and once you are done with the quiz you are done with learning that material.... I'm going to readopt those [quiz corrections and group homework] and, it's going to be extra time involved, but in my mind it's worth it.

Other Observed Outcomes

An unexpected yet valuable outcome of co-teaching was that informal discussions helped MF become acculturated to WMU in areas other than teaching.

> I would ask him [CH] everything, not just about teaching.... He was actually very helpful in a lot of areas including grant writing.... These discussions often sprang from side conversations during the first five minutes before class while waiting for people to mingle in the class.

As Boice (1991) and others (Cox, 2001; Rice et al., 2000) have noted, this additional support is frequently lacking for new faculty.

MF attributed some of his and CH's success with co-teaching to the kind of relationship CH built with him. It was collegial, rather than a student-teacher or mentor-mentee type of relationship.

> Well, the thing that I liked the most about this is it wasn't like I was Charles' protégé. He recognized me as a colleague and we were teaching this class together.... It wasn't like teacher-apprenticeship, which at this level might seem sort of insulting.

This collegial relationship differs from the K–12 model of co-teaching, in which the expert/novice differences are more explicit.

Discussion

We believe that there were three important components to the co-teaching design that made it successful: 1) it lasted an entire semester, 2) the course structure was set up in advance by the experienced instructor, and 3) there was a collegial, cooperative relationship between the co-teaching partners. Co-teaching changed MF's teaching beliefs and intentions consistent with the design principles of the reformed introductory physics courses at WMU. The predetermined course structure set up by CH allowed MF to adopt new (to him) teaching practices from the beginning of the semester. MF's beliefs about teaching and learning were largely aligned with the reform principles by the middle of the semester, while his plans for future teaching continued to change throughout the semester and ended compatible with the reforms. Thus, it appears the entire co-teaching semester was important. To just co-teach for the first half of the semester, for example, probably would not have been enough to complete the change.

The Benefits of Co-Teaching for New Faculty

As described earlier, new instructors are typically risk-averse and afraid of making mistakes in their teaching. Thus, any departure from traditional instruction must be made as risk-free as possible, in terms of both student satisfaction and time demands. Co-teaching, as enacted in this project, did this in two ways. First, it allowed the experienced instructor to set up a course structure that was known to work in the particular context, as well as to model and coach the new instructor within the context. Within this structure, the new instructor enjoyed a safe, low-risk setting to practice new ways of interacting in the classroom. In addition, since both instructors were listed as the instructor of record, neither could be held fully responsible for any negative student evaluations (although in this case evaluations were quite positive). The new instructor also saved precious time drawing on previously used materials and only having to do so for half of the classes. He then had more time and energy for the more reflective aspects of co-teaching. In addition, when teaching on his own the following semester, his co-teaching experience and the resources CH provided made it easier for him to continue teaching in the reformed manner than to fall back on the traditional manner and gave him an "ideal" baseline to which to compare his independent teaching.

The Cost of Co-Teaching

In the co-teaching model described here, the only cost is replacing an instructor for one class. In this case, the department hired an adjunct using external grant money. The recommended part-time rate for a four-credit class at WMU in fall 2005 was $2,800, a rate comparable to the national average for part-time faculty (Thornton, 2006). Departments that can absorb an extra class for one semester entail no cost at all. In comparison, Marder, McCullough, and Perakis (2001) calculated the cost of National Science Foundation–funded faculty development workshops (as an example of a common faculty development model) to be $4,200 per participant and found that only 40% of participants reported making moderate or greater changes to their teaching approaches. Institutions can run workshops on a cheaper scale, but the comparison demonstrates that co-teaching offers greater outcomes for less expenditure than other approaches.

Implementation Strategies for Faculty Development

The results of the co-teaching project reported here suggest that co-teaching can be a useful component of faculty development programs. Program directors can integrate co-teaching into their programming in various ways and play different roles in promoting and supporting it.

For example, co-teaching can be offered as an intensive new faculty development opportunity, with experienced faculty who have been recognized for their teaching excellence serving as ideal co-teaching partners. Co-teaching can also be used to build departmental capacity for research-based teaching approaches. In this case, a chair recruits multiple co-teaching pairs to promote fundamental teaching change across the unit. Finally, co-teaching can be incorporated into other faculty development approaches that support fundamental change, such as faculty learning communities (Cox, 2001, 2004) of co-teaching partners.

Faculty developers play a key role in the success of co-teaching. They can function as coaches and role models in the co-teaching relationship, helping faculty negotiate the details of their co-teaching plan and serving as a soundboard for their reflection. They can encourage both experienced and new faculty members to reflect on their teaching and their work together and to make explicit all of the implicit decision-making they do as teachers. Developers can also serve as research partners, just as AB did in this study, to create a scholarship of teaching and learning project that examines the process and outcomes of the co-teaching relationship.

Further Research

This study was of a single case. More examples of similar cases are needed to build a solid empirical foundation for co-teaching. We also need examples of disparate cases. For instance, how would co-teaching work for other populations, such as an experienced faculty member with an established traditional teaching routine? Would it help graduate students develop teaching expertise (Eddy & Mitchell, 2006)? Perhaps the success of the co-teaching experience depends on elements not identified here. Planning co-teaching experiences for research as well as faculty development can answer such questions.

Conclusion

Co-teaching is a cost-effective model that shows significant promise as an effective way to promote research-consistent instruction in new faculty. It seems to promote more change for much less money than the standard workshop model of faculty development because it immerses new faculty in their new instructional context and provides scaffolding and modeling to ensure success. Of course, co-teaching is only appropriate when a senior instructor knows how to teach the target course in a research-consistent manner. But with this key element in place, co-teaching can promote fundamental and lasting teaching change while supporting new faculty.

Author Note

This project was supported in part by the Physics Teacher Education Coalition (Phys-TEC), funded by the National Science Foundation, and jointly administered by the American Physical Society, American Association of Physics Teachers, and the American Institute of Physics.

References

Austin, A. E., & Baldwin, R. G. (1991). *Faculty collaboration: Enhancing the quality of scholarship and teaching.* Washington, DC: The George Washington University, School of Education and Human Development.

Barr, R. B., & Tagg, J. (1995, November/December). From teaching to learning—A new paradigm for undergraduate education. *Change, 27*(6), 12–25.

Ben-Peretz, M. (1995). Teacher stress and curriculum innovations in science teaching. In A. Hofstein, B. Eylon, & G. Giddings (Eds.), *Science education: From theory to practice* (pp. 429–435). Rehovot, Israel: Weizmann Institute of Science.

Berliner, D. C. (1987). Ways of thinking about students and classrooms by more and less experienced teachers. In J. Calderhead (Ed.), *Exploring teachers' thinking* (pp. 60–83). London, UK: Cassell Educational Limited.

Boice, R. (1991, March/April). New faculty as teachers. *Journal of Higher Education, 62*(2), 150–173.

Boyer Commission on Educating Undergraduates in the Research University. (1998). *Reinventing undergraduate education: A blueprint for America's research universities.* Retrieved May 17, 2007, from the Stony Brook University web site: http://naples.cc.sunysb.edu/Pres/boyer.nsf

Collins, A., Brown, J. S., & Holum, A. (1991, Winter). Cognitive apprenticeship: Making thinking visible. *American Educator, 15*(3), 6–11, 38–46.

Cox, M. D. (2001). Faculty learning communities: Change agents for transforming institutions into learning organizations. In D. Lieberman & C. Wehlburg (Eds.), *To improve the academy: Vol. 19. Resources for faculty, instructional, and organizational development* (pp. 69–93). Bolton, MA: Anker.

Cox, M. D. (2004). Introduction to faculty learning communities. In M. D. Cox & L. Richlin (Eds.), *New directions for teaching and learning: No. 97. Building faculty learning communities* (pp. 5–23). San Francisco, CA: Jossey-Bass.

Cuban, L. (1999). *How scholars trumped teachers: Change without reform in university curriculum, teaching, and research 1890–1990.* New York, NY: Teachers College Press.

Dancy, M. H., & Henderson, C. (2005). Beyond the individual instructor: Systemic constraints in the implementation of research-informed practices. In S. Franklin, J. Marx, & P. Heron (Eds.), *Proceedings of the 2004 Physics Education Research Conference* (Vol. 790, pp. 113–116). Melville, NY: American Institute of Physics.

Eddy, P. L., & Mitchell, R. (2006, May). Innovations: Co-teaching-training professionals to teach. *The National Teaching and Learning Forum, 15*(4), 1–7.

Elmore, R. F. (1996, Spring). Getting to scale with good educational practice. *Harvard Educational Review, 66*(1), 1–26.

Erby, K. (2001). Teaching and learning from an interdisciplinary perspective. *Peer Review, 3–4*(4–1), 28–31.

Farnham-Diggory, S. (1994, Autumn). Paradigms of knowledge and instruction. *Review of Educational Research, 64*(3), 463–477.

Felder, R. M., & Brent, R. (1996, Spring). Navigating the bumpy road to student-centered instruction. *College Teaching, 44*(2), 43–47.

Fullan, M. (2001). *The new meaning of educational change* (3rd ed.). New York, NY: Teachers College Press.

Handelsman, J., Ebert-May, D., Beichner, R., Bruns, P., Chang, A., DeHaan, R., et al. (2004, April). Education: Scientific teaching. *Science, 304*(5670), 521–522.

Henderson, C. (2005, August). The challenges of instructional change under the best of circumstances: A case study of one college physics instructor. *American Journal of Physics, 73*(8), 778–786.

Henderson, C., & Dancy, M. H. (2005). *When one instructor's interactive classroom activity is another's lecture: Communication difficulties between faculty and educational researchers.* Paper presented at the winter meeting of the American Association of Physics Teachers, Albuquerque, NM.

Hutchinson, J., & Huberman, M. (1993). *Knowledge dissemination and use in science and mathematics education: A literature review* (NSF 93–75). Arlington, VA: National Science Foundation.

Kezar, A. J. (2001). *Understanding and facilitating organizational change in the 21st century: Recent research and conceptualizations* (ASHE-ERIC Higher Education Report, 28[4]). San Francisco, CA: Jossey-Bass.

Loucks-Horsley, S., Hewson, P. W., Love, N., & Stiles, K. E. (1998). *Designing professional development for teachers of science and mathematics.* Thousand Oaks, CA: Corwin Press.

Marder, C., McCullough, J., & Perakis, S. (2001). *Evaluation of the National Science Foundation's Undergraduate Faculty Enhancement (UFE) program.* Arlington, VA: National Science Foundation.

Mazur, E. (1997). *Peer instruction: A user's manual.* Upper Saddle River, NJ: Prentice Hall.

Mitchell, J., & Marland, P. (1989). Research on teacher thinking: The next phase. *Teaching and Teacher Education, 5*(2), 115–128.

National Research Council. (2003). *Improving undergraduate instruction in science, technology, engineering, and mathematics: Report of a workshop.* Washington, DC: National Academies Press.

Piburn, M., & Sawada, D. (2000). *Reformed teaching observation protocol (RTOP): Reference manual* (Technical Rep. No. IN00–3). Tempe, AZ: Arizona Collaborative for Excellence in the Preparation of Teachers .

Rice, R. E., Sorcinelli, M. D., & Austin, A. E. (2000). *Heeding new voices: Academic careers for a new generation.* Washington, DC: American Association for Higher Education.

Roth, W.-M., Masciotra, D., & Boyd, N. (1999, October). Becoming-in-the-classroom: A case study of teacher development through coteaching. *Teaching and Teacher Education, 15*(7), 771–784.

Roth, W.-M., & Tobin, K. G. (2002). *At the elbow of another: Learning to teach by coteaching.* New York, NY: Peter Lang.

Saroyan, A., & Amundsen, C. (Eds.). (2004). *Rethinking teaching in higher education: From a course design workshop to a faculty development framework.* Sterling, VA: Stylus.

Schön, D. A. (1983). *The reflective practitioner: How professionals think in action.* New York, NY: Basic Books.

Seymour, E. (2001). Tracking the processes of change in U.S. undergraduate education in science, mathematics, engineering, and technology. *Science Education, 86,* 79–105.

Slater, T. F. (2003, October). When is a good day teaching a bad thing? *The Physics Teacher, 41*(7), 437–438.

Spillane, J. P. (2004). *Standards deviation: How schools misunderstand education policy.* Cambridge, MA: Harvard University Press.

Stake, R. E. (1998). Case studies. In N. K. Denzin & Y. S. Lincoln (Eds.), *Strategies of qualitative inquiry* (pp. 86–109). Thousand Oaks, CA: Sage.

Stigler, J. W., & Hiebert, J. (1999). *The teaching gap: Best ideas from the world's teachers for improving education in the classroom.* New York, NY: The Free Press.

Thornton, S. (2006, March–April). The devaluing of higher education: The annual report on the economic status of the profession 2005–06. *Academe, 92*(2), 24–35.

Van Driel, J. H., Verloop, N., Van Werven, H. I., & Dekkers, H. (1997, July). Teachers' craft knowledge and curriculum innovation in higher engineering education. *Higher Education, 34*(1), 105–122.

Wilson, S. M., Shulman, L. S., & Richert, A. E. (1987). "150 different ways" of knowing: Representations of knowledge in teaching. In J. Calderhead (Ed.), *Exploring teachers' thinking* (pp. 104–124). London, UK: Cassell Educational Limited.

Yerrick, R., Parke, H., & Nugent, J. (1997, April). Struggling to promote deeply rooted change: The "filtering effect" of teachers' beliefs on understanding transformational views of teaching science. *International Journal of Science Education, 81*(2), 137–159.

Yin, R. K. (2003). *Case study research: Design and methods* (3rd ed.). Thousand Oaks, CA: Sage.

14

Promoting Learning-Focused Teaching Through a Project-Based Faculty Development Program

Susanna Calkins, Greg Light
Northwestern University

This chapter describes how we incorporated project-based learning into a yearlong faculty development program at a research-intensive private university located in the Midwest. This inquiry-based approach fosters critical reflection on teaching and promotes learner-focused teaching in a manner that encourages deeper student approaches to learning. We use case studies, drawn from critical accounts of faculty projects, to illustrate a model that depicts how faculty understand improvement in their teaching and to identify key program elements that facilitated the adoption of learning-focused teaching practices by our participants.

For many faculty, finding the space and time to critically reflect on their teaching—and to consider how it relates to student learning—is a marginalized endeavor, especially when outweighed by demands of research, tenure, and promotion (Boice, 1992; Brew, 2003; Hattie & Marsh, 1996; Mullen & Forbes, 2000; Wolverton, 1998). Yet critical reflection is essential for developing sound teaching (Palmer, 1998), fostering professional development (Schön, 1983), and enhancing student learning (Light & Cox, 2001; McAlpine & Weston, 2000).

Since 1999, we have offered early-career faculty a structured space and time to reflect on their teaching through the Searle Fellows Program, a yearlong faculty development program that employs sustained reflective inquiry and project-based learning. Working individually and with peer groups, department colleagues, senior mentors, and faculty development staff, the faculty participants focus on exploring or resolving a relevant learning and teaching issue or problem. Not only does this process help faculty reflect on their teaching and student learning, but the projects also help the program staff to assess the participants' learning and sense of improvement and, in turn, to evaluate the program's effectiveness.

Program Overview

The faculty development program discussed here is a yearlong (eight-month) program for pre-tenure faculty at Northwestern University. The program seeks to provide faculty with the expertise and knowledge to critically assess and solve problems in their courses. To participate in the program, applicants must provide a description of a substantive teaching project related to a course they teach. In most cases, faculty are nominated for the program by deans or department chairs and self-select in or out according to their ability to participate in all program events. Since the program began in 1999, we have had 98 junior faculty from 9 out of 12 of the university's schools.

The program has two main goals: 1) to strengthen the participants' knowledge, understanding, and expertise in learning and teaching; and 2) to help them develop a project that will foster deep student learning (Entwistle, 1997). These projects usually focus on the development of a new course or curriculum, the revision of an existing course or curriculum, or the revision of a key assessment strategy in a course or curriculum.

Participants attend monthly dinner workshops, a two-day retreat led by the teaching center staff, three project group meetings, three or four teaching and learning workshops, and consultation meetings with senior faculty mentors and center staff. Rather than focusing simply on providing strategies, techniques, and tips, the program seeks to foster critical inquiry and professional reflection on teaching (Light & Cox, 2001).

Throughout the program we emphasized learning theory to promote student-focused, learning-oriented conceptions and approaches to teaching. These approaches aim to facilitate conceptual understanding and change in students rather than simple factual recall (Kember, 1997; Kember & Kwan, 2000; Prosser & Trigwell, 1999). They also promote deeper student learning (Entwistle, 1997; Marton & Booth, 1997; Ramsden, 2003) and improved learning outcomes (Kember & Gow, 1994; Prosser & Trigwell, 1999).

In addition, we highlighted core aspects of course design, encouraging our faculty to focus on learning outcomes, teaching methods, and assessments that moved them beyond traditional teacher-focused lectures and assessments. For example, participants learned about Kolb's (1984) Experiential Learning Cycle and student-focused taxonomies, such as Bloom's (1956) Taxonomy of Educational Objectives and Biggs's Structured Observation of Learning Outcomes taxonomy (Biggs & Collis, 1982), all of which promote critical thinking, active learning, and real-world relevance of course material. Throughout the program, we also publicized the benefits of student-active teaching methods (problem-based learning [PBL] and inquiry-based learning [IBL], case studies, role playing, small group work, discussion, etc.) and classroom assessment techniques (minute papers, concept maps, short reflections, self- and peer feedback, etc.).

Finally, we encouraged our faculty to have a small group analysis or midterm student focus group conducted in their classes to find out the students' perceptions of what aspects of the course were enhancing and impeding their learning, and to make adjustments accordingly. Along with their projects, these program components motivated our participants to reflect on and assess their development as teachers and, in many cases, to adopt a learning-focused approach to teaching.

Project-Based Learning

Project-based learning originated in PBL and IBL, two approaches that challenge learners with an ill-defined problem or set of problems and ask them to construct a reasonable solution, either over the duration of a course (PBL: Boud & Feletti, 2001; Ross, 2001; Schwartz, Mennin, & Webb, 2001) or in a single lesson or assignment (IBL: Lee, 2004). In both of these approaches, the learners, working individually or in collaborative groups, must be self-directed and construct knowledge for themselves. In our program, the faculty learner defines the problem to be resolved and tackles it through a process of active inquiry and deep critical thinking. This type of learning is also experiential and relies on doing (Kolb, 1984).

Project Goals and Description

As they develop their projects, participants are asked to identify learning outcomes, the methods they will use to help students achieve these outcomes, and their plans to assess their students' achievement. They work on their projects for several months, getting feedback from their fellow participants, department colleagues, and the center staff. At the end of the academic year, participants write up their projects ("critical accounts"), which we publish and bind in professional booklets. Participants present their final outcomes to the rest of their cohort and leading university administrators.

Case Study Analysis

We offer several program participant cases to illustrate how faculty understood improvement and experienced change in their teaching. We use a model (see Table 14.1) that differentiates three orientations, or categories, of how faculty understand teaching improvement. This model draws on several theoretical frameworks that distinguish teacher-focused/content-oriented and student-focused/learning-oriented teaching (Akerlind, 2003; Kember, 1997; Prosser & Trigwell, 1999).

TABLE 14.1

Improving Teaching: How Do Faculty Understand Improvement?

Category	Improvement Focus	Key Aspects of Focus
Transmission: Improving teaching	• Improve quality/quantity of content • Improve structure/organization of content • Acquire/increase experience of teaching • Expand practical teaching strategies/tips	*Teacher* focused
Acquisition: Improving student acquisition	• Develop teaching strategies that students perceive as working for them • Develop ways to improve students' acquisition of course content	*Student* and teacher focused
Engagement: Improving student learning	• Develop ways to improve students' conceptual understanding	*Learning*, student, and teacher focused

In the first category, faculty view teaching primarily as a means to transmit content and their own knowledge to passively receptive students, a process often referred to as information transmission. Faculty in this category, discussed in Cases 1 and 2, are likely to view improvement in teaching as improvement in the quality, quantity, and organization of the course content, and the way they structure and present this content to their students. The focus is still very much on the instructor and content knowledge, not on assessing whether students are actually learning.

In the second category, faculty begin to take a student-focused view of teaching, concentrating on ways of helping students acquire the course content. Such faculty often view teaching improvement as developing teaching strategies that students view as comfortable or effective. They are focused on the student, but they do not yet see teaching as being concerned with student learning as conceptual development or change (see Case 3).

At the more sophisticated end of the spectrum are faculty in the third category who regard teaching as facilitating student learning by promoting the students' own construction of knowledge or conceptual understanding. As discussed in Cases 4 and 5, such faculty are likely to view teaching improvement as improving students' achievement of deeper learning outcomes and their engagement in their own learning in a process of conceptual change.

While these views of teaching improvement can be more simply categorized as teacher focused, student focused, and learning focused, respectively, each successive category includes the one before. Thus, learning focused is student focused by definition, but the opposite is not necessarily the case. The following cases span the range of these categories.

Case 1: Improving Teaching as Improving the Quality of Course Content

For his project, Professor Gupta sought to revise a large lecture course on macroeconomics. In his opinion, the course had gone "relatively well" in the past but he thought it was too concept-heavy and did not contain enough content that was readily testable by rote learning, a method he relied on in his other courses. Since he considered the material in this course to be "somewhat abstract," he also found it hard to design appropriate assignments. Professor Gupta sought to revise the course by improving his delivery of content so that students would enjoy his presentations and the topics more. He collected new resources, especially PowerPoint and other multimedia, to present to the class, to jazz up the content delivery. As he explained:

> Instead of relying entirely on professor-led lectures, I want to rely only *almost* entirely on professor-led lectures. The change involves adding resources to the syllabus that land on students differently, such as graphics, videos, literature, demonstrations, and expert guests. Too much of these kinds of resources would likely undercut the seriousness of the class, so my goal is to just leaven the spoken word lectures with a sprinkling of other things.

In this case, the instruction is professor-led and the focus is on improving his course content and the organization of the course. One of Professor Gupta's main goals was to learn how to transmit course material more clearly to his students. He did pay some attention to backwards course design—a strategy endorsed frequently in the program. In his final project report, Professor Gupta explained:

I have tried to think of the course from the back to the front, in the sense of beginning with the kinds of questions I want students to be able to answer on a final exam and then thinking back through the course to be sure they are getting the information they need along the way. I am realizing that this approach is useful for thinking critically about what material I include, emphasize, or skip as I design the syllabus.

Yet the evidence from his critical account suggests that he still focused primarily on improving content delivery rather than developing the skills and learning of his students.

Case 2: Improving Teaching as Improving Instructor Performance

In his project, Professor Brown redesigned an introductory biology class for nonmajors and had several objectives in mind. He wanted his students to learn about the science of biology, including key terms and concepts. He also wanted to improve his lecturing, better convey his passion for the material and the discipline, and help his students become more comfortable with biology and feel "confident that their time was well-spent." Because he knew that most students signed up for the course because of a "fun" field trip conducted at the end of the term, he felt challenged to "maintain a high level of participation and enthusiasm" about the course material until the field trip.

Professor Brown primarily viewed improving teaching as expanding his knowledge of practical teaching strategies and tips in order to improve his own performance as an instructor. In his course redesign, Professor Brown trimmed what he termed "extraneous material" from his lectures to "liberate lecture time for other activities," including occasional in-class exercises and class presentations. For example, on one occasion, he had his students complete an ungraded, collaborative biology exercise to "change the pace of lecture" and to prepare them for the weekly lab. But when his students did not talk to each other as expected, he abruptly ended the exercise and showed the correct answer using a computer animation, as if the in-class exercise had never been attempted.

Even though Professor Brown was clearly reluctant to lose his sense of authority and control over the class, his introduction of new student-led teaching strategies and activities indicated a growing focus on how students acquire material. In his critical account, he stated that the next time he teaches the course, "I intend to create a before and after survey to better assess changing student beliefs, expectations, and understanding about biology. This information will allow me to better refine the course content." We viewed his goal to survey his students about their conceptual understanding of biology as promising and suggestive of someone moving into the transitional phase (discussed next), even though his current goal is "to better refine course content," rather than to promote student learning.

Case 3: Improving Teaching as Developing Teaching Strategies to Improve Student Acquisition of Course Content

Like many of our faculty participants, Professor Greene joined our program because she had received poor course evaluations and hoped to develop more confidence in her teaching. For her project, Professor Greene revised a large lecture course required for business majors, applying several lessons gleaned from the program. Unlike the first time she taught the course, in which she relied on "traditional" lectures to transmit central theoretical and empirical contributions of organizational theory, with little real-world application, this time she designed the course backwards, beginning with the student learning objectives (Light & Cox, 2001; McKeachie, 2002). She wanted her students to know more than content; she wanted them to know how to study social phenomena from a scientific perspective and be able to apply those principles and skills to other courses and in their future careers.

Professor Greene then set out to align these new learning objectives with her assessments and teaching methods. She structured the course around recent dramatic events (such as Hurricane Katrina) to make the course content and theory relevant to her students. She also employed ungraded, interactive short games and exercises to assess learning, to help her students acquire course content, and to give extensive feedback. For example, she used a common classroom assessment technique, the minute paper, to see if her students were grasping key concepts (Angelo & Cross, 1993). She felt rewarded when, in focus groups, her students later expressed their appreciation for these exercises; these assessments showed she cared about their learning.

Professor Greene falls into the transitional category, along with many other participants in our program. She adopted backwards course design and several active learning techniques used to make the course more relevant to her students, indicating that she was taking a much stronger student-focused approach to teaching. At the same time, her frequently expressed concerns about her teaching prowess, particularly whether her students would "like" her teaching methods, suggest that she was still not focusing on enhancing her students' learning. Nevertheless, she did start to concentrate on engaging her students more effectively and, as she gains confidence in her teaching, that focus may evolve into improving her students' conceptual understanding.

Case 4: Improving Teaching as Developing Students' Conceptual Understanding

For his project, Professor Lee developed a new assessment for a required introductory engineering course. As he explained in his critical account, "The stereotypical view of Engineering as 'problem solving' and Science as 'finding problems to solve' strongly persists in the students' mind and, in a larger context, society." His learning objectives for the course, then, were to enable students to connect their subject matter to the underlying science, to analyze complex material scientifically, and to assess their peers' and their own work. To help his students meet these objectives, Professor Lee designed a weekly "game quiz" that offered his students both formative and summative assessment, introduced them to complex material, and lowered the professor-student social barriers. As he has students playing in groups, he also sought to reduce the negative sense of competition often found in engineering classes.

In his game quiz, Professor Lee randomly assigned students to small groups. Each week, one group (the "Q-group") would develop a "nugget question" that would "encapsulate the essence of the topic of the week" and have multiple respectable answers in order to promote discussion. Group members assessed their own and each other's participation, and Professor Lee graded the group's question on its adherence to several criteria (relevance to topic, design, and clarity). The other groups would discuss the problem and submit a written solution or opinion. In class, the Q-group facilitated discussion of the various solutions and (with the assistance of Professor Lee) agreed on the best one. In the process, all of the students assessed their own understanding of the material in a formative way. According to Professor Lee, "The proposed activity generated a fun atmosphere for open discussion that should lead to a deeper understanding of the topics . . . and enhance the group learning process."

For Professor Lee, growth as a teacher meant learning to develop his students' conceptual understanding of the course content, even if it meant relinquishing some control to his students. He sought to engage his students deeply in their own learning by having them wrestle with difficult concepts, apply the concepts in the form of a question, and know the concepts well enough to help the other students weigh the merits of various solutions—all the while assessing their own and each other's performance.

Case 5: Improving Teaching as Developing Ways to Promote Conceptual Change

For her project, Professor Kung redesigned a required news writing course to help students learn how to practice journalism in a way that combines media forms (broadcast, magazine, newspaper, and new media). In her course revision, she focused on promoting problem solving and active learning and on refining her students' news editing and news writing skills. In addition, she gave her students power and voice in the classroom. As she explained, "The focus of the class needed to shift from an 'I lecture, now you write' approach in the bi-weekly three-hour lab sections to a more convivial newsroom atmosphere with the instructor acting as coach and editor."

In the past, Professor Kung had simply assigned stories for her students to write, which she would then critique. In the revised course, students were expected to generate their own original story ideas and sources and to take turns leading the class in making progress reports, providing updates, and reporting problems and solutions. They were also required to give each other feedback, publish their stories publicly on the web, and discuss their projects at the end of the term in a public student forum.

For Professor Kung, improvement in her teaching meant her students finding their own voices as journalists and changing their conception of journalism. In her critical account, she described what she termed the "profound" learning outcomes of the class: "By creating a newsroom atmosphere and demanding a professional level of work that will be published and seen on the university's Web site, the results are learning outcomes that move into the personal, intellectual, and social realms."

She purposely released control of the course so that her students could share responsibility for what they learned in the class. By actively engaging her students in the news creation process, the course mirrored the real world of journalism. By emphasizing relevance and student-led learning, she illustrated a holistic, learning-focused approach to teaching.

Analysis of Critical Accounts

We analyzed 41 critical accounts (drawn from the last three years of the program) more specifically in terms of the model described earlier. We found that nine participants' views of improvement in teaching could be construed primarily as content oriented and teaching focused. As described in Cases 1 and 2, participants in this category often expressed interest in developing teaching strategies or accruing new teaching tips in order to transmit course content more effectively or to improve their performance as a teacher. Eighteen participants fell into the transitional, or student-focused, category, as discussed in Case 3, in which instructors seek ways to improve students' acquisition of course content. Finally, 14 participants could be categorized at the highest conceptual level of enhancing student learning by promoting conceptual understanding and conceptual change, as described in Cases 4 and 5.

The following passages from the critical accounts represent commonly expressed views of teaching improvement that the participants developed by the end of the program, and this improvement definitely leans toward the student- and learning-focused end of the spectrum:

> Now my goal is to engage students and create a more dynamic environment for deeper learning . . . thus my focus now will be on critical thinking and problem-solving, rather than disseminating as much surface-learning material as I can. (Political science)

> I feel particularly strongly about [using] case studies because they enable students who are thoughtful and deep learners an opportunity to excel. Superficial and strategic learners would most likely focus on answering the questions on the assignment sheet, whereas deep learners may try different approaches and focus on the underlying problem and on providing a set of recommendations that are practical and substantiated with thorough analysis. (Engineering)

> One of the most welcome results of the conceptual changes underlying a new conception of myself as a facilitator . . . has been a new vision of the large lecture course. Instead of conceiving large lectures as something categorically different from small seminars, I now view both learning environments as situations suitable for active interaction between instructor and students and for small, peer-referenced learning as well as instructor-driven learning. (Foreign literature)

> Before I would tell the students they need to know this or that but now it's more "no, you don't need to know that." I am more selective in what material is important for the students to read. I get them to focus on the most important materials, get them to understand it. I focus on deep learning more than absorbing all the material. (Sociology)

General Discussion

Many of our faculty participants, typically short on teaching experience, enter our program holding the teacher-focused, transmission-focused view of teaching. Not only did our program foster their critical reflection, but it also launched them into a sustained inquiry into their teaching as they created or redesigned courses. Although the case studies represent each phase of the transmission engagement model of faculty improvement, very few participants stayed firmly entrenched in the transmission mode. The faculty who started there, like those described in Cases 1 and 2, came to find value in more student-focused teaching methods, albeit reluctantly at times. These findings echo Akerlind's (2003) contention that faculty who view growth in their teaching as primarily improving the quality and organization of content may be less open to more far-reaching change than those who define growth as improving student learning outcomes.

While many of our participants arguably fell into the transitional category—viewing improvement as developing teaching strategies that students perceive as working or as helping them to simply acquire concepts—a significant number clearly focused on deep learning as opposed to surface learning. As McKenzie (2002) suggests, faculty who are exposed to a range of teaching modes, allowing them to see the differences between teacher-focused, student-focused, and fully learning-focused modes, are more likely to develop sophisticated conceptions of teaching. Yet even the participants who adopted student-focused approaches did not necessarily achieve the highest, most sophisticated level of understanding of teaching growth—that is, viewing improvement as promoting deep conceptual development and change in their students. This may be due in part to faculty reluctance to adopt a more learner-centered orientation, whether from a lack of teaching experience, fear of deviating from traditional teaching methods, or even a low priority placed on good teaching (McAlpine & Weston, 2000).

Overall, requiring our faculty participants to conceptualize and implement a sustained, yearlong teaching project allows them to structure their experience of teaching using key theoretical frameworks. The project provides them with an area of focused inquiry into their teaching, with direct relevance and application, a crucial component of PBL (Boud & Feletti, 2001). Together with the written critical account, the project helps the participants reflect on and clarify their teaching and learning objectives and assess their overall practice. Moreover, we have found that the model described here allows us to better interpret the projects and critical accounts, helping us cultivate a deeper understanding of how our faculty members think about improvement. Clearly, our participants can and do improve within a category, but we use what we learn from these projects and accounts to develop our program so that more of our faculty will come to view improvement as developing learner-focused teaching and promoting students' conceptual change.

Author Note

All names and disciplines discussed in the case studies have been changed to ensure confidentiality.

References

Akerlind, G. S. (2003, October). Growing and developing as a university teacher—Variation in meaning. *Studies in Higher Education, 28*(4), 375–390.

Angelo, T. A., & Cross, K. P. (1993). *Classroom assessment techniques: A handbook for college teachers* (2nd ed.). San Francisco, CA: Jossey-Bass.

Biggs, J. B., & Collis, K. F. (1982). *Evaluating the quality of learning: The SOLO taxonomy.* San Diego, CA: Academic Press.

Bloom, B. S. (Ed.). (1956). *Taxonomy of educational objectives, handbook 1: Cognitive domain.* New York, NY: Longman.

Boice, R. (1992). *The new faculty member: Supporting and fostering professional development.* San Francisco, CA: Jossey-Bass.

Boud, D., & Feletti, G. (Eds.). (2001). *The challenge of problem-based learning* (2nd ed.). London, UK: Kogan Page.

Brew, A. (2003, May). Teaching and research: New relationships and their implications for inquiry-based teaching and learning in higher education. *Higher Education Research and Development, 22*(1), 3–18.

Entwistle, N. (1997). Contrasting perspectives on learning. In F. Marton, D. Hounsell, & N. Entwistle (Eds.), *The experience of learning* (pp. 3–22). Edinburgh, Scotland: Scottish Academic Press.

Hattie, J., & Marsh, H. W. (1996, Winter). The relationship between research and teaching: A meta-analysis. *Review of Educational Research, 66*(4), 507–542.

Kember, D. (1997, September). A reconceptualisation of the research into university academics' conceptions of teaching. *Learning and Instruction, 7*(3), 255–275.

Kember, D., & Gow, L. (1994, January/February). Orientations to teaching and their effect on the quality of student learning. *Journal of Higher Education, 65*(1), 58–74.

Kember, D., & Kwan, K.-P. (2000, September). Lecturers' approaches to teaching and their relationship to conceptions of good teaching. *Instructional Science, 28*(5–6), 469–490.

Kolb, D. A. (1984). *Experiential learning: Experience as the source of learning and development.* Upper Saddle River, NJ: Prentice-Hall.

Lee, V. S. (Ed.). (2004). *Teaching and learning through inquiry: A guidebook for institutions and instructors.* Sterling, VA: Stylus.

Light, G., & Cox R. (2001). *Learning and teaching in higher education: The reflective professional.* Thousand Oaks, CA: Sage.

Marton, F., & Booth, S. (1997). *Learning and awareness.* Mahwah, NJ: Lawrence Erlbaum.

McAlpine, L., & Weston C. (2000, September). Reflection: Issues related to improving professors' teaching and students' learning. *Instructional Science, 28*(5–6), 363–385.

McKeachie, W. J. (2002). *McKeachie's teaching tips: Strategies, research, and theory for college and university teachers* (11th ed.). Boston, MA: Houghton Mifflin.

McKenzie, J. (2002). Variation and relevance structures for university teachers' learning: Bringing about change in ways of experiencing teaching. In A. Goody, J. Herrington, & M. Northcote (Eds.), *Annual International Conference of Higher Education Research and Development Society of Australasia* (pp. 434–441). Perth, Australia: Higher Education Research and Development Society of Australasia.

Mullen, C. A., & Forbes, S. A. (2000, April). Untenured faculty: Issues of transition, adjustment and mentorship. *Mentoring and Tutoring, 8*(1), 31–46.

Palmer, P. J. (1998). *The courage to teach: Exploring the inner landscape of a teacher's life.* San Francisco, CA: Jossey-Bass.

Prosser, M., & Trigwell, K. (1999). *Understanding learning and teaching: The experience in higher education.* Buckingham, UK: Society for Research into Higher Education & Open University Press.

Ramsden, P. (2003). *Learning to teach in higher education.* New York, NY: Routledge-Falmer.

Ross, B. (2001). Towards a framework for problem-based curricula. In D. Boud & G. Feletti (Eds.), *The challenge of problem-based learning* (2nd ed., pp. 28–35). London, UK: Kogan Page.

Schön, D. A. (1983). *The reflective practitioner: How professionals think in action.* New York, NY: Basic Books.

Schwartz, P., Mennin, S., & Webb, G. (Eds.). (2001). *Problem-based learning: Case studies, experience and practice.* London, UK: Kogan Page.

Wolverton, M. (1998, Fall). Treading the tenure-track tightrope: Finding balance between research excellence and quality teaching. *Innovative Higher Education, 23*(1), 61–79.

15

Team Mentoring: An Alternative Way to Mentor New Faculty

Tara Gray
New Mexico State University

A. Jane Birch
Brigham Young University

Traditional mentoring programs usually have no mechanism for protégés to learn from each other, and they often match protégés with mentors sight unseen. Team mentoring is a less hierarchical program in which protégés mentor each other in a group while searching for more permanent and personal mentors. In this program, protégés and mentors are arguably better matched because mentors are chosen by the protégé. In addition, protégés benefit by tapping into the wisdom of their peers. As a result, team mentoring is a viable alternative to traditional mentoring programs.

Effective mentoring is a strong predictor of career success. One study showed that 15% of faculty without effective mentoring left campus early or were terminated, but this was true of none of the faculty who had effective mentoring (Boice, 2000). New faculty with mentors attained above average student evaluations by the second semester at a far higher rate than those without mentors (56% vs. 18%) (Boice, 1990). Effective mentoring also predicts greater political savvy, research productivity, and career success, as well as better teaching and leadership (Boice & Turner, 1989; Bova, 1995; Gaff & Simpson, 1994; Johnsrud & Atwater, 1993; Luna & Cullen, 1995).

Most faculty believe "the best mentoring occurs spontaneously" (Boice, 2000, p. 237). Unfortunately, spontaneous mentoring doesn't occur as often as needed, and it frequently doesn't occur at all for the faculty who most need it.

Spontaneous mentoring seems to occur for between 28% (Goodwin & Stevens, 1998) and one-third (Boice, 2000) of all new faculty. Worse, "nontraditional hires and newcomers who struggled most were even more likely to go unmentored" (Boice, 2000, p. 238). Spontaneous mentoring can work well, particularly when the bond between mentor and protégé is strong, but because spontaneous mentoring is not systematic, it has important disadvantages. It typically does not address the full range of faculty needs, and the relationship is easily terminated or neglected (Boice, 2000). One study found that most spontaneous mentoring pairs die a natural, early death due to "busyness" (Boice, 2000). Therefore, waiting for spontaneous mentoring to occur is often "no more effective than waiting at home for new romantic prospects" (Boice, 2000, p. 247).

Formal mentoring programs are not available everywhere, and the programs that do exist are imperfect. In one study, only 25% of the universities and colleges surveyed had mentoring programs (Kurfiss & Boice, 1990), and many mentoring programs have two problems. First, they often match mentors and protégés sight unseen before the program begins. When mentors and protégés are assigned this way, the mentoring relationship doesn't last as long as when the protégé chooses the mentor (Bode, 1999). In contrast, the most successful mentoring pairings occur after the protégé meets with several possible mentors before choosing one (Boice, 2000). Cox (1994) notes many advantages when the protégé selects the mentor:

> The protégé feels a sense of ownership of the decision; the mentor may feel a stronger connection to a protégé who has made a special effort to select her or him; the process of investigating and interviewing potential mentors broadens the exposure of the junior faculty member to other faculty; interviewing offers both members of the potential pair a more careful look at the possible relationship and minimizes the disappointment when a connection is not made; and finally, placing this responsibility with the junior faculty eases the program director's role in the selection process. (p. 251)

Second, there is much that new faculty can learn from each other, but there are no opportunities for this to happen in the traditional one-on-one programs. Just as it takes a village to raise a child, it takes more than one person to best support a protégé (Fayne & Ortquist-Ahrens, 2006; Sandler, 1993). Therefore, the best mentoring programs may involve opportunities for new faculty members to be supported by several other individuals, including their peers. Many universities are recognizing this in their mentoring programs, including Mutual Mentoring at the University of Massachusetts Amherst, which began in fall 2006, and Connecticut College's Christian A. Johnson Teaching Seminar for Incoming Faculty (Reder & Gallagher, 2007). At Connecticut College, second- and third-year faculty are actively involved as facilitators in the yearlong seminar for first-year faculty, and therefore serve as mentors for new faculty while continuing to benefit from the learning experiences provided.

Another such program is at the University of Texas at El Paso (UTEP). What started out in 2000 as a mentoring program that featured one-on-one mentoring evolved into a group mentoring program. During its early years, the program ran into a shortage of mentors. Even so, the power of peer mentoring became apparent as an important way to orient and support new women faculty. As a result, the UTEP program moved to group mentoring, with four to six protégés from the same college paired with two mentors (T. Reimers, personal communication, June 26, 2006).

In the Ithaca College group mentoring program, five to seven mentees, all from different departments, are grouped with at least one senior faculty member. This program's greatest challenge is finding common meeting times for group members. It follows a cultural immersion model as opposed to the coach model of individual mentoring (S. Morgan, personal communication, June 27, 2006).

One additional successful mentoring program is at Miami University, where protégés meet every three weeks for two-hour seminars, receive information on potential mentors, and ultimately select their own mentor (Cox, 1997).

All of these mentoring programs rely on protégé groups, and one of them has protégés choosing their individual mentors. As we developed our own program at New Mexico State University, we sought to build on the strengths of peer mentoring while helping protégés find their own mentors. The result was team mentoring, an alternative mentoring model in which protégés mentor each other while they search for more permanent and personal mentors. It offers two advantages over traditional mentoring models in that protégés benefit from the expertise of their peers and they are likely to be better matched with mentors.

Team Mentoring at New Mexico State University

Team mentoring at New Mexico State University, a Hispanic-serving research-extensive institution, is designed to serve faculty members, tenure track or not, during any of their first three years on campus. Each year the program supports about 14 participants, which is about one-third of the new faculty on campus, who volunteer to participate in one of two peer mentoring teams. With two teams available, new faculty have a choice of meeting times, and the teams remain small (seven faculty each). They are led by the teaching center director, who is also a tenured faculty member.

The yearlong program is designed to increase connection among new faculty by building a true cohort (fall semester) and helping them connect to some of the most supportive senior faculty across campus (spring semester). Originally, new faculty were told that their mentors could not come from their own departments as a strong argument can be made that being completely supportive of someone conflicts with judging the quality of his or her work (Boice, 2000). As the program has matured, however, we have relaxed this rule in view of research findings that some protégés are best served by departmental mentors (Boice, 1992; Boice & Turner, 1989; Cox, 1997; Jackson & Simpson, 1994). Protégés are given guidance for choosing mentors, such as to avoid faculty who are too busy for the task.

During the fall, the program brings new faculty together with their cohort (their "team") and the center director for four two-hour meetings. At the first meeting, team members get to know each other, write down questions they have about teaching, and receive copies of Boice's book *Advice for New Faculty Members* (2000). We chose this book because it focuses on managing time and balancing the demands of teaching, research, and service, which new faculty consistently rate as their biggest problems. The new faculty are asked to do several things during the two weeks before each meeting:

- Read the assigned section of the book and answer questions about that section. The questions help direct their reading and enable them to skim much of it if they prefer. (These questions, and other handouts mentioned in this chapter, are available upon request at tgray@nmsu.edu.)

- Choose one of Boice's ideas to put into action (such as writing daily for 15 to 30 minutes) and prepare to report on that action item at the next meeting. (New faculty are given a list of possible action items for each section of the book.)

- Have lunch (paid for by the teaching center) with one "potential mentor," a person whom they may eventually ask to be their mentor for this program. Each lunch is with a different potential mentor, so each protégé meets three potential mentors during the semester. About half of the new faculty protégés know whom they want to meet with from their own contacts on campus, and the other half request advice from the director, who has been on campus since 1993. At the first lunch meeting, protégés ask the potential mentor questions related to teaching; these questions can be drawn from the list of questions generated by all team members during the first team meeting.

Subsequent meetings have four parts, in which team members:

- Share their results of putting one of Boice's ideas into action, describe what went well and what did not, and explain whether they want to make it a regular habit.

- Discuss their answers to the questions for the assigned section of the book: teaching, scholarly writing, or service.

- Talk about what they learned from their meetings with the potential mentor the previous week. This activity takes up the bulk of the meeting because spirited discussions ensue about the advice given by the mentors.

- "Check in and check it out." "Checking in" consists of sharing some aspect about one's work, including recent successes and challenges. "Checking it out" involves suggesting a question for other team members to ask a potential mentor. A list of these questions is created so participants can use them when they have lunch with the next potential mentor.

By the end of the semester, each new faculty protégé chooses one of the three candidates to be his or her mentor for the spring semester. Enough potential mentors are available because of the personal way in which they are invited into the program, and mentors seem flattered to be asked. Mentors are oriented at the fifth and final meeting of the teams in a two-hour session. At this meeting, mentoring pairs are given some guidelines and help for having a successful mentoring experience and then given time to share their goals for the relationship and discuss and plan activities that will be useful to them.

Full participation in the fall program requires interviewing at least three potential mentors and attending each of the team meetings. Faculty who fully participate in the fall program are eligible for a free lunch program in the spring. Once a month during the spring semester, the protégé and his or her mentor have lunch after participating in a formal activity, such as exchanging syllabi, classroom visits, research papers, research agendas, and curricula vitae. Protégés receive guidelines for all of these activities. By having structured exercises before the one-on-one meetings, these meetings are more likely to take place and be productive. Protégés are also encouraged to check in with their mentors weekly to (briefly) tell them how they are doing in terms of their research, teaching, service, and selves.

To participate fully in the spring program, and to be reimbursed for the lunches, protégés must present the receipts for one lunch per month for five months (January to May). We hold faculty accountable in this program because accountability is the key to any successful faculty development program, including mentoring programs, and has been found to be even more important than the "worth and pleasure of the meetings" (Boice, 1990, qtd. in Boice, 2000, p. 241). Without accountability, most faculty development programs offer too little substance to be effective—that is, they become "puny interventions."

Results

The goals of team mentoring are to 1) provide useful answers to the new faculty members' questions, 2) increase their sense of community, 3) successfully pair protégés with mentors, and 4) ensure successful mentoring relationships. We survey the protégés at the end of the fall semester to assess how well the program achieved these goals. In Year 1 (2003), 13 of the 14 participants were surveyed (one participant was absent from this meeting). In Years 2 and 3 (2004 and 2005), all 11 and 15 participants were surveyed, respectively. In all, 39 participants were surveyed over three years, 65% of whom were female and 35% male, as shown in Table 15.1. In the first two years, more participants were female because the campus had an alternative National Science Foundation ADVANCE mentoring program for those in STEM (science, technology, engineering, and math) fields, so these faculty members were not invited to participate in team mentoring. In the third year, team mentoring opened to those in the STEM fields. As a result, the percentage of men in the program greatly increased.

TABLE 15.1

Gender of Participants

Year	Male	Female
Year 1	28%	72%
Year 2	9%	91%
Year 3	66%	33%
Average of 3 years	35%	65%

According to Table 15.2, the reactions of participants to the program were positive and the goals were reportedly met.

TABLE 2

Percent of New Faculty Who Agreed with Survey Statements About Team Mentoring

Survey Statement	Year 1	Year 2	Year 3	Average
Team mentoring increased my sense of community.	92%	100%	92%	95%
I got useful answers to my questions.	85%	100%	100%	95%
I found a mentor with whom I am excited to work.	92%	82%	85%	86%
I will recommend the program to my colleagues.	85%	100%	100%	95%
Team mentoring should be continued at New Mexico State University.	92%	100%	100%	97%

What did the protégés learn in the program? Responses to this question varied, but the following four representative responses indicate that the participants acquired some very specific knowledge and skills:

I no longer use power point for the whole class, which not only reduces my preparation but also increases the interaction with students.

I conducted a mid-term evaluation in one of my courses and this was a positive experience that gave me confidence and encouragement. I am writing more. I have a much better idea about the service component of my responsibilities and I feel better prepared to decide which opportunities will work for me.

I explain less material more thoroughly rather than covering more material more rapidly. I started to be more patient with my students.

I became more a practitioner of moderation and constancy in my research. I feel more confident in my research results because my research is done calmly, not last minute. Service: I thought more proactively about what service I might participate in rather than feeling pressured for time allocated away from my research and teaching.

At the end of the spring semester in the third year, we surveyed all three cohorts of protégés, giving away a $100 gift certificate to ensure a high response rate. We also used the online instrument SurveyMonkey, which allowed us to send reminders (three of them) to participants who had not responded. As a result of our efforts, our response rate was good: 69% (n = 25).

To determine whether the team mentoring program achieved its fourth and final goal, successful mentoring relationships, we presented to protégés a series of statements with which they could agree or disagree on a Likert scale. Many of these questions mirrored those we previously asked protégés about their peer mentoring team. As evident in Table 15.3, participants were very positive about how helpful the mentoring relationship had been.

TABLE 15.3

Percent of New Faculty Who Agreed with Survey Statements About the Mentoring Experience

Survey Statement	Agreed
My mentor helped me with my career.	92%
My mentor increased my sense of community.	84%
My mentor gave me useful answers to my questions.	84%
My mentor helped me with my research.	64%
My mentor helped me with my teaching.	68%
My mentor helped me with my service.	56%
I will recommend team mentoring to my colleagues.	92%
I think team mentoring should be continued at New Mexico State University.	92%

We also asked protégés, "What was least helpful about working with your mentor?" The most frequent answer (n = 7) was that nothing was "least helpful." The second most common answer (n = 5) was not being able to find time to work together.

Another survey question we posed was, "What was most helpful about working with your mentor?" As these representative answers imply, the honesty of the relationships and the listening skills of the mentors proved paramount:

The most important thing was honesty. Departmental relationships, as good as they can be, are filled with politics and there's always an evaluative aspect. It was nice to have someone to speak with openly.

She was a good listener and allowed me to talk through some of my ideas and provided input, which made them even better ideas.

I really liked the fact that she listened to me—and heard my concerns [regardless of the size of the issue]; she made me feel validated. She provided another vision of the university. . . . I would never have had the opportunity to meet her and spend time with her—had it not been for the Team Mentoring project. I still feel as if something would come up—I could contact her and she would make time for me.

Finally, we queried protégés about whether they would provide a signed testimonial to help us publicize the program. The following are two typical testimonials, both of which highlight the benefits of the classroom visits and exchange opportunities:

The Team Mentoring program has been extremely helpful to me. It has provided a structure within which I can work toward improving my research, teaching and service to the University. It also really forced me to think through who would be a good mentor, and to interview potential mentors, instead of simply taking it for granted. Although I initially did not really think that I would benefit much from a classroom visitation, I got a lot of valuable information about my teaching from my mentor, who facilitated a mini-feedback session in my class with my students. Likewise, I visited hers and found out some useful things about how to approach my own classes. Also, we are sharing our research and providing feedback. Having someone outside of your field to critique your writing is very instructive. My mentor, having recently gone through the tenure process, will be helping me to shape my dossier. I congratulate the staff of the Teaching Academy for implementing Team Mentoring, and hope that it continues to become a natural part of faculty development at New Mexico State University. (Judith Y. Weisinger, associate professor, management department)

My mentor . . . was engaging, reflective, and intuitive. Her questions to me, over our lunches, were sensitive, probing and they made me think—for hours and days after we met. We shared syllabi and vitaes, and she came to a class of mine and observed my students and my style. Her class visit provoked some great discussion between us. She was extremely valuable to me as I explored my college, other colleges, and the university as a whole, while coming to better understand the tenure process. She aided me in creating a more global form of thinking about New Mexico State University, academia in general, and how there can be a powerful and effective blending of the university and community. It was a wonderful partnership that evolved into a friendship. (Sue Forster-Cox, assistant professor, health science)

So far, the focus for all of the surveys has been on the protégés and whether the program was serving their needs. We have not yet surveyed mentors to see how they experience the program. Future studies will want to survey the mentors as well as protégés.

A program like team mentoring presents challenges that must be overcome to establish a successful program and maintain it year after year. First, it requires a faculty member or experienced faculty developer to facilitate the two mentoring teams. That person must give the program a great deal of time, but we have found that time spent this way is more enjoyable and productive than spending it matching mentoring partners. Second, the program needs a budget to pay for the eight lunches that each protégé eats with his or her potential mentors (three lunches) and ultimate mentor (five lunches). These lunches cost about $200 per participant, $5,000 in total. Of course, no mentoring program is without costs, and the benefits of this program greatly outweigh the costs.

Conclusion

Team mentoring is an alternative mentoring model in which protégés mentor each other in a group while they search for more permanent and personal mentors. Team mentoring has two key advantages over one-on-one mentoring models. First, the protégés mentor and learn from each other. Second, because protégés choose their own mentors, they and their mentors may be better matched. In sum, team mentoring is a viable and possibly more effective option than traditional mentoring programs.

Author Note

We thank Jean Conway, Milt Cox, Ereney Hadjigeorgalis, Laura Madson, Susanne Morgan, Leslie Ortquist-Ahrens, and Tine Reimers for their comments.

References

Bode, R. K. (1999). Mentoring and collegiality. In R. J. Menges & Associates, *Faculty in new jobs: A guide to settling in, becoming established, and building institutional support* (pp. 118–144). San Francisco, CA: Jossey-Bass.

Boice, R. (1990). Mentoring new faculty: A program for implementation. *Journal of Staff, Program, and Organizational Development, 8*(3), 143–160.

Boice, R. (1992). Lessons learned about mentoring. In M. D. Sorcinelli & A. E. Austin (Eds.), *New directions for teaching and learning: No. 50. Developing new and junior faculty* (pp. 51–61). San Francisco, CA: Jossey-Bass.

Boice, R. (2000). *Advice for new faculty members: Nihil nimus.* Boston, MA: Allyn & Bacon.

Boice, R., & Turner, J. L. (1989). The FIPSE-CSULB mentoring project for new faculty. In S. Kahn (Ed.), *To improve the academy: Vol. 8. Resources for student, faculty, and institutional development* (pp. 117–129). Stillwater, OK: New Forums Press.

Bova, B. M. (1995). Mentoring revisited: The Hispanic woman's perspective. *Journal of Adult Education, 23*(1), 8–19.

Cox, M. D. (1994). Reclaiming teaching excellence: Miami University's Teaching Scholars Program. In E. C. Wadsworth (Ed.), *To improve the academy: Vol. 13. Resources for faculty, instructional, and organizational development* (pp. 79–96). Stillwater, OK: New Forums Press.

Cox, M. D. (1997). Long-term patterns in a mentoring program for junior faculty: Recommendations for practice. In D. DeZure & M. Kaplan (Eds.), *To improve the academy: Vol. 16. Resources for faculty, instructional, and organizational development* (pp. 225–267). Stillwater, OK: New Forums Press.

Fayne, H., & Ortquist-Ahrens, L. (2006). Learning communities for first-year faculty: Transition, acculturation, and transformation. In S. Chadwick-Blossey & D. R. Robertson (Eds.), *To improve the academy: Vol. 24. Resources for faculty, instructional, and organizational development* (pp. 277–290). Bolton, MA: Anker.

Gaff, J. G., & Simpson, R. D. (1994, March). Faculty development in the United States. *Innovative Higher Education, 18*(3), 167–176.

Goodwin, L. D., & Stevens, E. A. (1998, Summer). An exploratory study of the role of mentoring in the retention of faculty. *Journal of Staff, Program, and Organizational Development, 16*(1), 39–47.

Jackson, W. K., & Simpson, R. D. (1994). Mentoring new faculty for teaching and research. In M. A. Wunsch (Ed.), *New directions for teaching and learning: No. 57. Mentoring revisited: Making an impact on individuals and institutions* (pp. 65–72). San Francisco, CA: Jossey-Bass.

Johnsrud, L. K., & Atwater, C. D. (1993, Spring). Scaffolding the ivory tower: Building supports for faculty new to the academy. *CUPA Journal, 44*(1), 1–14.

Kurfiss, J., & Boice, R. (1990). Current and desired faculty development practices among POD members. In L. Hilsen (Ed.), *To improve the academy: Vol. 9. Resources for student, faculty, and institutional development* (pp. 73–82). Stillwater, OK: New Forums Press.

Luna, G., & Cullen, D. L. (1995). *Empowering the faculty: Mentoring redirected and renewed* (ASHE-ERIC Higher Education Rep. No. 3). Washington, DC: The George Washington University, School of Education and Human Development.

Reder, M., & Gallagher, E. V. (2007). Transforming a teaching culture through peer mentoring: Connecticut College's Johnson Teaching Seminar for Incoming Faculty. In D. R. Robertson & L. B. Nilson (Eds.), *To improve the academy: Vol. 25. Resources for faculty, instructional, and organizational development* (pp. 327–344). Bolton, MA: Anker.

Sandler, B. R. (1993, March 10). Women as mentors: Myths and commandments. *The Chronicle of Higher Education*, p. B3.

16

A Research-Based Rubric for Developing Statements of Teaching Philosophy

Matthew Kaplan, Deborah S. Meizlish,
Christopher O'Neal, Mary C. Wright
University of Michigan

Despite its ubiquity as the way that instructors represent their views on teaching and learning, the statement of teaching philosophy can be a frustrating document to write and the results are often uneven. This chapter describes a rubric created at the University of Michigan's Center for Research on Learning and Teaching to help faculty and graduate students craft teaching statements. We describe the research that informed the creation of the rubric, talk about how we use the rubric in our consultations and workshops, and present an assessment that validates the use of the rubric to improve instructors' teaching statements.

The statement of teaching philosophy or teaching statement has emerged as a standard piece of academic writing in which instructors articulate their beliefs about, approaches to, and accomplishments in teaching and learning. Numerous resources are available about how to write teaching statements, both in print form (e.g., Chism, 1997–1998; Coppola, 2000; Ellis & Griffin, 2000; Goodyear & Allchin, 1998) and on teaching center web sites across the country. These articles also point out the practical benefits of teaching statements (e.g., for job searches and as part of teaching portfolios) and their potential for enhancing reflective practice, making implicit ideas about teaching and student learning explicit, and helping college teachers align their beliefs and their pedagogical practices.

Consultants at our teaching center have helped hundreds of graduate students and faculty write their own statements. As a result, we have come to agree that the process of writing a teaching statement can be quite valuable and lead to a document that provides needed insight into an instructor's pedagogical beliefs and behaviors. However, our experience has also shown that faculty and graduate students often find teaching statements difficult and frustrating to write and evaluate, and the quality of their efforts can be uneven despite the availability of resources and the genre's ubiquity. This frustration has led some academics to question the utility of teaching statements, criticizing them as empty, boilerplate, and uninformative (Montell, 2003; Pratt, 2005).

To remedy the problems associated with teaching statements, we crafted a rubric designed to guide authors through writing and editing their teaching statements and to help them give feedback to colleagues in workshops and seminars conducted by our center. The rubric's construction was informed by our own perceptions of what made for effective teaching statements and was later refined by a survey of search committee chairs' perceptions of the successful and unsuccessful qualities of teaching statements. The rubric has made the writing process more manageable by demystifying an unfamiliar genre that can seem overwhelming: The rubric's delineation of a fixed number of topics, along with clear criteria for each, helps writers focus their efforts.

In this chapter, we present evidence demonstrating the widespread use of teaching statements, discuss the development of the rubric, and then describe the various ways we use the rubric to help graduate students and faculty write their own teaching statements. We end with data from a brief assessment comparing clients' teaching philosophies in the pre-rubric and post-rubric eras, which appear to validate our approach.

Research Overview

Uses of Teaching Statements

Teaching statements can be used for both formative and summative evaluation. As just described, writing a teaching statement entails reflection on current practice, a necessary part of formative evaluation and a prerequisite for deciding on areas for improvement. However, statements of teaching philosophy are better known for their use in summative types of evaluation, in particular in vetting job candidates for faculty positions and evaluating faculty work in teaching for promotion and tenure.

In an attempt to learn more about teaching evaluation practices, we gathered information in spring 2006 from peer institutions concerning teaching evaluation methods mandated by their central administrations (i.e., provosts). For the purposes of this study, we defined peer institutions as those campuses with whom the University of Michigan collaborates in consortia of teaching center directors—members of the Committee on Institutional Cooperation and the Ivy Plus groups—as well as other flagship state universities. For a full list, see Figure 16.1.

FIGURE 16.1

Peer Institutions for Teaching Evaluation Survey

Berkeley	Illinois	Northwestern	UNC
Brown	Indiana	Ohio State	UVA
Chicago	Iowa	Penn	Washington
Columbia	Michigan	Penn State	Wisconsin
Cornell	Minnesota	Princeton	Yale
Dartmouth	MIT	Purdue	
Harvard	Michigan State	Stanford	

We gathered data from university web sites and then asked colleagues at teaching centers on those campuses to check and supplement the information. In all, we collected data from 26 institutions, 14 of which (53%) required some type of teaching statement for promotion and tenure (exact definitions and terminology varied and included self-evaluations, teaching philosophies, and comprehensive statements of a candidate's accomplishments in research, teaching, and service). Student ratings are the only type of evaluation required more frequently (18 universities, or 69%). Replicating this process on our own campus, we learned that all schools and colleges required some form of teaching statement. While there are obvious limitations to this study in terms of scope, it is clear that including some form of teaching statement in the review process has become standard practice, even at research-extensive universities.

Writing a statement of teaching philosophy has also become an integral part of the faculty job search. Our teaching center, like others around the country, includes sessions on the teaching statement in our campus-wide Preparing Future Faculty (PFF) Seminar as well as in customized, discipline-specific seminars. We also conduct numerous consultations with graduate students as they prepare their job applications.

To learn more about how graduate students use their statements, we did a follow-up survey of participants in our PFF Seminar, an intensive, month-long program with a particular emphasis on preparing documents for the job search. The results of that survey indicated that 90% of seminar participants used their teaching statements for the job market (Cook, Kaplan, Nidiffer, & Wright, 2001).

To determine the extent to which faculty search committees requested statements, two of the authors (Meizlish and Kaplan) conducted a survey of search committee chairs at colleges and universities across the country in spring and summer 2005. This survey was part of a larger project to examine the relative importance of teaching in faculty searches (for additional information on this study, see Meizlish & Kaplan, 2007). We began by collecting job ads from disciplinary databases for tenure-track assistant professors or open-rank positions in six disciplines (biology, chemistry, English, history, political science, and psychology), and then drew a random sample of those ads in each discipline for our follow-up survey. Of the 755 committee chairs who received the survey, 457 responded, a 61% response rate. Of those surveyed, 57% overall indicated that they requested a teaching statement at some point in the job search. Tables 16.1 and 16.2 report percentages by institutional type and disciplinary division. Differences by institutional type were not statistically significant: 60% of master's and bachelor's institutions and approximately 54% of doctoral universities requested statements. The disciplinary differences were statistically significant and somewhat surprising: Approximately 50% of humanities and social sciences committees requested statements, while close to 75% of natural sciences committees did so.

TABLE 16.1

Percentage of Respondents Requesting Statements of
Teaching Philosophy During the Hiring Process, by Institutional Type

Requested Teaching Philosophy During Hiring Process	Doctoral	Master's	Bachelor's
Yes	53.6%	61.5%	61.5%
No	46.4%	38.5%	38.5%

Note. Significance testing revealed no significant differences (p < .05) by institutional type.

TABLE 16.2

Percentage of Respondents Requesting Statements of Teaching Philosophy During the Hiring Process, by Division

Requested Teaching Philosophy During Hiring Process	Humanities	Social Sciences	Natural Sciences*
Yes	50.2%	49.6%	79.8%
No	49.8%	50.4%	20.2%

*Note. Results for the natural sciences are significantly different from those in the humanities and social sciences (p < .05).

It is clear from these responses that teaching statements are now commonly requested across the disciplinary and institutional spectrum. However, graduate students in our PFF Seminar often ask about the wisdom of sending an unsolicited teaching statement, and so our survey asked: "Based on your experience, how do you think a search committee would respond if the applicant submitted a statement of teaching philosophy even though a statement was not requested?" Respondents answered using a 6-point rating scale (from 1 = Extremely Unfavorable to 6 = Extremely Favorable) to express their views of unsolicited statements at three stages, the initial application, first-round interviews, and campus visits. Tables 16.3 and 16.4 report mean responses by institutional type and disciplinary division. At each stage, faculty viewed submission of an unsolicited statement in a generally positive light, with median responses of approximately 4.9 at each stage (5 = Favorable). Although there were slight differences by institutional type and disciplinary division, the overall conclusion remains unchanged: Submission of an unsolicited teaching statement is viewed quite positively by search committee chairs in our sample.

What Makes a Successful Statement?

In our survey, we asked search committee chairs to tell us what makes a statement of teaching philosophy successful or unsuccessful. Based on the responses, this is a topic of great interest to those who read teaching statements: 78% of respondents provided open-ended responses about successful statements and 76% about the unsuccessful ones.

In analyzing the 356 responses to the question "What makes a teaching statement successful?" we looked for common themes and language. We divided

TABLE 16.3

Mean Favorability of a Candidate's Submission of an Unsolicited Teaching Philosophy, by Institutional Type

Respondents rated each item on a 6-point Likert scale (6 = Extremely Favorable to 1 = Extremely Unfavorable)

Institutional Type^	Initial Application	First-Round Interview	Campus Visit
Doctoral extensive	4.73	4.70	4.79
Doctoral intensive	5.05*	5.12*	5.05
Master's	4.93*	4.93*	4.99
Bachelor's	5.00*	4.89	4.90
Overall	4.88	4.85	4.90

^ *Note.* Only differences between doctoral-extensive and other institutions were statistically significant at the ($p < .05$) level. These are indicated by an *.

TABLE 16.4

Mean Favorability of a Candidate's Submission of an Unsolicited Teaching Philosophy, by Disciplinary Division

Respondents rated each item on a 6-point Likert scale (6 = Extremely Favorable to 1 = Extremely Unfavorable)

Division ^	Initial Application	First-Round Interview	Campus Visit
Humanities	4.81	4.90	4.98
Social sciences	4.95	4.86	4.82
Natural sciences	4.88	4.68*	4.80
Overall	4.87	4.84	4.89

^ *Note.* Difference of means tests revealed statistically significant differences between the natural sciences and humanities during the first round ($p < .05$).

these themes into five major categories and then coded each response based on these categories:

- *Offers evidence of practice.* Search committees wanted to see how effectively a candidate could instantiate the philosophy of teaching. They sought specific examples of how the applicant linked theory with their actual teaching experiences (110 responses). This was by far the most commonly cited trait of successful statements. For example, a respondent in political science said the following: "Statements are most effective when they include specific and personal examples, experiences, etc. It makes the statement seem more than merely perfunctory." Similarly, a faculty member in psychology valued statements that were "Succinct; included examples of enactment of the philosophy."

- *Is student centered, attuned to differences in student ability, learning styles, or level* (65 responses). For example, a faculty member in biology was looking for "Clear expression of methods of instruction that go beyond the traditional lecture and testing methodology. Active learning and group problem solving appreciation are two valued components."

- *Demonstrates reflectiveness.* Search committees sought evidence that the writer was a thoughtful instructor. They looked for examples about how changes had been made in the classroom, how the instructor had grappled with instructional challenges, and how the applicant outlined his or her future development as a teacher (53 responses). For example, "They showed that the candidate had given much thought to their goals and approaches to teaching" (chemistry); "Indications that the candidate had reflected on his/her past experiences" (English).

- *Conveys valuing of teaching.* Survey respondents appreciated a tone or language that conveyed an enthusiasm for teaching or a vision of the applicant as a teacher. Conversely, they devalued philosophies that conceptualized teaching as a burden, a requirement, or as less of a priority than research (50 responses). For example "Successful statements demonstrated the candidate's enthusiasm for teaching" (chemistry); "Enthusiasm for teaching usually manifests itself as well as indications that it is as serious an undertaking as one's scholarly pursuits" (English).

- *Is well written, clear, readable* (39 responses).

In our analysis of the 347 responses to the question "What makes a teaching statement *unsuccessful*?" two characteristics were mentioned most frequently:

- *Is generic, full of boilerplate language, does not appear to be taken seriously.* By far the most commonly cited complaint was the use of jargon, buzzwords, or "teaching-philosophy speak" that made all statements sound alike and rather generic (134 responses). For example, "Failure to realize that much of what was in the statement was cliché" (history); "Tended to include all of the right 'buzz words' which made me wonder about the sincerity of the statement" (psychology); "Those that were formulaic, that seemed to include as many buzzwords as possible" (English).

- *Provides no evidence of practice.* Faculty wanted some sense that the ideas presented in the statement were actually grounded in the candidate's experience (74 responses). For example, "Most of it sounded highly theoretical and idealistic. I am not sure that the writers had ever tried some of those things with live students in actual classrooms" (history); "Global, vague statements that were not specific enough about exactly how the person would implement a teaching style" (psychology).

The Rubric

Clearly, the teaching statement is now a common part of faculty and graduate student work life. Just as obvious to us from our experience is the fact that academics are not prepared for this type of writing and, as a result, they find it difficult. The majority of our work on teaching statements occurs within the context of our month-long PFF Seminar, where one of the main requirements is the writing of a statement of teaching philosophy.

Unfortunately, during the first three years of the program (2000–2002) we were frequently disappointed with the quality of the statements participants were producing. These statements often sounded generic and theoretical, failing to convey the experiences and disciplinary contexts that emerged in discussions among the very talented graduate students in our program. Problems we were noting echoed issues raised by the faculty in our survey. The situation was particularly disheartening because the seminar already included several mechanisms to help participants develop successful statements, including readings, exercises for getting started, and feedback from peers in the seminar.

We began working on a rubric to make explicit to our PFF students our own perceptions of the strengths characteristic of effective teaching statements and the pitfalls to be avoided. Our assumption was that having a set of criteria would make the writing process more manageable.

Research on rubrics supports our approach. A rubric can be defined as "a scoring tool that lays out the specific expectations for an assignment. Rubrics divide an assignment into its component parts and provide detailed description of what constitutes acceptable or unacceptable levels of performance for each of those parts" (Stevens & Levi, 2005, p. 3). Andrade (1997) outlines four reasons why rubrics are effective, two of which are particularly applicable to our work with teaching statements. First, rubrics are useful for both teaching and assessment: "Rubrics can improve student performance . . . by making teachers' expectations clear and by showing students how to meet these expectations." Second, rubrics promote self-regulated learning and help students to develop their own judgment: "When rubrics are used to guide self- and peer-assessment, students become increasingly able to spot and solve problems in their own and one another's work" (Andrade, 1997). Rubrics have been shown to have positive impacts on high school and undergraduate students' writing and achievement (Andrade & Du, 2005). One may reasonably expect that students' uses of rubrics—to determine expectations, plan production, facilitate revision, and guide and prompt reflection (Andrade & Du, 2005)—would be mirrored by graduate students and faculty as they learn to write in this unfamiliar genre.

As mentioned earlier, the rubric we constructed drew on our own experience critiquing hundreds of teaching philosophies as well as the survey of search committee members. Our primary goals when writing it were 1) to provide a concrete structure that prompted and facilitated reflection on the key components of an instructor's philosophy and the articulation of that philosophy, and 2) to bring to the fore those characteristics that search committees found most meaningful and successful.

As we worked to refine and improve the rubric over different iterations, we also kept in mind those qualities that define successful rubrics. Mullinix (2003) presents a "rubric for rubrics" that we found informative in judging our own. We aimed for a rubric that could be called "exemplary" in all the criteria presented: clarity of criteria and expectations, distinction between levels of achievement, inter-rater reliability, support of metacognition, and ease of use in peer and self-evaluation (see also Popham, 1997, for an excellent discussion of the qualities of effective and ineffective rubrics).

We should note here that ours is not the first rubric created for the evaluation of teaching statements. Schönwetter, Sokal, Friesen, and Taylor (2002) outline a rubric in their paper on the development and evaluation of teaching statements. However, this rubric focuses on the statement as an articulation of instructors' understanding of the teaching and learning literature, rather than the areas highlighted by our survey research (e.g., the importance of specific evidence of practice).

The rubric (see Appendix 16.1) provides weak, average, and excellent descriptors of five categories of teaching philosophy characteristics:

1. Goals for student learning

2. Enactment of goals

3. Assessment of goals

4. Creating an inclusive learning environment

5. Structure, rhetoric, and language

The first three categories of the rubric were framed by theories of alignment across instructor goals, methods, and assessments. Alignment is a major focus of our PFF Seminar, and we have found that this approach leads to teaching statements that offer the fullest picture of an instructor's approach to teaching and learning. This model has the added benefit of prompting instructors to reflect on the degree to which their methods and assessments actually do align with their goals. As one seminar participant wrote,

> The rubric has actually gotten me thinking about my teaching and what I concentrate on in the classroom, in addition to developing a teaching philosophy statement. For example, how to reach all students in the class and how evaluation techniques tell me whether students are achieving goals.

Category 4 reflects our center's commitment to diversity and our belief that teaching that reaches students at the margins of the classroom is good for all students in the classroom. We have found this to be the most neglected component of teaching statements, and we have chosen to highlight this issue in its own category to draw particular attention to it. Descriptors for this category emphasize the integration of inclusive teaching and learning throughout the statement, thereby avoiding the isolated "diversity paragraph," another common weakness of teaching statements.

The last category (structure, rhetoric, and language) addresses some of the most common complaints about teaching statements. Descriptors for this category stress the elimination of teaching jargon that alienates many readers and weak thematic structures that make reading difficult.

A focus on specificity and disciplinary context is built into all of the categories in the rubric, and rich, illustrative examples are emphasized as well. For example, under "Enactment," the "Excellent" category includes the following descriptor: "Specific examples of the methods in use within the disciplinary context are given." A statement "needs work" in this category when "Methods are described but generically, [with] no example of the instructor's use of the methods within the discipline." Under "Structure, rhetoric, and language," excellence includes "Jargon is avoided and teaching terms (e.g., critical thinking) are given specific definitions that apply to the instructor's disciplinary context. Specific, rich examples are used to bolster statements of goals, methods, and assessments."

How Is the Rubric Used?

Because clients' needs differ depending on their rank and experience, as well as their disposition and ability to commit time to writing their teaching statement, the rubric is used as a consulting tool in a variety of different settings.

In *individual consultations* with graduate students and faculty, clients are typically interested in feedback on a teaching statement that they have already started. In this case, we typically ask clients to self-evaluate their own statement using the rubric. The consultant also evaluates the teaching statement before meeting the client, and the resulting consultation focuses on areas where the instructor and consultant agree and disagree and what the instructor needs to do to improve the statement in different categories of the rubric and holistically. Since beginning to use the rubric in this way we have noticed a drop in clients' anxiety about writing the statement and an increase in the quality of the teaching statements, even when our consultation clients were pressed for time (as is often the case).

The teaching philosophy rubric also forms the cornerstone of our 90-minute *Teaching Philosophy Workshop*. This workshop begins with a general introduction to the characteristics of the teaching statement, but then quickly introduces participants to the rubric. Within the first 15 minutes of the workshop, participants use the rubric to evaluate a sample teaching statement and use electronic classroom voting devices to rank the statement on each category of the rubric. We find that this anonymous voting helps workshop participants develop a shared understanding of how to use the rubric while leaving space for individual priorities and judgments as to the qualities of the statement most important to them. Due to the short length of this workshop, participants only have time to begin outlining their own teaching statements, but they have been effectively coached in using the rubric for evaluating their own statements.

The rubric is used most rigorously in our month-long *PFF Seminar*, held for 50 hours over 10 days in May each year. In this intensive workshop, 40–50 advanced graduate students learn about higher education, participate in and reflect on advanced teaching techniques, and write a statement of teaching philosophy and a sample syllabus, both for use in job applications. The seminar's coverage of the teaching statement begins in much the same way as the Teaching Philosophy Workshop. We introduce the characteristics of the teaching statement and the rubric. Participants then use the rubric and electronic voting devices to evaluate sample teaching statements. Thanks to the length of the seminar, participants are able to write and receive feedback from colleagues on multiple drafts of their teaching statements. The rubric guides this feedback, especially during earlier drafts. In all iterations, drafts and feedback are posted online for the benefit of all seminar participants.

Validation

To assess potential differences in the quality of teaching statements before and after the implementation of the rubric, philosophies from two years of the PFF Seminar were chosen for evaluation. A random sample of 20 philosophies was selected from the pool of all 80 statements, stratified by usage of the rubric (pre- and post-implementation) and discipline (see Table 16.5).

TABLE 16.5

Disciplinary Representation of Teaching Statements in the Study Sample

	Pre-Rubric (2002)		Post-Rubric (2006)	
Disciplinary Grouping	Number of All Statements	Number in Study Sample	Number of All Statements	Number in Study Sample
Science, technology, engineering, and math	16	4	18	4
Social sciences	11	4	9	2
Arts and humanities	4	2	15	4
Totals	31	10	42	10

These 20 teaching statements were then assessed from the perspective of job search committees based on the survey mentioned earlier. As a reminder, the following criteria were ranked as the top important constituents of a teaching statement:

- Offers evidence of practice

- Is student centered, attuned to differences in student ability, learning styles, or level

- Demonstrates reflectiveness

- Conveys valuing of teaching

- Is well written, clear, readable

One of the authors (Wright), a consultant in the university's Center for Research on Learning and Teaching not involved in the construction of the rubric, applied each of these criteria to the 20 statements. Statements were presented anonymously so that the rater would have no knowledge of which statements belonged to which cohort. Each standard received a rating of 1 (poor, or not addressed in the statement), 2 (good, or present in the statement but not extensively developed or well executed), or 3 (excellent, or present in the statement and well developed and executed). These scores were combined into an "effective philosophy index." For example, a statement that perfectly addressed all job search committee criteria would merit a score of 15.

Applying standards valued by job search committees, the evaluation of the 20 teaching statements found a dramatic increase in quality in the post-rubric statements. Before the rubric-based workshop became part of the PFF Seminar, the average evaluation score was 9.7 (see Table 16.6). After the introduction of the rubric, scores averaged 11.7, a statistically significant increase of 2.0 points ($p < .05$).

TABLE 16.6

Mean Evaluation Scores on the Effective Philosophy Index

	Pre-Rubric (2002) (SD)	Post-Rubric (2006) (SD)	Difference in Means
Overall Mean Score	9.7 (2.5) N = 10	11.7 (2.3) N = 10	2.0*

*$p < .05$

To illustrate the dramatic change in quality in another manner, 7 out of the 10 lowest-scoring philosophies were from 2002, while 7 out of the 10 highest-scoring philosophies were written in 2006. A more detailed analysis of the scoring reveals that the largest difference between the two years is found in the first category, "Offers evidence of practice" (2.7 mean in 2006 vs. 2.1 in 2002), a major focus of the rubric, while the smallest difference is found in the final category, "Is well written" (2.3 in 2006 vs. 2.1 in 2002), a more generic category that has less to do with the teaching philosophy than with the student's overall skill as a writer. Of the 10 statements from 2006, 8 were rated as excellent on evidence of practice, whereas only 4 received that rating in 2002.

The following is a typical example of the excellent use of evidence in the 2006 statements, in which rich examples of practice within a specific disciplinary context are woven in throughout the statement. This humanities graduate student writes about the goals of having students develop the ability to do close reading and of using writing to make connections between texts:

> *Close reading:* One way in which I try to "ease" students into close reading, then, is to pass out a small piece of familiar text. . . . I then begin to ask them questions about the text's specific imagery and diction, about the way its smaller elements work in service of an issue that surpasses their individual details. After modeling the close reading . . . I ask the class to spend 15 minutes writing notes for a close reading. . . . Once students finish writing, we compile a list of their "close-reading notes" on the board. The result each time has been an extraordinarily diverse and creative group of ways of looking at a small piece of text.

> *Using writing to connect texts:* I strive to engender a comparative spirit by requiring a variety of smaller writing assignments that concentrate on connecting individual readings . . . to other texts or issues that are meaningful to class members. One way I specifically go about this is to ask students to pick an anecdote, newspaper or magazine article whose themes speak to those in a particular text and to write a short reflective essay on the relationship. . . . One memorable essay from an American Novel course looked at . . .

The 2002 statements often have well-articulated ideas about teaching, but stop short of offering rich evidence for the implementation of these ideas. As a result, they tend to sound more generic, a main complaint of faculty in our survey. For instance, a student in the social sciences discusses the role of humor and the challenges of teaching core, multidisciplinary courses. While there are some examples, they are not nearly as rich or well developed, and they are not as firmly grounded in the discipline:

> *Humor:* I do not mean that all learning sessions must require "fun and games." Rather I use humor as a way of setting the tone for a session, or as a device to break the tension and frustration when the going gets rough. My use of humor has evolved over the years, relying less on "jokes" and more on an overall sense of good nature . . .

> *Core courses:* Students from these courses come from a variety of backgrounds and, for the most part, are highly motivated to learn. We require students to quickly learn concepts from a variety of disciplines and this can lead to frustration. . . . At times I have acted as a "translator" between disciplines explaining concepts in plain terms and helping students to draw connections between disciplines. I have found myself needing to explain basic computer data structures to students with humanities backgrounds, or introducing the basic components of a particular sociological theory to computer scientists.

Conclusion

Not surprisingly (for anyone who has used rubrics in their own teaching and assessment), the rubric-based consulting approach results in teaching statements that are more closely aligned with search committees' judgments of quality. Anecdotally, we can also report that authors' anxiety in writing statements is greatly reduced when they can rely on the concrete guidance of the rubric. As with many other instructional development interactions, we have found that a consulting approach focused on reflection and self-discovery is much more effective than just telling instructors what makes for a good statement. The rubric is a useful tool for facilitating this reflection and growth, as it provides an obvious structure for framing and gauging that reflection.

We do not, however, claim that the rubric offers a one-size-fits-all solution. Institutions, disciplines, and individuals differ in how they envision effective teaching and learning and its articulation. Consultants should see the rubric as a flexible tool that they can shape to their institution's or individual client's needs. Likewise, instructors must attain some degree of comfort with the ambiguities of the genre.

Finally, much, if not most, of our work on teaching statements has been with graduate students preparing for the job market. When applied to faculty teaching statements, the rubric-based approach raises some challenging questions for institutions. Should departments agree on a standard for teaching statements? How should statements be evaluated in tenure and promotion decisions? Should all faculty receive training in how to write in this unfamiliar genre? While it is unrealistic to expect that diverse and decentralized institutions such as ours could (or would want to) develop a uniform standard, individual departments might attempt to create their own rubrics for faculty teaching statements. This would provide faculty with a context-specific set of criteria and it would also open up a very significant conversation about the department's pedagogical values.

Appendix 16.1

Rubric for Statements of Teaching Philosophy

Developed by Matt Kaplan, Rosario Carillo,
Chris O'Neal, Deborah Meizlish, & Diana Kardia

Center for Research on Learning and Teaching, University of Michigan

Possible Components	*Excellent*	*Needs Work*	*Weak*
Goals for Student Learning: What knowledge, skills, and attitudes are important for student success in your discipline? What are you preparing students for? What are key challenges in the teaching-learning process?	Goals are clearly articulated and specific and go beyond the knowledge level, including skills, attitudes, career goals, etc. Goals are sensitive to the context of the instructor's discipline. They are concise but not exhaustive.	Goals are articulated although they may be too broad or not specific to the discipline. Goals focus on basic knowledge, ignoring skills acquisition and affective change.	Articulation of goals is unfocused, incomplete, or missing.
Enactment of Goals (teaching methods): What teaching methods do you use? How do these methods contribute to your goals for students? Why are these methods appropriate for use in your discipline?	Enactment of goals is specific and thoughtful. Includes details and rationale about teaching methods. The methods are clearly connected to specific goals and are appropriate for those goals. Specific examples of the method in use within the disciplinary context are given.	Description of teaching methods not clearly connected to goals or if connected, not well developed (seems like a list of what is done in the classroom). Methods are described but generically, no example of the instructor's use of the methods within the discipline is communicated.	Enactment of goals is not articulated. If there is an attempt at articulating teaching methods, it is basic and unreflective.

Possible Components	Excellent	Needs Work	Weak
Assessment of Goals (measuring student learning): How do you know your goals for students are being met? What sorts of assessment tools do you use (e.g., tests, papers, portfolios, journals), and why? How do assessments contribute to student learning? How do assessments communicate disciplinary priorities?	Specific examples of assessment tools are clearly described. Assessment tools are aligned with teaching goals and teaching methods. Assessments reinforce the priorities and context of the discipline both in content and type.	Assessments are described, but not in connection to goals and teaching methods. Description is too general, with no reference to the motivation behind the assessments. There is no clear connection between the assessments and the priorities of the discipline.	Assessment of goals is not articulated or mentioned only in passing.
Creating an Inclusive Learning Environment, Addressing One or More of the Following Questions: How do your own and your students' identities (e.g., race, gender, class, background, experience, and levels of privilege) affect the classroom? How do you account for diverse learning styles? How do you integrate diverse perspectives into your teaching?	Portrays a coherent philosophy of inclusive education that is integrated throughout the philosophy. Makes space for diverse ways of knowing and/or learning styles. Discussion of roles is sensitive to historically underrepresented students. Demonstrates awareness of issues of equity within the discipline.	Inclusive teaching is addressed but in a cursory manner or in a way that isolates it from the rest of the philosophy. Author briefly connects identity issues to aspects of his or her teaching.	Issues of inclusion are not addressed or addressed in an awkward manner. There is no connection to teaching practices.

Possible Components	*Excellent*	*Needs Work*	*Weak*
Structure, Rhetoric, and Language: How is the reader engaged? Is the language used appropriate to the discipline? How is the statement thematically structured?	The statement has a guiding structure and/or theme that engages the reader and organizes the goals, methods, and assessments articulated in the statement. Jargon is avoided and teaching terms (e.g., critical thinking) are given specific definitions that apply to the instructor's disciplinary context. Specific, rich examples are used to bolster statements of goals, methods, and assessments. Grammar and spelling are correct.	The statement has a structure and/or theme that is not connected to the ideas actually discussed in the statement, or organizing structure is weak and does not resonate within the disciplinary context. Examples are used but seem generic. May contain some jargon.	No overall structure present. Statement is a collection of disconnected thoughts about teaching. Jargon is used liberally and not supported by specific definitions or examples. Needs much revision.

References

Andrade, H., & Du, Y. (2005, April). Student perspectives on rubric-referenced assessment. *Practical Assessment, Research and Evaluation, 10*(3), 1–11.

Andrade, H. G. (1997). Understanding rubrics. *Educational Leadership, 54*(4). Retrieved May 21, 2007, from the Harvard Graduate School of Education, Active Learning Practices for Schools web site: http://learnweb.harvard.edu/ALPS/thinking/docs/rubricar.htm

Chism, N. V. N. (1997–1998). Developing a philosophy of teaching statement. *Essays on Teaching Excellence, 9*(3) 1–2.

Cook, C. E., Kaplan, M., Nidiffer, J., & Wright, M. C. (2001, March). Preparing future faculty—faster: A crash course guides students to the professoriate. *AAHE Bulletin, 54*(3), 3–7.

Coppola, B. (2000). How to write a teaching philosophy for academic employment. *American Chemical Society, Department of Career Services Bulletin,* 1–8.

Ellis, D., & Griffin, G. (2000). Developing a teaching philosophy statement: A special challenge for graduate students. *Journal of Graduate Teaching Assistant Development, 7*(1), 85–92.

Goodyear, G. E., & Allchin, D. (1998). Statements of teaching philosophy. In M. Kaplan & D. Lieberman (Eds.), *To improve the academy: Vol. 17. Resources for faculty, instructional, and organizational development* (pp. 103–121). Stillwater, OK: New Forums Press.

Meizlish, D. S., & Kaplan, M. (2007). *Valuing and evaluating teaching in academic hiring: A multi-disciplinary, cross institutional study.* Manuscript submitted for publication.

Montell, G. (2003, March 27). What's your philosophy on teaching, and does it matter? *The Chronicle of Higher Education.* Retrieved May 21, 2007, from http://chronicle.com/jobs/2003/03/2003032701c.htm

Mullinix, B. B. (2003). *A rubric for rubrics.* Retrieved May 21, 2007, from the Monmouth University, Faculty Resource Center web site: http://its.monmouth.edu/facultyresourcecenter/Rubrics/A%20Rubric%20for%20Rubrics.htm

Popham, W. J. (1997, October). What's wrong—and what's right—with rubrics. *Educational Leadership, 55*(2), 72–75.

Pratt, D. D. (2005, January–February). Personal philosophies of teaching: A false promise? *Academe, 91*(1), 32–35.

Schönwetter, D. J., Sokal, L., Friesen, M., & Taylor, K. L. (2002, May). Teaching philosophies reconsidered: A conceptual model for the development and evaluation of teaching philosophy statements. *International Journal for Academic Development, 7*(1), 83–97.

Stevens, D. D., & Levi, A. J. (2005). *Introduction to rubrics: An assessment tool to save grading time, convey effective feedback, and promote student learning.* Sterling, VA: Stylus.

17

Meeting the Challenges of Integrative Learning: The Nexia Concept

Jane Love
Furman University

Integrative learning challenges faculty developers to facilitate integrative and connective experiences not only for students, but for faculty as well. For many faculty, curricular requirements impede connective teaching, and the widespread assumption that connectivity must be taught on the course level also limits their ability to enrich students' learning through diverse perspectives and interactions. Nexia is an approach to this problem based on the concept of ad hoc connectivity, or small-scale, focused, short-term connections that allow students from two or more courses to interact around points of interest to both classes. By releasing connective teaching from expensive curricular constraints, the Nexia approach enables faculty and students to share interdisciplinary, integrative learning experiences within existing curricula.

> The courses being given at any moment on a campus represent any number of rich potential conversations within and across the disciplines. But since students experience these conversations only as a series of monologues, the conversations become actual only for the minority who can reconstruct them on their own. (Graff, 1992, p. 106)

Coming to Furman University from teaching at a community college and a large research institution, I first encountered the phrase *liberal arts moment* as used by both faculty and students to refer to just such an experience as Graff describes. What struck me about the usage of this phrase was the aura of preciousness surrounding it: For students, it was accompanied by surprise and delight, and for faculty as well, but for the latter these feelings were cast in more subdued tones of nostalgia for their own such moments and world-weariness, in recognition, I thought, of the elusive, capricious, and serendipitous integration of such moments. I could sense my colleagues thinking, "It's working; it's *actually working!*" and surmised that the "it" was the alchemical magic of liberal learning. Every conversation I recall having with colleagues about liberal arts moments seemed redolent with the unspoken yet shared knowledge of initiates, and the tacit understanding that these moments visit those whose deserving nature is thereby revealed as such.

In my early days at Furman, I often wondered where the tools for conjuring liberal arts moments were stored away, and what secret password was used to access them. I still wonder where in our institutional mission statement is the clear intention to teach students to connect disparate ideas on their own. At what point in their careers do liberal arts faculty profess and examine their intention to help students integrate their learning? What role can or should faculty developers and teaching and learning centers play in supporting this intention?

Defining the Problem: Initial Steps

Six years ago, when I first began thinking about these questions, the conversation about integrative learning had not yet appeared on Furman's radar, although faculty interest in connecting knowledge and disciplines through creative new courses already had an impressive history. Despite Furman's rigid and weighty general education curriculum, which consumed the better part of both students' and the faculty's time and energy in introductory-level departmental courses, individual faculty members had managed to design and teach innovative, experimental courses that brought together faculty from two or more departments in highly imaginative ways. The fate of these courses ultimately depended on whether or how they were able to meet general education requirements, so many of these efforts flourished for a brief semester or two before fading away. It wasn't that students weren't interested in these courses, but that they had no room left in their course schedules for them after meeting both general education and major requirements.

Clearly, the curriculum was unable to support the faculty's recognition of the value of connectivity. Faculty time and effort in developing and teaching these courses was not rewarded, and student time and effort in taking courses that did not count toward a major or the general education requirement was not specifically valued either. The institutional message seemed to be that connective, integrative learning is the icing on the cake, nice for an academically ludic curricular interlude amidst the more serious work of tapping departmental silos. Furman was far from unique in any of these respects. The time, effort, and expense associated with designing and teaching interdisciplinary courses pose challenges to virtually every institution, yet faculty interest in teaching these courses seems to outpace the curricular transformations that might reduce the friction between requirements and connective teaching. Indeed, this problem may well be endemic to the nature of educational institutions, whose structures, like the form of a sonnet, both enable and contain the intellectual life they nurture.

Refining the Problem: Recent Research

The Association of American Colleges and Universities and The Carnegie Foundation for the Advancement of Teaching have been particularly diligent in articulating this problem and in soliciting solutions. In their jointly sponsored three-year Integrative Learning Project, projects undertaken by 10 diverse institutions developed "advanced models and strategies to help students pursue learning in more intentional, connected ways" (The Carnegie Foundation, 2006). The projects (whose descriptions and outcomes are found in Huber et al., 2007) reveal the wide scope of connectivity within higher education, ranging from learning communities at the College of San Mateo, to an integrated capstone course at the Massachusetts College of Liberal Arts, to electronic portfolios at Portland State University. This broad range of initiatives, however, is implicit in the way the project's organizers answer the question, "What is integrative learning?"

> Fostering students' abilities to integrate learning—across courses, over time, and between campus and community life—is one of the most important goals and challenges of higher education. The undergraduate experience can be a fragmented landscape of general education courses, preparation for the major, cocurricular activities, and "the real world" beyond the campus. But an emphasis on integrative learning can help undergraduates put the pieces together and develop habits of mind that prepare them to make informed judgments in the conduct of personal, professional, and civic life. (Huber & Hutchings, 2004, p. 13)

One should anticipate that anything bearing the modifier "integrative" will tend to sprout tendrils of connectivity in every direction as it kudzus across the curriculum and beyond. Indeed, the term *integrative learning* appears to display this tendency in higher education at the moment. The conceptual logic of integration itself demands its own recursive, reflexive implementation. It is not enough simply to provide integrative learning opportunities for students, nor to help students connect them. Consistent, sustainable integrative learning requires the integration of these opportunities by integratively thinking faculty and administrators within integratively organized institutions. In other words, the process of creating integrative student learning is not only one of supplementation, but primarily one of transformation, for institutions, administrators, and faculty alike. The risk is that integrative efforts will languish within the conceptual sterility of "Departments of Integration," the tendrilly green safely quarantined from the sacred silos.

Huber and Hutchings (2004) explicitly recognize this difficulty:

> Many campuses today are creating opportunities for more integrative, connected learning. First-year seminars, learning communities, interdisciplinary studies, capstone experiences, portfolios, student self-assessment, and other innovations are increasingly in evidence. The bad news is that they often involve small numbers of students or exist in isolation, disconnected from other parts of the curriculum and from other reform efforts. Indeed, the very structures of academic life encourage students to see their courses as isolated requirements to complete.
>
> How, then, can campuses help students pursue learning in more intentionally connected ways? What does such learning look like? How might it be shaped by emerging cultural realities and by new thinking about learning and teaching? (p. 1)

The final report of the Integrative Learning Project (Huber et al., 2007) offers a wealth of provocative and inspiring ideas for how different institutions might craft unique approaches to integrating integration through programs and initiatives, many of them placing faculty conversations and connections in the spotlight (notably Carleton College, LaGuardia Community College, Salve Regina University, and the University of Charleston). These forward-thinking projects do much to "integrate integration" by supporting faculty in creating integrative opportunities for students. What may be missing here, though, are opportunities for faculty to experience integrative thinking for themselves, not primarily as teachers or scholars defined by expertise, but as amateurs, lovers of thinking for its own sake.

Recursive Integration

If integrative teaching and learning are to be authentic and sustainable, then faculty need to renew their sense of discovery and joy in making connections, and to allow these feelings to shape the integrative opportunities they create for students. Huber and Hutchings (2004) were aware of this need at the outset of the Integrative Learning Project:

> Behind these developments is a move toward asking students to "go meta" with their learning in order to identify, assess, and strategize about next directions. But many educators would argue that students are unlikely to develop such habits of reflection and intentionality if *faculty* do not do the same. Helping students to "go meta" involves designing better opportunities for students to connect their learning within and among courses and contexts. It involves faculty getting smarter about the look and feel of integrative learning so that students' efforts can be recognized and fostered. And it also involves faculty modeling, through their teaching, the thoughtful approach to learning that they want their students to develop. (pp. 8–9)

The authors are describing here, I think, the recursive property of integration and the role it plays in faculty development to support integrative learning. The natural corollary to active, creative, ubiquitous student integration is active, creative, ubiquitous faculty integration, released from curricular constraints and expressed through teaching. Faculty should not have to imagine what integrative learning looks like and feels like. They should be able to share the integrative processes of intellectual life with and alongside their students, through, and *as*, their teaching. I would, then, put yet a finer point on the role of faculty in "modeling . . . [a] thoughtful approach to learning": I would say that faculty need opportunities and support to engage in their own integrative thinking and learning, and that they especially need ways to actively explore and express integration, both their own and their students', through their teaching. More than anything, they need easy, agile ways of doing this that can directly involve their students, quick ways that can move in real time with the pace of their thinking and emerging current events. Some curricula are intentionally designed to enable this, but even for these institutions, curricular requirements often inhibit faculty in their ability to seamlessly fuse teaching with the unfurling excitement of intellectual life, for both themselves and their students. The pedagogy of integrative learning requires creative alternatives for teaching connectively that work independently of curricula or programs, and that is where Nexia begins.

Ad Hoc Connectivity

Initially, my idea was to help faculty at a small liberal arts institution, with limited resources and a limiting curriculum, bring the richness and excitement of cross-disciplinary connections to their classes without the time-consuming effort of designing, proposing, and teaching new courses. We often assume that teachable connections can only take place as full-fledged courses. My idea was to enable an interdisciplinary approach that works for creating courses, but also *below* the course level. In other words, instead of filtering potential connections for their suitability as course topics, why not include the smaller overlappings, convergences, and contiguities that could sustain a stimulating, enriching encounter between two or more classes for a shorter period of time?

For instance, a women's studies class exploring the difference between sex and gender might partner for a few days with a human physiology class to read Anne Fausto-Sterling's "The Five Sexes" (1993). It might be possible for the two classes to meet face to face, but it would not be necessary: They could just as easily use a blog or online discussion forum to compare and contrast disciplinary perspectives throughout the week. The two professors might choose to monitor the discussion closely, assigning students specific duties and topics and grading their efforts, or they might choose instead to have some students rotate as monitors, others as daily reporters who share a summary of the discussion in class meetings for reflection and analysis. Rather than grading their students' contributions, the professors might instead have each student identify a provocative question from the discussion for further research, either independently or in collaboration with a student from the other class.

In another example, students in neuroscience, psychology, information technology, and philosophy courses might cooperate to create an annotated bibliography on the ethics of artificial intelligence. Early in the connection, students might meet for a specially scheduled screening of the film *AI* (Spielberg, 2001) or to discuss a short, provocative text assigned in all four courses. This event would allow students to begin to frame research questions that cut across their respective courses, creating multidisciplinary teams around shared interests and purposes. Faculty might help students to work consciously at the intersection of disciplines by designing a review process for including materials in the bibliography that requires students to justify their selections to their respective groups, explaining their disciplinary significance as well as their value to the interdisciplinary nature of the bibliography. The project might culminate with another plenary event that challenges students collaboratively to apply their knowledge and understanding to complex case studies, thus demonstrating for themselves and others their understanding of both disciplinary and integrative methodologies. An even more expansive version might invite students from humanities and fine arts classes to examine the role played by cultural, artistic, and historical representations of artificial intelligence in contemporary ethical understandings of its challenges.

These are just two examples, but the possibilities for teaching connections range from brief, virtual conversations of a day or two, with students from different classes using email or blogs to explore a shared text or topic from the perspectives of their respective courses, to longer, more structured cross-course collaborations in which students form extended working relationships with students from other classes around a shared project.

The possibilities are indeed endless, and both logistically and pedagogically complex. I do not wish to imply that ad hoc connectivity (i.e., "connecting this to this" within the larger context of a course, or connections that operate below the organizational or curricular level of the course) is necessarily simple or easy; indeed, it will undoubtedly prove challenging on multiple levels. Regardless, these endless possibilities are, however, limited at the outset by faculty members' ability to see these connections in the conversations latent throughout the teaching of a day, a week, a term, from one side of campus to the other. The words of Gerald Graff that open this chapter are evocative for their suggestion that these unheard conversations *might inform teaching and learning*. Conversation is but a glimpse of thinking itself, not when preserved as knowledge, but when caught in flagrante delicto, as it were, in the act of being itself—spontaneous, fluid, inventive, speculative, and intrinsically, inherently ad hoc, anchored in specificity and enthralled by the moment. Perhaps the liberal arts moment is merely thinking catching itself in the act.

Conversations over lunch, at the gym, and at faculty or committee meetings often provide a faculty version of liberal arts moments, but just as often they lack the intentionality needed to see their influence expressed through teaching. Thematically organized curricular initiatives invite faculty to rethink their teaching from fresh perspectives, but also risk imposing confining programmatic requirements. Additionally, as a colleague recently opined, the connections that faculty think of on their own tend to remain within the cognitive and conceptual frameworks of their disciplines, thus defeating at least one purpose of connecting: the formation of new contexts, radical juxtapositions, and innovative ideas. The difficulty is not simply that connections do not occur, but that, when they do occur, we are missing a structure that recognizes the value of these connections and intentionally links them to teaching and learning, for faculty and students alike. Something more was needed.

Nexia: "Plugged" and "Unplugged"

Nexia began as both the concept of teaching connectively below the curricular radar, as it were, and as a technique for helping faculty discover intriguing connections for teaching, for research, and for the sheer joy of connecting. The technique we began with, which we've come to call "speed-linking," is simple and, because it requires no software or other technological support, completely "unplugged": groups of faculty from different divisions (roughly a dozen, but more were better than fewer) gathered to find connections among themselves. Working quickly, faculty paired off with instructions to find a teachable connection between their courses within a set time limit (usually seven minutes), after which they found new partners and repeated the sequence. Participants kept track of their connections on a worksheet, and, after several iterations of pairing and connecting, the entire group convened to share results.

Two things were notable about these sessions: First, most faculty enjoyed them tremendously. Not surprisingly, they bridled a bit at being kept to time limits for each pairing, but otherwise, they found the process inherently rewarding, both as a way of socializing with colleagues and as a form of "intellectual yoga."

The second, and perhaps more interesting, feature noted was the fascinating meta-connections that would emerge during the full-group processing at the end of the session. As faculty began to share the connections they'd discovered, others invariably chimed in with related connections, generating a hyper-connective dimension that stimulated provocative and lively discussion and insights into how knowledge is generalized across the curriculum. One faculty member noted that the speed-linking process was "how curriculum review ought to be done."

As useful and effective as these speed-linking sessions were, I was concerned that the face-to-face and personal nature of the sessions (which is one of their strengths) might well contribute to the institutional ephemerality of the connections. An ad hoc approach to connective teaching can have institutional significance only if a structure exists for recognizing, archiving, and building on the connections that faculty discover and articulate through their teaching. Developing such a structure became the next, and current, phase of Nexia.

I partnered with Kevin Treu, chair of Furman's computer science department, to seek funding from the Andrew W. Mellon Foundation for exploring and prototyping software that could both generate potential connections among faculty teaching and archive connections as they were implemented.

Using an unstructured database of faculty-submitted, teaching-related documents (such as syllabi, lecture notes, course web sites, PowerPoint slides, articles, course proposals and descriptions, coupled with research materials related to teaching, such as manuscripts, grant proposals and reports, book reviews, etc.), we have been working to adapt semantic search technology. This software will be able to return conceptual matches for queries to the database, rather than word-for-word matches or results based on meta-data. For example, a query of "biodiversity" might return potential connections with courses in earth and environmental sciences (unsurprisingly) and biology, but also with courses in women's and gender studies (physiological conceptions of sex and gender, or ecofeminism), psychology (neurodiversity), economics (the sustainability of models of global development), mathematics (complexity theory), religion (creation myths), computer science (systems theory and self-organizing intelligence), and so on. The software is still in development, but preliminary trials on test databases have been encouraging and exciting.

Our vision for the software includes a web-based interface to facilitate queries and uploading of documents into the database so that faculty may search for potential connections at any time, without having to rely on face-to-face events or serendipitous encounters. A variety of filters will enable searches to return results based on faculty member, department (inclusive or exclusive), academic term, and other relevant information. Results will be weighted according to user-specified parameters and thresholds. Faculty will also be able to register connections discovered independently of the Nexia software, as well as implemented connections so that indexing of the database incorporates and reflects the value of these faculty-supplied variables while also maintaining a durable archive of their connections. A graphical interface will allow visualization of connections as clouds, clusters, nodes, or maps.

A software tool such as this has the potential to support several institutional and faculty development functions, such as discovery of new areas of interest for curricular planning, initiatives, projects, and outside funding proposals, or for identification of emerging learning communities. Its primary purpose, however, is to serve as a stethoscope for faculty straining to hear the latent conversations across Furman's campus, and we will soon have the opportunity to use it: In fall 2008, Furman will implement a new general education curriculum, one that emphasizes the value of integration and encourages connective teaching. Already, Furman's Center for Teaching and Engaged Learning is working with faculty to envision "the look and feel" of their connected courses. Already, we are learning that connectivity poses far more complicated, sensitive challenges for faculty development than we ever imagined in our quest for more liberal servings of liberal arts moments.

Recommendations

The higher education community is still awakening to the importance of integration in undergraduate learning, and, along with it, the role of integration in faculty development. It is not too early, though, to share some preliminary recommendations for those wishing to explore creative ways of enhancing connectivity on their campuses.

For speed-linking or similar "unplugged" events, implementing the following recommendations will help to improve outcomes and maximize benefits:

- *Create context.* If possible, tie the event to a program or initiative that faculty are already thinking about, such as a curriculum change or an upcoming campus-wide theme.

- *Capture connections.* Provide faculty with worksheets for documenting the connections they discover at these events. Ask them to indicate which ones they find particularly compelling. Follow up on these with offers for consultation and support.

- *Anticipate anxieties; customize support.* Faculty who are interested in connecting their courses are often concerned about the additional time and effort that will be involved. To the extent possible, provide easy access to useful services and software, such as blogs and wikis. Investigate sources of student peer support on campus (e.g., the writing center or multimedia labs) for faculty who don't feel comfortable introducing their students to these technologies. Coordinated peer support may also facilitate group projects that involve students from two or more classes.

- *Build community.* Provide special recognition for faculty who actually teach their connections. Encourage them to create learning communities around shared issues, such as assessment of integrative learning and connective teaching.

- *Connect institutionally.* Summarize and share connections (with permission) with others who might benefit from this information (curriculum review or development groups, interdisciplinary studies departments, deans and provosts, grants offices, etc.) to highlight the institutional value of connective teaching.

Those interested in following the development of the Nexia software are welcome to visit our web site at http://nexia.furman.edu. We also encourage exploration and development of other software approaches to facilitated connectivity. The time is right for a community of developers to join together in envisioning technologies that will support, rather than replace, the integrative thinking skills our students so desperately need.

Conclusion

As we begin the work of creating pedagogies of integration, remembering what we already know and speculatively placing this knowledge within this new context may help to keep our expectations grounded and our perceptions clear. This is especially important as we approach connectivity, with its strong appeal to faculty imagination and its beguiling promise to leverage integrative benefits for student learning from existing curricula. Do not be deceived: Despite its warm and fuzzy surface, connectivity quickly cuts to the heart of deeply held personal assumptions and beliefs about the nature and value of teaching. Connectivity promises not so much to augment teaching as transform it and the teacher along with it. The vast array of possibilities for teaching connectively reflect the equally broad spectrum of teaching styles and philosophies. There is no one way of doing it; that is not what prompts transformation. Rather, the need to choose from among these possibilities brings to light our buried assumptions, values, and beliefs about teaching and about ourselves as teachers, often in confusing or perplexing ways. Connective teaching has much potential, not only as an integrative pedagogy, but as a path of deep reflection for faculty, a tool for conjuring liberal arts moments. As faculty and faculty developers begin the task of integrating integration, let the work proceed with care for what it asks of us, and with love for what it makes possible.

Author Note

The name "Nexia" derives from a conversation with Hal Abelson (MIT; co-founder of creativecommons.org) in 2003, in which he remarked on the similarity between our idea for a connectivity software tool and a 1950 science fiction novel by A. E. van Vogt, *The Voyage of the Space Beagle*. The central character of the novel, Dr. Elliott Grosvenor, is a pioneer in the field of "nexialism," or the science of integrating knowledge across disciplines. Nexialism is currently promoted by the Nexial Institute (www.nexial.org), with which Nexia has no formal relationship beyond the shared reference to van Vogt's novel.

References

The Carnegie Foundation for the Advancement of Teaching. (2006). *Integrative Learning Project: Opportunities to connect.* Retrieved May 21, 2007, from www.carnegiefoundation.org/programs/index.asp?key=24

Fausto-Sterling, A. (1993, March/April). The five sexes: Why male and female are not enough. *The Sciences,* 20–24.

Graff, G. (1992). *Beyond the culture wars: How teaching the conflicts can revitalize American education.* New York, NY: W. W. Norton.

Huber, M. T., Brown, C., Hutchings, P., Gale, R., Miller, R., & Breen, M. (Eds.). (2007). *Integrative learning: Opportunities to connect* (Public report of the Integrative Learning Project sponsored by the Association of American Colleges and Universities and The Carnegie Foundation for the Advancement of Teaching). Stanford, CA: The Carnegie Foundation for the Advancement of Teaching.

Huber, M. T., & Hutchings, P. (2004). *Integrative learning: Mapping the terrain.* Washington, DC: Association of American Colleges and Universities.

Spielberg, S. (Director, Producer). (2001). *AI* [Motion picture]. United States: Warner Bros.

18

The Teaching Resource Portfolio: A Tool Kit for Future Professoriate and a Resource Guide for Current Teachers

Dieter J. Schönwetter
University of Manitoba

Extensive annotated bibliographies have guided academic researchers over several years and in various disciplines, providing key resources to assist in the development of new ideas. However, less common are published annotated bibliographies on effective teaching resources, both general to teaching across various disciplines as well as specific to each discipline, that guide the academic in the teaching enterprise. This chapter focuses on a tool, the teaching resource portfolio, that helps the graduate student preparing for an academic career including teaching, the new faculty member desiring additional teaching resources, the academic wishing to have resources that support discipline-specific scholarship of teaching and learning initiatives, and the educational developer needing references to support his or her clients in teaching.

Annotated bibliographies are very common in research circles, providing researchers in various disciplines with the most current as well as the best resources for guiding research in a variety of disciplines and professions. However, less common are published annotated bibliographies on effective teaching resources, both general to teaching across various disciplines as well as specific to each discipline. The training of the future professoriate focuses more on the knowledge and skill development of a variety of critical teaching and learning dynamics than on the skill of finding discipline-specific teaching resources. The purpose of this chapter is to provide a tool for gathering teaching resources for the graduate student preparing for an academic career including teaching, for a new faculty member desiring additional teaching resources, for the academic wishing to have resources that support discipline-specific scholarship of teaching and learning initiatives, and for the educational developer seeking a reference-gathering tool to support his or her clients in teaching.

Literature Review

There are many annotated bibliographies supporting a variety of research topics in a variety of academic disciplines and professions. For instance, a World of Science search (conducted November 8, 2006) revealed 3,901 annotated bibliographic articles focusing on science research resources, a PsychInfo search (conducted November 8, 2006) revealed 1,208 annotated bibliographic articles focusing on psychological research resources, and a PubMed search (conducted November 7, 2006) revealed 541 annotated bibliographic articles focusing on medical and nursing research resources. Annotated bibliographic resources are prolific, supporting the work of researchers in various fields. However, annotated bibliographic articles supporting teaching in the college and university are less frequent in the literature, especially in disciplines outside of education.

When it comes to teaching in higher education, the field of education provides an abundance of annotated bibliographies, including varied teaching resources from the use of technology to dealing with classroom incivilities. For example, a recent ERIC search using the key words "annotated bibliography" and "teaching" and "college or university" (November 6, 2006) found 531 annotated bibliographic articles dealing with teaching issues in higher education. Unfortunately, most academics in disciplines outside of education and educational development are unaware of these resources, have limited access to them, and/or have inadequate discipline-specific teaching resources to rely on.

Most other academic disciplines have limited teaching resources. For instance, 29 annotated bibliographies have been identified in the social sciences. Of these, most are annual updated reports of teaching resources in psychology building on previous annotations, not independent reports (e.g., Berry & Daniel, 1985; Dagenbach, 1999; Daniel, 1981; Fulkerson & Wise, 1995; Johnson, Schroder, & Kirkbride, 2005; Morgan & Daniel, 1983; Mosley & Daniel, 1982; Wise & Fulkerson, 1996). Four of these support teaching sociology (e.g., Goldsmid & Goldsmid, 1982; Lindstrom, 1998; South, 1989) and three, teaching history (Barbuto & Kreisel, 1994; Brazier, 1985; Popp, 1996).

An additional 34 were found in the humanities, mainly on teaching English and/or literature. But here again, most of these are *annual updated* reports of teaching resources (e.g., Dieterich & Behm, 1984; Durst & Marshall, 1991; Jenkinson & Daghlian, 1968; Larson & Bechan, 1992; Larson & Saks, 1995; Marshall & Durst, 1991; McLaughlin & George, 1982; Saks & Larson, 1994; Speck, Hinnen, & Hinnen, 2003; Warren, 2005; Wiener & Sheckels, 1981). Other such reports are available for teaching law and technology (Goldman, 2001), teaching classical studies (McLaughlin & George, 1982), teaching revising and editing (Speck et al., 2003), and teaching geography (Banks, 1991; Bascom, 1994; Carey & Schwartzberg, 1969; Spencer & Hebden, 1982).

The sciences offer just a few teaching bibliographies: three for mathematics (Dubinsky, Mathews, & Reynolds, 1997; Herriott, 1925; King, 1981), two rather outdated ones for genetics (Barnes & Mertens, 1976; Laton & Bailey, 1939), one for chemistry (Carr, 2000), and one for engineering (Carter, 1986). In the medical sciences, five were identified in medical teaching (e.g., Billings, 1993; Browning, 1970; Cremens, Calabrese, Shuster, & Stern, 1995; MacKinney, 1994; Wright & Katcher, 2004), another seven for nursing ("Annotated bibliography," 1990; Cowan & Laidlaw, 1993; Heyden, Luyas, & Henry, 1990; MacVicar & Boroch, 1977; Mahon, 1997; Shen, 2004; Wylie, 1988), one in chiropractic education (Adams & Gatterman, 1997), one in residence training in medicine (Cremens et al., 1995), one in ethics training in psychiatry (Preisman et al., 1999), and one for teaching hospice care (Billings, 1993). Of the various annotated bibliographies on teaching, the earliest recorded ones, which hail from the early 1920s, deal with mathematics, language learning, and teaching students how to study (Buchanan & MacPhee, 1928; Herriott, 1925; Walker & Walker, 1928).

For the most part, these annotated bibliographies focus mainly on print resources, such as teaching reference books and journal articles. But teaching resources exist in many other forms: multimedia presentations, discipline-specific humor, teaching web sites and repositories, government sites, professional/trade associations and conference sites, and teaching and learning objects. These are typically overlooked in the annotated references just discussed.

Courses Preparing Future Faculty

Courses and programs preparing the future professoriate provide graduate students and new faculty with excellent knowledge and skill development. Based on a recent review of 155 Canadian and U.S. graduate courses taught during 2002–2004 to prepare graduate students for teaching in higher education, Schönwetter, Ellis, Taylor, and Koop (in press) found that course goal themes included "applied teaching skills, knowledge and understanding of teaching and learning, professional/philosophical/ethical issues, theory on teaching and learning, research on teaching and learning, and the principles of teaching/learning/design." The researchers went on to list the frequency of course requirements/assignments, beginning with the most common to the least common:

> Readings (N = 106), written reflection (N = 69), in-class presentations or teaching (N = 61), attendance and/or participation mark (N = 60), teaching philosophy (N = 51), course syllabus and/or outline (N = 44), teaching dossier or portfolio (N = 41), research paper or report (N = 38), micro teaching (N = 32), teaching observation (N = 32), critical essay or review (N = 22), peer review or assessment (N = 22), videotaped teaching or presentation (N = 22), learning assessment strategies or materials (N = 21), exam (N = 17), self-teaching assessment (N = 17), lesson plan (N = 16), interview a faculty member (N = 15), annotated bibliography or resources for teaching (N = 14), course or curriculum design (N = 10), course portfolio (N = 10), being mentored (N = 8),   case study (N = 7), curriculum vitae (N = 7), designing an assessment tool (N = 5), workshop and/or seminar participation (N = 5), Web page design (N = 4), and grading key or rubric (N = 4). (Schönwetter et al., in press)

Notice that of the 124 courses with assignments, only 14 (11.2%) required students to complete annotated bibliographies or resources for teaching. And of these 14 courses, most focused on print resources to the exclusion of electronic ones (Schönwetter et al., in press).

Guided by Schönwetter et al.'s study (in press), I developed a graduate course on teaching in the college and university to include a practical "tool kit" of resources that would benefit new teachers—the teaching resource portfolio (TRP). The common course requirements included micro-teaching, a teaching philosophy statement, a course design, and a reflection paper. As part of a pilot, students enrolled in the graduate teaching course were also encouraged to compile a list of potential teaching resources that they could consult in their future teaching. The first template required students to identify:

- Four general teaching texts spanning across disciplines (i.e., *McKeachie's Teaching Tips*)

- Ten general articles on teaching and learning issues

- Six specific articles on discipline-specific teaching and learning issues

- A list of conferences focusing on teaching and learning

As with many new ideas, most graduate students began the project with some reservations. They did not know how to go about compiling such a list, and they received only minimal instructor guidance. They perceived the task to require Herculean effort, and they had few models at that time (1993) and only one template to follow. As is usually the case with many keen graduate students who voluntarily attend a teaching and learning course, their motivation to achieve was strong. Ironically, students outside of the "traditional" teaching areas (i.e., engineering, medicine, nursing, mathematics, etc.) not only satisfied the basic requirements of this project, but also far exceeded their peers in education, the arts, and the social sciences. They found more new resource categories, such as multimedia presentations, humor sites, discipline-specific teaching handbooks and reference books, disciplinary conferences with teaching tracks, and journals dedicated to teaching in disciplines beyond the social sciences. As of today, the template has grown to more than 30 resource types, most recently Netcasts, as shown in Table 18.1. Readers interested in using this list in a college teaching course or a faculty workshop or project are welcome to use the template in Table 18.1 as a reference.

TABLE 18.1

Components of the TRP Template

Annotated bibliographies	General teaching journals
Assignment banks	General teaching texts
Case studies	Government publications and contacts
Community organizations	Laboratory tasks
Companies	Leading experts and practitioners
Conferences	Major employers
Course outlines	Marking rubrics
Creative works	Netcasts
• Poetry	Others
• Humor	Personal reflections on teaching and learning
• Image banks	Presentations
• Music	Props and where to get them
Discipline-specific research journals	Rubrics for class discussions, group work, etc.
Discipline-specific teaching journals	Stories
Discipline-specific teaching texts	Syllabi and course outline repositories
Educational support organizations and associations	Test banks
Exceptional journal articles on teaching	Videos
Funding opportunities	Web sites

Steps in TRP Development

The students in the course on teaching and learning in higher education are first introduced to the concept of the TRP in a workshop. The TRP is defined as "an annotated guide that lists essential resources for teaching from general teaching practices to innovative teaching tips" (Schönwetter & Taylor, 2003, p. 4). As such, it links to new developments and innovations in teaching across all disciplines as well as in specific disciplines. It varies in style and content across disciplines, providing an ideal resource list for first-time teachers and experienced teachers looking for new ways of teaching (Schönwetter, Taylor, & Duff, 2003).

Second, students are invited to explore the potential value of such a list of resources to improve their teaching. I draw on my personal experience to describe how such a tool can be used productively. To strengthen the perceived utility of this tool, students read testimonials from former students in the course on how their TRPs have helped in their teaching. Here are a few examples:

> As a novice lecturer, the teaching resource portfolio has been an invaluable tool to collect and organize teaching expertise. In collecting resources, I further identified my learning needs and developed my instructional skills, strategies, tools, and philosophies. (Elsie Duff, instructor, nursing, 2003)

> The TRP provided me an opportunity to consolidate material required to not only teach a course, but to extend beyond course content to include teaching and learning models, frameworks and tips. The TRP offered a framework to organize teaching materials and also to consider new resources that I may not have recognized as useful. The TRP has been well received by the Faculty of Nursing. Many colleagues were excited—waiting anxiously for publication! (Carol Enns, instructor, nursing, 2003)

> I have found my TRP to be an easy to access and update guide of relevant resources in my field of nursing. I have shared my TRP with students to show them how to organize resources as they become aware of them. This was a great assignment because at the end, students were left with a useful document that serves to assist them in their practice area. (Jamie Evancio, instructor, nursing, 2003)

> This was a great experience for me to work on my TRP and to exchange and discuss some material with another colleague. This year I

had a very well technologically equipped classroom which allowed me to use the web in my lectures. Some sites listed in our TRP helped to support visual ideas in calculus and provided online drills with instant hints if needed and feedback. Students found it very useful and many of them reported that those drills were a significant part of their study. Actually, a few students found the portfolio itself useful to find some interesting readings and internet material related to the course and math in general. (Margo Kondratieva, professor, mathematics, 2005)

The TRP has really become a document of my development as a teacher. I have also had numerous requests from faculty for a copy of it once it is published—there is substantial interest in this rather new form of teaching scholarship. (Karen Kampen, assistant professor, sociology, 2004)

Third, students have the opportunity to think of essential resources for their own TRPs. In groups of three to four, they identify a list, share it with the larger group, and compare it to the template shown in Table 18.1. As they generate new resource ideas, they add them to this template and the requirements of the teaching resource assignment.

Fourth, students examine examples of TRPs created by their peers over the last four years (Bowser, Duff, Enns, & Evancio, 2003; Kampen, 2004; Nighswander-Rempel & Kondratieva, 2005). I present selected excerpts from each example on PowerPoint slides and lead the students in discussing their utility for teaching (e.g., a mathematics web site that provides new problems requiring new solutions, a nursing humor web site). Next, groups of students brainstorm all possible places they might go to find their resources. These sources are listed alphabetically in Table 18.2. Again, as students think of new sources, they add them to this list.

Students are encouraged to follow up on some of the references they find. For instance, a journal article on effective teaching in their discipline usually has a list of references worth consulting. Google Scholar searches also yield good resources, especially for disciplines that are less likely to have a large repertoire of teaching resources. One resource often links to a variety of additional unexplored ones that print resources tend not to mention. Given that this assignment is first and foremost one of identifying teaching resources, students are permitted to capture the annotations that accompany the resources. For instance, a teaching reference book usually has an annotation written by the publisher that students may use verbatim. In the case of journal articles, the abstracts become the annotations. For other resources, such as web sites, teaching associations, and the like,

TABLE 18.2

Sources of Teaching Resources for the TRP

Associations	Materials for students
Bibliographies	Mentors
Bookstores	Networks
Clinics	Phone books
Conferences	Private organizations
Current media	Publishing companies
Emails	Recommended readings from courses
Excellent teachers	Resource sites with reviews: Amazon.com
Experts	Societies
Government libraries	Software descriptions
Government web sites	Student societies
Higher education facilities	Students
Humor sites	Teacher libraries
Industrial companies	Teaching manuals
Journals	Video stores
Lab work or lab assignments	Web
Library	

the home page descriptions of these resources serve as annotations. (Students are strongly advised to state clearly in their acknowledgments the original sources of their annotations.) Because time for this assignment is limited, having students read/view and critically evaluate the utility of every resource is impossible, so students need only collect resources at this point. They may follow up on reading/viewing and evaluating resources with a graduate reading/independent study course, if they choose.

Once students know how to locate teaching resources, their assignment is to limit their actual search to 40 hours. In the past, students have devoted between 60 and 100 hours to this project, a time investment few can afford. This course gives them a chance only to start their projects, after which these portfolios should become living documents, forever growing and changing as new resources become available. Many students have added new resources during the months after the course and have submitted their extensive lists for publication, some as monographs published by the university's teaching and learning center (Bowser et al., 2003; Kampen, 2004; Nighswander-Rempel & Kondratieva, 2005). Deans have asked about purchasing copies for their new faculty as well as keeping one copy as a reference in their own offices. This warm reception of our graduate students' work has raised their profile as teaching resource consultants.

The evaluation process is fairly straightforward, with students receiving formative feedback as they find bibliographic entries for each category. Often in newer disciplines, such as the natural resources, teaching resources are somewhat limited. Students need identify only a minimum number of entries of each type, and I adjust that minimum to the student's discipline as part of my formative feedback on the portfolio. Beginning as a simple course requirement, these living documents are intended to serve as an evolving resource for the students' entire teaching careers. Perhaps this is why students have turned in portfolios that far exceed the requirements of the assignment. Some have even collaborated with others to create extensive resource portfolios. Others have presented their portfolios at discipline-specific conferences (Durunna, Schönwetter, & Crow, 2006) and in one case published the portfolio in a discipline-specific research journal (Durunna, Schönwetter, & Crow, in press). It has been most rewarding to watch students enhance their fledgling careers with this resource.

The usefulness of these TRPs has even led some faculty members to network with each other across disciplines and to partner with librarians to create extensive TRPs for specific faculties. For instance, one of the most comprehensive TRPs to date was developed by an interdisciplinary team composed of a dental hygienist, a dentist, a librarian, a research assistant, and an education developer for the School of Dental Hygiene and the Faculty of Dentistry (Schönwetter, MacDonald, Mazurat, & Thornton-Trump, 2006). This monograph is currently being pursued by one of the professional associations whose leadership would like to distribute copies among its members.

These portfolios help not only those interested in enhancing their teaching, but also those involved in the scholarship of teaching and learning (Hutchings & Bjork, 1999; Hutchings, Bjork, & Babb, 2002). They can provide key references to guide research on teaching and learning issues in specific disciplines and professions. For example, the TRP for dental hygiene and dentistry (Schönwetter, MacDonald, et al., 2006) provided a solid foundation for research on the effective teaching of dental hygiene and dentistry (e.g., Schönwetter, Lavigne, Mazurat, & Nazarko, 2006), as well as the student tracking programs in both fields (e.g., Sileikyte, Schönwetter, Mazurat, & Nazarko, 2007).

The success of the TRP is in large part due to the many graduate students who have invested enormous effort, first to complete the course requirements, then to develop more extensive annotated bibliographies on discipline-specific teaching resources, either on their own or in collaboration with colleagues. Added to these students are the many workshop participants who have contributed new ideas and have refined the TRP development process (Schönwetter, MacDonald, et al., 2006; Schönwetter & Taylor, 2003; Schönwetter et al., 2003).

The Future Development of TRPs

Identifying lists of teaching resources in a discipline is just the first step in providing current and future teaching academics with effective instructional tools. What still remains is implementing a process of critically reviewing these resources to ensure that they are practical and of high quality. For that, readers are encouraged to suggest meaningful procedures to guide a rigorous review of such resources. In a college teaching course, students might be required to read/view at least some of the resources they collect and to critically analyze their utility as teaching resources. But instructors would also have to acquaint their students with relevant copyright laws in their jurisdiction, especially regarding creative resource items such as cartoons, video clips, and music clips. Resource users might benefit from some guidance on how to make the most of each resource, including how and where use them—for example, how and when to use content-appropriate humor to engage students in the lecture (Schönwetter, 1993; Schönwetter, Clifton, & Perry, 2002) and how best to employ multimedia resources, such as short movie segments and video demonstrations of clinical procedures (Murphy, Gray, Straja, & Bogert, 2004). These applications remain to be refined to maximize the value and utility of future TRPs.

Author Note

I would like to thank all of the graduate students who participated in completing their TRPs for the graduate teaching course at the University of Manitoba over the last 11 years, providing many unique ideas that have been incorporated into this edition. Many thanks also to the workshop participants at the Society for Teaching and Learning in Higher Education (STLHE) conference (Canada) and the Professional and Organizational Development Network in Higher Education (POD) conference (USA) for their insightful suggestions. Also, I am grateful to Dr. Linda Nilson for her helpful advice in writing this chapter. This chapter was supported by a University of Manitoba Social Sciences and Humanities Research Council of Canada Small Research Grant (329–4501–03), a Social Sciences and Humanities Research Council of Canada Standard Grant (410–2002–1584), and a POD Grant (2001–2002).

Parts of this chapter were presented at the 2006 POD conference, the 2006 American Dental Education Association annual meeting, and the 2003 STLHE conference. The idea presented in this chapter received the 2003 POD Bright Idea Award.

Further inquires or requests for reprints should be sent to Dieter J. Schönwetter, Ph.D., Education Specialist, Faculty of Dentistry, University of Manitoba, Winnipeg, Manitoba, Canada, R3E 0W2, telephone: 204-480-1302, fax 204-789-3912, email: schonwet@cc.umanitoba.ca.

References

Adams, A. H., & Gatterman, M. (1997, March/April). The state of the art of research on chiropractic education. *Journal of Manipulative Physiology Therapy, 20*(3), 179–184.

Annotated bibliography. (1990). *Recent Advances in Nursing, 26,* 193–215.

Banks, J. A. (1991). *Teaching strategies for ethnic studies* (5th ed.). Needham Heights, MA: Allyn & Bacon.

Barbuto, D. M., & Kreisel, M. M. (1994). "To keep the present and future in touch with the past": An annotated bibliography. *Behavioral & Social Sciences Librarian, 13*(1), 11–38.

Barnes, P., & Mertens, T. R. (1976, November/December). A survey and evaluation of human genetic traits used in classroom laboratory studies. *Journal of Heredity, 67*(6), 347–352.

Bascom, J. (1994). Southern exposure: Teaching 3rd-world geography. *Journal of Geography, 93*(5), 210–218.

Berry, K. A., & Daniel, R. S. (1985, December). Annotated bibliography on the teaching of psychology: 1984. *Teaching of Psychology, 12*(4), 231–236.

Billings, J. A. (1993, January). Medical education for hospice care: A selected bibliography with brief annotations. *Hospice Journal, 9*(1), 69–83.

Bowser, T., Duff, E., Enns, C., & Evancio, J. (2003). *Resource manual for instructors in nursing* (Vol. 1). Manitoba, Canada: University of Manitoba, University Teaching Services.

Brazier, P. (1985). *Art history in education: An annotated bibliography and history.* London, UK: University of London, Heinemann Educational Books for the Institute of Education.

Browning, P. L. (1970). *Evaluation of short-term training in rehabilitation.* Eugene, OR: University of Oregon, Department of Special Education.

Buchanan, M. A., & MacPhee, E. D. (1928). *An annotated bibliography of modern language methodology.* Toronto, Canada: University of Toronto Press.

Carey, G. W., & Schwartzberg, J. (1969). *Teaching population geography: An interdisciplinary ecological approach.* New York, NY: Teachers College Press.

Carr, C. (2000, March). Teaching and using chemical information: Annotated bibliography, 1993–1998. *Journal of Chemical Education, 77*(3), 412–422.

Carter, R. (1986). Teaching and learning in the 3rd culture: An annotated bibliography of issues in engineering education. *Studies in Higher Education, 11*(3), 323–324.

Cowan, D. H., & Laidlaw, J. C. (1993, Summer). A strategy to improve communication between health care professionals and people living with cancer: 1. Improvement of teaching and assessment of doctor-patient communication in Canadian medical schools. *Journal of Cancer Education, 8*(2), 109–117.

Cremens, M. C., Calabrese, L. V., Shuster, J. L., Jr., & Stern, T. A. (1995). The Massachusetts General Hospital annotated bibliography for residents training in consultation-liaison psychiatry. *Psychosomatics, 36*(3), 217–235.

Dagenbach, D. (1999). Some thoughts on teaching a pluralistic history in the history and systems of psychology course. *Teaching of Psychology, 26*(1), 22–28.

Daniel, R. S. (1981). Annotated bibliography on the teaching of psychology: 1980. *Teaching of Psychology, 8*(4), 249–253.

Dieterich, D. J., & Behm, R. H. (1984, May). Annotated bibliography of research in the teaching of literature and the teaching of writing. *Research in the Teaching of English, 18*(2), 201–218.

Dubinsky, E., Mathews, D., & Reynolds, B. E. (Eds.). (1997). *Readings in cooperative learning for undergraduate mathematics.* Washington, DC: Mathematical Association of America.

Durst, R. K., & Marshall, J. D. (1991, December). Annotated bibliography of research in the teaching of English. *Research in the Teaching of English, 25*(4), 497–509.

Durunna, O. N., Schönwetter, D. J., & Crow, G. H. (2006, March). *Teaching animal genetics and breeding: What are the resources available to instructors?* Paper presented at the 30th annual meeting of the Nigerian Society for Animal Production, Nigeria.

Durunna, O. N., Schönwetter, D. J., & Crow, G. H. (in press). Teaching animal genetics and breeding: What are the resources available to instructors? *Nigerian Journal of Animal Production.*

Fulkerson, F. E., & Wise, P. S. (1995). Annotated bibliography on the teaching of psychology: 1994. *Teaching of Psychology, 22*(4), 248–253.

Goldman, P. (2001). Legal education and technology: An annotated bibliography. *Law Library Journal, 93*(3), 423–467.

Goldsmid, C. A., & Goldsmid, P. L. (1982, April). The teaching of sociology, 1981: Review and annotated bibliography. *Teaching Sociology, 9*(3), 327–352.

Herriott, M. E. (1925). *How to make a course of study in arithmetic.* Urbana, IL: University of Illinois, College of Education.

Heyden, R., Luyas, G., & Henry, B. (1990, April). Development management for nursing administration. *Nursing Health Care, 11*(4), 179–181.

Hutchings, P., & Bjork, C. (1999). *An annotated bibliography of the scholarship of teaching and learning in higher education.* Philadelphia, PA: Carnegie Academy for the Scholarship of Teaching and Learning.

Hutchings, P., Bjork, C., & Babb, M. (2002). The scholarship of teaching and learning in higher education: An annotated bibliography. *Political Science & Politics, 35*(2), 233–236.

Jenkinson, E. B., & Daghlian, P. B. (1968). *Books for teachers of English: An annotated bibliography.* Bloomington, IN: Indiana University Press.

Johnson, D. E., Schroder, S. I., & Kirkbride, A. L. (2005). Annotated bibliography on the teaching of psychology: 2004. *Teaching of Psychology, 32*(4), 281–287.

Kampen, K. (2004). *Resource manual for instructors in sociology* (Vol. 1). Manitoba, Canada: University of Manitoba, University Teaching Services.

King, M. (1981). *The critical filter: Girls and mathematics: An annotated bibliography.* Adelaide, Australia: Adelaide College of the Arts and Education.

Larson, R. L., & Bechan, A. (1992, December). Annotated bibliography of research in the teaching of English. *Research in the Teaching of English, 26*(4), 446–465.

Larson, R. L., & Saks, A. L. (1993, December). Annotated bibliography of research in the teaching of English. *Research in the Teaching of English, 27*(4), 423–437.

Larson, R. L., & Saks, A. L. (1995, May). Annotated bibliography of research in the teaching of English. *Research in the Teaching of English, 29*(2), 239–255.

Laton, A. D., & Bailey, E. W. (1939). *Suggestions for teaching selected material from the field of genetics.* New York, NY: Columbia University, Teachers College.

Lindstrom, F. B. (1998, April). Teaching sociology with fiction: An annotated bibliography. *Sociological Inquiry, 68*(2), 281–284.

MacKinney, A. A., Jr. (1994, March). On teaching bedside diagnostic and therapeutic procedures to medical students: An annotated bibliography of audiovisual materials. *Journal of General Internal Medicine, 9*(3), 153–157.

MacVicar, J., & Boroch, R. (1977). Approaches to staff development for departments of nursing: An annotated bibliography. *National League for Nursing, 20*(1658), 1–38.

Mahon, P. Y. (1997, July/August). Transcultural nursing: A source guide. *Journal of Nurse Staff Development, 13*(4), 218–222.

Marshall, J. D., & Durst, R. K. (1991). Annotated bibliography of research in the teaching of English. *Research in the Teaching of English, 25*(2), 236–253.

McLaughlin, S. P., & George, E. V. (1982). Periodical literature on teaching the classics in translation, 1975–1979: An annotated bibliography. *Classical World, 75*(6), 341–354.

Morgan, L. I., & Daniel, R. S. (1983). Annotated bibliography on the teaching of psychology: 1982. *Teaching of Psychology, 10*(4), 248–253.

Mosley, C. E., & Daniel, R. S. (1982). Annotated bibliography on the teaching of psychology: 1981. *Teaching of Psychology, 9*(4), 250–254.

Murphy, R. J., Gray, S. A., Straja, S. R., & Bogert, M. C. (2004, August). Student learning preferences and teaching implications. *Journal of Dental Education, 68*(8), 859–866.

Nighswander-Rempel, S., & Kondratieva, M. (2005). *Resource manual for instructors in mathematics* (Vol. 1). Manitoba, Canada: University of Manitoba, University Teaching Services.

Popp, H. (1996). Studying and teaching ancient history: An introduction with annotated bibliography. *Gymnasium, 103*(1), 91–92.

Preisman, R. C., Steinberg, M. D., Rummans, T. A., Youngner, S. J., Leeman, C. P., Lederberg, M. S., et al. (1999, October). An annotated bibliography for ethics training in consultation-liaison psychiatry. *Psychosomatics, 40*(5), 369–379.

Saks, A. L., & Larson, R. L. (1994, December). Annotated bibliography of research in the teaching of English. *Research in the Teaching of English, 28*(4), 418–436.

Schönwetter, D. J. (1993). Attributes of effective lecturing in the college classroom. *Canadian Journal of Higher Education, 23*(2), 1–18.

Schönwetter, D. J., Clifton, R. A., & Perry, R. P. (2002, December). Content familiarity: Differential impact of effective teaching on student achievement outcomes. *Research in Higher Education, 43*(6), 625–655.

Schönwetter, D. J., Ellis, D., Taylor, K. L., & Koop, V. (in press). A review of graduate courses on college/university teaching in Canada and the USA. *Journal of Graduate Teaching Assistant Development.*

Schönwetter, D. J., Lavigne, S., Mazurat, R., & Nazarko, O. (2006). Students' perceptions of effective classroom and clinical teaching in dental and dental hygiene education. *Journal of Dental Education, 70*(6), 624–635.

Schönwetter, D. J., MacDonald, L., Mazurat, R., & Thorton-Trump, A. (2006). *Resources for teaching: Resource manual for faculty of dentistry and school of dental hygiene*. Manitoba, Canada: University of Manitoba, Faculty of Dentistry.

Schönwetter, D. J., & Taylor, K. L. (2003, October). *Bright ideas presentation: Transforming teaching through teaching resource portfolios*. Paper presented at the 28th annual meeting of the Professional and Organizational Development Network in Higher Education, Denver, CO.

Schönwetter, D. J., Taylor, K. L., & Duff, E. (2003, October). *Transforming teaching through teaching resource portfolios: Success stories from faculty and graduate students*. Paper presented at the annual meeting of the Society for Teaching and Learning in Higher Education, British Columbia, Canada.

Shen, Z. (2004). Cultural competence models in nursing: A selected annotated bibliography. *Journal of Transcultural Nursing, 15*(4), 317–322.

Sileikyte, R., Schönwetter, D. J., Mazurat, R., & Nazarko, O. (2007, March). *Competency at graduation: Assessment of graduating dental students' undergraduate educational experiences*. Paper presented at the annual meeting of the American Dental Education Association, New Orleans, LA.

South, S. J. (1989, October). Teaching sociology: An annotated bibliography. *Teaching Sociology, 17*(4), 515–516.

Speck, B. W., Hinnen, D. A., & Hinnen, K. (2003). *Teaching revising and editing: An annotated bibliography*. Westport, CT: Praeger.

Spencer, D., & Hebden, R. E. (1982). *Teaching and learning geography in higher education: An annotated bibliography*. Norwich, UK: Geo Books.

Walker, G. J., & Walker, B. (1928). Annotated bibliography on guidance through teaching how to study. *Vocational Guidance Magazine, 7*, 82–84.

Warren, T. (2005). Teaching revising and editing: An annotated bibliography. *Technical Communication, 52*(2), 225–226.

Wiener, H. S., & Sheckels, T. F. (1981). *The writing room: A resource book for teachers of English*. New York, NY: Oxford University Press.

Wise, P. S., & Fulkerson, F. E. (1996). Annotated bibliography on the teaching of psychology: 1995. *Teaching of Psychology, 23*(4), 257–264.

Wright, C. J., & Katcher, M. L. (2004, June). Pediatricians advocating for children: An annotated bibliography. *Current Opinion Pediatrics, 16*(3), 281–285.

Wylie, N. A. (Ed.). (1988). *The role of the nurse in clinical medical education*. Springfield, IL: Southern Illinois University, School of Medicine.

19

Reflecting and Writing About Our Teaching

Mark Weisberg
Queen's University

Reflecting on what we are doing can help us become better teachers and better people; yet in our increasingly busy and stressful lives, how can we find the space and time? This chapter describes and exemplifies two strategies that can help us and our colleagues become more reflective about our teaching and about our vocation: the Teachers' Reading Circle, meeting for regular discussions of provocative texts about teaching and learning, and the Teachers' Writing Circle, using prompts and examples of colleagues' writing to set participants on an extended course of writing about their own teaching.

It's 8:30 on a foggy October morning in Portland, Oregon. Twelve university teachers are gathered at four small round tables. They have come to reflect on and write about their teaching. It is a diverse group: in age, in experience, in academic discipline, in ethnic origin. Yet as they introduce themselves, explain why they are in the room, it's as if they speak in one voice: "No time," that voice says. "I want to reflect and to write, but I don't have time." "Too busy, too many obligations, at work and at home." "Too stressed; stretched too thin." "We have 3.5 hours; I'm hoping to find some inspiration."

They are not alone. These teachers are expressing what seems to be a constant in academic life. Many feel rushed, scattered, careening from email to meeting to class to crisis throughout the day, and consequently, unable to do what they most want to do. They yearn for time and space to reflect on their experiences, to learn from them and grow, occasionally at least, and even better, regularly. How to respond to this yearning?

As a teacher in a professional school, I have felt it crucial for students to reflect on what it might mean to lead an ethical life in law or in medicine and to carry that reflective practice into their working lives. I have tried to build into my courses structured opportunities for reflection, such as journal writing in and out of class, moments of silence, and provocative readings. And as a person working in faculty development, I've wondered how to offer colleagues similar opportunities.

One obvious way would be to facilitate extended reflection retreats, three or four days, enough time for people to become comfortable with each other and to establish a rhythm, and enough space for both individual and group reflection. I have co-facilitated three of these, and they work extremely well for people able to commit that much time and with resources to travel to a location conducive to reflection. Most participants have reported returning home with renewed energy for teaching and with a plan for building reflection into their lives.

Not everyone has that time and those resources. So for shorter periods, especially when working within a single university, I have found two approaches particularly promising. One is the Teachers' Reading Circle, monthly meetings focused on a provocative text about teaching and learning. Examples have included Mary Rose O'Reilley's books *The Peaceable Classroom* (1993) and *Radical Presence* (1998); Don Finkel's *Teaching With Your Mouth Shut* (2000); Parker Palmer's *The Courage to Teach* (1998); Jane Tompkins's *A Life in School* (1996); and Peter Elbow's *Embracing Contraries* (1986). Sessions typically are 1.5 hours. Before coming, participants will have read an assigned section of the book, or an article. The person facilitating might offer a prompt to help open the conversation, but after that, discussion remains relatively unstructured but always lively, as participants offer their responses to the readings and bring their own experiences into the room. Often isolated in their own departments, participants find a community of colleagues eager to listen to their experiences and perspectives and eager to share their own. And although enrollment has been limited, the series has been successful, running continuously for the past seven years.

The other approach involves a companion to the Teachers' Reading Circle —the Teachers' Writing Circle. Here the goal is to combine reflection with writing, to set participants on an extended course of writing about their teaching. Sessions might begin with the facilitator reading from one or two examples produced in similar sessions, or even examples of student writing (Allen, 1989). If someone would like to read from their own work, we would begin with that. Whereas hearing or reading examples from successful writers can overwhelm someone trying for the first time to write about his or her teaching, I have found that when writers experience what their peers can do, they feel encouraged to risk trying themselves. That approach certainly has worked with law students in my Legal Imagination class, eight of whom recently had their expressive writing published in a journal typically devoted to faculty work (Weisberg, 2003). It also has worked in writing workshops I've attended, two of which led to the publication of a book of pieces by national teaching award winners (Lerch, 2005), many of whom had attended one of these workshops and were sufficiently encouraged by their experience and by their colleagues' reception of their work to submit it for peer review.

In the workshop I'm describing, which occurred at the 2006 Professional and Organizational Development Network in Higher Education conference, colleagues have come both because they want time to write and reflect, and because as faculty developers they are interested in offering similar opportunities to their colleagues at home. Consequently, I have combined these two approaches, the Teachers' Reading Circle and the Teachers' Writing Circle.

We begin with an exercise designed to warm up our thinking and writing muscles:

> In front of you is a sheet with five quotations, each taken from a different book. Please read them through, find one that resonates for you, positively or negatively, and spend some time writing about it. I'll give you about eight minutes.

White Space

It requires a long time to take in a few words.

On either side of the word we need a patch of white, of silence, like the white space that defines a Chinese painting, or the rests in music that permit the notes to be heard.

By and large, our students are relentlessly over stimulated. They sing the body electric: plugged in, tuned out, motorized. And we are over stimulated, too. Many of us hate silence, especially in the classroom. It is the teacher's ultimate nightmare: what if I can't fill fifty minutes? And yet, if students spend twenty minutes in silence looking at ten lines of Homer, it can be time well spent.

I heard a student talking the other day about the difference between two sociology professors. "I love Professor Jones. He lectures from the moment he enters the room, without ever looking at his notes. You really get your money's worth in there. I don't know about Professor Smith. Sometimes you ask him a question and he looks out the window for a while before he answers."

An Experiment in Friendship

Attention: deep listening. People are dying in spirit for lack of it. In academic culture most listening is critical listening. We tend to pay attention only long enough to develop a counterargument; we critique the student's or the colleague's ideas; we mentally grade and pigeonhole each other. In society at large, people often listen with an agenda, to sell or petition or seduce. Seldom is there a deep, openhearted, unjudging reception of the other. And so we all talk louder and more stridently and with a terrible desperation. By contrast, if someone truly listens to me, my spirit begins to expand.

The Teacher Within

When we listen primarily to what we ought to be doing with our lives, we may find ourselves hounded by external expectations that can distort our identity and integrity.... In contrast ... Frederick Buechner offers a more generous and humane image of vocation as "the place where your deep gladness and the world's deep hunger meet."

In a culture that sometimes equates work with suffering, it is revolutionary to suggest that the best inward sign of vocation is deep gladness—revolutionary but true. If a work is mine to do, it will make me glad over the long haul, despite the difficult days.... If a work does not gladden me in these ways, I need to consider laying it down.

The Cloister and the Heart

Human beings, no matter what their background, need to feel that they are safe to open themselves to transformation. They need to feel a connection between a given subject matter and who they are in order for knowledge to take root. That security and connectedness are seldom present in a classroom that recognizes the students' cognitive capacities alone. People often assume that attention to the emotional lives of students, to their spiritual yearnings and their imaginative energies, will somehow inhibit the intellect's free play, drown it in a wash of sentiment, or deflect it into realms of fantasy and escape, that the critical and analytical faculties will be muffled, reined in, or blunted as a result. I believe the reverse is true.

The Danger of Softness

Teachers teach who they are as much as what they know.

"Would you please turn to a colleague and share with him or her whatever you'd like to share about what you've written."

A palpable buzz fills the room. People are reading what they wrote, engaged in intense discussion. Participating myself, I hear several incredible stories, beautifully expressed—people in midlife beginning new careers in faculty development, some doing so amid considerable personal stress, others wondering whether teaching really is their vocation and whether they should lay it down. The depth of personal revelation is startling, and refreshing.

Several respond to "White Space," noting how little of it is present in their teaching or collegial relations, and even in their lives. They want more, will try for more. This theme is often repeated in reflection workshops and in participants' evaluations.

Many volunteers contribute to the discussion, and more want to talk. To write is to commit, and when people have made those commitments, they're typically more willing, often anxious, to reveal them. We could continue discussing, but I want to suggest other strategies, allow people to experience them.

"In your materials you'll find a chapter from Mary Rose O'Reilley's book *Radical Presence*. I'd like to invite us to read it aloud, paragraph by paragraph. If someone would be willing to start us off, we can proceed—to make things easier, perhaps in a circle. The passage begins with the third paragraph on page 40."

Reading aloud in this fashion is a way of getting everyone's voice into the room. While scary, it is less threatening to most people, and usually more productive, than asking for a quick verbal response to a question or a prompt. As Peter Elbow (1986) puts it, "If you want to get people to seem dumber than they are, try asking them a hard question and then saying, 'Now think carefully'" (p. 56). Of course, one needs to be sensitive to those whose first language isn't English or who are unable to read.

Here is part of O'Reilley's (1998) passage:

> Some years ago I spent a sabbatical in a contemplative Quaker community that pretty much unfitted me for the academic world I had left behind. When I came back to my university, I was as confused and befuddled as some kind of alien from a neighboring galaxy. . . .
>
> The problem was, nothing I had learned on sabbatical had fitted me to sit at a desk. In fact, *I* had not come back from sabbatical. Someone had come back, but it was not the person who had left. . . .
>
> I tried very hard to do the work left behind for me by this woman who had gone away and not come back, but the harder I tried, the more I became physically or metaphysically ill. That woman, the for-

mer inhabitant of my body, lectured four days a week, three hours a day, just like her colleagues up and down the hall. When I opened my mouth to deliver her lectures, my chest started to hurt and a smothering sensation came over me. I ran out of breath and got faint. It has nothing to do with "getting used to it again," as my helpful colleagues suggested. I just didn't believe the words I was expected to deliver, and my vocal apparatus refused to make the sounds.

I was no longer able to tell my students what they needed to know, because I didn't know what they needed to know, though only a year ago, I had been quite sure.

What are you doing? What are you really doing? What is your deepest sense of call, your true vocation? My "consultant" (something like a spiritual director) in the contemplative community had asked me these questions week after week, and I had a vague answer. *To listen,* whatever that might mean. To find out what it might mean. On reentry into this galaxy, I quickly became aware of what it did *not* mean: lecturing on Joseph Conrad, schmoozing at academic cocktail parties. These activities and a few others (some of which were contractual obligations) brought on symptoms that felt like a heart attack. Heart break, maybe. It's easy for me to resist my deepest sense of call, especially if the call interferes with my ambitions about making a living and gaining prestige. . . . I was confused about priorities, about what I was supposed to be doing . . . and I was going home every day feeling that, no matter what I had accomplished, I had not done the right thing.

Somewhere in the middle of this crisis, the idea of composing a job description for myself occurred to me. I decided to write down a sentence that reflected my clearest sense of the task. Then I could feel that, whatever else got screwed up, I had been faithful to some inner light. *Peaceful listening,* I wrote on a three-by-five inch card, and tacked it up over my desk. The phrase helped me pull my days together. When all the phones were ringing, committees meeting, students lining up, I could tell myself, "The only thing that needs to happen is peaceful listening." This turned out to be a useful role for me. Since not too many people were listening to anybody, ever, around the university, I could take up a little slack. (pp. 40–42)

How would you respond to O'Reilley's invitation to compose your job description? How would your colleagues respond? What would a university look like if faculty members could collaborate on writing their job descriptions? Even if not individually, then collectively.

I have been challenged and intrigued by this thought experiment since I first encountered it several years ago. Here's my latest effort:

> *Giving permission*, or better, encouraging my students to give themselves permission. Permission to bring yourself to your work, to step forward, to risk being present in what you write and what you say. Permission to care. Permission to take your classmates and yourself seriously, as writers, as thinkers, as individuals responsible for the shape of the law. Permission to set your own goals and see what it might mean to work toward accomplishing them. (Weisberg, 2003, p. 435)

In the final segment of our workshop, I wanted to offer everyone an extended time to write, at least 20 minutes. Following Guy Allen's example (1989), I read two stories (reproduced in Appendix 19.1), powerful examples of expressive writing, one produced by a colleague in a similar writing workshop that later was published in *Making a Difference* (Connolly, 2005), the other by a law student, which begins with her discovering in class that the murder case in front of her that bears her family name is in fact about her father (Munro, 2003). What follows is an extraordinary meditation on her family, her fractured place in the legal world, expressing simultaneously what often is missing in legal adjudication: the people and their emotional lives.

Before setting everyone to work, I also stress how important it is for a writer to be detailed, not to hide behind abstractions, as academic prose often encourages us to do. As Natalie Goldberg (1990) reminds us,

> *Be specific.* Not car, but Cadillac. Not bird, but wren. Not fruit, but apple. Not a co-dependent, neurotic man, but Harry, who runs to open the refrigerator for his wife, thinking she wants an apple, when she is heading for the gas stove to light her cigarette. (p. 3)

And later:

> Mies van der Rohe, a twentieth-century architect, said God hides in the details. It is important as a writer to stay in the trenches with the details and not jump out because it is too scary to be there. Denial, repression, all those psychological adaptations we developed in childhood, were ways of not being there. Writing demands that we cut through and be where we are, and like a cat gripping the side of a cement wall at the top of a ten story building, stay there and look around and not blank out because it is too hard. This is it, here, whatever comes up. (p. 203)

I add, "You might want to write about a teaching or learning experience, positive or negative, a critical incident in teaching and learning, for example, a problem with a student or colleague. Or you might want to ask yourself this provocative question: What if I had nothing to prove? If that were true, what would my teaching and my personal life look like? We spend so much of our time and energy responding to and allowing ourselves to be controlled by real or imagined external demands, and trying to show ourselves worthy, that it might be interesting to reflect on what life would be like were we to give that up."

Twenty minutes later, several people still are writing. After several more minutes, they look up, and I invite people to read what they'd written. One person, who had published poetry years before but recently had been too busy to do so, found himself writing a poem. Another wrote this poem:

what if i had nothing to prove?

i wouldn't wear so much black
i wouldn't rush to get to work on time
i wouldn't worry that i haven't cleaned out my car since i don't know
    when
i wouldn't worry what my neighbors think when i sit on the driveway
    with
my daughter on a cold October evening rolling chalk back and forth
i wouldn't worry about faculty who criticize the readings i hand out at
    the lilly seminar
i wouldn't care when you-know-who sizes up the clothes i'm wearing
i wouldn't worry that my daughter is addicted to Elmo and will grow to
    hate reading
i would not wax facial hair
i would be more relaxed
i would be the envy of the world
i would never have to update my CV
i would work on my novel instead of trying to find the perfect job
i would not worry if my dahlia tubers don't get dug up before they freeze
i would not feel it necessary to put Ph.D. on my e-mail signature
                                                        —Justine Dymond

Reprinted with permission.

Funny, and also telling. In universities, and elsewhere, we tend to measure our success comparatively. Our differential salaries reflect external judgments of our "merit." We compete against each other for a fixed pool of financial resources. We measure ourselves by our success in being published in the most prestigious journals. And we pass that competitiveness on to our students. As Mary Rose O'Reilley (1993) puts it: "That's what teaching *should* be about . . . discerning the gift. Too often, by contrast, the central discipline of our craft is judging" (pp. 90–91). We discern the gifted, not the gift.

If we can give up that need to justify our lives to others, we might become more relaxed, less competitive, might not postpone writing the novel we yearn to write or the article we've avoided for fear our colleagues won't approve. Instead of having time as our enemy as we rush to work, we might make time our friend. Rather than ranking ourselves and each other, we might become freer to recognize, enjoy, and feel enriched by each person's gifts, and in the process become better teachers and better colleagues.

Hearing several colleagues read, another person volunteered, reporting that initially he had decided not to read because what he wrote was too personal. However, having experienced several equally personal pieces, he read his, in which he was concerned that in his research he had been neglecting the global issues he cared most about. The session had moved him to think seriously about how he was pursuing his vocation.

Another participant was encouraged by hearing others and also decided to share what she'd written. Let me share it with you.

Why Am I So Bothered About Class Attendance?

Dear Class,

I have been thinking long and hard about your poor attendance in class and why it bothers me so. I really have and now here I am in Portland at a teaching conference and I've been given 20 minutes to write. Oh, and to write reflectively. My first impulse was to write a lecture for Monday. I want to update that topic and am worried about when I'll have the time as I get back late on Sunday. Well, that's not really reflective and it was leading to cynical thoughts of why bother, half of you won't be there anyway!

That led me back to why the heck do I care? I get paid either way. The students getting As and Bs are always there. Is it that I have this great need to be important in your life? I don't think so. Oh, ok, a teensy bit. I like you. I don't even know you. The ratio in lecture is 178 to 1 and I'm not good with names and faces. But I do like you! You represent the very best of what life can be and you are at a wonderful passage in your life. And the bummer is, that some of you don't have the time to enjoy that. Your life stinks, you're angry or you're just too busy. I like you and care for you because you are 20-something and about to passage into the rest of your life. And, I know for some of you your performance in this class can make or break that event. And I figure some of you are angry and pissed off that this class is hard and requires work.

And that truly bothers me! You're seniors in majors that require this course and something has gone terribly wrong. And not just with you, but I fear with this institution or hell, with our whole society.

Here you are seniors and either you've reached this point without developing the learning skills needed to succeed or you've given up. That is the fault of the institution. Or, you're just here to get the degree and gee darn, now you're in a bit of a pickle, but you don't have the discipline to fix it.

Either way, that's what really, really bothers me—you are so damn disengaged. Whatever its cause this is the true heart of the matter and the challenge to me—To engage you!

And yet, I'm not sure how best to do this. What I must tell you regardless of how I tell you is that you're not working hard enough. And no one wants to hear that. I'm willing to soften the message and tell you that I'll help you with this. It's true and I will. Or am I just a push over and I need to tell you—get off your lazy butts and do it or you'll flunk. That's apparently what football coaches do at halftime and then the team goes out and wins. Well, I will take the former path if I speak of this to the class at all.

So, on Monday I'll lecture as I always do, even if you don't come. I can't help myself. I am compelled. There is a beauty to this subject that I can't help but share. And I think that is what bothers me the most when you don't come. You miss the beauty.

—Sharon Roberts

Reprinted with permission.

As these pieces demonstrate, with time and space to entertain it, and a willingness to set pen or pencil to paper and write continuously, a prompt such as "nothing to prove" can liberate the imagination, invite you to think beyond your usual constraints about your vocation. What you discover may be uplifting; it may be discouraging; it's likely to be challenging; and I hope it may set you on a path toward continuing reflection.

Working with the prompts I've described here and with others I've used or experienced (Peters & Weisberg, 2005), such as inviting participants to write their obituary or the eulogy for their funeral, what they'd like to have said about them at the end of their life, or invoking Saakvitne and Pearlman's (1996) invitation to visit their future self through a meditation featuring guided imagery, has affected many participants deeply, and in some cases led them to make radical changes in their teaching (Weisberg & Peters, in press).

Although our Portland workshop was relatively brief, the participants responded similarly. Asked what was most valuable about the session, they wrote, "The prompts were wonderful, really got us going." "Writing; hearing others." "Being able to write and knowing that I can write and that other people will read and are interested in my writing." "Thought provoking readings. Excellent framework for writing. Wonderful colleagues." These comments confirm my own experience that there are many people who will welcome the opportunity to write about and reflect on their teaching. They don't need much encouragement: someone willing to help them get started and one or two well chosen prompts, of which those I've mentioned here are only examples. If one or two people are willing to share their work, the rest may take care of itself.

I hope you can see the possibilities for reflection that these two approaches offer and that some of you will be tempted to try versions of them as facilitators in workshops with your colleagues, as a participant together with others similarly interested, even alone. There are many fascinating stories to be told and heard, and telling and hearing them can begin to provide the space and time many of us need.

Appendix 19.1

Two Stories

A Family's Criminal Legacy

Tanya Munro

I took a deep, unsettling breath. My throat seized. I swallowed hard and tried to force stalled pockets of air into my lungs. Even to inhale required concentration. Greasing my fingers with saliva, I flipped through the pages of my first-year criminal law book. My pulse quickened and I dropped my chin closer to the book to disguise the spreading color on my face, as I quietly prayed against the inevitable. Believing that god overlooked me, I have never been a religious person. Yet I hoped. My pleas for concealment were bargained without faith and proved futile. There it was, *R.* v. *Munro and Munro* broadcast in bold black ink. I stared at my name, branded on page 404. I wanted to escape my skin. MUNRO. Munro, my new, inexorable, and apparently unavoidable identity. A dispassionate judicial narration of my bloodline was here casually exposed in print, my family legacy succinctly summarized in two pages. Carswell, the book publisher, had resurrected my history and distributed it en masse to the entire law school community. What I felt most was fear and shame, thoroughly humbled by my "white trash" origins. I did not consider infamy to be flattering attire for professional school. Would I have to submit to autograph signings after class?

I expected my fellow students to find me guilty by association, that my presence in law school had smudged that imaginary line between "good guys" and "bad guys." Smart, educated, good people go to law school. Law students are borne from doctors, philanthropists, accountants, teachers, and other lawyers. They are not descended from callous murderers, rapists, and common thieves. Law students read about criminals; they don't share DNA with them. I had become a double agent, caught in the big lie. My secrets unveiled, broadcasted, and scrutinized . . .

I found it to be an odd experience, to read about my family from a stranger's perspective. First, I noticed that judicial ink indifferently stamps names and describes events. The real people are vacant from the sober presentation of case law. In a legal rendition of life there are no fathers, uncles, or daughters, no broken homes or beaten spirits. There are no stories of children kissing their father through walled prison plastic, or a child's silly preference for jails with vending machines that have their favorite candy. The pallid pages of the law books recite blunted facts and dramatize the logic of a legal argument. The reason the crime occurred, the real story the offender might tell, is nowhere to be found. In Stuart and Delisle's text, my criminal law book, *R.* v. *Munro and Munro* is lined up with the other cases in Chapter 3, "The Fault Requirement," nonchalantly placed under the heading, "Murder of a Police Officer." The placement may be logical but it seemed glaringly out of place to me.

I must say I know very little about my branch of the Munro family. My sister is the only Munro I have any kind of relationship with. Newspaper clippings, old court documents, and snippets of information pinched from private conversations have filled the gaps in my memory. My father was the oldest son of Lawrence and Francis Munro's eleven children. I derived this information from his death certificate, which I obtained from the registrar under false pretenses. It is a curious world that prevents a daughter from knowing where her father is buried. Of the eleven children in my father's family only three managed to avoid criminal sanctions. It was a family of habitual offenders leading self-destructive lives. The court did not ask why or how this happened. There will be some who attribute it to genetic predisposition, a hereditary propensity for violence. This answer frightens me, makes me wary of myself. But I'm not convinced it's the right answer. There was also chronic alcoholism and substance abuse, but how this got to be the norm in the family I cannot say. The better explanation is that it was a family that revolved around emotional and physical abuse. In the Munro household abuse often substituted for love. As a child my father had been beaten to the point of unconsciousness. It left him filled with hate and anger. Returning as an adult to that childhood home, he saturated its planks with gasoline and burnt it to the ground. A symbolic act, accomplishing nothing.

I often wonder what kind of person my father might have been if someone had tried to save him, or if anyone knew enough to try to save the children by removing them from harm. But no one did anything, and now nine siblings are criminal justice system darlings. The story of these children and the pain they must all bear is totally missing from the court records. It's ironic that the public and the government complain about the cost of maintaining the prison system, when their disregard helps create the people who inhabit it.

I remember walking the shiny halls of a correctional facility as a child, trying to stomp on the gleam reflected on the floor from the fluorescent lights overhead. I was oblivious to the fact that my father was in jail because he was a bad man. It was normal for me to speak to him through the awkward black phone hanging alongside the thick plastic wall separating us. Such things should never be normal, but then these things should never happen.

I now look upon *R. v. Munro and Munro* as a personal documentary, as a synopsis of a defunct lineage and my strained identity. Given that this case is of obvious personal significance, I have not tried to discuss its legal issues as would a law student. Instead of focusing on what is written in the judgment, I have been compelled by what it does not say. It may appear that I wish to shift the responsibility for my family's crimes to someone else. Perhaps I want to vindicate my father, or better, change the past. And I will always wonder whether a family of Munro children provided with a safe and loving home might not have averted the murder of police officer Sweet and many other crimes. I would have a father, and perhaps it is this unsatisfied desire that motivates my writing. Unfortunately, the past cannot be undone.

Note: The facts in this story are not completely accurate, but they reflect the author's understanding at the time it was written.

Reprinted with permission.

Distinguished, My Ass

Maureen Connolly

2003 3M Teaching Fellow

This narrative emerged from a workshop I had the privilege of attending as a 3M Teaching Fellow. It reminds me that whatever encounters I have with students, colleagues, and subject matter, I must always nurture the self-reflective vigilance at the heart of making a difference as a teacher.

The first time I experienced depression was the summer of 1997, when my partner's two sons—ages nine and eleven, bright, precocious, and somewhat devious—spent that summer with us. Before this, depression was something that other people, without my considerable strength of character and willpower, experienced. Nothing prepared me for that swift slide into worthlessness and unrequited rage. The real kicker was that the boys weren't all that bad. They were just boys. I would go to the bathroom, turn on the shower and cry and cry. I would cry in other places and times as well and the summer unfolded into a succession of driving, cooking, cleaning, and laundry commercials interrupted by daily rituals of tears and self-loathing.

Fast forward six years. The phone rings in my office. I find myself gazing around my space as I contemplate the consequences of answering the phone. Shelves are piled with books and files, the gifts of students, mugs, figurines, pictures of my nephew. There are unpacked boxes that reach the ceiling stacked on the corner of my long desk. A dresser sits in the corner, containing my fitness and training clothes. CDs and tapes are piled near the phone, my briefcase is hanging open, a mouth for papers, memos, and more work to finish at home. My students wonder if I am moving in or moving out. This semester's course and committee files are my only anchor to the here and now. And I am here, now. I am tired of here and now.

I feel the familiar and terrifying slide beginning. And it's not that things are that bad. It's a fairly regular semester, a fairly typical day. I answer the phone. It's Jill—her usual, damn chipper, high energy, see-the-good-in-every-moment self. She needs a title from me for the distinguished teaching award address I will give in May. I say to her, "How about the university's fucked and nothing that we do makes any difference?"

There is a long silence. Jill clears her throat. "Not a good time to ask you about this?" she asks. I wish that I had some magic button to stop the horrible ache in my throat and the tears in my eyes. I take off my glasses. The office fades to merciful fuzziness, the evidence of my incompetence temporarily, thankfully blurred.

"Give me a half hour," I tell her.

Author Note

Thanks to Gerry Hess and Susan Olding for encouragement and helpful conversation, and to Jean Koh Peters, without whose wonderful collaboration I could not have written this chapter.

References

Allen, G. (Ed.). (1989). *No more masterpieces: Short prose by new writers.* Toronto, Canada: Canadian Scholars Press.

Connolly, M. (2005). Distinguished, my ass. In M. Lerch (Ed.), *Making a difference/Toute la différence* (pp. 31–32). Ontario, Canada: Society for Teaching and Learning in Higher Education.

Elbow, P. (1986). *Embracing contraries: Explorations in learning and teaching.* New York, NY: Oxford University Press.

Finkel, D. L. (2000). *Teaching with your mouth shut.* Portsmouth, NH: Boynton/Cook.

Goldberg, N. (1990). *Wild mind: Living the writer's life.* New York, NY: Bantam.

Lerch, M. (Ed.). (2005). *Making a difference/Toute la différence.* Ontario, Canada: Society for Teaching and Learning in Higher Education.

Munro, T. (2003). A family's criminal legacy. *Legal Studies Forum, 27*(1), 403–405.

O'Reilley, M. R. (1993). *The peaceable classroom.* Portsmouth, NH: Boynton/Cook.

O'Reilley, M. R. (1998). *Radical presence: Teaching as contemplative practice.* Portsmouth, NH: Boynton/Cook.

Palmer, P. J. (1998). *The courage to teach: Exploring the inner landscape of a teacher's life.* San Francisco, CA: Jossey-Bass.

Peters, J. K., & Weisberg, M. (2005). *Reflecting on our teaching 2005.* Spokane, WA: Institute for Law School Teaching.

Saakvitne, K. W., & Pearlman, L. A. (1996). *Transforming the pain: A workbook on vicarious traumatization.* New York, NY: W. W. Norton.

Tompkins, J. (1996). *A life in school: What the teacher learned.* New York, NY: Perseus.

Weisberg, M. (2003). Epilogue: When (law) students write. *Legal Studies Forum, 27*(1), 421–435.

Weisberg, M., & Peters, J. K. (in press). Experiments in listening. *Journal of Legal Education.*

20

Breaking Down Barriers to the Use of Technology for Teaching in Higher Education

Erping Zhu
University of Michigan

This chapter examines the most common technologies used for teaching on college campuses and the most common barriers to advanced uses of technology tools. Survey results consistently show that the major barriers to incorporating technology into higher education are lack of faculty time, faculty doubts about the relevancy of technology to disciplinary learning, and inadequate technical support for faculty projects and technology uses. This chapter, then, proposes several approaches developed and assessed by the Center for Research on Learning and Teaching at the University of Michigan for removing those barriers to technology uses in higher education. Although providing flexible technology training schedules and formats helps address the problem of time, offering training that combines pedagogy and technology skills clarifies the link between technology and disciplinary knowledge acquisition. Finally, the collaborative approach to technology support enables faculty to enjoy continuous and coordinated technology support for their projects and technology uses in the classroom. This chapter also provides recommendations for supporting faculty in using technology to improve their teaching and student learning.

Technologies are now widely considered as essential tools for teaching, with a strong potential for enhancing teaching and learning (Mumtaz, 2000; Steel & Hudson, 2001). Technology integration, however, doesn't always result in finding effective pedagogy and innovative learning approaches to promote student-centered teaching and learning outcomes. Various barriers to integrating technology often prevent faculty from using it to promote knowledge construction and make changes in their teaching. This chapter reviews current technology uses in colleges and universities, identifies the major barriers that faculty members encounter when trying to integrate technology into classroom teaching, and recommends strategies that worked at the University of Michigan to effectively break down the barriers.

What Technologies Do Faculty Use in Teaching at Colleges and Universities?

Over the last decade some technology applications, such as the Internet, PowerPoint, email, word processing, and course management systems (CMSs), gained great acceptance in higher education. Faculty commonly use presentation technologies for lectures, electronically distribute lecture notes either before or after classes, manage student assignments and grades in CMSs, and communicate with students via email, discussion boards, and other communication technologies. Of all the technology tools used by faculty, communication technologies are probably the ones that faculty find most essential. Results from the Information Technology Survey at the University of Michigan (UMIT) show that most faculty believe that communication technologies keep them in close contact with students and colleagues and enable them to give students prompt feedback on their learning.

The landscape of technology use in higher education has not really changed over the years. Results from multiple years of UMIT surveys show that email, the web, word processing, presentation software, and CMSs are consistently the most frequently used applications (see Figure 20.1).

FIGURE 20.1

Technology Applications Frequently Used on College Campuses

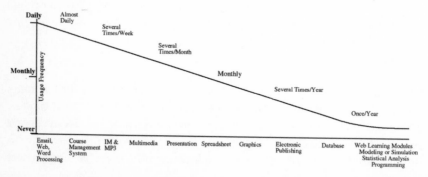

Since the adoption of CMSs on college campuses, their use has focused on distributing information, resources, and content (Morgan, 2003). The 2005 UMIT survey revealed that the most frequently used feature in a CMS is the "Resources" function where faculty can post syllabi, readings, and links to the library. These 2005 data mirror the 2001 findings, where the most frequently used features in a CMS were "Resources" and "Assignments," and the least used features were "Discussion" and "Student Profiles." ("Resources," "Assignments," "Discussion," and "Student Profiles" are features in CTools, a CMS used at the University of Michigan.)

The pace of adopting complex features in a CMS like "Discussion," "Quiz Tools," "Gradebook," and "Wikis and Blogs" is slow. In higher education, the usage of complex and interactive technologies such as instructional games, simulations, role-plays, and interactive learning modules and objects remains low. The changing nature of technology and emerging new technologies make it difficult for faculty to keep up with new learning tools and the pedagogies for using them. No doubt, time is another underlying factor. Over the years, we have found that our faculty often do not have the time to learn technology skills and to take on the task of developing technology-based instructional materials.

Our observations are supported by the UMIT survey findings, which consistently identified time and skills, technology support, and relevance to disciplinary learning as the faculty's biggest barriers to using technology more extensively. Acquiring the skills necessary for using many types of instructional technologies, such as creating technology-mediated learning modules, takes too much time. In addition, faculty do not see clear connections between their use of technology and their students learning more content knowledge. Yet another problem faculty have encountered is insufficient technology support. Indeed, faculty training and support is fifth on the top-ten list of current IT issues in higher education (Dewey, DeBlois, & Educause Current Issues Committee, 2006).

Breaking down these barriers has become one of the biggest challenges faced by instructional and faculty development units, such as centers for teaching and learning and centers for instructional technology. But these barriers are not insurmountable. A large Midwestern research university has taken successful measures to reduce or remove the barriers faculty face when they consider using technology in their teaching.

A Matter of Time: The Enriching Scholarship and Teaching with Technology Programs

Most college and university campuses offer scheduled faculty workshops in technological skills. These workshops usually focus on training faculty to use software packages such as PowerPoint, Microsoft Word, Dreamweaver, Photoshop, and Flash at a basic, intermediate, or advanced level. They provide general rather than customized training to meet individual needs. And the workshops work well for faculty who already have ideas on how to integrate technology into teaching. This training method imitates an industrial model (Brown, 2006) that maximizes efficiency, but doesn't necessarily meet faculty's needs or suit their learning styles. Many faculty develop specific technology skills only as or just before they work on projects that require them. Standard workshops that focus on software applications fail to provide faculty with sound ways that they can use the skills in their teaching and research.

Time is another issue. The typical faculty's workload far exceeds 40 hours per week. In fact, faculty report spending an average of 57.2 hours per week on their professorial responsibilities, which include teaching, student advising, and writing internal and external grant proposals, as well as research and writing articles for scholarly publications (Cook, Wright, & Hollenshead, 2000). Juggling these many duties makes it difficult for faculty to attend fixed-schedule workshops during the regular semesters.

Finding time to attend technology workshops and to reflect on teaching with technology seems to be the most challenging tasks for faculty during the semester. Because time is always limited for teaching, research, and other immediate commitments, attending a technology workshop is often pushed down or off a faculty member's to-do list. As the UMIT surveys find, time needed to learn and use new technology is one of the biggest barriers to faculty learning technology and using it in teaching, and other studies confirm this finding (Beggs, 2000; Butler & Sellbom, 2002; Dooley & Murphy, 2001; Hagner & Schneebeck, 2001; Steeples & Jones, 2001).

The perfect time to attend technology workshops doesn't exist, but there are times when faculty members are less busy and have some time to reflect on teaching. By analyzing faculty teaching load, work patterns, and the calendar of campus events, we found that the beginning of May seems to be the most available time for faculty at our institution. This period of time usually falls between the end of the winter semester and the beginning of the spring semester, an interim period during which faculty typically remain on campus.

This insight into the best timing for faculty technology training led to the development of a weeklong program called "Enriching Scholarship," which since 1998 has offered pedagogy training and hands-on technology sessions for faculty to explore the effective integration of technology into teaching, presenting material, conducting research, and publishing, as shown in Table 20.1.

TABLE 20.1

Sample Themes and Topics for the Enriching Scholarship Programs (1998–2006)

Themes		Topics
	Teaching and Presenting	• Design/use course web site
		• Create multimedia presentation
		• Engage in media conversion
		• Design new courses/curriculum
		• Online teaching and learning
		• Create interactive teaching or assessment modules
		• Innovative ways of teaching
	Researching and Publishing	• Evaluate the use of technology for teaching and learning
		• Explore different strategies and pedagogies for teaching
		• Use and evaluate various sources of information
		• Learn and manage information databases
		• Organize and manage notes and citations
		• Seek grants to promote teaching and learning

The Enriching Scholarship Program, a collaborative effort from several university technology offices, succeeded in capturing faculty's attention. Since the first program in spring 1998, this annual event has drawn hundreds of faculty and graduate student instructors, and the number of training sessions has grown from about 50 in 1998 to more than 100 in 2006. The program features a keynote session each year to set the stage for faculty reflection on the potential of technology innovations to enhance teaching, learning, and research. Then the training begins as a weeklong series of intensive sessions on technology and pedagogy. For many faculty, this compressed schedule is more productive than a series of monthly fixed-schedule workshops. As a supplement to this program, we make available our "just-in-time" training and coaching services to faculty who want to get a quick start on an application or who need to follow up on their workshop training. Thus, the technology training takes a three-tier approach: intensive technology training between semesters, regular workshop during semesters, and "just-in-time" training/coaching throughout the academic year, as shown in Figure 20.2.

FIGURE 20.2

Three-Tier Approach to Technology Skills Training

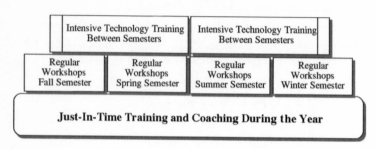

This three-tier approach creates more opportunities for faculty to learn technology skills at a time when they need those skills and have time to acquire them, thereby reducing the time barrier that inhibits faculty from learning and using technology for teaching. However, we encountered the unexpected problem of faculty attending the same workshop year after year. We wondered whether the workshop instructor had used the training time effectively and taught according to the plan. But it turned out that the faculty had not had the opportunity to implement the technology into their teaching immediately after learning it the previous year.

These returning faculty raised two issues. First, technology training may teach skills without making clear connections to disciplinary teaching and learning. Second, some faculty attend technology workshops without expecting the knowledge and skills to be relevant to their teaching. In this case, they may learn the skills for technology's sake rather than for advancing particular teaching and learning goals. Creative and innovative uses of technology in teaching and learning result from close connections between technology and disciplinary content. Providing training at a time faculty can attend is important, but its relevance to disciplinary teaching is highly pertinent to the successful integration of technology into teaching and learning.

A Question of Relevance: Connecting Technology and Disciplinary Learning

Questionable relevance has surfaced as a barrier to faculty's use of technology. Many faculty wonder whether it is worthwhile to master many of the available technologies (Butler & Sellbom, 2002). They also question whether technologies actually facilitate their students' learning of disciplinary content and skills. These concerns are not groundless. Technology can fail when carelessly planned or inappropriately used. To help faculty better appreciate technology's potential and connect it to disciplinary teaching, the Center for Research on Learning and Teaching (CRLT) established a five-day Teaching with Technology Institute that focuses on the connections among pedagogy, technology, and disciplinary learning.

Admission to the institute requires that interested faculty propose course-related technology projects. Each year, we select 10 faculty members based on such criteria as "inclusion of sound pedagogy in the plan for using technology in teaching" and "potential impact on student learning." Each participant receives a stipend of $2,500 for attending the institute and completing the project.

Institute participants define their course goals and learning objectives, design activities that assist students in meeting the learning objectives, identify technology tools that will facilitate student learning, and, finally, learn the technological skills they need. But each participant needs to be clear about what disciplinary knowledge, cognitive strategies (such as critical thinking or problem-solving skills), procedural skills, and attitudes he or she would like students to acquire in the course and what technologies may help students acquire them. A series of consultations helps the faculty identify the most relevant technologies. Of course, low-tech tools sometimes may prove useful for faculty projects as well. This approach of putting student learning first reverses the typical order of technology training, which often puts technology first. Figure 20.3 diagrams the steps through which each faculty project progresses.

As Figure 20.3 illustrates, institute faculty meet several times with CRLT instructional consultants, first to clarify project goals in terms of student learning outcomes, and then to design activities that engage students in learning content. The consultants help faculty explore a range of technology tools that can assist students to achieve the learning objectives, select the most appropriate technologies for the project, and identify ways to acquire the specific skills they need. Usually the faculty are advised to learn software applications like PowerPoint or a CMS before the institute starts, either through a "just-in-time" training service or by attending a training session if it fits his or her schedule. During the institute itself, faculty can then focus on mastering the particular features of a software application that aids in their designing teaching modules

FIGURE 20.3

Planning Stages for Faculty Technology Project

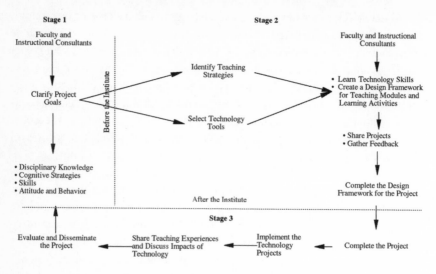

and learning activities. Participants also share their projects, discuss reasons for creating technology-based learning activities, and give and receive feedback. Most complete a framework for designing course materials, a template for teaching modules, or the actual teaching modules. Any remaining work is completed by the faculty member alone or with the help of a student assistant during the summer.

During the fall semester, participants implement their projects, teaching with either the chosen technology or the materials they created during the institute. Toward the end of the semester, they all meet to share their experiences, lessons learned, and the impacts of their technological innovations on their students' learning. Finally, they develop plans for project evaluation and dissemination.

Teaching with Technology projects range from multimedia presentations to interactive tools to web sites. For example, one professor created a multimedia and interactive PowerPoint presentation for a modern Latin American history lecture course. In his presentation, he uses images with audio and video clips, but he stops for student input in the middle, modeling a method of interactive presentation for engaging and involving an audience. Another project, "Interactive Education: Learning Pathology in the Context of the Patient," presents case histories to engage students in collaborative problem-based learning. The web-based and graphical cases pose specific questions that require students to research issues on their own outside of class, then to send to the instructor their questions and comments about the cases. These questions and comments add focus and a sense of student ownership to the class discussions.

Faculty feedback about the institute has been very positive. Participants report gaining a more comprehensive grasp of a range of technology tools available for enhancing teaching and learning experiences. Some faculty in the social sciences and humanities also appreciate obtaining new perspectives on approaching their disciplinary materials.

In summary, the institute brings technology to faculty and connects it to teaching disciplinary knowledge. With the faculty projects deeply grounded in genuine teaching contexts and focused on disciplinary knowledge acquisition, the link between technology and the disciplines is more obvious. Therefore, learning technology skills takes on meaning and relevance to faculty.

Taking a Collaborative Approach to Technology Support

Faculty sometimes feel threatened by unexpected technology glitches, and the resulting loss of class time, when they use technologies in unfamiliar instructional settings (Berge, 1998), and they often complain about the irregular and inconsistent support they receive from technology units on campus. This kind of support impedes their uses of technology in teaching and their completion of technology projects (Berge, 1998). For example, when a faculty member creates and uses multimedia presentations or interactive learning activities for lectures, he or she may have problems in running the presentations smoothly, projecting them correctly, and getting technology to work well enough to engage students.

The support systems on most college campuses are designed to foster the earlier adopters' technology integration into teaching (Johnston & McCormack, 1996), also known as the "first wave" (Hagner, 2001). They are usually technologically savvy risk-takers and self-starters and "they will come if you build it" (Hagner, 2001). However, they do not constitute the majority of faculty at any institution. Faculty who attend technology workshops and propose projects for a technology institute may have some characteristics in common with the first wave, but they usually want to focus on teaching and learning and regard the technology as just a means to an instructional end (Hagner & Schneebeck, 2001).

Large universities usually run technology skills training out of one or more centrally supported computer labs, and at this level technology support tends to be high quality. But when faculty go back to their offices, they may find that college or departmental support staff are ill prepared to advise on using certain software in teaching.

Therefore, CRLT takes a collaborative approach to planning, organizing, and supporting projects initiated in the Teaching with Technology Institute. Collaboration is necessary for several reasons: the decentralized support structure of a large university; the high-level expertise needed to support faculty technology projects; and the impossibility that a single unit can offer expertise over as wide a range of areas as faculty development, instructional design, software training, and classroom/facility support. For instance, CRLT has expertise in faculty development, course design, and pedagogy for using technologies in teaching, and other central and departmental technology units have support staff specialized in hardware and software applications and training, as well as in network infrastructure. Neither CRLT nor the technology unit alone is able to provide comprehensive support for faculty in their uses of technology in teaching.

The collaborative approach enables us to introduce faculty to a community of supporters. The pedagogy specialists in faculty development get involved in the faculty technology projects first, then collaborate with technology support staff, software trainers, and hardware and classroom equipment support staff. During the development stage, the projects are already building in their future support, increasing the likelihood that they will be implemented smoothly into the classroom. For instance, with all levels of support poised to serve a given project, faculty can use multimedia instructional materials in different environments without encountering glitches. The CMS support staff will check that the system supports various video formats, the classroom support staff will ensure that appropriate equipment like a sound system and data projector are available in rooms where the course will be taught, and the infrastructure support personnel will provide instructions for configuring students' personal computers.

Sometimes faculty members use technology in their teaching without informing local technology support staff until support is actually needed. When this happens, the local support staff are in no position to give guidance and timely assistance, and both the staff and the faculty are frustrated. By involving technology support staff from various levels and informing them of the project goals, technology needs, and expected usage in all instructional settings, faculty enjoy continuous and coordinated support.

This issue may not prove so devastating in a small institution, but in a large one with thousands of faculty members, the problem snowballs if one part of the support system fails.

For instance, when a faculty member decided to make his lectures available to students, the instructional consultant discussed with the faculty the implications of podcasting for teaching and student preparation for lectures, and the classroom support staff checked the audio output on the teaching podium to ensure the system's recording capability or recommended the use of certain wireless microphones in classrooms without teaching podiums. Finally, the CMS staff created an "iTunes U," a special place in the CMS to store these lecture podcasts so that students can retrieve them from the course web site. If any of these elements were missing, the podcast project would not be successful. A collaborative support approach for faculty-driven technology projects, as described in Figure 20.4, is critical in large institutions with many decentralized colleges, schools, departments, and technology support units.

FIGURE 20.4

Collaborative Approach to Technology Support

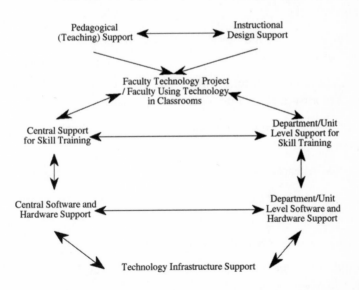

The collaborative support model starts at the bottom of the diagram with the technology infrastructure, which interfaces with both central and departmental hardware and software support structures, as indicated by two sets of double-headed arrows. The central software and hardware support staff then work closely with department/unit-level software/hardware support staff. Those in charge of the centralized technology training coordinate their sessions with the college and departmental trainers, and both training units assist faculty in developing their technology projects and using technology in classrooms. Faculty also receive pedagogical and instructional design support for developing new curricula and courses and for creating technology-enabled learning activities. This final layer of support directs the faculty's attention to student learning, assessment, and project evaluation.

Recommendations for Supporting Faculty in Using Technology

Based on our experience in teaching, guiding, and supporting faculty in their instructional use of technology, we recommend the following strategies to facilitate the use of technology for enhancing teaching and learning in higher education:

- Have flexible technology training schedules and formats.

- Take technology training to faculty rather than having them come to computer labs.

- Contextualize technology skills training in disciplinary knowledge acquisition.

- Focus on student learning rather than technology tools, and link technology to course goals and student learning outcomes.

- Let course goals and learning outcomes drive the selection of technology tools.

- Provide instructional design guidance for faculty technology projects.

- Integrate teaching strategies and learning theories into the use of technology tools.

- Prepare faculty to change teaching practices with the use of technology.

- Build in assessments of student learning or an evaluation plan for the technology projects.

- Take a collaborative approach to supporting faculty's technology projects.

- Ensure ongoing and continuing support for uses of technology in teaching.

- Promote the scholarship of teaching and learning with technology.

Conclusion

Claims that technology can enhance education are popular (Niemi & Gooler, 1987) and potential benefits and anecdotal success stories also abound (Massy & Zemsky, 1995), but inducing most faculty to use technology in teaching has never been easy or free of obstacles. The approaches the CRLT takes to break down the barriers have worked well at the University of Michigan, and they should export well to other contexts with some simple modifications. Integrating technology into higher education does involve skill training, but such training must be made convenient for faculty and contextualized to learning disciplinary knowledge to make it meaningful to faculty. Beyond skill acquisition, technology integration often demands changes in teaching practices and curricular design so pedagogical experts must be involved as well. Given the complexity of technology integration, we recommend enlisting a collaborative community of support staff and various experts to help faculty improve their teaching and their students' learning experiences, which is, after all, the ultimate goal of technology integration into higher education.

Author Note

I wish to thank my colleague, Crisca Bierwert, associate director of the CRLT, who collaborated with me on the design and implementation of the Teaching with Technology Institute. I also wish to thank Ryan Hudson, program coordinator of the CRLT, for her excellent editing of this chapter.

References

Beggs, T. A. (2000, April). *Influences and barriers to the adoption of instructional technology.* Paper presented at the Mid-South Instructional Technology Conference, Murfreesboro, TN.

Berge, Z. L. (1998, Summer). Barriers to online teaching in post-secondary institutions: Can policy changes fix it? *Online Journal of Distance Learning Administration, 1*(2). Retrieved May 21, 2007, from www.westga.edu/~distance/Berge12.htm

Brown, J. S. (2006, September/October). New learning environments for the 21st century: Exploring the edge. *Change, 38*(5), 26–33.

Butler, D. L., & Sellbom, M. (2002, Summer). Barriers to adopting technology for teaching and learning. *Educause Quarterly, 25*(2), 22–28.

Cook, C. E., Wright, M. C., & Hollenshead, C. S. (2000). *More than a research university: The importance of teaching at the University of Michigan* (Center for Research on Learning and Teaching Occasional Paper No. 14). Ann Arbor, MI: University of Michigan.

Dewey, B. I., DeBlois, P. B., & Educause Current Issues Committee. (2006, Summer). Current IT issues survey report, 2006. *Educause Quarterly, 29*(2). Retrieved May 21, 2007, from www.educause.edu/eq/eqm06/eqm0622.asp

Dooley, K. E., & Murphy, T. H. (2001). College of agriculture faculty perceptions of electronic technologies in teaching. *Journal of Agricultural Education, 42*(2), 1–10.

Hagner, P. R. (2001). *Interesting practices and best systems in faculty engagement and support* (NLII White Paper). Retrieved May 21, 2007, from www.educause.edu/ir/library/pdf/NLI0017.pdf

Hagner, P. R., & Schneebeck, C. A. (2001). Engaging the faculty. In C. A. Barone & P. R. Hagner (Eds.), *Technology-enhanced teaching and learning: Leading and supporting the transformation on your campus* (pp. 1–12). San Francisco, CA: Jossey-Bass.

Johnston, S., & McCormack, C. (1996, October). Integrating information technology into university teaching: Identifying the needs and providing the support. *International Journal of Educational Management, 10*(5), 36–42.

Massy, W. F., & Zemsky, R. (1995). *Using information technology to enhance academic productivity.* Washington, DC: Educom.

Morgan, G. (2003). *Key findings: Faculty use of course management systems.* Retrieved May 21, 2007, from www.educause.edu/ir/library/pdf/ERS0302/ekf0302.pdf

Mumtaz, S. (2000). Factors affecting teachers' use of information and communications technology: A review of the literature. *Journal of Information Technology for Teacher Education, 9*(3), 319–341.

Niemi, J. A., & Gooler, D. D. (Eds.). (1987). *New directions for continuing education: No. 34. Technologies for learning outside the classroom.* San Francisco, CA: Jossey-Bass.

Steel, J., & Hudson, A. (2001, May). Educational technology in learning and teaching: The perceptions and experiences of teaching staff. *Innovations in Education and Teaching International, 38*(2), 103–111.

Steeples, C., & Jones, C. (Eds.). (2001). *Networked learning: Perspectives and issues.* New York, NY: Springer.

Bibliography

Adams, A. H., & Gatterman, M. (1997, March/April). The state of the art of research on chiropractic education. *Journal of Manipulative Physiology Therapy, 20*(3), 179–184.

Adams, M., Bell, L. A., & Griffin, P. (1997). *Teaching for diversity and social justice: A sourcebook.* New York, NY: Routledge.

Adams, T. A. (2005). Establishing intellectual space for black students in predominantly white universities through black studies. *Negro Educational Review, 56*(4), 285–299.

Aitken, N. D., & Sorcinelli, M. D. (1994). Academic leaders and faculty developers: Creating an institutional culture that values teaching. In E. C. Wadsworth (Ed.), *To improve the academy: Vol. 13. Resources for faculty, instructional, and organizational development* (pp. 63–77). Stillwater, OK: New Forums Press.

Akerlind, G. S. (2003, October). Growing and developing as a university teacher—Variation in meaning. *Studies in Higher Education, 28*(4), 375–390.

Alexander, B. B., Burda, A. C., & Millar, S. B. (1997). A community approach to learning calculus: Fostering success for underrepresented ethnic minorities in an emerging scholars program. *Journal of Women and Minorities in Science and Engineering, 3*(3), 145–159.

Allen, C. (1999). Wiser women: Fostering undergraduate success in science and engineering with a residential academic program. *Journal of Women and Minorities in Science and Engineering, 5*(3), 265–277.

Allen, G. (Ed.). (1989). *No more masterpieces: Short prose by new writers.* Toronto, Canada: Canadian Scholars Press.

Ambady, N., Paik, S., Steele, J., Owen-Smith, A., & Mitchell, J. P. (2004). Deflecting negative self-relevant stereotype activation: The effects of individuation. *Journal of Experimental Social Psychology, 40*(3), 401–408.

American Association for Higher Education & Carnegie Campus Cluster. (2004). *T and P SoTL language.* Retrieved May 15, 2007, from www.cfkeep.org/html/snapshot.php?id=9244212

Andrade, H., & Du, Y. (2005, April). Student perspectives on rubric-referenced assessment. *Practical Assessment, Research and Evaluation, 10*(3), 1–11.

Andrade, H. G. (1997). Understanding rubrics. *Educational Leadership, 54*(4). Retrieved May 21, 2007, from the Harvard Graduate School of Education, Active Learning Practices for Schools web site: http://learnweb.harvard.edu/ALPS/thinking/docs/rubricar.htm

Angelo, T. A. (1996). Relating exemplary teaching to student learning. In M. D. Svinicki & R. J. Menges (Eds.), *New directions for teaching and learning: No. 65. Honoring exemplary teaching* (pp. 57–64). San Francisco, CA: Jossey-Bass.

Angelo, T. A., & Cross, K. P. (1993). *Classroom assessment techniques: A handbook for college teachers* (2nd ed.). San Francisco, CA: Jossey-Bass.

Annotated bibliography. (1990). *Recent Advances in Nursing, 26,* 193–215.

Ardizzone, A., Breithaupt, F., & Gutjahr, P. (2004). Decoding the humanities. In D. Pace & J. Middendorf (Eds.), *New directions for teaching and learning: No. 98. Decoding the disciplines: Helping students learn disciplinary ways of thinking* (pp. 50–55). San Francisco, CA: Jossey-Bass.

Aronson, E., & Patnoe, S. (1997). *The jigsaw classroom: Building cooperation in the classroom* (2nd ed.). New York, NY: Longman.

Aronson, J. (2004, November). The threat of stereotype. *Educational Leadership, 62*(3), 14–19.

Aronson, J., Quinn, D. M., & Spencer, S. J. (1998). Stereotype threat and the academic underperformance of minorities and women. In J. Swim & C. Stangor (Eds.), *Prejudice: The target's perspective* (pp. 83–103). San Diego, CA: Academic Press.

Aronson, J., & Salinas, M. F. (1997). *Stereotype threat, attributional ambiguity, and Latino underperformance.* Unpublished manuscript.

Aronson, J., & Williams, J. (2004). *Stereotype threat: Forewarned is forearmed.* Unpublished manuscript.

Arreola, R. A. (2000). *Developing a comprehensive faculty evaluation system: A handbook for college faculty and administrators on designing and operating a comprehensive faculty evaluation system* (2nd ed.). Bolton, MA: Anker.

Austin, A. E. (2002, January/February). Preparing the next generation of faculty: Graduate school as socialization to the academic career. *Journal of Higher Education, 73*(1), 94–122.

Austin, A. E., & Baldwin, R. G. (1991). *Faculty collaboration: Enhancing the quality of scholarship and teaching.* Washington, DC: The George Washington University, School of Education and Human Development.

Austin, A. E., Brocato, J. J., & Rohrer, J. D. (1997). Institutional missions, multiple faculty roles: Implications for faculty development. In D. DeZure & M. Kaplan (Eds.), *To improve the academy: Vol. 16. Resources for faculty, instructional, and organizational development* (pp. 3–20). Stillwater, OK: New Forums Press.

Badran, S. (2004). Honoring exemplary teaching: Departmental teaching awards in mathematics departments of research institutions. *Dissertation Abstracts International, 67* (4), 96. (UMI No. 3217013)

Baker, P. (1998). Students' perception of classroom factors that impact success for African-American students in higher education settings (Doctoral dissertation, Northern Illinois University, 1998). *Dissertation Abstracts International, 59,* 1434.

Baldwin, R. G., & Chang, D. A. (2006, Fall). Reinforcing our "keystone" faculty: Strategies to support faculty in the middle years of academic life. *Liberal Education, 92*(4), 28–36.

Bandura, A. (1986). *Social foundations of thought and action: A social cognitive theory.* Englewood Cliffs, NJ: Prentice Hall.

Bandura, A. (1997). *Self-efficacy: The exercise of control.* New York, NY: W. H. Freeman.

Banks, J. A. (1991). *Teaching strategies for ethnic studies* (5th ed.). Needham Heights, MA: Allyn & Bacon.

Barbuto, D. M., & Kreisel, M. M. (1994). "To keep the present and future in touch with the past": An annotated bibliography. *Behavioral & Social Sciences Librarian, 13*(1), 11–38.

Barlow, A. E. L., & Villarejo, M. R. (2004). Making a difference for minorities: Evaluation of an educational enrichment program. *Journal of Research in Science Teaching, 41*(9), 861–881.

Barnes, P., & Mertens, T. R. (1976, November/December). A survey and evaluation of human genetic traits used in classroom laboratory studies. *Journal of Heredity, 67*(6), 347–352.

Barr, R. B., & Tagg, J. (1995, November/December). From teaching to learning—A new paradigm for undergraduate education. *Change, 27*(6), 12–25.

Barrows, H. D., & Tamblyn, R. M. (1980). *Problem-based learning: An approach to medical education.* New York, NY: Springer.

Bartlett, T. (2003, December 12). What makes a teacher great? *The Chronicle of Higher Education,* p. A8.

Bascom, J. (1994). Southern exposure: Teaching 3rd-world geography. *Journal of Geography, 93*(5), 210–218.

Bass, R. (1999, February). The scholarship of teaching: What's the problem? *Inventio, 1*(1). Retrieved May 15, 2007, from the George Mason University, Division of Instructional Technology web site: www.doit.gmu.edu/Archives/feb98/randybass.htm

Beggs, T. A. (2000, April). *Influences and barriers to the adoption of instructional technology.* Paper presented at the Mid-South Instructional Technology Conference, Murfreesboro, TN.

Ben-Peretz, M. (1995). Teacher stress and curriculum innovations in science teaching. In A. Hofstein, B. Eylon, & G. Giddings (Eds.), *Science education: From theory to practice* (pp. 429–435). Rehovot, Israel: Weizmann Institute of Science.

Berge, Z. L. (1998, Summer). Barriers to online teaching in post-secondary institutions: Can policy changes fix it? *Online Journal of Distance Learning Administration, 1*(2). Retrieved May 21, 2007, from www.westga.edu/~distance/Berge12.htm

Berheide, C. W., & Marx, M. S. (2004). *Thinking about thinking: Using an idea notebook to develop critical thinking skills.* Retrieved May 14, 2007, from www.cfkeep.org/html/snapshot.php?id=68820745934565

Berliner, D. C. (1987). Ways of thinking about students and classrooms by more and less experienced teachers. In J. Calderhead (Ed.), *Exploring teachers' thinking* (pp. 60–83). London, UK: Cassell Educational Limited.

Berry, K. A., & Daniel, R. S. (1985, December). Annotated bibliography on the teaching of psychology: 1984. *Teaching of Psychology, 12*(4), 231–236.

Biggs, J. B., & Collis, K. F. (1982). *Evaluating the quality of learning: The SOLO taxonomy.* San Diego, CA: Academic Press.

Billings, J. A. (1993, January). Medical education for hospice care: A selected bibliography with brief annotations. *Hospice Journal, 9*(1), 69–83.

Blaidsell, M. L., & Cox, M. D. (2004). Mid-career and senior faculty learning communities: Learning throughout faculty careers. In M. D. Cox & L. Richlin (Eds.), *New directions for teaching and learning: No. 97. Building faculty learning communities* (pp. 137–148). San Francisco, CA: Jossey-Bass.

Bloom, B. S. (Ed.). (1956). *Taxonomy of educational objectives, handbook 1: Cognitive domain.* New York, NY: Longman.

Blumberg, P. (2004). Documenting the educational innovations of faculty: A win-win situation for faculty and the faculty development center. In C. M. Wehlburg & S. Chadwick-Blossey (Eds.), *To improve the academy: Vol. 22. Resources for faculty, instructional, and organizational development* (pp. 41–51). Bolton, MA: Anker.

Bode, R. K. (1999). Mentoring and collegiality. In R. J. Menges & Associates, *Faculty in new jobs: A guide to settling in, becoming established, and building institutional support* (pp. 118–144). San Francisco, CA: Jossey-Bass.

Bogdan, R. C., & Biklen, S. K. (1998). *Qualitative research for education* (3rd ed.). Needham Heights, MA: Allyn & Bacon.

Bogdan, R. C., & Biklen, S. K. (2003). *Qualitative research for education* (4th ed.). Boston, MA: Allyn & Bacon.

Boice, R. (1990). Mentoring new faculty: A program for implementation. *Journal of Staff, Program, and Organizational Development, 8*(3), 143–160.

Boice, R. (1991, March/April). New faculty as teachers. *Journal of Higher Education, 62*(2), 150–173.

Boice, R. (1992). Lessons learned about mentoring. In M. D. Sorcinelli & A. E. Austin (Eds.), *New directions for teaching and learning: No. 50. Developing new and junior faculty* (pp. 51–61). San Francisco, CA: Jossey-Bass.

Boice, R. (1992). *The new faculty member: Supporting and fostering professional development.* San Francisco, CA: Jossey-Bass.

Boice, R. (2000). *Advice for new faculty members: Nihil nimus.* Boston, MA: Allyn & Bacon.

Boice, R., & Turner, J. L. (1989). The FIPSE-CSULB mentoring project for new faculty. In S. Kahn (Ed.), *To improve the academy: Vol. 8. Resources for student, faculty, and institutional development* (pp. 117–129). Stillwater, OK: New Forums Press.

Borich, G. D. (1999). Dimensions of self that influence effective teaching. In R. P. Lipka & T. M. Brinthaupt (Eds.), *The role of self in teacher development* (pp. 92–117). Albany, NY: State University of New York Press.

Bosson, J. K., Haymovitz, E. L., & Pinel, E. C. (2004). When saying and doing diverge: The effects of stereotype threat on self-reported versus non-verbal anxiety. *Journal of Experimental Social Psychology, 40*(2), 247–255.

Boud, D., & Feletti, G. (Eds.). (2001). *The challenge of problem-based learning* (2nd ed.). London, UK: Kogan Page.

Bova, B. M. (1995). Mentoring revisited: The Hispanic woman's perspective. *Journal of Adult Education, 23*(1), 8–19.

Bowser, T., Duff, E., Enns, C., & Evancio, J. (2003). *Resource manual for instructors in nursing* (Vol. 1). Manitoba, Canada: University of Manitoba, University Teaching Services.

Boyer Commission on Educating Undergraduates in the Research University. (1998). *Reinventing undergraduate education: A blueprint for America's research universities.* Retrieved May 17, 2007, from the Stony Brook University web site: http://naples .cc.sunysb.edu/Pres/boyer.nsf

Boyer, E. L. (1990). *Scholarship reconsidered: Priorities of the professoriate.* Princeton, NJ: The Carnegie Foundation for the Advancement of Teaching.

Bransford, J. D., Brown, A. L., & Cocking, R. R. (Eds.). (2000). *How people learn: Brain, mind, experience, and school* (Expanded ed.). Washington, DC: National Academy Press.

Brazier, P. (1985). *Art history in education: An annotated bibliography and history.* London, UK: University of London, Heinemann Educational Books for the Institute of Education.

Brew, A. (2003, May). Teaching and research: New relationships and their implications for inquiry-based teaching and learning in higher education. *Higher Education Research and Development, 22*(1), 3–18.

Brinko, K. T., Atkins, S. S., & Miller, M. E. (2005). Looking at ourselves: The quality of life of faculty development professionals. In S. Chadwick-Blossey & D. R. Robertson (Eds.), *To improve the academy: Vol. 23. Resources for faculty, instructional, and organizational development* (pp. 93–110). Bolton, MA: Anker.

Brookfield, S. D. (2007). A critical theory perspective on faculty development. In D. R. Robertson & L. B. Nilson (Eds.), *To improve the academy: Vol. 25. Resources for faculty, instructional, and organizational development* (pp. 55–69). Bolton, MA: Anker.

Brown, J. S. (2006, September/October). New learning environments for the 21st century: Exploring the edge. *Change, 38*(5), 26–33.

Browning, P. L. (1970). *Evaluation of short-term training in rehabilitation.* Eugene, OR: University of Oregon, Department of Special Education.

Buchanan, M. A., & MacPhee, E. D. (1928). *An annotated bibliography of modern language methodology.* Toronto, Canada: University of Toronto Press.

Burstyn, J. N., Sellers, S. L., Friedrich, K. A., & Gunasekera, N. (2006). [Workshop evaluations of CIRTL Diversity Resources]. Unpublished raw data.

Butler, D. L., & Sellbom, M. (2002, Summer). Barriers to adopting technology for teaching and learning. *Educause Quarterly, 25*(2), 22–28.

Cabrera, A. F., Crissman, J. L., Bernal, E. M., Nora, A., Terenzini, P. T., & Pascarella, E. T. (2002, January/February). Collaborative learning: Its impact on college students' development and diversity. *Journal of College Student Development, 43*(1), 20–34.

Cabrera, A. F., Doyon, K., Friedrich, K., Roberts, J., Saleem, T., & Giovanetto, L. (2004). *Literature review.* Retrieved May 16, 2007, from the University of Wisconsin–Madison, Center for the Integration of Research, Teaching and Learning web site: http://cirtl.wceruw.org/DiversityInstitute/resources/annotated%2Dbibliography

Cabrera, A. F., & Nora, A. (1994). College students' perceptions of prejudice and discrimination and their feelings of alienation: A construct validation approach. *Review of Education/Pedagogy/Cultural Studies, 16*(3–4), 387–409.

Cahn, S. M. (2004, January–February). Taking teaching seriously. *Academe, 90*(1), 32–33.

Cambridge, B. L. (Ed.). (2004). *Campus progress: Supporting the scholarship of teaching and learning.* Sterling, VA: Stylus.

Camic, P. M., Rhodes, J. E., & Yardley, L. (Eds.). (2003). *Qualitative research in psychology: Expanding perspectives in methodology and design.* Washington, DC: American Psychological Association.

Carey, G. W., & Schwartzberg, J. (1969). *Teaching population geography: An interdisciplinary ecological approach.* New York, NY: Teachers College Press.

Carey, S. J. (2006, Fall). From the editor. *Peer Review: Learning & Technology, 8*(4), 3.

The Carnegie Foundation for the Advancement of Teaching. (2001). *The Carnegie classification of institutions of higher education, 2000 edition.* Menlo Park, CA: Author.

The Carnegie Foundation for the Advancement of Teaching. (2006). *CASTL campus program.* Retrieved May 15, 2007, from www.carnegiefoundation.org/programs/sub.asp?key=21&subkey=68&topkey=21

The Carnegie Foundation for the Advancement of Teaching. (2006). *Integrative Learning Project: Opportunities to connect.* Retrieved May 21, 2007, from www.carnegiefoundation.org/programs/index.asp?key=24

Carr, C. (2000, March). Teaching and using chemical information: Annotated bibliography, 1993–1998. *Journal of Chemical Education, 77*(3), 412–422.

Carter, D., & Tuitt, F. (2006, October). *Black achievers' experiences with and responses to stereotype threat and racial microaggressions.* Paper presented at the BOTA Think Tank, Atlanta, GA.

Carter, R. (1986). Teaching and learning in the 3rd culture: An annotated bibliography of issues in engineering education. *Studies in Higher Education, 11*(3), 323–324.

Carusetta, E., & Cranton, P. (2005, July). Nurturing authenticity through faculty development. *Journal of Faculty Development, 20*(2), 79–86.

Cashin, W. E. (1990). Assessing teaching effectiveness. In P. Seldin & Associates, *How administrators can improve teaching: Moving from talk to action in higher education* (pp. 89–103). San Francisco, CA: Jossey-Bass.

Center for Innovation in the Liberal Arts Associates. (2001–2006). *Proposals and final reports* (0102A–0506B). Northfield, MN: St. Olaf College.

Centra, J. A. (1996). Identifying exemplary teachers: Evidence from colleagues, administrators, and alumni. In M. D. Svinicki & R. J. Menges (Eds.), *New directions for teaching and learning: No. 65. Honoring exemplary teaching* (pp. 51–56). San Francisco, CA: Jossey-Bass.

Chickering, A., & Ehrmann, S. C. (1996, October). Implementing the seven principles: Technology as lever. *AAHE Bulletin, 49*(2). Retrieved May 17, 2007, from www.tltgroup.org/programs/seven.html

Chism, N. V. N. (1997–1998). Developing a philosophy of teaching statement. *Essays on Teaching Excellence, 9*(3) 1–2.

Chism, N. V. N. (2006, July/August). Teaching awards: What do they award? *Journal of Higher Education, 77*(4), 589–617.

Chism, N., & Mintz, J. (1998). *Who's developing the developers? A survey of job satisfaction, challenges, and disappointments of North American educational developers.* Paper presented at the International Consortium of Educational Developers, Austin, TX.

Clarebout, G., Elen, J., Luyten, L., & Bamps, H. (2001, March). Assessing epistemological beliefs: Schommer's questionnaire revisited. *Educational Research and Evaluation: An International Journal on Theory and Practice, 7*(1), 53–77.

Clark, R. E. (1983, Winter). Reconsidering research on learning from media. *Review of Educational Research, 53*(4), 445–459.

Cohen, G. L., Steele, C. M., & Ross, L. D. (1999). The mentor's dilemma: Providing critical feedback across the racial divide. *Personality and Social Psychology Bulletin, 25*(10), 1302–1318.

Cohen, P. A. (1980a). Effectiveness of student-rating feedback for improving college instruction: A meta-analysis of findings. *Research in Higher Education, 13*(4), 321–341.

Cohen, P. A. (1980b). A meta-analysis of the relationship between student ratings of instruction and student achievement. *Dissertation Abstracts International, 41* (05), 2012. (UMI No. 8025666)

Cohen, W. A. (2006). *The marketing plan* (5th ed.). Hoboken, NJ: John Wiley & Sons.

Collins, A., Brown, J. S., & Holum, A. (1991, Winter). Cognitive apprenticeship: Making thinking visible. *American Educator, 15*(3), 6–11, 38–46.

Connolly, M. (2005). Distinguished, my ass. In M. Lerch (Ed.), *Making a difference/Toute la différence* (pp. 31–32). Ontario, Canada: Society for Teaching and Learning in Higher Education.

Cook, C. E., Kaplan, M., Nidiffer, J., & Wright, M. C. (2001, March). Preparing future faculty—faster: A crash course guides students to the professoriate. *AAHE Bulletin, 54*(3), 3–7.

Cook, C. E., Wright, M. C., & Hollenshead, C. S. (2000). *More than a research university: The importance of teaching at the University of Michigan* (Center for Research on Learning and Teaching Occasional Paper No. 14). Ann Arbor, MI: University of Michigan.

Coppola, B. (2000). How to write a teaching philosophy for academic employment. *American Chemical Society, Department of Career Services Bulletin,* 1–8.

Cornwall, A., & Jewkes, R. (1995, December). What is participatory research? *Social Science and Medicine, 41*(12), 1667–1676.

Cox, M. D. (1994). Reclaiming teaching excellence: Miami University's Teaching Scholars Program. In E. C. Wadsworth (Ed.), *To improve the academy: Vol. 13. Resources for faculty, instructional, and organizational development* (pp. 79–96). Stillwater, OK: New Forums Press.

Cox, M. D. (1995). The development of new and junior faculty. In W. A. Wright & Associates, *Teaching improvement practices: Successful strategies for higher education* (pp. 283–310). Bolton, MA: Anker.

Cox, M. D. (1997). Long-term patterns in a mentoring program for junior faculty: Recommendations for practice. In D. DeZure & M. Kaplan (Eds.), *To improve the academy: Vol. 16. Resources for faculty, instructional, and organizational development* (pp. 225–267). Stillwater, OK: New Forums Press.

Cox, M. D. (2001). Faculty learning communities: Change agents for transforming institutions into learning organizations. In D. Lieberman & C. Wehlburg (Eds.), *To improve the academy: Vol. 19. Resources for faculty, instructional, and organizational development* (pp. 69–93). Bolton, MA: Anker.

Cox, M. D. (2004). Introduction to faculty learning communities. In M. D. Cox & L. Richlin (Eds.), *New directions for teaching and learning: No. 97. Building faculty learning communities* (pp. 5–23). San Francisco, CA: Jossey-Bass.

Cox, M. D., & Richlin, L. (2004). Editor's notes. In M. D. Cox & L. Richlin (Eds.), *New directions for teaching and learning: No. 97. Building faculty learning communities* (pp. 1–4). San Francisco, CA: Jossey-Bass.

Cox, M. D., & Sorenson, L. D. (2000). Student collaboration in faculty development: Connecting directly to the learning revolution. In M. Kaplan & D. Lieberman (Eds.), *To improve the academy: Vol. 18. Resources for faculty, instructional, and organizational development* (pp. 97–127). Bolton, MA: Anker.

Cowan, D. H., & Laidlaw, J. C. (1993, Summer). A strategy to improve communication between health care professionals and people living with cancer: 1. Improvement of teaching and assessment of doctor-patient communication in Canadian medical schools. *Journal of Cancer Education, 8*(2), 109–117.

Cranton, P. (1998). *No one way: Teaching and learning in higher education.* Dayton, OH: Wall & Emerson.

Cremens, M. C., Calabrese, L. V., Shuster, J. L., Jr., & Stern, T. A. (1995). The Massachusetts General Hospital annotated bibliography for residents training in consultation-liaison psychiatry. *Psychosomatics, 36*(3), 217–235.

Creswell, J. W. (2003). *Research design: Qualitative, quantitative, and mixed methods approaches* (2nd ed.). Thousand Oaks, CA: Sage.

Cross, K. P., & Steadman, M. H. (1996). *Classroom research: Implementing the scholarship of teaching.* San Francisco, CA: Jossey-Bass.

Cuban, L. (1999). *How scholars trumped teachers: Change without reform in university curriculum, teaching, and research 1890–1990.* New York, NY: Teachers College Press.

Dagenbach, D. (1999). Some thoughts on teaching a pluralistic history in the history and systems of psychology course. *Teaching of Psychology, 26*(1), 22–28.

Damron, J. (2003). What's the problem? A new perspective on ITA communication. *Journal of Graduate Teaching Assistant Development, 9*(2), 81–88.

Dancy, M. H., & Henderson, C. (2005). Beyond the individual instructor: Systemic constraints in the implementation of research-informed practices. In S. Franklin, J. Marx, & P. Heron (Eds.), *Proceedings of the 2004 Physics Education Research Conference* (Vol. 790, pp. 113–116). Melville, NY: American Institute of Physics.

Daniel, R. S. (1981). Annotated bibliography on the teaching of psychology: 1980. *Teaching of Psychology, 8*(4), 249–253.

Davies, P. G., Spencer, S. J., & Steele, C. M. (2005). Clearing the air: Identity safety moderates the effects of stereotype threat on women's leadership aspirations. *Journal of Personality and Social Psychology, 88*(2), 276–287.

Davis, B. G. (1993). *Tools for teaching.* San Francisco, CA: Jossey-Bass.

Denzin, N. K., & Lincoln, Y. S. (Eds.). (2000). *Handbook of qualitative research* (2nd ed.). Thousand Oaks, CA: Sage.

Désert, M., Gonçalves, G., Leyens, J.-P. (2005). *Stereotype threat effects upon behavior: The role of actual control.* Manuscript submitted for publication.

Dewey, B. I., DeBlois, P. B., & Educause Current Issues Committee. (2006, Summer). Current IT issues survey report, 2006. *Educause Quarterly, 29*(2). Retrieved May 21, 2007, from www.educause.edu/eq/eqm06/eqm0622.asp

deWinstanley, P. A., & Bjork, R. A. (2002). Successful lecturing: Presenting information in ways that engage effective processing. In D. F. Halpern & M. D. Hakel (Eds.), *New directions for teaching and learning: No. 89. Applying the science of learning to university teaching and beyond* (pp. 19–31). San Francisco, CA: Jossey-Bass.

Dieterich, D. J., & Behm, R. H. (1984, May). Annotated bibliography of research in the teaching of literature and the teaching of writing. *Research in the Teaching of English, 18*(2), 201–218.

Dooley, K. E., & Murphy, T. H. (2001). College of agriculture faculty perceptions of electronic technologies in teaching. *Journal of Agricultural Education, 42*(2), 1–10.

Dorsey, R. (2006). *Decoding creative plot development.* Unpublished manuscript, Indiana University, Bloomington.

Dubinsky, E., Mathews, D., & Reynolds, B. E. (Eds.). (1997). *Readings in cooperative learning for undergraduate mathematics.* Washington, DC: Mathematical Association of America.

Dunkin, M. J., & Precians, R. P. (1992, December). Award-winning university teachers' concepts of teaching. *Higher Education, 24*(4), 483–502.

Durisen, R., & Pilachowski, C. (2004.) Decoding astronomical concepts. In D. Pace & J. Middendorf (Eds.), *New directions for teaching and learning: No. 98. Decoding the disciplines: Helping students learn disciplinary ways of thinking* (pp. 33–43). San Francisco, CA: Jossey-Bass.

Durst, R. K., & Marshall, J. D. (1991, December). Annotated bibliography of research in the teaching of English. *Research in the Teaching of English, 25*(4), 497–509.

Durunna, O. N., Schönwetter, D. J., & Crow, G. H. (2006, March). *Teaching animal genetics and breeding: What are the resources available to instructors?* Paper presented at the 30th annual meeting of the Nigerian Society for Animal Production, Nigeria.

Durunna, O. N., Schönwetter, D. J., & Crow, G. H. (in press). Teaching animal genetics and breeding: What are the resources available to instructors? *Nigerian Journal of Animal Production.*

Dweck, C. S. (1986, October). Motivational processes affecting learning. *American Psychologist, 41*(10), 1040–1048.

Eddy, P. L., & Mitchell, R. (2006, May). Innovations: Co-teaching-training professionals to teach. *The National Teaching and Learning Forum, 15*(4), 1–7.

Ehrmann, S. C. (n.d.). *Asking the right question: What does research tell us about technology and higher learning?* Retrieved May 17, 2007, from www.tltgroup.org/resources/Flashlight/AskingRightQuestion.htm

Elbow, P. (1986). *Embracing contraries: Explorations in learning and teaching.* New York, NY: Oxford University Press.

Elliot, D. L., Skeff, K. M., & Stratos, G. A. (1999). How do you get to the improvement of teaching? A longitudinal faculty development program for medical educators. *Teaching and Learning in Medicine, 11*(1), 52–57.

Ellis, D., & Griffin, G. (2000). Developing a teaching philosophy statement: A special challenge for graduate students. *Journal of Graduate Teaching Assistant Development, 7*(1), 85–92.

Elmore, R. F. (1996, Spring). Getting to scale with good educational practice. *Harvard Educational Review, 66*(1), 1–26.

Entwistle, N. (1997). Contrasting perspectives on learning. In F. Marton, D. Hounsell, & N. Entwistle (Eds.), *The experience of learning* (pp. 3–22). Edinburgh, Scotland: Scottish Academic Press.

Erby, K. (2001). Teaching and learning from an interdisciplinary perspective. *Peer Review, 3–4*(4–1), 28–31.

Farnham-Diggory, S. (1994, Autumn). Paradigms of knowledge and instruction. *Review of Educational Research, 64*(3), 463–477.

Fausto-Sterling, A. (1993, March/April). The five sexes: Why male and female are not enough. *The Sciences,* 20–24.

Fayne, H., & Ortquist-Ahrens, L. (2006). Learning communities for first-year faculty: Transition, acculturation, and transformation. In S. Chadwick-Blossey & D. R. Robertson (Eds.), *To improve the academy: Vol. 24. Resources for faculty, instructional, and organizational development* (pp. 277–290). Bolton, MA: Anker.

Felder, R. M. (1996). Teaching to all types: Examples from engineering education. *ASEE Prism, 6*(4), 18–23.

Felder, R. M., & Brent, R. (1996, Spring). Navigating the bumpy road to student-centered instruction. *College Teaching, 44*(2), 43–47.

Feldman, K. A. (1977). Consistency and variability among college students in rating their teachers and courses: A review and analysis. *Research in Higher Education, 6*(3), 223–274, 277.

Feldman, K. A. (1978). Course characteristics and college students' ratings of their teachers: What we know and what we don't. *Research in Higher Education, 9*(3), 199–242.

Feldman, K. A. (1987). Research productivity and scholarly accomplishment of college teachers as related to their instructional effectiveness: A review and exploration. *Research in Higher Education, 26*(3), 277–291.

Feldman, K. A. (1989a). The association between student ratings of specific instructional dimensions and student achievement: Refining and extending the synthesis of data from multisection validity studies. *Research in Higher Education, 30*(6), 583–645.

Feldman, K. A. (1989b). Instructional effectiveness of college teachers as judged by teachers themselves, current and former students, colleagues, administrators, and external (neutral) observers. *Research in Higher Education, 30*(2), 137–194.

Feldman, K. A. (1996). Identifying exemplary teaching: Using data from course and teacher evaluations. In M. D. Svinicki & R. J. Menges (Eds.), *New directions for teaching and learning: No. 65. Honoring exemplary teaching* (pp. 41–50). San Francisco, CA: Jossey-Bass.

Ferreira, M. M. (2002). The research lab: A chilly place for graduate women. *Journal of Women and Minorities in Science and Engineering, 8*(1), 85–98.

Ferrett, T. (2006). *First year students "go beyond" with integrative inquiry into abrupt change.* Retrieved May 14, 2007, from www.cfkeep.org/html/snapshot.php?id=28615862064637

Fink, L. D. (2003). *Creating significant learning experiences: An integrated approach to designing college courses.* San Francisco, CA: Jossey-Bass.

Fink, L. D. (2005). *Major new ideas that can empower college teaching.* Unpublished manuscript. Retrieved May 14, 2007, from www.finkconsulting.info/files/Fink2006 MajorNewIdeasToEmpowerCollegeTeaching.doc

Finkel, D. L. (2000). *Teaching with your mouth shut.* Portsmouth, NH: Boynton/Cook.

Firmin, M., Hwang, C., Copella, M., & Clark, S. (2004, Summer). Learned helplessness: The effect of failure on test-taking. *Education, 124*(4), 688–694.

Forsythe, G. B., & Gandolfo, A. (1996). Promoting exemplary teaching: The case of the U.S. Military Academy. In M. D. Svinicki & R. J. Menges (Eds.), *New directions for teaching and learning: No. 65. Honoring exemplary teaching* (pp. 99–104). San Francisco, CA: Jossey-Bass.

Fraenkel, J. R., & Wallen, N. E. (2003). *How to design and evaluate research in education* (5th ed.). New York, NY: McGraw-Hill.

Franklin, J. (2001). Interpreting the numbers: Using a narrative to help others read student evaluations of your teaching accurately. In K. G. Lewis (Ed.), *New directions for teaching and learning: No. 87. Techniques and strategies for interpreting student evaluations* (pp. 85–100). San Francisco, CA: Jossey-Bass.

Frantz, A. C., Beebe, S. A., Horvath, V. S., Canales, J., & Swee, D. E. (2005). The roles of teaching and learning centers. In S. Chadwick-Blossey & D. R. Robertson (Eds.), *To improve the academy: Vol. 23. Resources for faculty, instructional, and organizational development* (pp. 72–90). Bolton, MA: Anker.

Fulkerson, F. E., & Wise, P. S. (1995). Annotated bibliography on the teaching of psychology: 1994. *Teaching of Psychology, 22*(4), 248–253.

Fullan, M. (2001). *The new meaning of educational change* (3rd ed.). New York, NY: Teachers College Press.

Gaff, J. G., & Simpson, R. D. (1994, March). Faculty development in the United States. *Innovative Higher Education, 18*(3), 167–176.

Gale, R. (2003). *Portfolio assessment and student empowerment.* Retrieved May 14, 2007, from www.cfkeep.org/html/snapshot.php?id=2478563

Gibson, G. W. (1992). *Good start: A guidebook for new faculty in liberal arts colleges.* Bolton, MA: Anker.

Gillespie, K. H., Hilsen, L. R., & Wadsworth, E. C. (Eds.). (2002). *A guide to faculty development: Practical advice, examples, and resources.* Bolton, MA: Anker.

Glaser, B. G. (1978). *Theoretical sensitivity: Advances in the methodology of grounded theory.* Mill Valley, CA: Sociology Press.

Goldberg, B., & Finkelstein, M. (2002, Summer). Effects of a first-semester learning community on nontraditional technical students. *Innovative Higher Education, 26*(4), 235–249.

Goldberg, N. (1990). *Wild mind: Living the writer's life.* New York, NY: Bantam.

Goldman, P. (2001). Legal education and technology: An annotated bibliography. *Law Library Journal, 93*(3), 423–467.

Goldsmid, C. A., & Goldsmid, P. L. (1982, April). The teaching of sociology, 1981: Review and annotated bibliography. *Teaching Sociology, 9*(3), 327–352.

Gonzales, P. M., Blanton, H., & Williams, K. J. (2002). The effects of stereotype threat and double-minority status on the test performance of Latino women. *Personality and Social Psychology Bulletin, 28*(5), 659–670.

Good, C., Aronson, J., & Inzlicht, M. (2003, December). Improving adolescents' standardized test performance: An intervention to reduce the effects of stereotype threat. *Journal of Applied Developmental Psychology, 24*(6), 645–662.

Goodwin, L. D., & Stevens, E. A. (1998, Summer). An exploratory study of the role of mentoring in the retention of faculty. *Journal of Staff, Program, and Organizational Development, 16*(1), 39–47.

Goodyear, G. E., & Allchin, D. (1998). Statements of teaching philosophy. In M. Kaplan & D. Lieberman (Eds.), *To improve the academy: Vol. 17. Resources for faculty, instructional, and organizational development* (pp. 103–121). Stillwater, OK: New Forums Press.

Graf, D., & Wheeler, D. (1996). *Defining the field: A survey of the membership of the Professional and Organizational Development Network.* Colorado Springs, CO: Professional and Organizational Development Network.

Graff, G. (1992). *Beyond the culture wars: How teaching the conflicts can revitalize American education.* New York, NY: W. W. Norton.

Gray, M., & Bergmann, B. R. (2003, September–October). Student teaching evaluations: Inaccurate, demeaning, misused. *Academe, 89*(5), 44–46.

Gray, P., Froh, R., & Diamond, R. (1992). *A national study of research universities: On the balance between research and undergraduate teaching.* Syracuse, NY: Syracuse University, Center for Instructional Development.

Hagner, P. R. (2001). *Interesting practices and best systems in faculty engagement and support* (NLII White Paper). Retrieved May 21, 2007, from www.educause.edu/ir/library/pdf/NLI0017.pdf

Hagner, P. R., & Schneebeck, C. A. (2001). Engaging the faculty. In C. A. Barone & P. R. Hagner (Eds.), *Technology-enhanced teaching and learning: Leading and supporting the transformation on your campus* (pp. 1–12). San Francisco, CA: Jossey-Bass.

Handelsman, J., Ebert-May, D., Beichner, R., Bruns, P., Chang, A., DeHaan, R., et al. (2004, April). Education: Scientific teaching. *Science, 304*(5670), 521–522.

Hattie, J., & Marsh, H. W. (1996, Winter). The relationship between research and teaching: A meta-analysis. *Review of Educational Research, 66*(4), 507–542.

Henderson, C. (2005, August). The challenges of instructional change under the best of circumstances: A case study of one college physics instructor. *American Journal of Physics, 73*(8), 778–786.

Henderson, C., & Dancy, M. H. (2005). *When one instructor's interactive classroom activity is another's lecture: Communication difficulties between faculty and educational researchers.* Paper presented at the winter meeting of the American Association of Physics Teachers, Albuquerque, NM.

Herriott, M. E. (1925). *How to make a course of study in arithmetic.* Urbana, IL: University of Illinois, College of Education.

Heyden, R., Luyas, G., & Henry, B. (1990, April). Development management for nursing administration. *Nursing Health Care, 11*(4), 179–181.

Holmgren, R. A. (2005). Teaching partners: Improving teaching and learning by cultivating a community of practice. In S. Chadwick-Blossey & D. R. Robertson (Eds.), *To improve the academy: Vol. 23. Resources for faculty, instructional, and organizational development* (pp. 211–219). Bolton, MA: Anker.

Houston, T. K., Clark, J. M., Levine, R. B., Ferenchick, G. S., Bowen, J. L., Branch, W. T., et al. (2004, December). Outcomes of a national faculty development program in teaching skills. *Innovations in Education and Clinical Practice, 19,* 1220–1227.

Huber, M. T., Brown, C., Hutchings, P., Gale, R., Miller, R., & Breen, M. (Eds.). (2007). *Integrative learning: Opportunities to connect* (Public report of the Integrative Learning Project sponsored by the Association of American Colleges and Universities and The Carnegie Foundation for the Advancement of Teaching). Stanford, CA: The Carnegie Foundation for the Advancement of Teaching.

Huber, M. T., & Hutchings, P. (2004). *Integrative learning: Mapping the terrain.* Washington, DC: Association of American Colleges and Universities.

Huber, M. T., & Hutchings, P. (2005). *The advancement of learning: Building the teaching commons.* San Francisco, CA: Jossey-Bass.

Hutchings, P. (Ed.). (2000). *Opening lines: Approaches to the scholarship of teaching and learning.* Menlo Park, CA: The Carnegie Foundation for the Advancement of Teaching.

Hutchings, P. (Ed.). (2002). *Ethics of inquiry: Issues in the scholarship of teaching and learning.* Menlo Park, CA: The Carnegie Foundation for the Advancement of Teaching.

Hutchings, P., & Bjork, C. (1999). *An annotated bibliography of the scholarship of teaching and learning in higher education.* Philadelphia, PA: Carnegie Academy for the Scholarship of Teaching and Learning.

Hutchings, P., Bjork, C., & Babb, M. (2002). The scholarship of teaching and learning in higher education: An annotated bibliography. *Political Science & Politics, 35*(2), 233–236.

Hutchings, P., & Shulman, L. S. (1999, September/October). The scholarship of teaching: New elaborations, new developments. *Change, 31*(5), 10–15.

Hutchinson, J., & Huberman, M. (1993). *Knowledge dissemination and use in science and mathematics education: A literature review* (NSF 93–75). Arlington, VA: National Science Foundation.

Inzlicht, M., & Ben-Zeev, T. (2000). A threatening intellectual environment: Why females are susceptible to experiencing problem-solving deficits in the presence of males. *Psychological Science, 11*(5), 365–371.

Jackson, W. K., & Simpson, R. D. (1994). Mentoring new faculty for teaching and research. In M. A. Wunsch (Ed.), *New directions for teaching and learning: No. 57. Mentoring revisited: Making an impact on individuals and institutions* (pp. 65–72). San Francisco, CA: Jossey-Bass.

Jenkinson, E. B., & Daghlian, P. B. (1968). *Books for teachers of English: An annotated bibliography.* Bloomington, IN: Indiana University Press.

Jenrette, M., & Hays, K. (1996). Honoring exemplary teaching: The two-year college setting. In M. D. Svinicki & R. J. Menges (Eds.), *New directions for teaching and learning: No. 65. Honoring exemplary teaching* (pp. 77–83). San Francisco, CA: Jossey-Bass.

Johnson, C., & Middendorf, J. (2007). *Decoding geologic time*. Manuscript submitted for publication.

Johnson, D. E., Schroder, S. I., & Kirkbride, A. L. (2005). Annotated bibliography on the teaching of psychology: 2004. *Teaching of Psychology, 32*(4), 281–287.

Johnsrud, L. K., & Atwater, C. D. (1993, Spring). Scaffolding the ivory tower: Building supports for faculty new to the academy. *CUPA Journal, 44*(1), 1–14.

Johnston, S., & McCormack, C. (1996, October). Integrating information technology into university teaching: Identifying the needs and providing the support. *International Journal of Educational Management, 10*(5), 36–42.

Jones, L. F. (2005). Exploring the inner landscape of teaching: A program for faculty renewal. In S. Chadwick-Blossey & D. R. Robertson (Eds.), *To improve the academy: Vol. 23. Resources for faculty, instructional, and organizational development* (pp. 130–143). Bolton, MA: Anker.

Kampen, K. (2004). *Resource manual for instructors in sociology* (Vol. 1). Manitoba, Canada: University of Manitoba, University Teaching Services.

Kegan, R., & Lahey, L. L. (2001). *How the way we talk can change the way we work: Seven languages for transformation*. San Francisco, CA: Jossey-Bass.

Kember, D. (1997, September). A reconceptualisation of the research into university academics' conceptions of teaching. *Learning and Instruction, 7*(3), 255–275.

Kember, D., & Gow, L. (1994, January/February). Orientations to teaching and their effect on the quality of student learning. *Journal of Higher Education, 65*(1), 58–74.

Kember, D., Jenkins, W., & Ng, K. C. (2004, March). Adult students' perceptions of good teaching as a function of their conceptions of learning—Part 2. Implications for the evaluation of teaching. *Studies in Continuing Education, 26*(1), 81–97.

Kember, D., & Kwan, K.-P. (2000, September). Lecturers' approaches to teaching and their relationship to conceptions of good teaching. *Instructional Science, 28*(5–6), 469–490.

Kember, D., & Wong, A. (2000, July). Implications for evaluation from a study of students' perceptions of good and poor teaching. *Higher Education, 40*(1), 69–97.

Kezar, A. J. (2001). *Understanding and facilitating organizational change in the 21st century: Recent research and conceptualizations* (ASHE-ERIC Higher Education Report, 28[4]). San Francisco, CA: Jossey-Bass.

King, K. P. (2004). Both sides now: Examining transformative learning and professional development of educators. *Innovative Higher Education, 29*(2), 155–174.

King, M. (1981). *The critical filter: Girls and mathematics: An annotated bibliography*. Adelaide, Australia: Adelaide College of the Arts and Education.

Kolb, D. A. (1984). *Experiential learning: Experience as the source of learning and development.* Upper Saddle River, NJ: Prentice-Hall.

Kreber, C. (1999). *Defining and implementing the scholarship of teaching: The results of a Delphi study.* Paper presented at the annual meeting of the Canadian Society for the Study of Higher Education, Sherbrooke, Quebec.

Kreber, C. (2001a). Observations, reflections, and speculations: What we have learned about the scholarship of teaching and where it might lead. In C. Kreber (Ed.), *New directions for teaching and learning: No. 86. Scholarship revisited: Perspectives on the scholarship of teaching* (pp. 99–104). San Francisco, CA: Jossey-Bass.

Kreber, C. (2001b). The scholarship of teaching and its implementation in faculty development and graduate education. In C. Kreber (Ed.), *New directions for teaching and learning: No. 86. Scholarship revisited: Perspectives on the scholarship of teaching* (pp. 79–88). San Francisco, CA: Jossey-Bass.

Kreber, C., & Cranton, P. (1997). Teaching as scholarship: A model for instructional development. *Issues and Inquiry in College Learning and Teaching, 19*(2), 4–12.

Kreber, C., & Cranton, P. (2000, July/August). Exploring the scholarship of teaching. *Journal of Higher Education, 71*(4), 476–495.

Kurfiss, J., & Boice, R. (1990). Current and desired faculty development practices among POD members. In L. Hilsen (Ed.), *To improve the academy: Vol. 9. Resources for student, faculty, and institutional development* (pp. 73–82). Stillwater, OK: New Forums Press.

Lang, H. G., & DeCaro, J. J. (1989). Support from the administration: A case study in the implementation of a grassroots faculty development program. In S. Kahn (Ed.), *To improve the academy: Vol. 8. Resources for student, faculty, and institutional development* (pp. 71–79). Stillwater, OK: New Forums Press.

Larson, R. L., & Bechan, A. (1992, December). Annotated bibliography of research in the teaching of English. *Research in the Teaching of English, 26*(4), 446–465.

Larson, R. L., & Saks, A. L. (1993, December). Annotated bibliography of research in the teaching of English. *Research in the Teaching of English, 27*(4), 423–437.

Larson, R. L., & Saks, A. L. (1995, May). Annotated bibliography of research in the teaching of English. *Research in the Teaching of English, 29*(2), 239–255.

Laton, A. D., & Bailey, E. W. (1939). *Suggestions for teaching selected material from the field of genetics.* New York, NY: Columbia University, Teachers College.

Lattuca, L. R., Voigt, L. J., & Faith, K. Q. (2004, Fall). Does interdisciplinarity promote learning? Theoretical support and researchable questions. *Review of Higher Education, 28*(1), 23–48.

LeCompte, M. D., Millroy, W. L., & Preissle, J. (Eds.). (1992). *The handbook of qualitative research in education.* San Diego, CA: Academic Press.

Lee, V. S. (Ed.). (2004). *Teaching and learning through inquiry: A guidebook for institutions and instructors.* Sterling, VA: Stylus.

Lerch, M. (Ed.). (2005). *Making a difference/Toute la différence.* Ontario, Canada: Society for Teaching and Learning in Higher Education.

Levinson-Rose, J., & Menges, R. J. (1981, Fall). Improving college teaching: A critical review of research. *Review of Educational Research, 51*(3), 403–434.

L'Hommedieu, R., Menges, R. J., & Brinko, K. T. (1988). *The effects of student ratings feedback to college teachers: A meta-analysis and review of research.* Unpublished manuscript.

L'Hommedieu, R., Menges, R. J., & Brinko, K. T. (1990, June). Methodological explanations for the modest effects of feedback from student ratings. *Journal of Educational Psychology, 82*(2), 232–241.

Lieberman, D. A., & Guskin, A. E. (2003). The essential role of faculty development in new higher education models. In C. M. Wehlburg & S. Chadwick-Blossey (Eds.), *To improve the academy: Vol. 21. Resources for faculty, instructional, and organizational development* (pp. 257–272). Bolton, MA: Anker.

Light, G., & Cox R. (2001). *Learning and teaching in higher education: The reflective professional.* Thousand Oaks, CA: Sage.

Lincoln, Y. S., & Guba, E. G. (1985). *Naturalistic inquiry.* Newbury Park, CA: Sage.

Lindholm, J. A., Szelény, K., Hurtado, S., & Korn, W. S. (2005). *The American college teacher: National norms for the 2004–2005 HERI faculty survey.* Los Angeles, CA: University of California–Los Angeles, Higher Education Research Institute.

Lindstrom, F. B. (1998, April). Teaching sociology with fiction: An annotated bibliography. *Sociological Inquiry, 68*(2), 281–284.

Linnenbrink, E. A., & Pintrich, P. R. (2002). Motivation as an enabler for academic success. *School Psychology Review, 31*(3), 313–327.

Loeher, L. (2006, October). *An examination of research university faculty evaluation policies and practices.* Paper presented at the 31st annual meeting of the Professional and Organizational Development Network in Higher Education, Portland, OR.

Lopez, B. (1986). *Arctic dreams.* New York, NY: Vintage Books.

Lopez, T. B., & Lee, R. G. (2005). Five principles for workable client-based projects: Lessons from the trenches. *Journal of Marketing Education, 27*(2), 172–188.

Loucks-Horsley, S., Hewson, P. W., Love, N., & Stiles, K. E. (1998). *Designing professional development for teachers of science and mathematics.* Thousand Oaks, CA: Corwin Press.

Lowman, J. (1996). Characteristics of exemplary teachers. In M. D. Svinicki & R. J. Menges (Eds.), *New directions for teaching and learning: No. 65. Honoring exemplary teaching* (pp. 33–40). San Francisco, CA: Jossey-Bass.

Luna, G., & Cullen, D. L. (1995). *Empowering the faculty: Mentoring redirected and renewed* (ASHE-ERIC Higher Education Rep. No. 3). Washington, DC: The George Washington University, School of Education and Human Development.

Lunde, J. P., & Barrett, L. A. (1996). Decentralized/departmental reward systems. In M. D. Svinicki & R. J. Menges (Eds.), *New directions for teaching and learning: No. 65. Honoring exemplary teaching* (pp. 93–98). San Francisco, CA: Jossey-Bass.

MacKinney, A. A., Jr. (1994, March). On teaching bedside diagnostic and therapeutic procedures to medical students: An annotated bibliography of audiovisual materials. *Journal of General Internal Medicine, 9*(3), 153–157.

MacVicar, J., & Boroch, R. (1977). Approaches to staff development for departments of nursing: An annotated bibliography. *National League for Nursing, 20*(1658), 1–38.

Maguire, P. (1987). *Doing participatory research: A feminist approach.* Amherst, MA: University of Massachusetts, Center for International Education.

Mahon, P. Y. (1997, July/August). Transcultural nursing: A source guide. *Journal of Nurse Staff Development, 13*(4), 218–222.

Major, B., Spencer, S., Schmader, T., Wolfe, C., & Crocker, J. (1998). Coping with negative stereotypes about intellectual performance: The role of psychological disengagement. *Personality and Social Psychology Bulletin, 24*(1), 34–50.

Marder, C., McCullough, J., & Perakis, S. (2001). *Evaluation of the National Science Foundation's Undergraduate Faculty Enhancement (UFE) program.* Arlington, VA: National Science Foundation.

Markus, H. R., Steele, C. M., & Steele, D. M. (2002). Color blindness as a barrier to inclusion: Assimilation and nonimmigrant minorities. In R. Shweder, M. Minow, & H. R. Markus (Eds.), *Engaging cultural differences: The multicultural challenge in liberal democracies* (pp. 453–472). New York, NY: Russell Sage Foundation.

Marsh, H. W. (1984). Students' evaluations of university teaching: Dimensionality, reliability, validity, potential biases, and utility. *Journal of Educational Psychology, 76*(5), 707–754.

Marsh, H. W. (1987). Students' evaluations of university teaching: Research findings, methodological issues, and directions for future research. *International Journal of Educational Research, 11*(3), 253–388.

Marsh, H. W., & Dunkin, M. J. (1992). Students' evaluations of university teaching: A multidimensional approach. In J. C. Smart (Ed.), *Higher education: Handbook of theory and research, Vol. VIII* (pp. 143–234). New York, NY: Agathon Press.

Marshall, J. D., & Durst, R. K. (1991). Annotated bibliography of research in the teaching of English. *Research in the Teaching of English, 25*(2), 236–253.

Marton, F., & Booth, S. (1997). *Learning and awareness.* Mahwah, NJ: Lawrence Erlbaum.

Marx, D. M., Brown, J. L., & Steele, C. M. (1999, Fall). Allport's legacy and the situational press of stereotypes. *Journal of Social Issues, 55*(3), 491–502.

Marx, D. M., & Goff, P. A. (2005, December). Clearing the air: The effect of experimenter race on target's test performance and subjective experience. *British Journal of Social Psychology, 44*(4), 645–657.

Marx, D. M., & Roman, J. S. (2002, September). Female role models: Protecting women's math test performance. *Personality and Social Psychology Bulletin, 28*(9), 1183–1193.

Massy, W. F., & Zemsky, R. (1995). *Using information technology to enhance academic productivity.* Washington, DC: Educom.

Maton, K. I., Hrabowski, F. A., & Schmitt, C. L. (2000, September). African American college students excelling in the sciences: College and post-college outcomes in the Meyerhoff Scholars Program. *Journal of Research in Science Teaching, 37*(7), 629–654.

Mazur, E. (1997). *Peer instruction: A user's manual.* Upper Saddle River, NJ: Prentice Hall.

McAlpine, L., & Weston C. (2000, September). Reflection: Issues related to improving professors' teaching and students' learning. *Instructional Science, 28*(5–6), 363–385.

McFarland, L. A., Lev-Arey, D. M., & Ziegert, J. C. (2003). An examination of stereotype threat in a motivational context. *Human Performance, 16*(3), 181–205.

McKeachie, W. J. (2002). *McKeachie's teaching tips: Strategies, research, and theory for college and university teachers* (11th ed.). Boston, MA: Houghton Mifflin.

McKenzie, J. (2002). Variation and relevance structures for university teachers' learning: Bringing about change in ways of experiencing teaching. In A. Goody, J. Herrington, & M. Northcote (Eds.), *Annual International Conference of Higher Education Research and Development Society of Australasia* (pp. 434–441). Perth, Australia: Higher Education Research and Development Society of Australasia.

McKinney, K., Broadbear, J., Gentry, D., Klass, P., Naylor, S., & Virgil, N. (2003). *Summary of on-line questionnaire study on the status of SoTL at Illinois State University.* Retrieved May 15, 2007, from the Illinois State University, Scholarship of Teaching and Learning web site: www.sotl.ilstu.edu/downloads/pdf/sotlonlinequest.pdf

McLaughlin, S. P., & George, E. V. (1982). Periodical literature on teaching the classics in translation, 1975–1979: An annotated bibliography. *Classical World, 75*(6), 341–354.

Meizlish, D. S., & Kaplan, M. (2007). *Valuing and evaluating teaching in academic hiring: A multi-disciplinary, cross institutional study.* Manuscript submitted for publication.

Menges, R. J., & Austin, A. E. (2001). Teaching in higher education. In V. Richardson (Ed.), *Handbook of research on teaching* (4th ed., pp. 1122–1156). Washington, DC: American Educational Research Association.

Mezirow, J. (1991). *Transformative dimensions of adult learning.* San Francisco, CA: Jossey-Bass.

Miami University. (2004). *Faculty learning communities: Participating institutions and their communities and directors.* Retrieved May 16, 2007, from the Miami University, Faculty Learning Communities web site: www.units.muohio.edu/flc/participating.shtml

Miller, E. (1995). Rewarding faculty for teaching excellence/effectiveness: A survey of currently available awards including faculty comments and desires in regard to the whole process of rewards. *Dissertation Abstracts International, 56* (6), 2133. (UMI No. 9534400)

Mitchell, J., & Marland, P. (1989). Research on teacher thinking: The next phase. *Teaching and Teacher Education, 5*(2), 115–128.

Mooney, K. M., Fordham, T., & Lehr, V. D. (2005). A faculty development program to promote engaged classroom dialogue: The Oral Communication Institute. In S. Chadwick-Blossey & D. R. Robertson (Eds.), *To improve the academy: Vol. 23. Resources for faculty, instructional, and organizational development* (pp. 220–235). Bolton, MA: Anker.

Mooney, K., Reder, M., & Holmgren, R. (2005, January). *Transforming teaching cultures: The need for teaching and learning programs at liberal arts colleges.* Paper presented at the annual meeting of the Association of American Colleges and Universities, San Francisco, CA.

Moore, J. L., III, Madison-Colmore, O., & Smith, D. M. (2003, Fall). The prove-them-wrong syndrome: Voices from unheard African-American males in engineering disciplines. *Journal of Men's Studies, 12*(1), 61–73.

Montell, G. (2003, March 27). What's your philosophy on teaching, and does it matter? *The Chronicle of Higher Education.* Retrieved May 21, 2007, from http://chronicle.com/jobs/2003/03/2003032701c.htm

Morgan, G. (2003). *Key findings: Faculty use of course management systems.* Retrieved May 21, 2007, from www.educause.edu/ir/library/pdf/ERS0302/ekf0302.pdf

Morgan, L. I., & Daniel, R. S. (1983). Annotated bibliography on the teaching of psychology: 1982. *Teaching of Psychology, 10*(4), 248–253.

Mosley, C. E., & Daniel, R. S. (1982). Annotated bibliography on the teaching of psychology: 1981. *Teaching of Psychology, 9*(4), 250–254.

Mullen, C. A., & Forbes, S. A. (2000, April). Untenured faculty: Issues of transition, adjustment and mentorship. *Mentoring & Tutoring, 8*(1), 31–46.

Mullinix, B. B. (2003). *A rubric for rubrics.* Retrieved May 21, 2007, from the Monmouth University, Faculty Resource Center web site: http://its.monmouth.edu/facultyresourcecenter/Rubrics/A%20Rubric%20for%20Rubrics.htm

Mullinix, B. B. (2006, April). *Trends across the HE landscape: The faculty status of faculty developers.* Paper presented at the annual meeting of the American Educational Research Association, San Francisco, CA.

Mullinix, B. B., & Akatsa-Bukachi, M. (1998). Participatory evaluation: Offering Kenyan women power and voice. In E. T. Jackson & Y. Kassam (Eds.), *Knowledge shared: Participatory evaluation in development cooperation* (pp. 167–176). West Hartford, CT: Kumarian Press.

Mullinix, B. B., & Chism, N. V. N. (2005, October). *The faculty status of faculty developers: A collaborative construction and collective explorations.* Paper presented at the 30th annual meeting of the Professional and Organizational Development Network in Higher Education, Milwaukee, WI.

Mumtaz, S. (2000). Factors affecting teachers' use of information and communications technology: A review of the literature. *Journal of Information Technology for Teacher Education, 9*(3), 319–341.

Munro, T. (2003). A family's criminal legacy. *Legal Studies Forum, 27*(1), 403–405.

Murphy, P. K., & Alexander, P. A. (2002, Spring). What counts? The predictive powers of subject-matter knowledge, strategic processing, and interest in domain-specific performance. *Journal of Experimental Education, 70*(3), 197–214.

Murphy, R. J., Gray, S. A., Straja, S. R., & Bogert, M. C. (2004, August). Student learning preferences and teaching implications. *Journal of Dental Education, 68*(8), 859–866.

National Research Council. (1997). *Science teaching reconsidered: A handbook.* Washington, DC: National Academy Press.

National Research Council. (2003). *Improving undergraduate instruction in science, technology, engineering, and mathematics: Report of a workshop.* Washington, DC: National Academies Press.

National Science Foundation, Division of Science Resources Statistics. (2003). *Science and engineering doctorate awards: 2002* (NSF Publication No. 04–303). Arlington, VA: Author.

Nauta, M. M., Epperson, D. L., & Kahn, J. H. (1998, October). A multiple-groups analysis of predictors of higher level career aspirations among women in mathematics, science, and engineering majors. *Journal of Counseling Psychology, 45*(4), 483–496.

Niemi, J. A., & Gooler, D. D. (Eds.). (1987). *New directions for continuing education: No. 34. Technologies for learning outside the classroom.* San Francisco, CA: Jossey-Bass.

Nighswander-Rempel, S., & Kondratieva, M. (2005). *Resource manual for instructors in mathematics* (Vol. 1). Manitoba, Canada: University of Manitoba, University Teaching Services.

Nyquist, J. D. (1986). CIDR: A small service firm within a research university. In M. Svinicki, J. Kurfiss, & J. Stone (Eds.), *To improve the academy: Vol. 5. Resources for student, faculty, and institutional development* (pp. 66–83). Stillwater, OK: New Forums Press.

Nyquist, J. D., Manning, L., Wulff, D. H., Austin, A. E., Sprague, J., Fraser, P. K., et al. (1999, May/June). On the road to becoming a professor: The graduate student experience. *Change, 31*(3), 18–27.

Oblinger, D. G., & Oblinger, J. L. (Eds.). (2005). *Educating the net generation.* Boulder, CO: Educause.

O'Connor, T. (2006). *Decoding a philosophical argument.* Unpublished manuscript, Indiana University, Bloomington.

Olsen, D., & Sorcinelli, M. D. (1992). The pretenure years: A longitudinal perspective. In M. D. Sorcinelli & A. E. Austin (Eds.), *New directions for teaching and learning: No. 48. Developing new and junior faculty* (pp. 15–25). San Francisco, CA: Jossey-Bass.

O'Reilley, M. R. (1993). *The peaceable classroom.* Portsmouth, NH: Boynton/Cook.

O'Reilley, M. R. (1998). *Radical presence: Teaching as contemplative practice.* Portsmouth, NH: Boynton/Cook.

Osborne, J. W. (2001, July). Testing stereotype threat: Does anxiety explain race and sex differences in achievement? *Contemporary Educational Psychology, 26*(3), 291–310.

Pace, D., & Middendorf, J. (Eds.). (2004). *New directions for teaching and learning: No. 98. Decoding the disciplines: Helping students learn disciplinary ways of thinking.* San Francisco, CA: Jossey-Bass.

Palmer, P. J. (1998). *The courage to teach: Exploring the inner landscape of a teacher's life.* San Francisco, CA: Jossey-Bass.

Parkes, J., & Harris, M. B. (2002, Spring). The purposes of a syllabus. *College Teaching, 50*(2), 55–61.

Patton, M. Q. (2002). *Qualitative research and evaluation methods* (3rd ed.). Thousand Oaks, CA: Sage.

Paulsen, M. B. (1999). How college students learn: Linking traditional educational research and contextual classroom research. *Journal of Staff, Program, and Organizational Development, 16*(2), 63–71.

Paulsen, M. B. (2001). The relation between research and the scholarship of teaching. In C. Kreber (Ed.), *New directions for teaching and learning: No. 86. Scholarship revisited: Perspectives on the scholarship of teaching* (pp. 19–29). San Francisco, CA: Jossey-Bass.

Perry, R. P., Hladkyj, S., Pekrun, R. H., Clifton, R. A., & Chipperfield, J. G. (2005, August). Perceived academic control and failure in college students: A three-year study of scholastic attainment. *Research in Higher Education, 46*(5), 535–569.

Peters, J. K., & Weisberg, M. (2005). *Reflecting on our teaching 2005.* Spokane, WA: Institute for Law School Teaching.

Piburn, M., & Sawada, D. (2000). *Reformed teaching observation protocol (RTOP): Reference manual* (Technical Rep. No. IN00–3). Tempe, AZ: Arizona Collaborative for Excellence in the Preparation of Teachers .

Pintrich, P. R., Marx, R. W., & Boyle, R. A. (1993, Summer). Beyond cold conceptual change: The role of motivational beliefs and classroom contextual factors in the process of conceptual change. *Review of Educational Research, 63*(2), 167–199.

Popham, W. J. (1997, October). What's wrong—and what's right—with rubrics. *Educational Leadership, 55*(2), 72–75.

Popp, H. (1996). Studying and teaching ancient history: An introduction with annotated bibliography. *Gymnasium, 103*(1), 91–92.

Pratt, D. D. (2005, January–February). Personal philosophies of teaching: A false promise? *Academe, 91*(1), 32–35.

Preisman, R. C., Steinberg, M. D., Rummans, T. A., Youngner, S. J., Leeman, C. P., Lederberg, M. S., et al. (1999, October). An annotated bibliography for ethics training in consultation-liaison psychiatry. *Psychosomatics, 40*(5), 369–379.

Professional and Organizational Development Network in Higher Education. (2006). *POD institutional membership by Carnegie classification.* Internal POD Network Document.

Prosser, M., & Trigwell, K. (1999). *Understanding learning and teaching: The experience in higher education.* Buckingham, UK: Society for Research into Higher Education & Open University Press.

Quinn, D. M., & Spencer, S. J. (2001, Spring). The interference of stereotype threat with women's generation of mathematical problem-solving strategies. *Journal of Social Issues, 57*(1), 55–71.

Quinn, J. (1994, January). *Teaching award recipients' perceptions of teaching award programs.* Paper presented at the second annual American Association for Higher Education Forum on Faculty Roles and Rewards, New Orleans, LA.

Ralph, E. G. (1998). *Motivating teaching in higher education: A manual for faculty development.* Stillwater, OK: New Forums Press.

Ramsden, P. (2003). *Learning to teach in higher education.* New York, NY: RoutledgeFalmer.

Random House. (2006). *Random House unabridged dictionary.* Retrieved May 17, 2007, from http://dictionary.reference.com/browse/task

Reder, M., & Gallagher, E. V. (2007). Transforming a teaching culture through peer mentoring: Connecticut College's Johnson Teaching Seminar for Incoming Faculty. In D. R. Robertson & L. B. Nilson (Eds.), *To improve the academy: Vol. 25. Resources for faculty, instructional, and organizational development* (pp. 327–344). Bolton, MA: Anker.

Reder, M., & Mooney, K. (2004, November). *Getting started in small college faculty development.* Roundtable at the 29th annual meeting of the Professional and Organizational Development Network in Higher Education, Montreal, Canada.

Rice, R. E. (1992). Toward a broader conception of scholarship: The American context. In T. G. Whiston & R. L. Geiger (Eds.), *Research and higher education: The United Kingdom and the United States* (pp. 117–129). Buckingham, UK: Society for Research into Higher Education & Open University Press.

Rice, R. E. (2006, Fall). From Athens and Berlin to LA: Faculty work and the new academy. *Liberal Education, 92*(4), 6–13.

Rice, R. E. (2007). It all started in the Sixties: Movements for change across the decades—A personal journey. In D. R. Robertson & L. B. Nilson (Eds.), *To improve the academy: Vol. 25. Resources for faculty, instructional, and organizational development* (pp. 3–17). Bolton, MA: Anker.

Rice, R. E., Sorcinelli, M. D., & Austin, A. E. (2000). *Heeding new voices: Academic careers for a new generation.* Washington, DC: American Association for Higher Education.

Richards, L. (1999). *Using NVivo in qualitative research.* Thousand Oaks, CA: Sage.

Richlin, L. (2001). Scholarly teaching and the scholarship of teaching. In C. Kreber (Ed.), *New directions for teaching and learning: No. 86. Scholarship revisited: Perspectives on the scholarship of teaching* (pp. 57–68). San Francisco, CA: Jossey-Bass.

Richlin, L., & Essington, A. (2004). Overview of faculty learning communities. In M. D. Cox & L. Richlin (Eds.), *New directions for teaching and learning: No. 97. Building faculty learning communities* (pp. 25–39). San Francisco, CA: Jossey-Bass.

Riley, D. (2003). Employing liberative pedagogies in engineering education. *Journal of Women and Minorities in Science and Engineering, 9*(2), 137–158.

Roberts, R., Sweet, M., Walker, J., Walls, S., Kucsera, J., Shaw, S., et al. (2006, October). *Teacher mistakes: A window into teacher self-efficacy.* Paper presented at the annual meeting of the American Psychological Association, New Orleans, LA.

Ross, B. (2001). Towards a framework for problem-based curricula. In D. Boud & G. Feletti (Eds.), *The challenge of problem-based learning* (2nd ed., pp. 28–35). London, UK: Kogan Page.

Rosser, S. V. (1993). Female friendly science: Including women in curricular content and pedagogy in science. *Journal of General Education, 42*(3), 191–220.

Roth, W.-M., Masciotra, D., & Boyd, N. (1999, October). Becoming-in-the-classroom: A case study of teacher development through coteaching. *Teaching and Teacher Education, 15*(7), 771–784.

Roth, W.-M., & Tobin, K. G. (2002). *At the elbow of another: Learning to teach by coteaching.* New York, NY: Peter Lang.

Rubin, B., & Krishnan, S. (2004.) Decoding applied data in professional schools. In D. Pace & J. Middendorf (Eds.), *New directions for teaching and learning: No. 98. Decoding the disciplines: Helping students learn disciplinary ways of thinking* (pp. 67–73). San Francisco, CA: Jossey-Bass.

Russell, T. (2001). *The "no significant difference phenomenon"* (5th ed.). Montgomery, AL: International Distance Education Certification Center.

Saakvitne, K. W., & Pearlman, L. A. (1996). *Transforming the pain: A workbook on vicarious traumatization.* New York, NY: W. W. Norton.

Saks, A. L., & Larson, R. L. (1994, December). Annotated bibliography of research in the teaching of English. *Research in the Teaching of English, 28*(4), 418–436.

Sandler, B. R. (1993, March 10). Women as mentors: Myths and commandments. *The Chronicle of Higher Education*, p. B3.

Saroyan, A., & Amundsen, C. (Eds.). (2004). *Rethinking teaching in higher education: From a course design workshop to a faculty development framework.* Sterling, VA: Stylus.

Savin-Baden, M., & Major, C. H. (2004). *Foundations of problem-based learning.* New York, NY: Open University Press.

Schön, D. A. (1983). *The reflective practitioner: How professionals think in action.* New York, NY: Basic Books.

Schönwetter, D. J. (1993). Attributes of effective lecturing in the college classroom. *Canadian Journal of Higher Education, 23*(2), 1–18.

Schönwetter, D. J., Clifton, R. A., & Perry, R. P. (2002, December). Content familiarity: Differential impact of effective teaching on student achievement outcomes. *Research in Higher Education, 43*(6), 625–655.

Schönwetter, D. J., Ellis, D., Taylor, K. L., & Koop, V. (in press). A review of graduate courses on college/university teaching in Canada and the USA. *Journal of Graduate Teaching Assistant Development.*

Schönwetter, D. J., Lavigne, S., Mazurat, R., & Nazarko, O. (2006). Students' perceptions of effective classroom and clinical teaching in dental and dental hygiene education. *Journal of Dental Education, 70*(6), 624–635.

Schönwetter, D. J., MacDonald, L., Mazurat, R., & Thorton-Trump, A. (2006). *Resources for teaching: Resource manual for faculty of dentistry and school of dental hygiene.* Manitoba, Canada: University of Manitoba, Faculty of Dentistry.

Schönwetter, D. J., Sokal, L., Friesen, M., & Taylor, K. L. (2002, May). Teaching philosophies reconsidered: A conceptual model for the development and evaluation of teaching philosophy statements. *International Journal for Academic Development, 7*(1), 83–97.

Schönwetter, D. J., & Taylor, K. L. (2003, October). *Bright ideas presentation: Transforming teaching through teaching resource portfolios.* Paper presented at the 28th annual meeting of the Professional and Organizational Development Network in Higher Education, Denver, CO.

Schönwetter, D. J., Taylor, K. L., & Duff, E. (2003, October). *Transforming teaching through teaching resource portfolios: Success stories from faculty and graduate students.* Paper presented at the annual meeting of the Society for Teaching and Learning in Higher Education, British Columbia, Canada.

Schraw, G., Bendixen, L. D., & Dunkle, M. E. (2002). Development and validation of the Epistemic Belief Inventory (EBI). In B. K. Hofer & P. R. Pintrich (Eds.), *Personal epistemology: The psychology of beliefs about knowledge and knowing* (pp. 261–275). Mahwah, NJ: Lawrence Erlbaum.

Schroeder, C. M. (2005). Evidence of the transformational dimensions of the scholarship of teaching and learning: Faculty development through the eyes of the SoTL scholars. In S. Chadwick-Blossey & D. R. Robertson (Eds.), *To improve the academy: Vol. 23. Resources for faculty, instructional, and organizational development* (pp. 47–71). Bolton, MA: Anker.

Schwartz, P., Mennin, S., & Webb, G. (Eds.). (2001). *Problem-based learning: Case studies, experience and practice.* London, UK: Kogan Page.

Sekerka, L. E., & Chao, J. (2003, Winter). Peer coaching as a technique to foster professional development in clinical ambulatory settings. *Journal of Continuing Education in the Health Professions, 23*(1), 30–37.

Seldin, P. (1984). *Changing practices in faculty evaluation.* San Francisco, CA: Jossey-Bass.

Seldin, P., & Associates. (1999). *Changing practices in evaluating teaching: A practical guide to improved faculty performance and promotion/tenure decisions.* Bolton, MA: Anker.

Sellers, S. L., & Friedrich, K. A. (2006). *Unmasking inequality: A self-guided workshop on educational success.* Retrieved May 17, 2007, from the University of Wisconsin–Madison, Center for the Integration of Research, Teaching and Learning web site: http://cirtl.wceruw.org/DiversityInstitute/resources/workshops/

Sellers, S. L., Friedrich, K., Gunasekera, N., Saleem, T., & Burstyn, J. (2006). *Case studies in inclusive teaching in science, technology, engineering, and mathematics.* Madison, WI: University of Wisconsin–Madison, Center for the Integration of Research, Teaching, and Learning.

Sellers, S. L., Roberts, J., Giovanetto, L., & Friedrich, K. (2005). *Reaching all students: A resource for teaching in science, technology, engineering, and mathematics.* Madison, WI: University of Wisconsin–Madison, Center for the Integration of Research, Teaching, and Learning.

Seymour, E. (2001). Tracking the processes of change in U.S. undergraduate education in science, mathematics, engineering, and technology. *Science Education, 86,* 79–105.

Seymour, E., & Hewitt, N. M. (1997). *Talking about leaving: Why undergraduates leave the sciences.* Boulder, CO: Westview Press.

Shen, Z. (2004). Cultural competence models in nursing: A selected annotated bibliography. *Journal of Transcultural Nursing, 15*(4), 317–322.

Shenk, G. (2001). *California history and political action.* Retrieved May 14, 2007, from www.carnegiefoundation.org/programs/project_summary.asp?scholar=114

Shih, M., Pittinsky, T., & Ambady, N. (1999, January). Stereotype susceptibility: Identity salience and shifts in quantitative performance. *Psychological Science, 10*(1), 80–83.

Shulman, L. S. (1987, February). Knowledge and teaching: Foundations of the new reform. *Harvard Educational Review, 57*(1), 1–22.

Shulman, L. S. (1993, November/December). Teaching as community property: Putting an end to pedagogical solitude. *Change, 25*(6), 6–7.

Shulman, L. S. (2002). Foreword. In M. T. Huber & S. P. Morreale (Eds.), *Disciplinary styles in the scholarship of teaching and learning: Exploring common ground* (pp. v–ix). Sterling, VA: Stylus.

Shulman, L. S. (2004). Visions of educational leadership: Sustaining the legacy of Seymour Fox. In M. Nisan & O. Schremer (Eds.), *Educational deliberations: Festschrift in honor of Seymour M. Fox* (pp. 451–472). Jerusalem: Keter Publishers.

Sileikyte, R., Schönwetter, D. J., Mazurat, R., & Nazarko, O. (2007, March). *Competency at graduation: Assessment of graduating dental students' undergraduate educational experiences.* Paper presented at the annual meeting of the American Dental Education Association, New Orleans, LA.

Skinner, M. E., & Welch, F. C. (1996, Fall). Peer coaching for better teaching. *College Teaching, 44*(4), 153–156.

Slater, T. F. (2003, October). When is a good day teaching a bad thing? *The Physics Teacher, 41*(7), 437–438.

Smallen, D., & Leach, K. (2004). *Information technology benchmarks: A practical guide for college and university presidents.* Washington, DC: Council of Independent Colleges.

Smith, C. E., & Hopkins, R. (2004, March). Mitigating the impact of stereotypes on academic performance: The effects of cultural identity and attributions for success among African American college students. *Western Journal of Black Studies, 28*(1), 312–321.

Smith, K. S. (2001, Fall). Pivotal events in graduate teacher preparation for a faculty career. *Journal of Graduate Teaching Assistant Development, 8*(3), 97–105.

Smith, R. (2001). Expertise and the scholarship of teaching. In C. Kreber (Ed.), *New directions for teaching and learning: No. 86. Scholarship revisited: Perspectives on the scholarship of teaching* (pp. 69–78). San Francisco, CA: Jossey-Bass.

Sorcinelli, M. D., Austin, A. E., Eddy, P. L., & Beach, A. L. (2006). *Creating the future of faculty development: Learning from the past, understanding the present.* Bolton, MA: Anker.

South, S. J. (1989, October). Teaching sociology: An annotated bibliography. *Teaching Sociology, 17*(4), 515–516.

Speck, B. W., Hinnen, D. A., & Hinnen, K. (2003). *Teaching revising and editing: An annotated bibliography.* Westport, CT: Praeger.

Spencer, D., & Hebden, R. E. (1982). *Teaching and learning geography in higher education: An annotated bibliography.* Norwich, UK: Geo Books.

Spencer, S. J., Steele, C. M., & Quinn, D. M. (1999). Under suspicion of inability: Stereotype vulnerability and women's math performance. *Journal of Experimental Social Psychology, 35*, 4–28.

Spielberg, S. (Director, Producer). (2001). *AI* [Motion picture]. United States: Warner Bros.

Spillane, J. P. (2004). *Standards deviation: How schools misunderstand education policy.* Cambridge, MA: Harvard University Press.

Stahl, J. M. (2005, January). Research is for everyone: Perspectives from teaching at historically black colleges and universities. *Journal of Social and Clinical Psychology, 24*(1), 85–96.

Stake, R. E. (1998). Case studies. In N. K. Denzin & Y. S. Lincoln (Eds.), *Strategies of qualitative inquiry* (pp. 86–109). Thousand Oaks, CA: Sage.

Steel, J., & Hudson, A. (2001, May). Educational technology in learning and teaching: The perceptions and experiences of teaching staff. *Innovations in Education and Teaching International, 38*(2), 103–111.

Steele, C. M. (1997). A threat in the air: How stereotypes shape intellectual identity and performance. *American Psychologist, 52*(6), 613–629.

Steele, C. M. (1999, August). Thin ice: Stereotype threat and black college students. *The Atlantic Monthly, 284*(2), 44–54.

Steele, C. M. (2004). Kenneth Clark's context and mine: Toward a context-based theory of social identity threat. In G. Philogène (Ed.), *Racial identity in context: The legacy of Kenneth B. Clark.* Washington, DC: American Psychological Association.

Steele, C. M., & Aronson, J. (1995, November). Stereotype threat and the intellectual test performance of African Americans. *Journal of Personality and Social Psychology, 69*(5), 797–811.

Steeples, C., & Jones, C. (Eds.). (2001). *Networked learning: Perspectives and issues.* New York, NY: Springer.

Stein, R. B., & Short, P. M. (2001, Summer). Collaboration in delivering higher education programs: Barriers and challenges. *Review of Higher Education, 24*(4), 417–435.

Steinert, Y., Nasmith, L., McLeod, P. J., & Conochie, L. (2003, February). A teaching scholars program to develop leaders in medical education. *Academic Medicine, 78*(2), 142–149.

Stevens, D. D,, & Levi, A. J. (2005). *Introduction to rubrics: An assessment tool to save grading time, convey effective feedback, and promote student learning.* Sterling, VA: Stylus.

Stevens, M. C. (2004). *What makes a faculty learning community effective?* Unpublished manuscript.

Stewart, J. L. (2006). *Integrative learning in the sciences: Decision making at the intersection of science knowledge and student beliefs and values.* Retrieved May 14, 2007, from www.cfkeep.org/html/snapshot.php?id=70824690508493

Stigler, J. W., & Hiebert, J. (1999). *The teaching gap: Best ideas from the world's teachers for improving education in the classroom.* New York, NY: The Free Press.

Stimpert, J. L. (2004, July/August). Turbulent times: Four issues facing liberal arts colleges. *Change, 36*(4), 42–49.

St. Olaf College, Office of Academic Research and Planning. (2005). *Faculty development survey results: Quantitative and qualitative results.* Northfield, MN: Author.

Stone, J., Lynch, C. I., Sjomeling, M., & Darley, J. M. (1999). Stereotype threat effects on Black and White athletic performance. *Journal of Personality and Social Psychology, 77*(6), 1213–1227.

Strauss, A., & Corbin, J. (1998). *Basics of qualitative research: Techniques and procedures for developing grounded theory* (2nd ed.). Thousand Oaks, CA: Sage.

Svinicki, M. D., & Menges, R. J. (1996). Consistency within diversity: Guidelines for programs to honor exemplary teaching. In M. D. Svinicki & R. J. Menges (Eds.), *New directions for teaching and learning: No. 65. Honoring exemplary teaching* (pp. 109–113). San Francisco, CA: Jossey-Bass.

Takacs, D. (2001). *Teaching to inspire political participation in communities.* Retrieved May 14, 2007, from www.carnegiefoundation.org/programs/project_summary.asp?scholar=115

Taylor, E., & Antony, J. S. (2000, Summer). Stereotype threat reduction and wise schooling: Towards the successful socialization of African American doctoral students in education. *Journal of Negro Education, 69*(3), 184–198.

Theall, M., & Centra, J. A. (2001). Assessing the scholarship of teaching: Valid decisions from valid evidence. In C. Kreber (Ed.), *New directions for teaching and learning: No. 86. Scholarship revisited: Perspectives on the scholarship of teaching* (pp. 31–43). San Francisco, CA: Jossey-Bass.

Thornton, S. (2006, March–April). The devaluing of higher education: The annual report on the economic status of the profession 2005–06. *Academe, 92*(2), 24–35.

Tobias, S. (1990, July/August). They're not dumb. They're different. A new "tier of talent" for science. *Change, 22*(4), 10–30.

Tompkins, J. (1996). *A life in school: What the teacher learned.* New York, NY: Perseus.

Treisman, U. (1992, November). Studying students studying calculus: A look at the lives of minority mathematics students in college. *College Mathematics Journal, 23*(5), 362–372.

Tschannen-Moran, M., & Hoy, A. W. (2001, October). Teacher efficacy: Capturing an elusive construct. *Teaching and Teacher Education, 17*(7), 783–805.

Tuitt, F. (2003). *Black souls in an ivory tower: Understanding what it means to teach in a manner that respects and cares for the souls of African American graduate students.* Unpublished doctoral dissertation, Harvard University, Cambridge, MA.

U.S. Department of Education. (2006). *A test of leadership: Charting the future of U.S. higher education.* Washington, DC: Author.

Van Driel, J. H., Verloop, N., Van Werven, H. I., & Dekkers, H. (1997, July). Teachers' craft knowledge and curriculum innovation in higher engineering education. *Higher Education, 34*(1), 105–122.

Walker, G. J., & Walker, B. (1928). Annotated bibliography on guidance through teaching how to study. *Vocational Guidance Magazine, 7,* 82–84.

Ward, K., & Wolf-Wendel, L. (2004, Winter). Academic motherhood: Managing complex roles in research universities. *Review of Higher Education, 27*(2), 233–257.

Warren, T. (2005). Teaching revising and editing: An annotated bibliography. *Technical Communication, 52*(2), 225–226.

Weimer, M. (1995). Why scholarship is the bedrock of good teaching. In R. J. Menges, M. Weimer, & Associates, *Teaching on solid ground: Using scholarship to improve practice.* San Francisco, CA: Jossey-Bass.

Weimer, M. (2001). Learning more from the wisdom of practice. In C. Kreber (Ed.), *New directions for teaching and learning: No. 86. Scholarship revisited: Perspectives on the scholarship of teaching* (pp. 45–56). San Francisco, CA: Jossey-Bass.

Weimer, M. (2006). *Enhancing scholarly work on teaching and learning: Professional literature that makes a difference.* San Francisco, CA: Jossey-Bass.

Weisberg, M. (2003). Epilogue: When (law) students write. *Legal Studies Forum, 27*(1), 421–435.

Weisberg, M., & Peters, J. K. (in press). Experiments in listening. *Journal of Legal Education.*

Wergin, J. (1993, July/August). Departmental awards. *Change, 25*(4), 24.

Weston, C. B., & McAlpine, L. (2001). Making explicit the development toward the scholarship of teaching. In C. Kreber (Ed.), *New directions for teaching and learning: No. 86. Scholarship revisited: Perspectives on the scholarship of teaching* (pp. 89–97). San Francisco, CA: Jossey-Bass.

Whitt, E. J. (1991, Winter). "Hit the ground running": Experiences of new faculty in a school of education. *Review of Higher Education, 14*(2), 177–197.

Wiener, H. S., & Sheckels, T. F. (1981). *The writing room: A resource book for teachers of English.* New York, NY: Oxford University Press.

Wilson, S. M., Shulman, L. S., & Richert, A. E. (1987). "150 different ways" of knowing: Representations of knowledge in teaching. In J. Calderhead (Ed.), *Exploring teachers' thinking* (pp. 104–124). London, UK: Cassell Educational Limited.

Wineburg, S. (2003, April 11). Teaching the mind good habits. *The Chronicle of Higher Education*, p. B20.

Wise, P. S., & Fulkerson, F. E. (1996). Annotated bibliography on the teaching of psychology: 1995. *Teaching of Psychology, 23*(4), 257–264.

Wolverton, M. (1998, Fall). Treading the tenure-track tightrope: Finding balance between research excellence and quality teaching. *Innovative Higher Education, 23*(1), 61–79.

Wright, C. J., & Katcher, M. L. (2004, June). Pediatricians advocating for children: An annotated bibliography. *Current Opinion Pediatrics, 16*(3), 281–285.

Wylie, N. A. (Ed.). (1988). *The role of the nurse in clinical medical education.* Springfield, IL: Southern Illinois University, School of Medicine.

Yanowitz, K. L. (2004). Do scientists help people? Beliefs about scientists and the influence of prosocial context on girls' attitudes towards physics. *Journal of Women and Minorities in Science and Engineering, 10*(4), 393–399.

Yerrick, R., Parke, H., & Nugent, J. (1997, April). Struggling to promote deeply rooted change: The "filtering effect" of teachers' beliefs on understanding transformational views of teaching science. *International Journal of Science Education, 81*(2), 137–159.

Yin, R. K. (2003). *Case study research: Design and methods* (3rd ed.). Thousand Oaks, CA: Sage.

Zahorski, K. J. (1996). Honoring exemplary teaching in the liberal arts institution. In M. D. Svinicki & R. J. Menges (Eds.), *New directions for teaching and learning: No. 65. Honoring exemplary teaching* (pp. 85–92). San Francisco, CA: Jossey-Bass.